CW00401670

Finance and Accounting

Related Macmillan titles

R. Anderson, *Management, Information Systems and Computers*
C. Jones, *The Computer Handbook – A Businessman's Guide*
P. Turner and D. Turner, *GCSE Accounting*
J. Harvey, *Mastering Economics, 3rd edition*
E. C. Eyre, *Mastering Basic Management*
D. P. Whiting, *Mastering Banking*
D. Foster, *Mastering Marketing*
G. Bright and M. Herbert *Mastering Accounting*
A. Simmonds, *Mastering Financial Accounting*
L. A. Woolcott and W. R. Unwin, *Mastering Business Communication*
C. Boyle, *Mastering Statistics with your Microcomputer*
D. E. Avison, *Mastering Business Computing with your Microcomputer*
P. Bailey, *Mastering Office Practice, 2nd edition*
P. Stevens, *Work Out Principles of Accounts*
T. Burley and G. O'Sullivan, *Work Out Operational Research*
J. Bingham, *Professional Masters: Data Processing*
R. Oldcorn, *Professional Masters: Management*
G. Lindt, *Professional Masters: Financial Management*
R. Oldcorn, *Professional Masters: Company Accounts*
R. Chapman, A. Norman and M. Norman, *The Student Guide to BTEC Business and Finance*

FINANCE AND ACCOUNTING
2ND EDITION

R. S. Giles

Assisted by J. W. Capel

Bournemouth & Poole College
of Further Education
Lansdowne, Bournemouth

MACMILLAN

First edition 1987
Reprinted 1990
Second edition 1991

Published by
MACMILLAN EDUCATION LTD
Houndmills, Basingstoke, Hampshire RG21 2XS
and London
Companies and representatives
throughout the world

Typeset and Illustrated by TecSet Ltd, Wallington, Surrey
Printed in Hong Kong

British Library Cataloguing in Publication Data
Giles, R. S. (Richard S.)
Finance and accounting – 2nd. ed.
1. Great Britain. Accounting
I. Title   II. Capel, J. W. (John W.)
657.0941
ISBN 0–333–54164–2

Contents

Seven assignments to challenge students, three of them integrated with people in organisations and the organisation in its environment.

Preface

This book is suitable for students embarking on a BTEC National course in Business Studies. It has also been found successful on other courses including GCSE and 'A' level accounting, the Institute of Bankers and other examining bodies.

The response to the First Edition was very encouraging and we have followed it up with this current work, improving the quality by up-dating relevant information, incorporating a full computer-based accounting section and including many further questions with which to stimulate and challenge students.

As a summary, the text has been used on the following courses:

GCSE	Accounting
'A' Level	Accounting
CIOB Foundation	Structure of Accounts
IPS	Business Accounting
BTEC HNC/D	Business & Finance
ICM	Accounting
AAT	Accounting

Richard Giles and John Capel
1991

Acknowledgements

For this Second Edition, we would like to take the opportunity to thank both students and staff of the Business Studies and Computing Department at Bournemouth & Poole College for their guidance and assistance. In particular, Royston Carlton, Christine Freer, Douglas Lewis, Graham Whitehall and also a former colleague, David Balfour (Stafford College).

We would also like to express our thanks to Pegasus Software Ltd and to Microsoft Ltd for the use of the software in the computer-based accounting sections.

Introduction

This book is divided into eight sections. These sections cover the BTEC National first year 'Finance Unit' and the second year 'Accounting Option'. At the front of each of these sections the objectives/indicative content is stated.

The first four sections develop financial accounting from basic book-keeping, using the balance sheet approach, to analysis and interpretation of financial statements.

Throughout the text, the importance of finance in different business organisations is emphasised. This also includes a full exposition of public sector accounts for both Central and Local Government.

Section V contains a comprehensive treatment of personal finance, while section VI concentrates on costing and management accounts, emphasising the contribution made by accountants in the decision-making process. Section VII develops the further aspects of accounting required for the second year option.

Section VIII contains a programme of assignments that lecturers may find useful. Abbreviated answers to the questions in the text and also a glossary of accounting terms, which students should find useful, are sited at the end of the book. Abbreviated answers have been included in order that students working on their own can check if they are 'on the right track'.

The text uses both the traditional and running balance methods of ledger recording and the vertical presentation of final accounts. As far as is necessary for a text at this level, it conforms to the requirements of the *1985 Companies Act*, and includes the *1989 Companies Act* which supplements the 1985 Act. Therefore, the only data likely to date quickly are the tax rates and the tax bands referred to in the section for personal finance.

The assignment programme should be of value to lecturers and contains a mix of both financial and fully integrated assignments which combine with 'People in Organisations' and 'The Organisation in its Environment'. The integrated assignments also develop business skills in finance, accounts, communication, administration and economics.

The Financing of Resources

Objectives
To understand the importance of finance in different types of organisations.

To recognise the 'sources of finance' in both the Private and Public Sectors of business.

To be aware of the role of the Accountant and the type of responsibilities found in an Accounts Office.

To recognise the importance of the Balance Sheet showing the resources of an organisation and the financing of those resources.

PART 1

An Introduction to Finance and Accounting

Finance

Finance may be defined as management of money. The money resources of a person, or of an organisation, or of a nation, need to be managed efficiently otherwise they may easily be wasted or lost.

All of us, individually or as part of an organisation, need to have some understanding of finance from the point of view of:

(a) Sources of finance. Where do we get the money from?
(b) Application of finance. What do we do with the money once we get it? How is the money to be used?

For an individual, personal finance primarily comes from the income which is earned from doing a job of work. Individuals also buy many goods and services on credit at a time when many credit organisations are busily promoting the use of the credit card. Money is used to pay for personal expenditure like accommodation, food, clothes, transport and other incidentals of life.

From an organisation's point of view, the sources of finance will come from the owner or owners of the enterprise (capital), from borrowing money and from the profits of the business. It will use the money to pay for resources such as premises, equipment and stock and also to pay for the running expenses of the business like wages and salaries.

From the nation's point of view, the Government needs to raise substantial finance from the various sources of taxation, in order to spend the money on behalf of the nation, on programmes such as health, social security, education and defence.

If we are to understand anything at all about the world of finance, we need to know something about the basic principles of recording and managing money and how money may be used and evaluated.

People go into business ventures for all kind of reasons. For some, they want independence. They want to be their own boss. For others, it may be because they have a competitive and ambitious spirit and want to earn a high income.

For many business enterprises, the motive for being in business is to make PROFITS, either for themselves if they are sole owners of the business (sole-traders), or as a partner in a partnership, or as a shareholder of a company wanting a share of profits in the form of dividends.

Most businesses are involved in trading. Buying or selling goods or services like shop-keepers or making products and selling them as manufacturers of food, drink, clothing, household goods, television sets and cars. Whatever the type of business, all businesses are heavily dependent on finance, not only to commence operations, but also to sustain their very existence.

Accounting

Every type of business enterprise needs to keep financial records. Book-keeping and accounting are part of the world of finance involving the keeping of financial records and using their records (of accounts) to help the owners and management of businesses to run their enterprises more efficiently.

Every business needs to understand the importance of handling its finances soundly otherwise it can soon be in difficulty and lose its resources.

Book-keeping's basic function is to make sure that financial information is accurately recorded and to classify and group this information into sets of accounts.

Accounting uses the book-keeping records as the foundation for preparing financial statements and to help owners and management in their decisions concerning the handling of the business. They will want to know if the business is profitable. Profits mean success but losses indicate failure. The more profitable a business, the greater its success and confidence will increase. They will also need to know whether the business is financially secure, in other words, can it adequately meet its debts when the debts are due to be paid. Is the business financially stable so that it is not only trading next week but also next year. Profits without stability are like the summer without sunshine. And suddenly, even good profits can end!

It is the function of accounting to provide the interested parties of a business with the appropriate financial statements which will indicate the business's performance in terms of profit and financial stability. These reports or statements basically concern the profit and loss account and the balance sheet.

Types of Business Organisations in the Private Sector

In the private sector of business, as distinct from the public sector (State-owned enterprises), there are three basic types of organisations which are primarily profit-motivated:

(a) Sole-trader;
(b) Partnership;
(c) Limited Company.

The essential difference between these lies in the size of the business. This is directly related to the initial investment in the business—that is, the provision of capital, the most important ingredient in determining the size of a business enterprise.

The sole-trader is a one-man business unit. Capital is raised by the resources of one person, including any borrowing from banks, building societies or other financial institutions.

Partnerships may have as many as twenty partners and subsequently have the greater potential to raise more capital if each partner contributes a share. The more partners, the more capital is available for use in the business.

Limited companies are basically of two types. They are either public limited or private limited companies. Although there is no restriction on the number of shareholders who can contribute capital in either type of company, the private company may only sell its shares privately (that is, without resort to advertising) and therefore the number of shareholders is likely to be limited, shares being sold within the boundaries of family, friends and business acquaintances.

A public limited company has no such restriction and can raise its capital by issuing a prospectus (an invitation to the public to buy its shares). A merchant bank or issuing house can act on behalf of the company and make the necessary arrangements for the sale. In this way, very large amounts of capital can be raised and public companies can take credit for being responsible for stimulating growth in capital investment during the last 100 years. For a public company, at least £50,000 of share capital must be registered with the company, of which at least 25% must be issued and paid for before it can start operating.

Shareholders are part-owners of their companies. The reward for owning shares may come from the payment of dividends from company profits, or from the increase in value of the shares (capital gain). Dividends are paid on the nominal value of shares (their face value) and not their market value. Dividends are usually determined as so much in the £; for example, 12p/£ would gain £12 per 100 shares.

Limited companies have the advantage of having 'limited liability' but sole-traders and partnerships are disadvantaged by not having this. This means that in the event of a company's collapse, shareholders are protected against the debts of the company up to the value of their paid-up capital, but nothing more. Sole-traders or partnerships are unlimited, which means they are personally liable for all debts. This could involve the selling of personal possessions in order to settle business debts.

Sources of Finance

To begin a business requires money. This is known as *capital*. The money, or capital, is provided by the owner or owners of a business and includes any money which may be borrowed, this being referred to as *borrowed* or *loan capital*.

The owner or owners of a business may borrow money from a bank or a building society or any other financial institution prepared to lend them money. Building societies will normally lend money for mortgages on land and buildings.

The Owner's Capital

When a business enterprise begins, the owner or owners puts his or their resources into the business, this representing their capital. The capital may be in the form of money, equipment, tools, premises, or indeed any other resource. The total value of these resources will be expressed in monetary terms and will establish the initial capital (or net worth) of the owner or owners, at the commencement of business. Capital may stay the same or either increase or decrease depending on how successful the business is and what the owner decides to do.

Limited companies have shareholders who have subscribed share capital and are therefore part-owners of a business. The more shares they own, the more of the business they own. A shareholder of a public limited company whose shares are listed on the stock exchange may sell his shares if he wishes. Shares listed are 'marketable' securities and may be bought or sold by shareholders or by new investors to the market. Private limited companies are not listed on the stock exchange and are therefore not marketable securities. Transfer of shares is restricted to those members who can sell their shares privately.

A company must register with the Registrar of Companies at Companies House, London, and state the amount of capital it wants to raise. This is known as the *authorised capital*. The shares issued and purchased by shareholders are known as *issued and paid-up capital*, which may be less than the authorised capital. A company may wish to issue further shares at a later date when it may require more capital for future investment and growth.

Classes of Shares

There are basically two distinct classes of shares:

Ordinary shares. These are the most common type of shares and are often referred to as *equities*. The rate of dividend depends on how much profit the company has made and how much the directors decide to pay out as dividends and how much they want to retain in the company (in what is known as *reserves*). Ordinary shareholders are paid last, after preference shareholders, the rate of dividend depending on how much the directors recommend. Large companies may pay an 'interim' dividend half-way through the financial year and a final dividend at the end of the financial year.

Preference shares. These entitle shareholders to a fixed rate of dividend (for example, 8% preference shares). These shares may be more suitable to the investor who wants a regular and fixed dividend and a more reliable investment than that offered by ordinary shares. Share capital is part of the shareholders funds (or net worth) and represents ownership capital and not loan capital.

Borrowing: Loan Capital

Loans may come from a variety of different sources but the most significant source is the bank. The commercial (or High Street) banks are generally recognised as the 'Big Five' — Barclays, National Westminster, Lloyds, Midland, and now the TSB.

A loan may be short-term (for example, within one year) like a bank overdraft or a medium-term to long-term loan (for example, two to twenty years), used for specific capital purposes.

Loans on short-term credit are usually required to finance the day-to-day running of the business — for example, to purchase materials, to pay wages, to pay for overhead costs. It is unlikely that a long-term loan would be negotiated to finance short-term expenditure. An overdraft arrangement with the bank usually allows a person or business to reach a certain fixed limit in the current account — for example, £5000 'in the red'. If the limit is exceeded, the bank may take steps to reduce the overdraft facility or even cancel it. Interest is charged on a daily basis and is usually a percentage above what is termed the bank's *base rate*.

A business bank loan is for a specific period of time with arrangements to repay by regular instalments over the period of the loan. For medium-term to long-term loans, the loan capital may be required for specific projects, for example.

to purchase machinery or equipment
to mortgage buildings or land
to develop new products
to finance an export campaign.

There is also a Government-sponsored scheme which was started in 1981. Termed the *Loan Guarantee Scheme* it operates via the clearing banks and is designed to assist small firms to obtain finance for new projects and ventures, especially in the areas of technology and manufacturing. The maximum that can be lent under this scheme is £75,000, the Government reimbursing the bank 70% of the sum lent if the company subsequently fails.

Debenture Issues

Debentures represent loan capital. Debentures may be issued by companies for the purpose of raising finance over a specific period of time (for example, 5, 10, 15 years). Interest payment to creditors (Debenture Holders) is a fixed percentage of the nominal value of the stock and is payable even if profits are not made. They are usually secured on the assets of the company in that if the company goes into liquidation, the Debenture Holders can be paid from the proceeds of the asset sales. These are often known as *Mortgage Debentures*.

The nominal value of a 'block' of Debenture Stock is £100 and it is this figure which is paid back to the stock holder when the Debenture matures. However, it is possible to sell one's stock on the Stock Exchange before the maturity date — that is, they are marketable just like shares. But, unlike shares, the value of Debentures are not dependent on the current and expected profits of the company. Their value is primarily determined by the rate of interest paid on the stock in relation to current rates of interest elsewhere, say in a bank; generally, if interest rates are 'high' in relation to the rate paid on the stock, then the market value will be below £100. When interest rates fall, therefore, the value of the stock can rise to £100 or sometimes even more if interest rates are very low.

Profits

The profits of a business are one of the most important sources of business finance. For sole-traders and partners, most of the profits may be withdrawn from the business through the financial year as part of their income.

Companies need to pay corporation tax to the Inland Revenue and dividends to shareholders. Any profit which is left can be ploughed back into the business to finance its expansion or to provide for specific projects or replacement of assets like machinery, equipment and plant. Companies who retain their profits usually transfer them to what is known as *reserves*.

Some Other Sources of Finance

Equipment Leasing

Here a company does not buy its capital equipment outright but leases it for a pre-determined rental, say quarterly.

The firm doing the leasing is known as the *lessor*, which always has legal possession of the equipment; sometimes it is the actual supplier or manufacturer of the equipment that does the leasing. In other cases a leasing company buys the equipment and then leases it to the firm. The firm which is leased the equipment is known as the *lessee*. Paying a fixed rental charge to the lessor helps the lessee manage its expenditure cash-budget more easily; it has the use of the equipment without first having to find or borrow the money to purchase the equipment. Leasing contracts also have servicing arrangements so that the lessee is saved the expense of a regular servicing bill as well as the future costs of the equipment's replacement. Essentially, all this means that the lessee has more funds at its disposal to finance its activities.

Factor Finance

This has become a very popular way by which firms ensure an adequate cash flow and thus short-term finance coming into the business to meet current expenditure. It involves a firm employing a debt factoring company. The firm employing the company passes all its invoices (trade debts) on to the factoring company which pays a major percentage of their value immediately and the rest when the debt is paid. In this way the firm has immediate funds (liquidity) because its funds or a major part of them are not tied up in debtors. The factoring company charges interest on the sum advanced until the debt is cleared; administration charges are payable too. A considerable number of factor financing arrangements are 'without recourse' — that is, the factoring company bears any losses occurring as a result of bad debts. Both large and small firms will employ factoring companies on a fairly continuous basis — the kind of financing provided can be a 'lifeline' to small firms who are experiencing cash-flow problems because of slow debtors.

Creditors

Suppliers of goods and services to business enterprises provide firms with an important source of short-term finance. If credit facilities are granted to a business for the purpose of buying goods or services allowing say, two months to pay, the two months' credit is a short-term loan without interest charged.

Investors in Industry

This organisation was originally set up in 1945 as two separate bodies — the Industrial and Commercial Finance Corporation, and the Finance Corporation for Industry. In 1975 the two companies were merged and renamed Finance for Industry, and in 1983 that name was changed to Investors in Industry.

The whole purpose of this body is to sponsor small, medium-sized, and large companies who are seeking 'venture capital' for projects which are not likely to yield a profitable return for many years to come. Backed by the English and Scottish Clearing Banks and the Bank of England, Investors in Industry has sufficient capital backing to take the longer-term view — lending money for periods of up to fifteen years. It thus plays an essential role in helping the development of British Industry, especially in the highly competitive world of computer technology.

The major source of finance for business is the initial capital invested by the owner or owners of the enterprise. The size of the initial capital investment is determined by the nature of the business, whether it is a sole-trader, partnership or company. The larger the input of capital the larger the business is likely to be. It is therefore not surprising that most sole-traders are small business enterprises, especially popular in the retail trade where they earn their living as shop-keepers. Public companies on the other hand, represent the large business enterprises because there is no restriction on the number of shareholders who can subscribe capital.

Public Finance

Public finance refers to Government (or State) finances. It involves the raising of money through taxation and borrowing for the purpose of spending money on public goods and services such as health, social security, education and defence. Public finance helps to support the nationalised industries like coal, steel and transport using taxation or allowing them to borrow, particularly when these industries fail to meet financial targets set by the Government.

Local Authority Finance

In April 1990, the Government introduced its controversial system of applying a community charge (poll tax) to replace the rates, in England and Wales. The system had been introduced in Scotland a year earlier. Rates were a local tax paid by owner-occupiers of land and property which was levied by the local authorities to meet part of the cost of running their local services, a large proportion going to pay for education, roads, housing, police and social services.

Local authorities were also supported by the Rate Support Grant (RSG) which had provided about 45–55% of their spending. Specific grants from Central Government provided finance for capital projects such as roads, schools and housing. If local authorities wanted more money, they could borrow from various sources such as issuing local authority bonds or using the Stock Exchange to sell local authority stock.

The Community Charge is the replacement of the domestic rates. A charge is now set by each of the local authorities which is payable by every resident adult. A sum of money is fixed by the authority payable by each adult. This sum is based on the calculations for expenditure by each authority. The Government also supports this tax by way of a grant system that is intended to compensate for differences in local authorities' needs.

There are wide differences between authorities in the fixing of the community charge. In some regions the charge may be as high as £600 a head; in others, it may be half this sum and this has caused a great deal of conflict.

This system should benefit those people who live alone and only have to pay a single adult charge, but heavily weighs against the family which may have a number of occupants who are of adult age. The controversy also lies in the type of dwellings people occupy. Should a pensioner in a tiny flat pay the same community charge as a wealthy resident owning a large property?

The tax was resented on its introduction because the Government 'got its sums wrong'. The average English rates bill in 1989 had been levied at £269 per head. In 1990, this average had increased substantially by 35% to £362.

Nearly half of local authority spending comes from Central Government grants which broadly relate to the needs of the local authority, for example, the number of children to be educated, the number of schools, hospitals and roads to be built. Each authority's finance comes from these grants, plus the money which comes from imposing its community charge, plus its share of revenue which comes from the uniform business rate.

Local businesses were also rated on the rateable value of their properties. Since the introduction of the community charge, the Government introduced a uniform business rate. Local authorities no longer controlled the rate of tax to be paid by businesses in their region, this now being under the control of the Department of the Environment. A uniform business rate is paid by each business across the whole of the nation and the money goes into a central pool. Each authority receives its share from the pool in relation to the number of adults residing in its area. Thus central Government is able to exercise greater control of local authority spending.

Local authorities raise other forms of revenue from housing rents and a variety of service sales such as car parking, entertainment centres and other leisure activities, planning charges, search fees and interest payments received.

The system of raising local authority finance is discussed further in Section III, Part 6, Public Sector Accounts.

Raising Government Finance

The majority of Central Government finance comes from taxation in one form or another, including National Insurance contributions. Any short-fall in raising Government finance is made up by borrowing money. The Treasury is the Government department responsible for the control of public finance. The Bank of England acts in the capacity of financial advisor to the Treasury as well as functioning as the Government's bank, keeping the records of its receipts and expenditure in what is called the 'Exchequer Account'.

The finance raised is used to pay for the vast programme of public spending as mentioned above. The projected forecast of spending for 1990–1991 has been set at approximately £180 billion, rising to £203 billion for 1992–1993.

The aim of the Government is to control public expenditure and borrowing as a proportion of national output, so that if expenditure is held more or less level in real terms (allowing for inflation), any growth in the economy will lead to the required reduction of Government expenditure as a percentage of National Income.

The following table of public finance shows where the money comes from and where it goes.

Public finance: Projected figures for 1990–1991 based on spending of approx. £180 billion

Where money is from	pence/£	Where money is spent	pence/£
Income tax	23p	Social Security	26p
Corporation tax	10p	Health and personal	
North Sea revenues	1p	Social Services	11p
National Insurance	17p	Education and Science	10p
Rates [Poll tax]	10p	Defence	10p
VAT	14p	Environment and	
Duties on fuel,		Transport	7p
tobacco and alcohol	11p	Home Office	4p
Other sources	5p	Other Government	
Expenditure taxes	6p	departments	8p
Capital taxes	3p	Wales, Scotland and	
		Northern Ireland	10p
		Other payments	4p
		Interest payments	10p
	100p		100p

Public Sector Borrowing

The Government's medium-term financial strategy (MTFS) is to reduce public borrowing as a percentage of national output from about 2% in 1985–86 to approximately 1% between 1989–1993.

Borrowing is necessary, when public expenditure is more than public receipts. If the Government did not resort to borrowing, the increases in taxation levels needed to pay for expenditure would be relatively high and largely unacceptable to the public.

The Treasury is responsible for borrowing (generally known as the PSBR – Public Sector Borrowing Requirement), and via the Bank of England uses the Stock Exchange to sell Government Stock (or Gilts). The Government raises about 70% of its borrowing in this way, most of the stock being taken up by insurance companies and pension funds because there is little risk of the

Government defaulting. The other 30% of borrowing comes in the form of National Savings via the Post Office, selling National Savings Certificates, Income Bonds, Premium Savings Bonds, Deposit Bonds and the accounts of the National Savings Bank. Both Government Stock and National Savings are at fixed interest rates, the difference being that the former is marketable on the Stock Exchange and the latter non-marketable.

The Government's reform of the nationalised industries during the 1980's meant that a massive privatisation programme transferred many of the public sector industries into the private sector.

Proceeds from the sale of public sector businesses boosted the finances of the Treasury to a sum approaching £20 billion which helped to not only reduce the PSBR, but positively to replace it with PSDR (Public Sector Debt Repayment). These repayments commenced in the latter part of the 1980's and the Chancellor's forecast for the early years of the 1990's was about £6–£8 billion per annum. This has not only reduced the National Debt of the nation, but significantly has helped to reduce the massive interest payments made each year on the total debt.

When the Government requires short-term funds to meet its current expenditure, as it often does, it arranges to sell Treasury Bills via the Bank of England. Each Treasury Bill has a nominal or part value, say £10,000, and each has a maturity period of 91 days.

However, unlike virtually all other kinds of fund-raising by the Government, Treasury Bills do not carry a rate of interest. In reality, no one is going to lend the Government money 'for free' so every week the Bank of England actions off the Bills – invites tenders – to the highest bidders. The bidders include foreign banks, financial institutions and discount houses, but not the UK clearing banks. The higher the bids or tenders (that is, the nearer to the Bill's part value), the greater the chance an institution has of receiving some Bills). In practice, the financial institutions are adept at putting in tenders such that the difference between what they pay for the bills and the money they get back after 91 days – the par value – reflects the current cost of borrowing. For example, a £50,000 Treasury Bill might be sold for £48,500. The annualised cost to the Government is

$$£50,000 - £48,500 = £1500$$

$$\frac{£\ 1500}{£48,500} \times \frac{100}{1} \times \frac{365}{91} = 12.4\%$$

The 12.4% is likely to reflect the current costs of borrowing from banks and financial markets.

The Budget

The Budget relates to the proposals planned by Government for changes in taxation and is also an annual review of the Government's economic policies for the year.

The Budget proposals are laid down in the Budget statement prepared by the Chancellor of the Exchequer, usually in March each year, and presented to the House of Commons. How will the Government finance its expenditure programme? What changes in taxation are to be made and how is it to be spent?

In the 1990–1991 proposals, income from direct taxes (taxes on income such as income tax and corporation tax), will account for about 35%. Indirect taxes (taxes on goods and services such as VAT and customs and excise duties) are estimated to be 32%. Local rates (community charge) and National Insurance are another 27%. The remaining 6% comes from other sources.

As far as public expenditure is concerned, at least half of it will finance health, social security, education and defence.

The Budget is not only a means of financing public expenditure. It is also a very important statement that reviews the Government's economic proposals for the year and is a means of implementing its policies. It has been the policy of successive Governments to make the control of inflation its primary objective through the use of both monetary and fiscal measures. Other significant objectives include invigorating the economy to make it more productive and competitive, and developing an economy which relates strongly to market forces so as to provide opportunities for growth and employment.

Finance for Nationalised Industries

After the Second World War the newly elected Labour Government set about its vast nationalisation programme to ensure that the nation had what they considered essential needs and services under public control. Acts of Parliament took over private sector industries such as coal (1946), railways and electricity (1947) and gas (1948). The shareholders of these former companies were paid off either in cash or Government securities at fixed interest rates or a combination of both.

Government ministers were made responsible for appointing the chairman and members of each board running the nationalised industries. Today they have the responsibility of agreeing with the management of each board the general planning and direction of how the industries should be run — for example, the general standard of services to be provided, the pricing policy and so forth. However, the day-to-day running of the industries is left to the individual management of each of the boards.

Over the years, Governments have issued guidelines to the nationalised industries to ensure, as far as possible, that they are run in the same way as commercial enterprises in the private sector, and hence make profits or break even. Some nationalised industries like the Post Office make very good returns on capital while others including coal, steel and railways tend to struggle from year to year and often make losses which need to be supported by funds from the Exchequer (in other words, the taxpayers).

The rate of return on capital before taxation is currently 5% per annum, although financial targets are individualised for each industry depending to a great extent on what services they need to provide the public. The Government also sets external financing limits when it comes to the industries borrowing capital, to ensure they stay within specific targets and do not over-reach their spending powers.

Financing for nationalised industries basically comes from:

(a) Revenue from sales of goods and or services.
(b) Profits which are used to pay back interest and loans, and/or retained in the industry to improve services.
(c) Government grants and subsidies. Grants tend to be used for specific purposes such as capital projects (for example, building programmes) or reduce the price of certain services (for example, Post Office charges).
(d) Loans from Government. This comprises the bulk of the boards' borrowing requirements, using the National Loans Fund.
(e) Temporary borrowing needs from the finance markets, including loans and overdrafts.
(f) Loans from foreign sources (such as banks), but subject to Treasury approval.

Nationalised industries are monopolies subject to public scrutiny. The House of Commons Select Committee on Nationalised Industries is responsible for examining the reports and accounts of the industries and for making recommendations to Government. Findings from the annual reports and accounts can then be subject to debate in the House.

The interests of the industry's consumers are also protected by Consumers' Councils (such as the Post Office Users National Council) which deal with a wide range of complaints and suggestions from consumers.

The Privatisation of the Public Sector

The Conservative Government, since it came to power in May, 1979, set out its major policy of reforming the nationalised industries throughout the 1980's. The Conservative Party saw this as one of its essential methods of economic recovery. At the same time, it saw an opportunity to pursue its policy of wider share ownership by the general public and the employees of the nationalised industries.

The 1980's saw a massive privatisation programme where the public was offered the sale of shares for the ownership of the following industries:

British Aerospace	Enterprise Oil
British Airways	Britoil
British Gas	Associated British Ports
British Telecom	British Shipbuilders
Cable & Wireless	Rolls Royce
The National Freight Consortium	British Airports Authority
The Rover Group	The Regional Water Authorities
Jaguar	The Electricity Boards [1990]

In all, almost $\frac{3}{4}$ of a million jobs have been transferred from the public to the private sector, thereby reducing the 'balance' between public and private ownership. The process has not been without its critics. The former Conservative Prime Minister, the late Harold Macmillan (first Earl Stockton), criticised the Government for selling the 'family silver', and upsetting the balance of Britain's mixed economy, between the private and public sectors of business.

Other privatisations in the pipeline include British Coal, the British Steel Corporation and perhaps British Rail.

Proceeds from these sales have brought about £20 billion into the Treasury and have helped to increase the budget surplus in the late 1980's and early 1990's. The surplus funds from the domestic budgets have in turn helped to repay our National Debt. The PSBR has been reduced and replaced by the PSDR. Billions of pounds have been repaid, reducing not only the National Debt, but significantly, reducing the high cost of borrowing through interest rates.

PART 2

The Role of the Accountant and the Accounts Office

The accountant's work is often varied and interesting, as well as far reaching. Many people think they have a boring job to do, recording figures all day long and checking the work of others.

Accountants do this of course as part of their work but more importantly, they are managers of finance whether they work in private practice or in an organisation where accounting is one of a number of departments like sales, marketing, production and personnel. Not only are they concerned with recording financial information, they are also interested in planning and forecasting results. They are financial consultants helping other managers to decide the way ahead, playing a critical part in evaluating business problems and being part of a team which plans, controls and takes decisions in an organisation.

Accountants, when qualified, may take on different roles. There are four main accounting qualifications:

The Institute of Chartered Accountants (letters ACA);
The Chartered Association of Certified Accountants (letters ACCA);
The Chartered Institute of Public Finance and Accountancy (letters CIPFA);
The Chartered Institute of Management Accountants (letters ACMA).

An ACA may work in a private practice, providing auditing and financial accounting services, such as preparing annual accounts for clients, and advising on taxation matters. In fact, the large professional firms of accountants engage in a whole range of Financial Consultancy work. Many ACAs work as Senior Accountants in Industry and Commerce. An ACCA may similarly work in a private practice, and is qualified to audit and provide the

17

same services as an ACA. Probably, a higher proportion of ACCA qualified accountants work in industry and commerce than do so in private practice.

A CIPFA accountant will mainly work for local authorities, where a specialist knowledge of public sector financial accounting is required. An ACMA is not qualified to audit, consequently most ACMA's work in industry and commerce as Management Accountants, concerned with assisting management to assess business performance and cost-effectiveness. However, some ACMAs are employed in private practice as Management Consultants. Much of the Management Accountant's work is involved with assessing future performance.

The Accounts Office

The role of the accountant either in private practice or working in an organisation may be listed as:

(a) The collection and recording of financial data.
(b) The organisation of financial data into books of account.
(c) The control of cash resources.
(d) The preparation of financial statements, such as profit and loss account and balance sheet.
(e) The assessment of financial performance through the analysis and evaluation of accounting reports.
(f) The examination of accounts in the role of auditor.
(g) The preparation of budgets to forecast estimation of expenditure against income for planning, control and evaluation of trading performance.
(h) The preparation of costing estimates including marginal costing and break-even.
(i) The preparation of cash flow to ensure that sufficient cash is available to meet day-to-day expenditure.
(j) The arrangement and negotiation for raising capital including loans or overdraft facilities.
(k) The role of financial advisor or consultant.

The recording of financial information is the key function of an accounts office. Customers' and suppliers' records must be accurately recorded by the sales and bought ledger clerks, information for these records coming from business documents like the invoice and credit note as well as from the receipts and payments of cash.

The cashier is responsible for all matters involving the receipt and payment of money and the checking of statements with the business's bank account records. There may be a junior clerk delegated to take care of petter cash payments.

Wages must also be calculated for each of the firm's employees, including payments for overtime or bonus schemes. Appropriate deductions need to be made for taxation, National Insurance and other stoppages from pay.

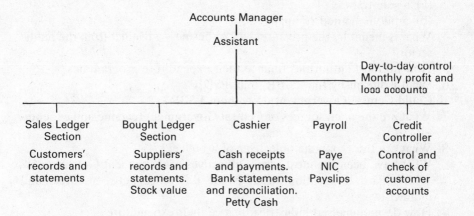

Stock must be recorded either on stock record cards or using a stock program on the computer, showing both the quantity and type of stock in balance as well as its value.

The accountant and his assistant will have overall control of the staff and be responsible for preparing monthly statements of profit and loss as well as the final accounting reports at the end of the financial period. They may also be involved in the preparation of budget acounts which are used to forecast and control income and epxenditure figures for all departments of the business.

The computer is playing an important role in the recording of financial information. Computer programs are available for sales and bought ledgers, stock control, payroll and the preparation of final accounts.

The accounts clerk will tend to type in data on a computer keyboard rather than traditionally writing the information in the accounting books.

Finance is one of the most important aspects of an organisation because the whole of it is dependent on its expertise. The preparation of accounts helps to explain what is happening in the business: whether it is successful or not, whether it has sufficient cash to pay its way, whether it should make this decision or that. It should also be noted that accountants do look ahead and help management make better informed decisions which concern the organisation, at the same time ensuring that finances are under sound control.

Exercises

1. How does the function of book-keeping differ from the function of accounting?

2. Why does the provision of capital influence the size of a business organisation? Can you think of any other factor which may influence the size of a business?
3. What do you consider the main sources of finance for
   (a) a sole-trader
   (b) a public limited company?
4. What is meant by the private sector of business a distinct from the public sector?
5. How do local authorities finance their expenditure programmes?
6. What is meant by the 'PSBR' and 'PSDR'?
   Could Central Government do without PSBR?
7. What are the main sources of Central Government revenue and expenditure?
8. What are the economic objectives of a budget?
   What have been the most recent objectives of the present Government?
   With regard to taxation, what is the difference between direct and indirect taxes?
9. How do nationalised industries finance their expenditure?
   What kind of control can Central Government exert on a public corporation?
10. Outline the role of the accountant in a small-to-medium accounts department.

PART 3

Introducing the Balance Sheet

The balance sheet is a statement which lists the assets, the liabilities and the capital of a business organisation.

Assets represent a business's resources. They may be financed by a combination of the owner's capital and any capital borrowed, referred to in accounting as 'liabilities'. One of the major functions of a business is to make profits and this is achieved by financing resources which will make money and in turn, produce more resources.

The following figures represent the assets and the liabilities of G. Harrison who is the owner of a small retail shop. He has recently started in business and is learning by experience. He left his job in a bank because he felt more than a little adventurous and wanted to make a success of being in business for himself.

ASSETS: THE RESOURCES OWNED BY A BUSINESS.

G. Harrison's assets:

	£	£
Premises	12,000	
Fixtures & Fittings	2,000	
Equipment	3,000	
Stock	—	
Debtors (customers who owe money)	—	
Bank Account	3,000	
Total Assets:		20,000

LIABILITIES: THE FINANCE OWED BY A BUSINESS.

G. Harrison's liabilities:

	£	£
• Creditors (money owed to suppliers)	—	
Mortgage on Premises	8,000	
Bank Loan	2,000	
Total Liabilities:		10,000

WHAT IS G. HARRISON WORTH?
Simply the *difference* between assets and liabilities.

Total Assets:		20,000
Less		
Total Liabilities:		10,000
Harrison's 'Net Worth' (his Capital)	=	10,000

The balance sheet is simply a list of assets, liabilities and capital of a business at any given time. These are constantly changing in response to the business's trading activity.

The balance sheet of G. Harrison on 1 January is as follows:

	£	£
Fixed Assets (at cost)		
Premises	12,000	
Fixtures and Fittings	2,000	
Equipment	3,000	17,000
Current Assets		
Stock	—	
Debtors	—	
Bank	3,000	
		3,000
Total Assets		20,000

less
Current Liabilities
Creditors   —

Long-term Liabilities
Mortgage on Premises   8,000
Bank Loan   2,000
                                             ———
                                             10,000
                    Total Liabilities   10,000
                                                    ———
                                                    10,000
                                                    ———
Financed by
Capital: G. Harrison   10,000
                                                    ———

These figures are represented by the accounting equation:

Capital	=	Assets	—	Liabilities
£10,000	=	£20,000	—	£10,000

Alternatively, the equation may be represented as

Assets	=	Capital	+	Liabilities
£20,000	=	£10,000	+	£10,000

The first equation $(C = A - L)$ tends to emphasise the net worth of the owner. The alternative equation $(A = C + L)$ tends to emphasise the business as financed by a combination of the owner's capital + borrowed capital.

The Accounting Equation

       Capital   =   Assets

Or in words: the capital provided by the owner = the resources owned by the business.

       Capital   +   Liabilities   =   Assets

That is, the combination of the owner's capital plus what is borrowed = the financing of the assets.
From the owner's point of view:

       Capital   =   Assets   —   Liabilities

Categories of Assets and Liabilities

The two main categories of **assets** are

FIXED   that is, those more or less used permanently in the business: premises, equipment, fixtures and fittings, motor vehicles.

CURRENT   that is, those assets used for trading purposes and constantly circulating from cash, bank, stock and debtors. Current assets have a higher liquidity than fixed assets because they can be converted into cash more quickly.

Other types:

INTANGIBLE ASSETS
               that is, those assets not included above which tend to be 'invisible'. For example, *goodwill* – a business willing to pay to purchase another business may have to include a sum for the reputation or good name of that business.

INVESTMENTS
               that is, when a business buys property, stocks or shares in other business enterprises.

There are two main categories of **liabilities**:

LONG-TERM (deferred)
               for example, Bank loans, mortgages.
               The debt to be repaid runs longer than the business's financial year. That is, creditors after 12 months.

CURRENT   for example, creditors, banks overdraft, bills still outstanding. Short-term debts which will be repaid within the business's financial year. That is, creditors within 12 months.

Try this exercise:
The following represents the assets and liabilities of H. Brown, a retail proprietor, as on 1 January:

Assets	£
Land and Buildings	15,000
Bank a/c	2,500
Stock at cost	3,000
Equipment	1,800
Motor Van	750
Debtors	150
Cash	100
Fixtures	1,750

Liabilities

Mortgage on Land and Buildings	10,000
Bank Loan (4 years)	2,000
Creditors	1,850
Bills outstanding	120

Required

(a) Place the above in their appropriate categories.
(b) Calculate the net worth (or capital) of H. Brown.
(c) Prepare a balance sheet as at 1 January.
(d) Show the accounting equation from the point of view of the proprietor, including the figures.
(e) Show the alternative equation including the figures.

The assets are the resources of the business:

Which parties are financing the resources of the business?

Make a list of the financial institutions where a businessman can borrow money to finance his enterprise.

Check your answers below.

(a)

Assets		*Liabilities*	
Fixed:	Current:	Long-term:	Current:
Land and Buildings	Stock	Mortgage	Creditors
Equipment	Debtors	Bank Loan	Bills outstanding
Fixtures	Bank		
Motor Van	Cash		

(b) Net Worth: the owner's capital

$$C = \text{Assets} - \text{Liabilities}$$
$$£11,080 = £25,050 - £13,970$$

(c) *Balance Sheet of H. Brown as on 1 January*

	£	£
Fixed Assets		
Land and Buildings	15,000	
Fixtures	1,750	
Equipment	1,800	
Motor Van	750	19,300

Current Assets

Stock	3,000	
Debtors	2,500	
Bank	150	
Cash	100	5,750
Total Assets		25,050

less
Current Liabilities

Creditors	1,850	
Bills outstanding	120	
	1,970	

Long-term Liabilities

Mortgage on L and B	10,000	
Bank Loan	2,000	
	12,000	
Total Liabilities		13,970
Net Assets		11,080

Financed by

Capital: H. Brown	11,080

(d)
Capital	=	Assets	–	Liabilities
£11,080		£25,050		£13,970

(e)
Assets	=	Capital	+	Liabilities
£25,050		£11,080		£13,970

Parties financing the resources

H. Brown	£11,080	
Total		
Liabilities	13,970	£25,050

Some of the financial institutions where a businessman could borrow capital to help finance his enterprise:

(i) The Banks (for example, loans and overdrafts).
(ii) The building societies (for example, mortgages on premises).
(iii) The insurance companies (for example, mortgages and loans on policies).
(iv) The finance companies (for example, loans and hire-purchase finance).

The following is an incomplete Balance Sheet of Arthur Smith. Complete the exercise yourself.

Balance Sheet of Arthur Smith as on 1 June

Fixed Assets	£	
Premises	19,500	
Fixtures and Fittings	1,750	
Motor Vehicle	800	
tools, Equipment	500	*22550*
Current		
Stock	1,650	
Debtors	1,020	
Bank	–	
Cash	150	*2820*
		25370
Current Liabilities		
Creditors	1,245	
Bank Overdraft	875	
Bills due	80	*2200*
Long-term		
Mortgage on Premises	10,000	
Hire-Purchase Finance	1,200	*11200* *13400*
Financed by	?	
Capital: Arthur Smith	——	*11970*

Complete the accounting equation figure: C = A − L

11970 = 25370 − 13400.

Changes in the Balance Sheet

When G. Harrison started his business, he had £10,000 of his own money which he put into his business bank account. The accounting equation is

$$
\begin{aligned}
\text{Capital} &= \text{Assets} \\
£10{,}000 &= £10{,}000 \text{ (Bank a/c)}
\end{aligned}
$$

He then used his capital to finance the business resources:

(a) He bought the shop for £12,000 by depositing £4000 cash and getting a mortgage from the local building society for the balance of £8000.
(b) He paid a £2000 cheque for Fixtures and fittings.
(c) He paid a further £3000 cheque for Equipment.
(d) He needed to borrow £2000 from the bank on a 2 year loan to ensure he had sufficient resources for future expenditure.

What did his financial position look like after these transactions?

Bank Account	£	£
Balance		10,000
less Payments:		
Premises	4,000	
Fixtures	2,000	
Equipment	3,000	9,000
		1,000
Add Loan		2,000
New balance		3,000

What does G. Harrison's Balance Sheet look like now?

Fixed Assets	£	£
Premises	12,000	
Fixtures and fittings	2,000	
Equipment	3,000	17,000
Current Assets		
Bank	3,000	3,000
		20,000
less		
Long-term Liabilities		
Mortgage	8,000	
Bank Loan	2,000	10,000
		10,000
Financed by		
Capital: G. Harrison		10,000

Check the accounting equation:

$$A = C + L$$
$$\text{or } C = A - L$$

The balance sheet of Mr. Harrison has changed because of the financial transactions. His balance sheet still balanced, however, because for each transaction there were *two* aspects to record: for example
  When he bought the equipment for £3000

He *received* the equipment	(Asset +)	Equipment a/c	£3,000
He *gave* the cheque	(Asset −)	Bank a/c	−£3,000

This is the basic convention in accounting: there is a *dual-aspect* for each transaction.

In the next part of the text, the dual-aspect of recording will be shown by using the ledger (that is, the book of financial accounts).

Alternative presentation of the balance sheet

The balance sheet has been presented in a vertical format relating to the accounting equation:

Assets − Liabilities = Capital

This method has the distinct advantage of having figures listed in columnar form which makes it easier for comparison purposes. The vertical method of presentation is the most commonly used.

The alternative format is a horizontal layout listing assets on the left and capital and liabilities on the right. This method relates to the alternative accounting equation:

Assets = Liabilities + Capital

G. Harrison's balance sheet

Fixed Assets	£	£	Liabilities	£	£
Premises	12,000		Long-term		
Fixtures and fittings	2,000		Mortgage	8,000	
Equipment	3,000	17,000	Bank Loan	2,000	10,000
Current Assets			Capital		
Bank		3,000	G. Harrison		10,000
		20,000			20,000

Both formats are acceptable in accounting practice. One of the conventions of accounting is consistency. Once a particular method of doing things is decided, then that method is applied consistently. The text will follow the vertical format because of the advantage of showing comparison figures if required.

The following is an example showing the balance sheet changes of a trader, H. Jones. He commenced business on 1 January when he inherited a small retailing business from his uncle:

Transaction	A* (£)	L* (£)	C* (£)	Result (£)
1. Started business: inherited premises £20,000 and also put £5,000 into bank	25,000		25,000	Capital: 25,000 Assets: 25,000
2. Bought £3,500 of stock on credit from XYZ	3,500	3,500		A: 28,500 L: 3,500
3. Bought £1,500 of stock by cheque	+1,500 −1,500			No change
4. Bought a motor vehicle £2,500: cheque £500 (deposit); balance from Jack's Garage on credit	+2,500 − 500	2,000		A: 30,500 L: 5,500
5. Put another £500 cash into bank from own resources	+500		500	A: 31,000 L: 5,500 C: 25,500
6. Bought equipment £2,000 by cheque	+2,000 −2,000			No change
7. Paid £1,000 to Jack's Garage on account	−1,000	−1,000		A: 30,000 L: 4,500

*A = Assets, L = Liabilities, C = Capital.

Note: For every transaction, *two* aspects are recorded:

> One account *receives*
> The corresponding account *gives*

This enables the balance sheet to balance.

Balance Sheet of H. Jones after the transactions in January took place:

	£	£	£
Fixed Assets			
Premises	20,000		
Equipment	2,500		
Motor Vehicle	2,000		24,500
Current Assets			
Stock	5,000		
Bank	500	5,500	
Current Liabilities			
Creditors		3,500	
Working Capital			2,000
			26,500
Deferred Liabilities			
Garage (2 years)			1,000
			25,500
Financed by			
Capital: H. Jones			25,500

Accounting Equation:
$$C = A - L$$
$$25,500 = 30,000 - 4,500$$

G. Harrison's Balance Sheet as at 31 December (see p. 32)

After a year's trading Harrison's financial position is shown through his balance sheet. Note that he has made a profit of £5,500. (The calculation of profit is shown in the part concerning trading and profits and loss account.) He has also drawn money from his business for his own living expenses. This is the proprietor's 'drawings' which is deducted from his capital.

In this presentation. Harrison's *working capital* is also shown by simply deducting current liabilities from current assets. Working capital is an important concept because it indicates the business's ability to pay off its current debts. The business must have sufficient liquidity to trade comfortable without wondering if there is money available to pay off creditors. Harrison is in a sound position on 31 December because there is twice the value of current assets over current liabilities.

	£	£	£
Fixed Assets (at cost)			
Premises	10,000		
Fixtures and fittings	3,000		
Equipment	5,000		18,000
Current Assets			
Stock	8,000		
Debtors	1,500		
Bank	2,400		
Cash	100	12,000	
less			
Current Liabilities			
Creditors	5,500		
Bills outstanding	500	6,000	
Working Capital			
			6,000
			24,000
less			
Long-term Liabilities			
Mortgage on Premises	7,750		
Bank Loan	4,250		12,000
Net Assets			12,000
Financed by			
Capital (1 January)	10,000		
+ Profit	5,500	15,500	
− Drawings		3,500	12,000

Note : This presentation of the balance sheet is a little more sophisticated than the earlier examples and will be used as the standard format in the remainder of the text.

Exercises

1. Place these assets, liabilities of J. Smith, hardware merchant, in the form
    of a Balance Sheet.

Shop	8,000		
Equipment	1,500	Bank mortgage	7,000
Motor van	900	Creditors*	115
Bank	120	Loan from	
		Insurance Company	500
Cash	35		
		Capital:	
Stocks	1,175	J. Smith	4,335
Debtors*	220		

Notes — debtors represent people who owe Mr Smith money.
          creditors represent people whom Mr Smith owes money.

A. Illustrate Mr Smith's figures by means of the accounting equation.
B. Which party holds the most claim on the business's assets?
C. If Mr Smith paid off his creditors by cheque, how would this affect his
    balance sheet?
D. Could he buy £125 worth of stock without money in the bank? How
    could the transaction be financed?
E. Prepare a new balance sheet incorporating the changes in C. and D.
    above.

2. John Jones started up in business during the first week of April with a
    motor vehicle worth £800 and deposited £3,000 in the bank as his
    investment in the business.
        The accounting equation would therefore be:

Capital	=	Assets	−	Liabilities
£3,800	=	£3,800	−	0

During the month of April, John Jones's initial transactions were
involved in using the capital to commence business operations:

	£
(a) Bought stock, paying by cheque	1,500
(b) Bought equipment on credit from Jackson & Co. Ltd	2,000
(c) Paid £300 cheque for tools and other equipment	300
(d) Paid a cheque for a trailer to be used on the motor vehicle	240
(e) Borrowed from the bank a loan extended over two years	1,000
(f) Paid Jackson & Co. Ltd 10% of the sum owing	

Required:

(a) Show the dual-effect of each of John Jones's transactions during April. The first one is done for you:

Stock a/c increases £1,500 (asset +)
Bank a/c decreases £1,500 (asset −)

(b) Prepare a statement to show how much John has in his bank account after the above transactions have been completed.
(c) Prepare a balance sheet for John Jones as at 30 April listing his resources and the financing of them.
(d) Calculate John's working capital on 30 April. Do you consider it sufficient? Give a brief explanation.

3. The following accounts represent the financial interests of M. Crooks on 1 June 1988. He runs a small business associated with the building trade.

	£
Premises	33,500
Machinery and Equipment	12,500
Tools	1,500
Motor Vehicle	4,200
Furniture in the Office	1,500
Stocks (at cost)	15,000
Debtors	1,275
Cash	100
Bank Overdraft	1,750
Creditors for supplies	13,450
Bills outstanding	750
Interest payments due	125
Mortgage on Premises	22,500
Hire-purchase loan on Motor Vehicle (2 years)	1,000
Bank Loan (5 years)	10,000
Capital a/c: M. Crooks	20,000

Required:

(a) Group the above accounts in their appropriate categories — for example, current asset, fixed asset, etc.
(b) Prepare the balance sheet of M. Crooks as at 1 June 1988.
(c) Show the accounting equation which would emphasise the ownership of M. Crooks.
(d) The liabilities of the owner look rather excessive. Has he sufficient funds to meet his current debts?
(e) Crooks must find at least £2,000 by the end of the month to pay off bills and creditors outstanding. Suggest how he could pay them!

4. Complete the following table. Enter the figures in the appropriate columns.

	Assets		Liabilities		Capital
	Current	Fixed	Current	Fixed	
	£	£	£	£	£
(a) Proprietor's Capital: Robert David £ 13,985					
(b) Plant, Equipment 4,000					
(c) Premises 12,000					
(d) Debtors 3,725					
(e) Creditors 4,630					
(f) Loan from P. Jackson 3,500					
(g) Building Society Loan 8,000					
(h) Drawings for proprietor's personal use* 2,000					
(i) Stocks 6,500					
(j) Bank 1,850					
(k) Cash 40					

*Drawings are a *deduction* from proprietor's capital. Anything taken from the business for *personal* use reduces the owner's capital.

Required:

(a) Prepare a balance sheet on 1 June for the proprietor — Robert David. Show working capital as part of the presentation.
(b) The loans from P. Jackson and the Building Society are both longer than 12 months and therefore are to be treated as long term.
(c) Why is adequate working capital important?

5. Redraft the balance sheet below of Harry Smith as at 30 June in vertical form: it is a poor presentation which needs adjustment.

Capital		£	Assets	£
H. Smith		12,000	Premises	25,500
Liabilities			Motor Vehicles	4,500
Loan from Frank		24,000	Drawings of Harry	1,000
Overdraft		1,505	Office Equipment	3,000
Creditors	4,500		Cash	100
−Debtors	3,490	1,010	Stocks	3,780
Gas Bill due		55	Fixtures and fittings	1,050
HP on vehicles				
outstanding ($\frac{1}{2}$ year)		360		
		38,930		38,930

Also required:

(a) A brief comment regarding the extent of liabilities in relation to Harry's own capital.
   The loan from Frank is over a period of 5 years.
(b) An opinion as to whether Harry's cash resources are adequate.
(c) A comment on Harry's capital tied up in fixed assets relative to capital tied up in his trading assets (current assets).
(d) Show the accounting equation illustrating C = A − L.

6. The following represents the financial figures of R. James as at year ended 30 June.

Assets	£	Capital a/c	£
Land and Buildings	25,000	R. James 1 January	20,000
Furniture and fittings	5,500		
Equipment	7,000	*Liabilities*	
Motor Van	6,500	Mortgage	15,500
Bank	2,500	Bank loan (5 years)	10,500
Cash	50	Interest owing	750
Debtors	1,450	Creditors	4,500
Stock	8,000	Bills outstanding	1,000
Profit from trading	8,250		
Proprietor's personal			
expenses	4,500		

Required:

(a) Prepare a balance sheet for R. James as at 30 June. Show his working capital as part of the presentation.
(b) Comment on the owner's working capital.

(c) On a capital outlay of £20,000 on 1 January, would you say that the profit was reasonable?
What would you receive in income if the money was invested in the bank or building society at current rates?
(d) What other motives are there for going into business besides making profit?

7. *Balance Sheet of J. Robertson as on 31 December, 1989*

Assets	£	Capital	£	£
Plant & Machinery	7,075	J. Robertson (1/1)?		
Motor Vans	8,350	Net Loss	3,850	
Tools & Equipment	1,875	Drawings	2,910	17,740
Stocks	51,450			
Debtors	2,421	Liabilities		
Cash	904	Loan a/c (8 years)		11,460
		H–P Finance (3 years)		9,293
		Creditors		20,170
		Bank Overdraft		14,212
	72,875			72,875

Required:

(a) Calculate J. Robertson's capital on 1 January, 1989.
(b) Prepare the balance sheet of J. Robertson in the vertical method showing the amount of working capital.
(c) What kind of trading year do you consider Robertson has had? Make a brief comment.

8. The information below relates to the summarised balance sheets of R.D. Andrews:

	Year 1 £	Year 2 £	Year 3 £
Stock	800	1,040	2,920
Debtors	740	700	620
Bank/Cash	440	300	–
Premises	16,000	16,000	16,000
Other fixed assets	1,300	1,300	1,380
	19,280	19,340	21,000
Capital	18,000	18,220	19,180
Bank O/D			1,020
Creditors	1,280	1,120	800
	19,280	19,340	21,000

Required:
(a) Calculate the working capital of R.D. Andrews at the end of each year.
(b) Calculate the working capital ratio correct to 1 decimal place.
(c) In which of the 3 years do you consider R. D. Andrews is best able to meet his current debts? Explain why.

The Development, Purpose and Function of Accounting

Objectives

To understand the principles of recording financial transactions in the ledger system.

To recognise the need for several ledgers as the business expands.

To be aware of the source documents for financial information (for example, invoices, credit notes, statements) for entry to the day books and ledgers.

To recognise the need of the cash book for cash transactions.

To prepare a bank reconciliation statement to cross-check the cash book with the bank statements.

To prepare a petty cash book for minor cash payments.

To be aware of the importance of the computer for the recording of financial information.

By keeping records of accounts it is possible to know more accurately and efficiently the state of affairs of a business. It is essential to know the exact balances of accounts because when the time comes to, say, pay a creditor or collect money from a debtor, accurate figures must be available to ensure the right amount is paid at the right time.

In a small business of a sole-trader or partnership, the keeping of formalised accounts may be absent. Financial record-keeping may be restricted to the basic and simple: for example, a book for receipts and payments of money (cash book); the processing of documents like the invoice and credit note relating to sales and purchases and the filing of all bills relating to the business.

In larger business enterprises, the paper work expands as the business expands and becomes more complex. The financial accounts of the enterprise must be prepared in a more formalised way. Accurate records must be kept in order to provide the business with day-to-day information. Relevant information can then be extracted from the records and passed on to those persons who need to use it. Suppliers' accounts can then be paid at the right time and customers can be chased up if their accounts are overdue.

One of the most important functions of accounting is to summarise financial information periodically in order to prepare profit and loss reports and balance sheets for owners and management and other interested parties such as the Inland Revenue. From these records, the performance of the business can be evaluated, giving those interested parties vital information on which to base their decisions.

In this section, the ledger is the key to the recording process. It is based on the principle of *double-entry* which simply means that each transaction has a dual-aspect and each aspect must be recorded in an account in the ledger.

The recording of accounts in the ledger system enables the business to be better organised and controlled.

Large businesses have several ledgers for the purpose of organising their accounts more efficiently. Sales ledgers are used to record debtors only, purchase (bought) ledgers for creditors only, cash ledgers for cash transactions, and a general ledger for other groups of accounts. In this way, accounting serves the needs of the organisation, providing a framework for the collection and recording of financial data.

PART 1

The Ledger System

The section will concentrate on recording transactions involving assets, liabilities and capital accounts.

The Balance Sheet could be used to record all changes brought about by financial transactions. However, this would be very tedious and time-consuming because the Balance Sheet would change after every transaction. The Ledger is used instead. The Balance Sheet is only used to show the business's financial position at any specific time required by the owner or management of the business.

The Ledger is a system in accounting to record all financial transactions. It is a book or collection of accounts and provides the fundamental basis of keeping accounting records. It is from these accounts that reports of profit and loss and financial position can be prepared.

The Ledger is designed to record the principle of 'double-entry' – that is, every financial transaction has two aspects and each aspect is recorded in an account; for example.

Paid a cheque of £500 for Equipment

Equipment account is one aspect because the value of equipment will increase by £500. The Bank account is the other because the cheque paid will reduce the amount in the bank.

The following is an example of the traditional ledger headings where the page is divided into two to show debits on the left side and credits on the right.

Debit   Credit

Date	Particulars	Amount £	Date	Particulars	Amount £
			The Name of the Account		

Analysis of the Ledger

(a) The ledger has two sides.
(b) The left side is the *DEBIT* side.
(c) The right side is the *CREDIT* side.
(d) The name of an account is placed in the centre of the ledger page.
(e) The particulars column is used to record the details of a transaction.

Key Points in Recording Ledger Transactions

Double-entry recording is a method in which *two* entries are recorded for every transaction.
   Every transaction has two aspects to it:

(a) the receiving of goods or services is one aspect, and
(b) the payment for these by cash or credit is the other.

Each of these aspects is recorded in an account. One account will record:

(a) the value received on the *DEBIT* side (Dr.), and
(b) the value given on the *CREDIT* side (Cr.).

A Basic Rule in Accounting is:

   All *ASSET* accounts received are debited and
   All *CAPITAL* and *LIABILITY* accounts received are credited.

   Therefore, if an asset is increased, it is a debit entry and if it is decreased, it is a credit entry. For example, furniture £200, is purchased for cash:

   Furniture Account   Debit   £200
   Cash Account   Credit   £200

   Two entries are recorded for each transaction and in this case, the asset furniture is increased (Dr) and cash decreased (Cr).

Conversely, when either a capital or liability account is increased, it represents a credit entry and when decreased, a debit entry. For example, if a motor van was purchased on credit terms for £3,000 from Henley Ford Ltd:

Motor Van Account   Debit   £3000
Henley Ford Ltd. a/c   Credit   £3000

The asset, motor van, is increased (Dr), and the liability, Henley Ford Ltd. is also increased (Cr).

The Ledger of G. Harrison – An Example

	Account Dr.	Account Cr.
1/1 G. Harrison started business with £10,000 in the bank. Which account is Dr and which account is Cr?	Bank (A+)	Capital (C+)
5/1 Harrison paid a £3,000 cheque for Equipment and £4,000 cheque as a Deposit on Premises.	Equipment (A+) Premises (A+)	Bank (A−) Bank (A−)
Obtained a Mortgage £8,000 over 10 years, on the Premises.	Premises (A+)	Mortgage (L+)
7/1 Obtained a Bank Loan £2,000 from NatWest over 3 years.	Bank (A+)	Bank Loan (L+)
10/1 Paid £2,000 cheque for Fixtures.	Fixtures (A+)	Bank (A−)

A = Asset
L = Liability

A business transaction may be any financial activity which involves the business as in the examples above. Each transaction has 2 aspects, one debit, the other credit, which must be recorded in order to get the full picture of the ledger accounts.

The ledger entries of G. Harrison are as follows:

Debit					Credit

Date	Particulars	Amount £	Date	Particulars	Amount £
			Bank a/c		
Jan. 1	Capital	10,000	Jan. 5	Equipment	3,000
7	Bank loan	2,000	5	Premises	4,000
			10	Fixtures	2,000
			Capital a/c		
			Jan. 1	Bank	10,000
			Equipment a/c		
Jan. 5	Bank	3.000			
			Premises a/c		
Jan. 5	Bank	4,000			
	B.S. Mortgage	8,000			
			Building Society Mortgage a/c		
			Jan. 5	Premises	8,000
			Bank Loan a/c		
			Jan. 7	Bank	2,000
			Fixtures a/c		
Jan. 10	Bank	2,000			

Note: (a) Where an asset increases, the entry is debited.
  Where it decreased (Bank a/c) the entries are credited.
  (b) Where capital or liability accounts increase, the entries are credited.
  (c) What is the *BALANCE* of each account? That is, the difference in values between the debit and credit entries (Bank a/c £3,000).

Balancing the Accounts in the Ledger

The balance of each account is the *difference* between the two sides of an account. The balance of Harrison's bank account is £3,000 because the debit side is greater than the credit side by this amount.

Procedure

(a) Enter 'Balance c/d' (carried down) on the lesser value of the two sides.
(b) This has the effect of making both sides equal. The total amounts of both sides must appear on the same line.
(c) Once the totals have been entered, the word 'Balance b/d' (brought down) is entered under the totals, on the opposite side of 'Balance c/d'. This shows the value standing in an account at a particular time.
(d) Accounts in the Ledger may be balanced as frequently as the volume of transactions allow. The greater the volume of transactions, the greater the need to keep accounts up to date and therefore balanced.

The balancing of G. Harrison's Bank a/c

Debit (Dr.)   Credit (Cr.)

£   £

Bank a/c

Jan.	1	Capital	10,000	Jan.	5	Equipment	3,000
	7	Bank loan	2,000		5	Premises	4,000
					10	Fixtures	2,000
					12	Balance c/d	3,000
			12,000				12,000

Jan. 13   Balance b/d   3,000

Where entries occur on one side of an account only, these need only be added:

Premises a/c

Jan.	5	Bank	4,000
		B.S. Mortgage	8,000
			12,000

The Ledger of ABC Company: An Example Exercise

On 1st July, the ledger account balances of ABC Company were:

Dr.   Cr.

Premises a/c

1/7 Balance 25,000	

Fixtures & Fittings a/c

1/7 Balance 12,500	

Motor Vehicle a/c

1/7 Balance 2,750	

Stock a/c

1/7 Balance 1,500	

Bank a/c

1/7 Balance 2,500	

R. Jones a/c (creditor)

	1/7 Balance 4,500

Interest Owing a/c

	1/7 Balance 1,750

Mortgage on Premises a/c

	1/7 Balance	15,000

Capital a/c

	1/7 Balance	23,000

Note: 1. All asset account balances are DEBIT.
   2. All liability and capital account balances are CREDIT.
   3. What is the balance of ABC's Capital a/c?

   $$C \quad = \quad A \quad - \quad L$$
   $$23,000 \quad = \quad 44,250 \quad - \quad 21,250$$

   4. Below, transactions occur on 3 July which are then posted to the Ledger.

Using the existing accounts of ABC Company on this page, which ledger entries would be required for the following transactions:
All transactions on 3 July:

	£
(a) ABC purchased stock paying by cheque	1,000
(b) £450 cheque paid against the interest owing	450
(c) A new trailer for the motor vehicle paying by cheque	250
(d) ABC purchased additional equipment on credit terms from XYZ Co.	1,500
(e) Stock was purchased on credit from Jones	750

Double-entries

	Debit £	Credit £
(a) Stock a/c (A+)	1.000	
Bank a/c (A−)		1,000
(b) Interest owing a/c (L−)	450	
Bank a/c (A−)		450
(c) Motor Vehicle a/c (A+)	250	
Bank a/c (A−)		250
(d) Equipment a/c (A+)	1,500	
XYZ Co. Ltd. (L+)		1,500
(e) Stock a/c (A+)	750	
R. Jones a/c (L+)		750
Total debits and credits	3,950	3,950

A = Asset
L = Liability

Note: For each transaction there is a double entry.
One account is debited, its corresponding account is credited.

Why is it so important to record both accounts?
Because when a transaction occurs, something is received and something is
given. In (a), for example, the Stock a/c increased by £1,000 and therefore it
was debited to show the increase. At the same time, the bank a/c was reduced
after the payment of the cheque.

Ledger Accounts of ABC Company – after transactions on 3 July.

On 3rd July, the ledger account balances of ABC Company were:

Dr.   Cr.

Premises a/c

1/7 Balance	25,000		

Fixtures & Fittings a/c

1/7 Balance	12,500		

Motor Vehicle a/c

1/7 Balance	2,750		
3/7 Bank	250		

Stock a/c

1/7 Balance	1,500		
3/7 Bank	1,000		
3/7 Jones	750		

Bank a/c

1/7 Balance	2,500	3/7 Stock	1,000
		3/7 Motor V	250
		3/7 Interest	450

R. Jones a/c (creditor)

	1/7 Balance 4,500
	3/7 Stock 750

Interest Owing a/c

3/7 Bank 450	1/7 Balance 1,750

Mortgage on Premises a/c

	1/7 Balance 15,000

Capital a/c

	1/7 Balance 23,000

Equipment a/c

3/7 XYZ Co. 1,500	

XYZ Co. Ltd.

	3/7 Equipment 1,500

Find out the balance of each account.

   Check: Bank a/c   = £800 Debit.

                Interest a/c   = £1300 Credit.

From the above ledger accounts, a Balance Sheet has been prepared for ABC Company as on 3 July:

Balance Sheet of ABC Company as at 3 July

	£	£	£
Fixed Assets			
Premises	25,000		
Fixtures and Fittings	12,500		
Equipment	1,500		
Motor Vehicle	3,000		42,000
Current Assets			
Stock	3,250		
Debtors	—		
Bank	800	4,050	
less Current Liabilities			
Creditors (Jones)	5,250		
Interest owing	1,300	6,550	
*Working Capital			(2,500)
			39,500
less Deferred Liabilities			
Mortgage	15,000		
XYZ Co. (2 years)	1,500		16,500
Net Assets			23,000
Financed by			
Capital: ABC Co.			23,000

Note: *Working Capital is a negative figure because current liabilities exceed current assets. On 3 July, ABC Co. is not in a position to meet current debt. This is known as *insolvency*. The business needs to inject more liquid capital otherwise it may meet financial difficulties. All the capital is tied up in fixed assets rather than current assets.

Exercises

1. Which of the following accounts have Debit balances? Which have Credit balances? Tick the appropriate column.

Account	Debit	Credit
Fixtures and Fittings		
Debtors		
Creditors		
Bank		
Motor Vehicles		
Stock		
Mortgage		
Premises		
Bank Overdraft		
Cash		
Capital		
Equipment		

2. Balance the following accounts on 31 January; bring down the balances the next day.

R. Green a/c (creditor)

		£				£
Jan. 10	Bank	500	Jan. 1	Balance		1,180
30	Bank	1,830	20	Goods		1,000
			27	Goods		150

Bank a/c

Jan. 1	Balance	3,500	Jan. 3	ABC Ltd	850
3	R. Smith	500	4	Southern Gas	275
			8	Rent	85
			10	R. Green	500
			12	Wessex Water	125
			30	R. Green	1,830
			31	Goods	200

Goods a/c (Purchases)

Jan. 1	Balance	250
20	R. Green	1,000
27	R. Green	150
31	Bank	200

3. The following transactions are to be recorded in the ledger of R. David during the month of June:

    June
    1   Commenced business with a motor van valued at £600 and a bank account of £1,500.
    2   Bought stock on credit from XYZ Co. £1,800.
    4   Bought tools and equipment, paying by cheque £300.
    8   Paid XYZ Co. £500 on account.
    11 Arranged a loan from Barclay's bank for £2,500 which was entered in the business bank account.
    14 Won £500 on the races and put it into the business!
    15 Sold the motor van for £600 on credit to J. Briggs.
    21 Briggs sent a cheque £250 on account.

    Balance each account at the end of the month and bring down the balance on 1 July.

4. Record the following transactions of J. Bird for the month of January in his ledger:

    January
    1   The owner invested £60,000 in the business by depositing the money into his bank account
    5   A cheque of £26,000 was paid for premises
    11 A motor van was purchased on credit from Jackson, a local car salesman, valued at cost £5,000
    15 Office equipment was paid by cheque £1,750
    23 Paid £1,250 by cheque to a local builder for fixtures and fittings
    25 Arranged a loan from the local bank for £4,000

    Balance each account at the end of the month and bring down the balance.

5. Jack Jones put £5,000 into the Bank on 1 January for the purpose of setting up business. Ledger entries would be:

    bank a/c   £5,000   Debit
    capital a/c   £5,000   Credit

    The following are details of his transactions during the month of January:

    January
    5   Bought a new typewriter for the office, £250 cheque
    6   Bought stock from ABC Co. on credit terms £3,000

7 Bought a second-hand motor van £800. This was financed by a cheque of £250 as a deposit and the rest is on credit from Jake Smith (Car Dealers)

10 Paid £500 cheque to ABC Co. on account

12 The proprietor decides to put another £2,000 in the business from his own savings

15 Purchased fixtures and fittings for the office which was paid by cheque, £750

20 Paid the garage the balance owing on the motor vehicle

21 More stock was purchased for his business:
some of the stock was paid by cheque £254 and there was also £1,125 stock on credit from the supplier, ABC Co.

25 Paid a cheque to ABC Co. on the balance outstanding. On the same day, the owner ordered another £2,400 of stock on credit terms

Required:

(a) Enter each transaction in the ledger of Jack Jones for the month of January.

(b) Balance the accounts on 31 January, bring down the balances.

Introducing Revenue and Expenses in the Ledger

There are *FIVE* distinct groups of accounts:

ASSETS
CAPITAL
LIABILITIES
REVENUE
EXPENSES

The first three of these groups have already been recorded in the ledger: asset balances shown as debits and capital and liability balances shown as credits.

What are Revenue and Expense Accounts?

REVENUE Refers to the income earned by a business by selling its goods or services. Sales is the main form of revenue earned by a business enterprise. Manufacturers make goods to sell.

Wholesalers and retailers form part of the distribution chain to sell the goods to consumers. Professional and trades people sell their services — for example, solicitor's fees, estate agent's commission, an electrician's services.

Income may also come from other sources — for example, rent received, bank interest, dividends, discount received are some of these sources. Banks earn the major part of their revenue from the interest they charge their borrowers, while insurance companies earn their income from selling premiums to their clients. Income may also be invested to earn more income.

EXPENSES   Refers to goods and services paid for by a business. Expenses (or costs) basically fall into three categories: the cost of labour (wages and salaries), the cost of goods or materials (purchases), and the general running expenses of the business (such as light and heat, rates and insurances, advertising, distribution expenses, administration expenses, stationery, printing, and a good number of other overhead costs).

The Recording of Revenue and Expenses

Which Side of the Ledger to Record Expenses?
Expenses are debited in the same way as asset accounts: when an expense is increased, it is a debit entry. When an expense is decreased, it is credited.

Which Side of the Ledger to Record Revenue?
When revenue accounts are increased, they are credited in the same way as for capital and liability accounts.
A decrease in revenue will therefore be a debit entry.

The Ledger of G. Harrison	Account Dr.	Account Cr.
15/1 Paid wages by cheque, £125.	Wages (E+)	Bank (A−)
18/1 Purchased goods by cheque, £500.	Purchases (E+)	Bank (A−)
27/1 Paid gas bill, cheque, £75 30/1 and electricity, cheque, £40	Light & Heat (E+)	Bank (A−)

21/1 Purchased goods from J. Jones £250, a supplier, on credit.	Purchases (E+)		J. Jones (L+)	
10/1 Cash sales paid into bank £750.	Bank (A+)		Sales (R+)	
14/1 Sold goods on credit to J. Hunt, a customer, £285.	J. Hunt (A+)		Sales (R+)	

The ledger account entries of G. Harrison are as follows:

Dr.   Cr.

BANK A/C

8/1	Balance	3,000	15/1	Wages	125
10/1	Sales	750	18/1	Purchases	500
			27/1	Light & Heat	75
			30/1	Light & Heat	40
			31/1	Balance c/d	3,010
		3,750			3,750
1/2	Balance b/d	3,010			

WAGES A/C

15/1	Bank	125

LIGHT & HEAT A/C

27/1	Bank (gas)	75
30/1	Bank (elect.)	40
		115

PURCHASES A/C

18/1	Bank	500
21/1	Jones	250
		750

SALES A/C

			10/1	Bank	750
			14/1	Hunt	285
					1,035

JONES, J. A/C (creditor)

			21/1	Purchases	250

HUNT, J. A/C (debtor)

14/1	Sales	285

The Recording of Stock

The value of unsold stock is an asset to the organisation. At stock-taking time, which takes place at the end of a financial period, the stock is valued usually at cost price and recorded in the stock account.

When the purchasing and selling of stock takes place within the financial period, it is recorded in the purchases and sales accounts respectively and *NOT* in the stock account. In the purchases account it is recorded at its cost price, while in the sales account it is recorded at its selling price.

Example

			£
Jan.	1	Value of unsold stock	1,500
	5	Purchased stock from Brown	1,000
	10	Cash purchases by cheque	400
	12	Sold stock to Jackson	250
	17	Purchased stock from Brown	1,750
	18	Sold stock to Jackson	485
	27	Cash sales paid to Bank	1,250

Note: always assume transactions of
personal accounts of debtors and
creditors to be on a *credit* basis
unless otherwise stated.

Recording Stock in the Ledger

Dr.   Cr.

STOCK A/C

5/1	Balance	1,500		

PURCHASES A/C

5/1	Brown	1,000		
10/1	Bank	400		
17/1	Brown	1,750		
		3,150		

SALES A/C

	12/1 Jackson 250
	18/1 Jackson 485
	27/1 Bank 1,250
	1,985

BANK A/C

27/1 Sales 1,250	10/1 Purchases 400

BROWN A/C

	5/1 Purchases 1,000
	17/1 Purchases 1,750
	2,750

JACKSON A/C

12/1 Sales 250	
18/1 Sales 485	
735	

Review of the FIVE Groups

Assets	Things of value *OWNED* by the busines enterprise; for instance, land, buildings, equipment, bank, cash, debtors, etc.
Liabilities	Things of value *OWING* by the business enterprise; for instance, creditors, overdrafts at the bank, loans, mortgages, etc.
Capital	The difference between the two above is what is owned less what is owed:

$$C \ = \ Assets \ - \ Liabilities$$

This is the basic accounting equation
and may alternatively be written:

$$Assets \ = \ Capital \ + \ Liabilities$$
$$Thus \ C \ = \ A \ - \ L$$
$$or \ A \ = \ C \ + \ L$$

Revenue	The value of goods and services sold; for instance, sales, commission received.
Expenses	The value of goods and services paid; for example, purchases, wages, rent, salaries, heating, etc.

Review of Recording Procedure

Accounting Group	Type of Balance Dr. or Cr.		Increase in the A/C	Decrease in the A/C
Assets	Debit		Debit	Credit
Capital		Credit	Credit	Debit
Liabilities		Credit	Credit	Debit
Revenue		Credit	Credit	Debit
Expenses	Debit		Debit	Credit

A transaction has TWO ASPECTS:

One aspect will be *debited*
the corresponding aspect will be *credited*.

The Trial Balance

The trial balance may be defined as:

'A summary of all the account balances in the ledger to prove the arithmetical accuracy of double-entry recording.'

In other words, there should be a debit entry as well as a credit entry for every transaction. This is the double-entry principle.

At frequent intervals, ledger account balances are listed in the trial balance to prove that the recording process is arithmetically correct.

Mr G. Harrison prepares a trial balance at the end of each month. At 31 January, his trial balance is:

Trial balance of G. Harrison at 31 January

	Dr. £	Cr. £
Bank	3,010	
Premises	12,000	
Fixtures and Fittings	2,000	
Equipment	3,000	
Mortgage		8,000
Bank loan		2,000
Capital G. Harrison		10,000
Wages	125	
Light and Heat	115	
Purchases	750	
Sales		1,035
Creditors		250
Debtors	285	
	21,285	21,285

The totals agree and therefore the arithmetical accuracy of double-entry recording has proved to be correct. If the principle of double-entry is not recorded, the trial balance will fail to balance.

Example

Prepare from the following accounts, a trial balance for P. Jackson, as on 1 January, 1990:

	£		£
Bank Overdraft	300	Sales	48,575
Cash	200	Purchases	35,450
Motor Van	2,420	General Exps.	2,485
Debtors	515	Motor Exps.	850
Creditors	1,225	Rent Received	840
Capital	10,500		
Bank Loan	3,400		
Premises	25,300		
Mortgage	8,950		
Equipment	6,570		

Trial Balance of P. Jackson as on 1/1/90

	Dr. £	Cr. £
Bank Overdraft		300
Cash	200	
Motor Van	2,420	
Debtors	515	
Creditors		1,225
Capital: P. Jackson		10,500
Bank Loan		3,400
Premises	25,300	
Sales		48,575
Purchases	35,450	
General Expenses	2,485	
Motor Expenses	850	
Rent Received		840
Mortgage		8,950
Equipment	6,570	
	73,790	73,790

Exercises

1. The balances of R. James extracted from his ledger on 31 January were as follows:

Account	£
Capital: R. James	12,125
Premises	11,900
Fixtures and Fittings	800
Stock	320

Debtors	1,020
Creditors	890
Sales	6,950
Purchases	4,050
General expenses	1,875

Required:

(a) Prepare a trial balance for R. James as on 31 January.
(b) Categorise each account into one of the five accounting groups.
(c) Which of the above accounts would be listed in the balance sheet?

2. The balances of D. Andrew were taken from the ledger on 30th June:

Account	£
Bank	3,305
Stock	750
Equipment	4,000
Motor Van	1,750
Sales	2,095
Purchases	1,115
Wages	880
Rent	565
General overheads	480
Debtors	955
Creditors	1,560
Bank loan	1,250
Bills outstanding	55
Capital: D. Andrew	8,840

Required:

Prepare the trial balance on 30 June.

3. The following balances were taken from the books of P. McCartney (Music Publisher) on 1st June, 1988:

		£
Bank	Dr. Balance	1,240
Stock	Dr. Balance	2,150
Motor Vehicle	Dr. Balance	1,175
J. Jones	Dr. Balance	248
N. Diamond	Cr. Balance	152
B. Manilow	Cr. Balance	502
Capital: P. McCartney		4,159

Enter the six accounts in Mr McCartney's ledger. The transactions below relate to the month of June. Make appropriate entries in McCartney's ledger.

Assume transactions to be on a credit basis unless otherwise stated.

			£
June	2	Bought stock from N. Diamond	258
	4	J. Jones paid on account	100
	5	Bought stock from B. Manilow	374
	10	The proprietor paid N. Diamond the balance owing 1 June	
	15	Sold vehicle receiving the full book value to Harry Belafonte on credit	
	18	Paid by cheque 10% deposit on a new vehicle costing	2,750
		The balance is on credit from Jake's Garage	
	20	Paid a cheque to B. Manilow $33\frac{1}{3}$% of his outstanding balance	
	28	Paid N. Diamond on account	158
	30	Paid cheque for new stereo equipment to be used on premises	399

Required:

(a) Balance each of the above accounts on 30 June 1988. Ensure that after entering 'balance c/d' that totals are on the same line.

(b) Bring down the balances on 1 July to begin the new month's transactions.

(c) Extract a trial balance as at 30 June 1988.

4. The following represents the ledger entries of Jack Jones, Music Publisher:

Balances of Debtors   *1 April*:

Smith	£250
Lillee	£115
Thomson	£25

Balances of Creditors   *1 April*:

May	£85
Cowdrey	£172

Capital a/c: J. Jones   1 April: £18
Bank a/c: £115 [overdraft]

Transactions occurring during April

April	2	Sold goods to Lillee £287 and to Smith £415
	5	Bought goods from Cowdrey £150
	10	Sold goods to Thomson £37
	15	Settled May's account of 1 April
	17	Smith settled his account of 1 April
	21	Paid £75 to Cowdrey on account

22 Sold goods to Thomson £156
25 Thomson paid £62 on account
26 Bought goods from May £195
29 Paid Cowdrey a further £95 on account
30 Received £201 cheque from Lillee.

Required:

(a) Enter all the above information in Jack's ledger.
(b) Extract a trial balance for the month ending 30 April.

5. *Preparation of Balance Sheets and Ledger recording of A, L and C*

The following represents the financial position of Harry Smith, shop proprietor, on 1 June 1988

Assets	£	Liabilities	£	Capital
Premises	15,000	Long-term		?
Stock	2,150	Bank loan	10,000	
Equipment	1,500			
Bank	463			
		Creditors:		
Debtors:		Brown	1,247	
White	1,150	Jackson	353	
Jones	1,037			

Required:

(a) Draw up a balance sheet as on 1 June to illustrate Harry's financial position.
(b) Using traditional two-sided ledger paper, enter the above account balances as on 1 June 1988.

The transactions below relate to Harry's business during June. Enter them in the ledger.

Note: For every transaction there is a debit entry and a corresponding credit.

			£
June	2	Bought stock from Jackson	1,500
	3	Bought stock by cheque	275
	4	Jones paid £750 cheque on account	
	5	Harry paid Jackson on account	600
	8	Bought stock from Brown	550
	10	Purchased a motor vehicle valued	2,400
		Paid 10% Deposit by cheque	
		The balance outstanding from Jake's Garage Co.	

13	Paid a cheque to Brown	500
	and to Jackson on a/c	300
16	Harry needed to inject a further £1500 into the business from his own resources	
18	Sold £1000 of his old equipment to Gordon on credit	
20	Bought new equipment on credit from ABC Co. Ltd	1,750
21	Gordon sent a cheque to cover 50% of his debt	
25	Paid Jake's garage a cheque which would leave a balance of £1500 owing	
27	Agreed to pay £25 extra for installing new equipment to ABC Co. Ltd (Asset to be dr.)	
30	Paid ABC Co. Ltd £775 on account	
30	Received a cheque from White	337

(c) Extract a trial balance for Harry Smith as on 30 June 1988.

PART 2

The Running Balance Method of Recording Accounts

This method of recording ledger accounts is more updated. Computerised systems use this format rather than the traditional method of dividing ledger pages in half with Dr. entries on the left and Cr. entries on the right.

The Ledger is designed to look more like the page of a bank statement. Dr. and Cr. columns appear side-by-side with the balance column at the end:

Date	Particulars	Dr.	Cr.	Balance
Jan 1	Balance			200 dr.
4	Sales	150		350
15	Sales	100		450
28	Bank		300	150
Feb 1	Balance			150 dr.

(a) After each transaction the balance is updated and has the distinct advantage of balances instantly being known.

(b) In the traditional method of ledger recording, balances may have been brought down at frequent intervals but not with the instant result of having a balance after each entry.

(c) Is the ledger account above a debtor or a creditor?
    What information tells you it is a debtor/creditor?

(d) Were the sales made for cash or on a credit basis?

Below there are four ledger accounts entered in the traditional method.

The bank account at the bottom is in the running balance style which can be checked with the bank account above.

The bank balance of £2,610 ends up the same of course, only the method of recording is different.

Bank A/c

Jan. 1	Capital	8,000	Jan. 3	Premises	4,000
			7	Stock	750
			12	Equip.	380
			19	Stock	80
			27	Tools	180
			31	Balance c/d	2,610
		8,000			8,000
Feb. 1	Balance b/d	2,610*			

Premises A/c

Jan. 1	Bank	4,000

Stock A/c

Jan. 7	Bank	750
19	Bank	80
		830

Equipment and tools A/c

Jan. 12	Bank	380
27	Bank	180
		560

The Bank A/c using the running balance method

		Debit	Credit	Balance
Jan. 1	Capital	8,000		8,000 Dr.
3	Premises		4,000	4,000
7	Stocks		750	3,250
12	Equipment		380	2,870
19	Stock		80	2,790
27	Tools		180	2,610 *

Note: The Bank A/c finishes the month with the identical balance irrespective of the method of ledger recording.

Enter Premises, Stock and Equipment and tools accounts in the running balance format.

An Example Exercise — Ledger and Trial Balance

The ledger uses the running balance method of recording transactions.

J. Jones, the proprietor of a small business enterprise, had £5,000 in his Bank a/c and also a Motor vehicle value £585 on 1 May.

Transactions during May:

May 2 Paid rent for premises £25 per week paying by cheque, 4 weeks in advance
3 Paid for shop fixtures by cheque £475
5 Bought on credit terms goods for resale from:
   J. Randle £150
   T. Smith £225

7 Cash Sales £125 into Bank
8 Shop assistant's wages £55 paid by cheque
9 Cash Sales £85 into Bank
12 Paid by cheque:
   J. Randle £100 on account
   T. Smith £75 on account

15 Shop assistant's wages £55 paid by cheque
16 Cash Sales £98 into Bank
20 Bought on credit terms from J. Randle £300 goods
24 Sold goods on credit to Corfe Mullen Social Club £120
27 Shop assistant's wages £82 by cheque
30 Received from Corfe Mullen Social Club £50 on account
31 Cash Sales £84 into Bank

Required:

(a) The ledger of J. Jones using the running balance method of recording for the month ending 31 May (this is done for you).
(b) Enter the figures for the Trial Balance as on 31 May. The Trial Balance will fail to balance because of an error in the ledger. Find the error and adjust the balance in the ledger.

LEDGER OF J. JONES

Date	Particulars	DR.	CR.	Balance	
Capital a/c					
1/5	Bank		5,000	5,000 (Cr.)	Capital
	Motor Vehicle		585	5,585	
Bank a/c					
1/5	Capital	5,000		5,000 (Dr.)	Asset
2	Rent		100	4,900	
3	Fixtures		475	4,425	
7	Sales	125		4,550	
8	Wages		55	4,495	
9	Sales	85		4,580	
12	Randle, J.		100	4,480	
	Smith, T.		75	4,405	
15	Wages		55	4,350	
16	Sales	98		4,448	
27	Wages		82	4,366	
30	Corfe Mullen Social Club	50		4,416	
31	Sales	84		4,500	
Motor Vehicle a/c					
1/5	Capital	585		585 (Dr.)	Asset
Fixtures a/c					
3/5	Bank	475		475 (Dr.)	Asset
Corfe Mullen Social Club a/c (Debtor)					Asset
24/5	Sales	120		120 (Dr.)	
30	Bank		50	70	
Rent a/c					
2/5	Bank	100		100 (Dr.)	Expenses
Purchases a/c					
5/5	Randle, J.	150		150 (Dr.)	Expenses
	Smith, T.	225		375	
20/5	Randle, J.	300		675	

Note: The final column is not part of the ledger. It indicates, for information only, the group to which the account belongs.

Date	Particulars	DR.	CR.	Balance	
Sales a/c					
7/5	Bank		125	125 (Cr.)	Revenue
9	Bank		85	210	
16	Bank		98	308	
24	Corfe Mullen		120	428	
31	Bank		84	512	
Wages a/c				Expenses	
8/5	Bank	55		55 (Dr.)	
15	Bank	55		110	
27	Bank	82		192	
J. Randle a/c					Liability
5/5	Purchases		150	150 (Cr.)	
12	Bank	100		50	
20	Purchases		300	450	
T. Smith a/c					Liability
5/5	Purchases		225	225 (Cr.)	
12/5	Bank	75		150	

Trial Balance of J. Jones as at month ending 31 May

	Dr.	Cr.
	£	£
Capital — J. Jones		
Bank		
Motor Vehicle		
Fixtures		
Rent		
Purchases		
Wages		
Sales		
J. Randle		
T. Smith		
Corfe Mullen Social Club		

Divisions of the Ledger

The ledger is the book of accounts; or rather, the ledgers are the books of account. When a business enterprise expands its trading operations, invariably the paper work increases too. There is a greater volume of accounts to handle. It may be that the business has a great number of debtors and creditors and wants to keep these in separate ledgers.

To improve the organisation of accounting, the ledger may be divided into four main sections:

Personal ledgers:
1. *The Sales ledger* to record all transactions of customers who are sold goods or services on a credit basis. The ledger for debtors only.
2. *The Bought ledger* (or Purchase ledger) to record all transactions of suppliers for the supply of goods or services on a credit basis. The ledger for creditors only.

The personal ledgers are for PERSONAL accounts — that is, individual debtors and creditors.

3. *The Nominal ledger* (or General ledger). To record all impersonal accounts, that is
(i) All the nominal accounts which are the revenue and expense accounts of the business, such as rent, wages, sales, purchases, etc.
(ii) All the REAL accounts which are the tangible assets of the business (those which can be seen), such as Premises, Equipment, Stock, Bank, etc.
(iii) The capital account of the owner or owners.

4. *The Cash ledger (or Cash Book)* to record all cash and cheque receipts and payments. It may also include the recording of cash discounts — that is, a discount from a sum owing, given for prompt payment.

The three categories of accounts from the above information are:

(a) Personal accounts — names of individual debtors and creditors.
(b) Nominal accounts — impersonal accounts of the revenue and expenses of a business.
(c) Real accounts — asset accounts of a business — that is the value of the business's resources such as premises, stock, bank/cash.

The following is a list of accounts taken from the ledgers of G. Harrison. Make a tick in the appropriate column for each account.

Account	Cash Book	Sales Ledger	Bought Ledger	Nominal Ledger
Debenhams PLC (supplier)			✓	
T. Smith (customer)		✓		
Stock				✓
Bank	✓			
Sales				✓
Purchases				✓
Plant and Machinery				✓
Cash	✓			
Marks & Spencer (supplier)			✓	
Cash discount	✓			
Wages				✓
Light and Heat				✓
Commission				✓
Premises				✓
Admin. Expenses				✓

Nominal accounts: Sales, Purchases, Cash Discount, Wages, Light and Heat, Commission, Admin. Expenses.
Personal accounts: Debenhams, Smith, Marks & Spencer.
Real accounts: Stock, Bank, Plant and Machinery, Cash and Premises.

Exercises

1. The following information relates to the ledger accounts of David Robert as on 31 December 1988.

	£
Premises	15,000
Furniture and Fittings	2,750
Equipment, Tools	2,375
Motor Van	1,340
Bank (Dr.)	320
Purchases	14,050
Sales	16,950
R. Smith (Dr.)	800
J. Hunt (Dr.)	220
S. Jones (Cr.)	1,890
N. Fox (Cr.)	2,000
Wages	3,000
General Expenses	985
Bank Loan: Southern Bank	5,000
Capital: D. Robert (1/1/88)	15,000

Required:

(a) Extract a trial balance as on 31 December 1988.

(b) If more than a single ledger was used, list the accounts which would be entered in each ledger.

(c) Which of the above accounts would not be entered in the balance sheet?

2. Roger Lee has the following accounts in his ledger on 1 May 1988:

	£	
Jackson, P	336	Dr.
Newman, J.	450	Cr.
Sales	1,755	Cr.
Purchases	1,565	Dr.
Bank	525	Dr.
Capital: R. Lee	221	Cr.

The transactions below took place during the month of May. Enter them in the ledger using the running balance method of recording.

			£
May	3	Paid a cheque to Newman on account	275
	5	Sold goods to Jackson	122
	8	Jackson paid on account	168
	10	Cash Sales	375
	12	Bought goods from Newman	227

15	Sold goods to Jackson	210
16	Cash Sales	280
21	Bought goods, paying by cheque	187
23	Bought further goods from Newman	156
25	Paid Newman a cheque on account	125
28	Received a cheque from Jackson which would leave £250 outstanding in his account	
30	Cash Sales	156
	Cash Purchases paid by cheque	450
	New account opened. Sold goods to R. Fanshawe	300

Required:

(a) Enter the opening accounts in the ledger of R. Lee on 1 May 1988.

(b) Enter the above transactions in Lee's ledger for the month of May and also extract a trial balance as at 31 May 1988. Assume transactions of personal a/c's on credit unless otherwise stated.

3. Freddy Smith had the following ledger balances on 1 January 1988:

	£	
Premises (cost)	20,000	(dr.)
Motor Van	1,875	(dr.)
Stock	1,900	(dr.)
Bank	850	(dr.)
Debtors:		
Rollin	420	(dr.)
Vines	268	(dr.)
Mortgage on Premises	16,750	(cr.)
Creditors:		
Boston	1,950	(cr.)
Turner	350	(cr.)

The transactions for the month of January were as follows:

		£
January		
1	General expenses paid by cheque	35
2	Cash sales	125
4	Goods from Boston	2,000
5	Sold to Rollin goods	500
7	Cash sales	225
9	Insurance by cheque	84
11	Purchases by cheque, goods	100
14	Rollin settles account balance of 1 January, by cheque	
15	Cash sales	585
16	Paid cheque to Boston on account	1,000
18	Bought from Turner, goods	750
22	Paid general expenses, cheque	80

24	Sold goods to Vines	450
26	Cash sales	378
27	Vines paid cheque to clear balance owing on 1 January	
30	Cash sales	225
31	Paid Turner £500 on account	

Required:

(a) Extract a trial balance as on 1 January for Freddy Smith, including your calculation of his capital a/c. Enter the balances in his ledger.
(b) Enter the above transaction in the ledger of Freddy Smith using the running balance method. Assume all cash received entered in Smith's bank a/c.
(c) Extract a trial balance for Freddy Smith as at 31 January 1988.

4. On January 1, Jack Brigg's financial position was as follows:

	£	
Premises	17,000	(dr.)
Fixtures	1,500	(dr.)
Stocks	1,200	(dr.)
Bank (overdraft)	675	(cr.)
Cash	150	(dr.)

Debtors

J. Collins	1,100	(dr.)
D. Smith	925	(dr.)

Creditors

R. Jones	1,200	(cr.)

Required:

(a) Find the Capital a/c of J. Briggs and enter the figure in his ledger.
(b) Enter all other accounts in the ledger listed above.

Transactions during JANUARY

Jan.	3	Sold goods to Collins £2,850
	5	Cash Sales £1,300 into Bank
	8	Purchased goods from Jones £1,605
	12	Paid salaries by cheque £300
	13	Owner withdrew £20 cash for personal use (drawings a/c)
	14	Paid £260 cheque for general repairs
	16	Cash Sales £455. Banked £400
	19	Sold goods to Smith £720

26   Paid salaries by cheque £300
27   Cash purchases £90
29   Received cheques from:
       Collins and Smith in settlement of their accounts of Jan. 1
30   Paid Jones by cheque £1,750 on a/c
31   Paid purchases of goods by cheque £175
31   Sold £500 of fixtures cash

Required:

(c) Enter all the above transactions in the ledger of Jack Briggs.
(d) Extract a trial balance as at 31 January 1988.

5. On 1 July the following balances were extracted from the books of George Harrison — record shop owner.

	£	
Capital George Harrison	1,860	(cr.)

As represented by:

Cash/Bank	1,812	(dr.)
Lloyd, C.	440	(dr.)
Jones, D.	168	(dr.)
Bloggs, H.	560	(cr.)

(a) You are required to enter the above information in George's ledger.
(b) Enter the transactions below in the ledger for the month of July. Use the running balance method of recording.

Transactions during July

July 1   Cash Sales £140
     2   General expenses cheque £30
     3   Harrison drew a cheque for personal use £40
     6   Sold to Lloyd £250 goods on credit and to Jones £156 goods on credit
     7   Purchased from Bloggs £400 goods on credit
     8   Cash Sales £160
     9   Paid for purchases of goods by cheque £215
    10   Purchased a motor vehicle £350 cash
    15   Paid by cheque:
           Salaries   £85
           General expenses   £27
           Insurance   £54

    21   Cash Sales £85

22   Sold further goods to Jones on credit £44
24   Cash Sales £80
26   Paid by cheque Bloggs a/c — settled 1 July balance
27   Received cheques from:
       Lloyd having settled the 1 July balance
       Jones £100 on account
28   Paid Bloggs another £150 on account
29   Bought goods on credit from T. Jones £580
30   Paid salaries by cheque £80

(c) Extract a trial balance as at month ending 31 July.

6.   Mr Les Dawson commenced business on 1 January 1987 with Capital of £30,000. He put £28,000 into a business bank account and kept the remainder in a cash account as cash in hand.

      During the first two weeks in January the following business transactions occurred:

Jan. 1   Credit purchases: Green & Co. £4,000 Black & Co. £2,500
      2   Purchased fixtures and fittings £6,200, paying by cheque
      5   Paid by cheque £56, advertising in the local paper
      6   Paid rent six months in advance £6,000 by cheque
      7   Cash sales £400. Credit sales: Redhill & Co. £3,500
      8   Wages paid by cheque £86
      9   Paid insurance premium for 12 months £400, by cheque
      12   Credit purchases: Green & Co. £3,000
      13   Paid postage and stationery by cash £38
      14   Withdrew cash £500 for personal use
      15   Paid Green & Co. 50% of his outstanding balance
      15   Wages paid by cash £84
      16   Cash sales £880. Credit sales: Redhill & Co. £4,600 Shaw Ltd. £2,100
      17   Redhill & Co. send a cheque £5,000 on account
      18   Paid Black & Co. in full, by cheque

Required:

(a) Open appropriate ledger accounts for the business, recording the above transactions. Extract a trial balance as at 17 January 1987.
(b) Why is it necessary to have more than a single ledger system for different types of business organisations?

PART 3

The Sales Day Book (or Sales Journal)

Accounts are compiled from business documents like the invoice and credit note as well as from actual receipts and payments of money. These may first be recorded in the Day Books, or books of prime entry. They are subsidiary books in the accounting system which help to 'feed' information in a collective way to the ledgers.

The function of the day books is to list and summarise all goods and services bought and sold on credit. When these are bought or sold on credit, the invoice acts as the bill of sale and is the evidence of the transaction. When goods are returned to a supplier, the credit note is the documentary evidence of the return.

The day books (or journals) may be listed as:

1. *The Sales Day Book*
   Records all sales on credit to customers by listing the key figures of the invoices sent to customers.
2. *The Purchases Day Book*
   Records all purchases from suppliers on credit by listing all the key figures from the invoices received from suppliers.
3. *The Returns Day Book*
   There are two of these to record:
   (a) Returns Inward Day Book
       Records all returns from customers (sales return).
       Credit notes sent to customers are listed with the key figures.
   (b) Returns Outward Day Book
       Records all returns back to suppliers (purchases return).
       Credit notes received from suppliers are listed with the key figures.

4. *The Cash Book*
   This is the cash ledger and records all receipts and payments of cash or cheques. The cash book 'doubles up' as both subsidiary book and ledger. The petty cash book which records small payments of cash falls into the same category.

5. *The Journal*
   This is also a subsidiary book, but it is not dealt with in this chapter. It is a book to record transactions that are outside the scope of the above books. See Section VII

The Accounting System

So far it has been stated that the recording of transactions is the basis of preparing accounts in a business organisation. Financial transactions are basically by payment of cash or on credit terms, which are then fed through the system via the day books and cash book to the ledger system. The trial balance is a check of the ledger system.

From these records it then becomes possible to prepare accounting statements, particularly at the end of a financial period, to show whether the

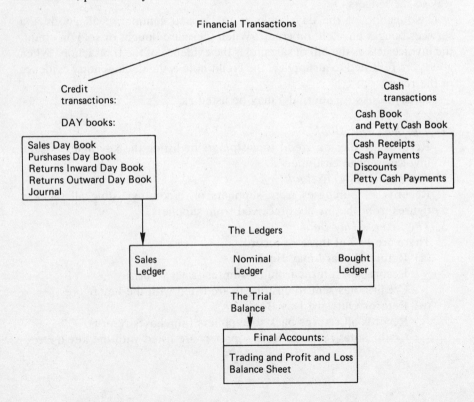

business has made a profit or loss. The statement showing profit or loss is called the Trading and Profit and Loss Account. The Balance Sheet may also be prepared at the same time to show the firm's financial position at that time. These statements are referred to as the 'Final Accounts' of the business.

The Sales Day Book

The sales ledger clerk usually records the sale on credit to the customer from the copy of the invoice sent from the Sales Department. The invoice copy is checked for accuracy before entry.

Details from the invoice to record in the sales day book are:

(a) Date of sale.
(b) name of customer.
(c) Invoice No.
(d) The sales total net (that is, gross sales *less* trade discount).
(e) VAT if applicable.
(f) The total net sales + VAT (if applicable).

If customers return goods, these are recorded in the Returns Inward Book when a copy of the credit note sent to the customer is received by the sales ledger clerk.

The Sales Day Book may be totalled when convenient. This may be daily or weekly or monthly, depending on the volume of sales on credit.

Posting from the Day Book to the Ledgers

The Sales Ledger:

Debit   each debtor account with the net sales value + VAT where applicable (asset +).

The Nominal Ledger:

Credit   the total value of net sales to Sales a/c
the total value of VAT   to VAT a/c   (revenue +)

Where a Sales Ledger Control is used (Debtors Control) to check the Sales Ledger, the Control a/c is Debited with the total of net sales + VAT (where applicable).

The following pages illustrate:

(a) A simplified Sales Day Book without VAT.
(b) A Sales Day Book with VAT.

A Simplified Day Book (without VAT)

Sales Day Book

Date	Customer's a/c	Invoice No.	Amount
1 May	J. Smith	1285	300 Dr.
5 May	R. Jones	1286	255 Dr.
7 May	F. Brown	1287	100 Dr.
15 May	J. Smith	1288	125 Dr.
26 May	F. Brown	1289	120 Dr.
		SALES (CR.)	900

Ledger posting

Date	Particulars	Debit	Credit	Balance
J. Smith a/c				
1 May	Sales	300		300 dr.
15 May	Sales	125		425
R. Jones a/c				
5 May	Sales	255		255 dr.
F. Brown a/c				
7 May	Sales	100		100 dr.
26 May	Sales	120		220
Sales a/c				
31 May	Debtors		900	900 cr.

Note:
The double-entry

(1) Each individual customer (debtor) is debited (Asset +).
(2) The *total* of Sales for the month is credited (Revenue +).

The Sales Invoice

An invoice sent from Mr G. Harrison to one of his customers, R. Thomson:

```
                        I N V O I C E

                           G  Harrison
                    214 The High Street
                           Poole
                           Dorset

  To:  R Thomson
       14 West Way
       Broadstone
       Poole
                                      VAT Reg: 424 28422 56
                                      Invoice No:INV/ 1136
```

Date: 4th June 1987	Your Order Ref: 30 May Despatch Date : 4 June 87	Terms: 10% Trade Carriage Paid

Code Number	Qty	Description	Unit Price	Total Price	Less Trade	Net
1042Z	10	SLAZENGER MK5 tennis rackets	20	200	20	180

```
                                                 ======
                                    TOTAL NET:£180
E&OE                                VAT @15 %:£ 27
```

| Delivery Address: as above | |
| Payment within 28 days of invoice date | TOTAL VALUE:£207 |

*Trade discount refers to a deduction to the customer allowing him to buy the goods at a reduced price. It is normally given to people who are traders.

Cash discount is offered to customers to encourage them to pay their accounts promptly. Mr Harrison offers trade discount but not cash.

Illustrated Example

Sales with VAT and also using the control a/c

On June 1 the balances in the ledgers of Mr G. Harrison were as follows:

Sales Ledger:	£		Nominal Ledger	£	
Thomson	45	Dr.	Sales a/c	8,500	Cr.
Simpson	110	Dr.	VAT a/c	350	Cr.
Jackson	180	Dr.	Sales Ledger		
	335		Control a/c*	335	Dr.

During June, sales invoices (all + 15% VAT) were sent to the following customers:

	Invoice No.	Date	Net Sales £	VAT £
Thomson	1136	4/6	180	
Simpson	1137	10/6	200	
Thomson	1138	11/6	100	
Jackson	1139	15/6	360	
Simpson	1140	20/6	160	

Cheques received from customers at the end of June were:

	£	£
Thomson	300	
Simpson	450	
Jackson	500	1,250

Required:

(a) Enter the opening balances on June 1 in the ledgers of G. Harrison.
(b) Prepare the Sales Day Book for June, calculating the VAT.
(c) Post from the day book to the appropriate ledgers.
(d) Enter the cheques received in the appropriate accounts, including the control account.
(e) Prepare a schedule of debtors to cross-check with the sales ledger control account.

*Sales Ledger Control a/c: [S/L Control a/c]
This is a total a/c representing the total individual accounts in the Sales Ledger (£335). It may be used for both sales and purchases ledgers and is a measure of control; that is, a check can be made to ensure that total balances in the sales ledger (or purchases ledger) = the control a/c balance. *The sales ledger control a/c is also referred to as the debtors' control a/c.*

Sales Day Book: Harrison

Date	Customer's Account	Invoice No.	Sales A/C £	VAT A/C £	Total Debtors A/C £
4/6	Thomson	1136	180	27	207 Dr.
10/6	Simpson	1137	200	30	230 Dr.
11/6	Thomson	1138	100	15	115 Dr.
15/6	Jackson	1139	360	54	414 Dr.
20/6	Simpson	1140	160	24	184 Dr.
			1,000	150	1,150
			(Cr.)	(Cr.)	(Dr.)

Sales Ledger: Harrison

Date	Particulars	Folio	Dr. £	Cr. £	Balance £
Thomson a/c					
1/6	Balance				45 Dr.
4/6	Sales	*S 25	180		
	VAT		27		252
11/6	Sales	S 25	100		
	VAT		15		367
30/6	Bank			300	67
1/7	Balance				67 Dr.
Simpson a/c					
1/6	Balance				110 Dr.
10/6	Sales	S 25	200		
	VAT		30		340
20/6	Sales	S 25	160		
	VAT		24		524
30/6	Bank			450	74
1/7	Balance				74 Dr.
Jackson a/c					
1/6	Balance				180 Dr.
15/6	Sales	S 25	360		
	VAT		54		594
30/6	Bank			500	94
1/7	Balance				94

*Folio cross-reference to the page number of the day book.

Schedule of Debtors (June)

	£
Thomson	67 Dr.
Simpson	74
Jackson	94
	*235

General Ledger: Harrison

Date	Particulars	Folio	Dr.	Cr.	Balance
Sales a/c			£	£	£
1/6	Balance				8,500 Cr.
30/6	Debtors	S 25		1,000	9,500
1/7	Balance				9,500 Cr.
VAT a/c					
1/6	Balance				350 Cr.
30/6	Debtors	S 25		150	500
1/7	Balance				500 Cr.
*S/L Control a/c					
1/6	Balance				335 Dr.
30/6	Sales	S 25	1,000		
	VAT		150		1,485
30/6	Bank			1,250	235
1/7	Balance				*235 Dr.

Note: (a) The key figures from the invoice are entered in the day book — invoice number, sales, VAT and total cost.

(b) Debtors' accounts are debited with their individual totals in the Sales Ledger.

(c) Total for Sales and VAT accounts are credited in the General Ledger.

(d) Total debtors accounts will be debited to the S/L Control account. The Control account is simply a means of cross-checking the total individual balances in the Sales Ledger.

*Sales Ledger Control a/c

Exercises

1. The credit sales of Alan Smith were listed for the week ending 8 June. You need to calculate the VAT (15%) for each of them:

No. 27

	Customer's Account	Invoice No.	Amount £
4/6	Thomson	1136	180
5/6	Jackson	1137	200
6/6	Brown	1138	380
7/6	Warren	1139	300
7/6	Thomson	1140	420
8/6	Wilson	1141	60
8/6	Jones	1142	150

Required:

(a) Prepare the Sales Day Book for the week ending 8 June.
(b) What ledger are the individual debtors posted to?
    On which side of their account?
(c) What ledger are the totals of the day book posted to?
    On which side of the relevant account is each of the totals posted to?
(d) What purpose has the Sales ledger control account?
    Why is it not part of the double-entry?

2. Debtor's balances on 1 June in G. Harrison's Sales Ledger were:

	£
Arthur	100 Dr.
Brian	120 Dr.
Colin	150 Dr.

During the month of June, Harrison sold on credit:

		Invoice	£
5/6	Arthur	421	250
8/6	Brian	422	160
15/6	Arthur	423	200
20/6	Colin	424	280

On 28 June, Harrison received cheques from A, B and C settling their accounts on 1 June.

Required:

1. The Sales Day Book for the month of June.
2. Sales Ledger accounts of Arthur, Brian and Colin for June.
3. The sales account as it would appear in the Nominal Ledger (Opening balance £1,240 Cr.).

3. Prepare the *same* information as above in the books of G. Harrison with the following exceptions:
   (a) 15% VAT is charged on the sale of goods.
   (b) A Sales Ledger Control account is opened in the Nominal Ledger with a balance of £370 Dr. on 1 June (that is, the three debtors).
   (c) The Nominal Ledger have the following balances on 1 June:

Sales a/c	£1,240 Cr.
VAT a/c	£ 125 Dr.
Sales Ledger Control a/c	£ 370 Dr.

   (d) Prepare a schedule of debtors to check with the control account balance as on 30 June.

4. The balances on 1 May in the sales ledger of Norman Hunter were:

	£
Bremner W.	575 (dr.)
Lorimer P.	255 (dr.)
Jones M.	250 (dr.)
Gray E.	100 (dr.)
	1,180

Sales Ledger Control a/c	1,180

   The sales invoices issued for the month of May were as follows:

	Customer	Invoice No.	Amount	VAT
1 May	Bremner	2742	200	+15%
6 May	Gray	2743	280	+15%
14 May	Bremner	2744	450	+15%
18 May	Jones	2745	180	+15%
21 May	Lorimer	2746	800	+15%
22 May	Giles (New a/c)	2747	100	+15%
24 May	Bremner	2748	300	+15%
28 May	Jones	2749	150	+15%

Required:

(a) Prepare the Sales Day Book for the month of May.
(b) Prepare the individual debtors accounts in the sales ledger.
(c) Prepare the debtors control account for the month of May.

5. The following represents the Sales Day Book of XYZ Ltd for the month of June:

CUSTOMER	TOTAL	BATS	BALLS	PADS
	£	£	£	£
Brearley, M.		172	12.50	35.00
Botham, I.		60	4.25	20.50
Boycott, G.		250	43.75	55.80
Bailey, T.		78	12.50	70.00
Benaud, R.		195	38.75	61.50

(a) Complete the totals for the Sales Day Book for the month of June (no VAT).
(b) Enter the opening balances in XYZ's Sales Ledger for each of the following (1 June):

Brearley	£200.96
Botham	15.00
Boycott	66.30
Bailey	27.88
Benaud	40.25

(c) Post the additional transactions for June to the personal accounts of the above.
(d) Make the necessary postings to the General Ledger using a *separate* sales a/c for each of the above items. The Debtors Control balance 1 June was £350.39 (dr.).
(e) Check the individual debtors total with the Debtors control as at 30 June.

PART 4

The Purchases Day Book (or Purchases Journal)

The Purchases Day Book

The function of the purchases day book is to list, summarise and, where applicable, analyse all purchase invoices over a period of time. The total of purchases may be required daily, weekly or monthly depending on the number of credit purchases made from suppliers.

The Buying Department is responsible for ensuring that invoices received from suppliers are checked against the original purchase orders and that the stores have checked that the goods received comply with the details of the delivery note.

The invoice, stamped and initialled by the persons responsible for checking the appropriate details, will then be sent to the Accounts Department for recording.

The Bought Ledger clerk does not take action in recording until the supplier's invoice is fully checked and initialled.

Any returns sent back to a supplier must await the credit note which will be received by the Buying Department and checked for accuracy. It is then sent to Accounts to be debited to the supplier's account.

Monthly Statements received from suppliers stating the sum owing to them is not paid by the Accounts Department until it is checked against the supplier's account in the Bought Ledger.

Posting from the Purchases Day Book to Ledgers:

(a) *The Purchase or Bought Ledger. Credit* each creditor account with the net purchase plus VAT if applicable.
(b) *The Nominal Ledger. Debit* the total value of purchases a/c and *debit* VAT where applicable.

The Purchase Invoice

Below is an invoice from ROCCO Sports supplier of sports goods. The details are:

```
                    R O C C O     S P O R T S          INVOICE
                      15 - 47 Cheviot Lane            B/ 184285
                           Wakefield
                           Yorkshire
                     Telephone  0602 5571
  VAT Reg 584 5691 48
```

Area	Customer Order details	Fwd		Date	Account No.	Invoice No.	Page
16	O/15672 2.MAY.88			25.5.88	H1452	184285	1/1

Invoice Address
  G HARRISON
  214 HIGH STREET
  POOLE   DORSET

Consignee

Code	Qty	Description		Price	Goods value	VAT rate%	VAT
Z451 F	10	SWINGBALL SET		8.41	84.10	15.00	12.10

Total Goods	84.10	
Total VAT	12.10	← 12.10
INVOICE TOTAL	96.20	

Terms: cash discount 4% within 7 days or 2% payment by 20th of following month.

Name of Supplier	ROCCO Sports Co.
Date of Invoice	25 May
No. of Invoice	184285
Quantity/description of goods	10 Swingball sets
Price	£8.41 each plus VAT 15%
Terms	No trade discount offered.
	Cash discount: 4% within 7 days or 2% for payment by 20th of month following invoice date

VAT 15%   The VAT calculated is £12.1. It is
                                 not based on the goods value of
                                 £84.10 because cash discount has
                                 been offered. This allows the VAT to
                                 be calculated on the lower figure of
                                 £60.74 (£84.10 − £3.36), that is, less
                                 4% cash discount.

The following pages illustrate:

(a) A simplified Purchases Day Book without VAT.
(b) A Purchases Day Book with VAT.

A Simplified Purchases Day Book (without VAT)

Date	Supplier's a/c	Invoice No. Received	Amount £
4 May	R. Bates	415	155
12 May	J. Snow	0276	276
15 May	R. Bates	627	359
20 May	J. Sorrell	A253	180
28 May	J. Sorrell	A322	190
		Purchases (Dr.)	1,160

Ledger posting

Date	Particulars	Debit	Credit	Balance
R. Bates a/c				
4 May	Purchases		155	155 (cr.)
15 May	Purchases		359	514
J. Snow a/c				
12 May	Purchases		276	276 (cr.)
J. Sorrell a/c				
20 May	Purchases		180	180 (cr.)
28 May	Purchases		190	370
Purchases a/c				
31 May	Creditors	1,160		1,160 (dr.)

Double-entry:
(1) Each supplier (creditor) is credited with the amount of the purchase (Liability +).
(2) The *total* purchases is debited (Expense +).

Example Illustrated

Purchases with VAT and also using the control a/c
The following represents the Purchase Day Book of G. Harrison for the
month of June: Page No. 42

Date	Supplier	Invoice No.	Purchases	VAT	Total
			£	£	£
June 4	Decca	4,242	450	67.50	517.50 Cr.
8	Decca	5,789	200	30.00	230.00 Cr.
15	EMI	687	360	54.00	414.00 Cr.
22	Jacksons	1,425	120	18.00	138.00 Cr.
			1,130.00	169.50	1,299.50
			(Dr.)	(Dr.)	(Cr.)

1 June Balances from Ledgers:

			£
General Ledger:	Purchases a/c	(debit)	3,576.50
	VAT a/c	(credit)	421.25
	Purchase Ledger:		
	Control Account	(credit)	5,646.50

			£
Purchase Ledger:	Decca	(credit)	3,465.00
	EMI	(credit)	1,572.50
	Jacksons	(credit)	609.00

Required:

(a) Enter the above balances on 1 June in the ledger of G. Harrison.
(b) Post the month's details from the Day Book to the appropriate ledger
     accounts. The Purchase Ledger control a/c [P/L Control] is also referred
     to as the Creditors' Control a/c.

(c) Enter the payment details: all cheques on 30 June.

 £1,500 to Decca on a/c
 £1,000 to EMI on a/c
 £200 to Jacksons on a/c.

General Ledger

Date	Particulars	Folio	Debit	Credit	Balance
			£	£	£
Purchases a/c					
June 1	Balance				3,567.50 (Dr)
30	Creditors	P 42	1,130		4,697.50
VAT a/c					
June 1	Balance				421.25 (Cr)
30	Creditors	P 42	169.50		251.75
P/L Control a/c					
June 1	Balance				5,646.50 (Cr)
30	Purchases	P 42		1,130.00	
	VAT			169.5	6,946.00
	Bank		2,700		4,246.00

Purchase Ledger:

Date	Particulars	Folio	Debit	Credit	Balance
			£	£	£
Decca Records a/c					
June 1	Balance				3,465.00 (Cr)
4	Purchases	P 42		450.00	
	VAT			67.50	3,982.50
8	Purchases	P 42		200.00	
	VAT			30.00	4,212.50
30	Bank		1,500		2,712.50
EMI Records a/c					
June 1	Balance				1,572.50 (Cr)
15	Purchases	P 42		360.00	
	VAT			54.00	1,986.50
30	Bank		1,000		986.50

Jacksons a/c			Debit	Credit	Balance
June 1	Balance				609 (Cr)
22	Purchases	P 42		120.00	
	VAT			18.00	747.00
30	Bank		200		547.00

Check the control a/c with the Purchase Ledger:

June 30	P/L Control a/c		£4,246 Cr.
30	Purchase Ledger Schedule:		

	£	
Decca	2,712.5	
E.M.I.	986.5	
Jacksons	547	
	———	£4,246 Cr.

Balances agree:

When preparing the Trial Balance, the control accounts represent the totals of both debtors and creditors. They are useful because if control accounts cross-check with personal ledgers it is assumed that double-entry recording is correct. In the event that the Trial Balance failed to balance, personal accounts need not be checked to locate the error(s) if they already agree with the control accounts.

Note: (a) The Purchase Ledger: each creditor account is credited with the purchase + VAT.

      (b) The Nominal Ledger: totals for both purchases a/c and VAT a/c are debited. The total of the Purchases Day Book is credited to the P/L Control a/c.

      The Purchase Ledger is commonly referred to as the Bought Ledger.

Application of the Accounting System

Prepare the Day Book of ABC Shoes Ltd using analysis columns for Men's Women's and Children's shoes – from the following information:

Date	Supplier	Invoice No.	Description	Value £
3/2	Footwear Ltd	F223674	5 Pairs men's casuals @ £24 pair + VAT	120
6/2	Freeman, Hardy + Willis	08476	10 pairs of kiddies sandals @ £9.50 + VAT	95
7/2	Country Casuals Ltd	14279K	5 pairs of ladies dress shoes @ £15 + VAT	75
14/2	Footwear Ltd	F223989	10 pairs of men's brogues @ £21 pair + VAT	210
16/2	Freeman, Hardy + Willis	08979	20 pairs of children's school casuals @ £9.50 + VAT	190
21/2	Footwear Ltd	F224028	25 pairs of country casuals for men @ £21 + VAT	525
28/6	Jones Leather Goods	26011	18 pairs ladies dress shoes @ £15 + VAT	270

Day Book columns:
  Use the following –

Invoice No.	Men's Shoes	Women's Shoes	Child's Shoes	VAT	Total Creditor

Purchases Day Book: ABC Company

Date	Supplier	Invoice No.	Mens Shoes	Womens Shoes	Child's Shoes	VAT	Total Creditor
			£	£	£	£	£
3/2	Footwear Ltd.	F2236	120			18	138
6/2	F.H.&W.	08476			95	14.25	109.25
7/1	Country Cas'l	14279		75		11.25	86.25
14/2	Footwear Ltd.	F2239	210			31.50	241.50
16/2	F.H.&W.	08979			190	28.50	218.50
21/2	Footwear Ltd.	F2240	525			78.75	603.75
28/2	Jones Leather	26011		270		40.50	310.50
			855	345	285	222.7	1,707.75

How would these entries be posted to the ledgers?

1. Each Supplier's account is Credited with the total sum.

2. The total sum of Men's, Women's and Child's shoes is Debited to the Purchase account of each category:

Purchases a/c		
(Men's)	£855	Dr.
(Women's)	£345	Dr.
(Child's)	£285	Dr.

3. VAT a/c   £222.75   Dr.

4. Purchase Ledger Control a/c   £1,707.75   Cr.

Exercises

1. See Invoice No. 1185 from G. Harrison to R. Jones. Answer the following listed below from the point of view of R. Jones receiving the invoice from Harrison.

    (a) In which book is the invoice entered?
    (b) Complete the totals across. Trade Discount is 25%.
    (c) Calculate the VAT (15%). Note $2\frac{1}{2}$% cash discount is offered.
    (d) Complete the totals of the invoice at the bottom.
    (e) How would you complete the postings to the ledgers?

```
                    I N V O I C E

                    G  Harrison
                214 The High Street
                      Poole
                      Dorset

To:  R Jones
     14 Ship Road
     The Quay                          VAT Reg: 424 28422 56
     Poole                             Invoice No:INV/ 1185
```

Date: 10 June 1988	Your Order Ref: 275	Terms: 25% Trade
	Despatch Date : 10 June	Carriage Paid

Code Number	Qty	Description	Unit Price	Total Price	Less Trade	Net
1042	4	Tennis Rackets (Slazenger) (special edition)	32			
1070	10	Squash Rackets (Dunlop)	8.25			

```
                                                    ======
                                          TOTAL NET:£
E&OE                                      VAT @ 15 %:£
```

Delivery Address: as above	TOTAL VALUE:£
Payment within 28 days of invoice date, Cash Discount 2½%	

2. The following supplier's invoices were received by G. Harrison for the week ending 29 May.

No. 26

	Supplier's Account	Invoice No.	Amount £	VAT £
25/5	Rocco Sports Co.	184285	84.10	12.10
26/5	Arena	4556	152.	22.80
26/5	Sondico	X4443	350.	52.50
28/5	Rocco Sports Co.	184789	126.	18.14
29/5	Arena	5287	80.	12.
29/5	Dunlop Sports Co.	199774	215.	32.25

Required:

(a) Prepare the Purchases Day Book of G. Harrison for the week ending 29 May.
(b) What ledger would the individual suppliers be posted to? On which side of their respective accounts? Explain why it is on the side you have chosen.
(c) What ledger is used to post the totals of the purchases day book? On which side of the account for each of the three totals?
(d) What is the purchases control account used for?
(e) Which of the above suppliers offers a cash discount?

3. Creditor's balances on 1 June in G. Harrison's Bought Ledger were:

	£
Dick	280 Cr.
Eric	100 Cr.
Fred	120 Cr.

During the month of June, Harrison bought on credit from his suppliers:

		Invoice	£
8/6	Dick	3478	400
12/6	Eric	51729	220
15/6	Eric	51915	160
23/6	Fred	283	100

On 29 June Harrison sent cheques to:

	£
Dick	180
Eric	100
Fred	60

Required:

1. The Purchases Day Book for June.
2. Bought Ledger accounts of Dick, Eric and Fred for June.
3. The Purchases a/c as it would appear in the Nominal Ledger (opening balance £1,100 Dr.) at the end of June.

4. Prepare the *same* information as above in the books of G. Harrison with the following exceptions:

(a) 15% VAT is charged on goods purchased.
(b) A Bought Ledger Control a/c is opened in the Nominal Ledger with a balance of £500 Cr. on 1 June.

(c) The Nominal Ledger has the following balances on 1 June:

	£
Purchases a/c	1,100 Dr.
VAT a/c	125 Dr.
Bought Ledger Control a/c	500 Cr.

(d) Prepare a schedule of creditors to check with the control account balance on 30 June.

5. The following represents the transactions of Harry Smith — a retailer — during the month of July:

			Invoice Nos
July	1	Bought goods from ABC: 200 units @ £5 units less 25% trade discount	27491
	2	Bought goods from XYZ: 150 units @ £2 units less 20% trade discount	X427
	7	Sold to R. Green 100 units @ £7 less 10% trade discount	142
	9	Sold to R. Jones 100 units @ £5.50 less 10% trade discount	143
	12	Bought goods from ABC: 500 units @ £4 unit less 25% trade discount	9278
	14	Sold goods to F. Smith 100 units @ £3.50 trade discount nil	144
	17	Bought goods from XYZ: 200 units @ £2 unit less 20% trade discount	X588
	21	Sold to R. Green 150 units @ £7 less 10% trade discount	145
	26	Bought from ABC: 500 units @ £4.50 less 25% trade discount	10429

Required:

(a) Enter the above in Harry Smith's Purchases and Sales Day Books (no VAT).
(b) Post to the ledgers:
   Personal ledger for individual debtors and creditors.
   General ledger for total sales and total purchases.

6. The personal accounts in Harry Smith's ledger were as follows:

May 1st balances

	£
R. Mellows	200 Cr.
Paterson Bros.	150 Cr.
J. Hudson	95 Cr.
D. Moorcroft	24 Cr.

The following invoices were received from the above suppliers during May:

		Invoice No.	Net Purchase	VAT (+ 15%)
MAY			£	£
3	Mellows	2784	200.00	
7	Hudson	149	150.00	
10	Paterson Bros	87632	400.00	
14	Hudson	251	180.00	
20	Mellows	3219	350.00	
21	Hudson	267	225.00	
26	Moorcroft	4929	100.00	

On May 30th Harry Smith paid off the opening balances of each creditor.

Required:

(a) The purchases day book for the month of May. You need to calculate the VAT 15% on each purchase.
(b) The personal ledger accounts of Smith as they would appear on 31st May.

PART 5

The Returns Day Books

The Returns Day Books

The two books to record returns are:

1. The Returns Inward Day Book — to record sales returns from customers (debtors).
2. The Returns Outward Day Book — to record purchases returns to suppliers (creditors).

Situations arise in business where goods may be returned to the seller for a variety of reasons. They may have been damaged in transit, the wrong type may have been sent, or the buyer may have changed his mind and sent them back. The invoice could have been added incorrectly and overcharged. There may be bottles, crates or barrels involved where a credit is given for the return of them.

The *Credit Note* is the documentary evidence for any return or allowance. It signifies that a reduction is to be made from the account where the credit note is sent.

The Returns Inward Day Book: the credit notes sent to customers to cover their returns are listed in sequence (numerically) and in date order. Posting to the ledgers will include:

(a) the Sales Ledger. *Credit* the debtor's a/c with the value of the return plus VAT if applicable.
(b) The Nominal Ledger. *Debit* the Returns Inward a/c and Debit the VAT if VAT is charged.
     Where a Control a/c is used, *Credit* the total value of returns plus VAT if charged, to the Sales Ledger Control a/c (in line with crediting individual debtors).

The Returns Outward Day Book: credit notes received from suppliers cover the return of purchases to them. The credit notes are listed in date order.

Posting to ledgers will include:

(a) The Purchase Ledger. *Debit* the creditor's a/c with the value of the return plus VAT if applicable.

(b) The Nominal Ledger. *Credit* the Returns Outward a/c and Credit VAT if VAT charged.

Where a Control a/c is used, *debit* the total value of returns plus VAT if charged, to the Purchase Ledger Control a/c (in line with debiting individual creditors).

Mr. G. Harrison — documents

A Credit Note sent to a customer of G. Harrison:

```
┌──────────────────────────────────────────────────┐
│  C R E D I T   N O T E                             │
├────────────────────────────────┬───────────────── │
│ From  G Harrison               Credit No.:         │
│       214 High Street            B/  427           │
│       Poole                                        │
│       Dorset                                       │
│                                                    │
│ To    T Smith                                      │
│       56-57 Ringwood Road                          │
│       Poole                                        │
├────────────────────────────────┬───────────────── │
│ Credit in respect of           │ Date 7 May        │
│  ☒ Retd Goods   ☐ Error        │ Inv  253          │
│  ☐ Discount     ☐ O'chge       │ Order 67231       │
│  ☐ Shortage     ☐             │ Ref               │
├──────────────────────────┬──────┬────┬──────       │
│ Date    Details          │      │ £  │ p           │
│ June 15  200 Tennis Balls│      │ 32 │ 00          │
│          (poor quality)  │      │    │             │
│       Less 25% Trade     │      │  8 │ 00          │
│                          │      │ 24 │ 00          │
│       Plus 15% VAT       │      │  3.│ 60          │
├──────────────────────────┴──────┴────┴──────       │
│        Total Credit:£    27 . 60                   │
└──────────────────────────────────────────────────┘
```

The Credit Note is the documentary evidence for returns and allowances. A credit note sent to a customer has the effect of reducing the customer's account. In this case Mr. Smith's a/c will be credited by £27.

ILLUSTRATED EXAMPLE

The Returns Inward Day Book

The debtor's balances in G. Harrison's Sales Ledger on 1 June were:

	£
J. Jones	156 Dr.
T. Smith	385 Dr.
T. Dooley	224 Dr.

The Returns Inward Day Book for the month of June:

No. 4

	Customer's a/c	C/N No.	Returns Inward a/c	VAT a/c	Total Debtor's a/c
			£	£	£
June 15	T. Smith	427	24	3.60	27.60 Cr.
23	T. Dooley	428	60	9.00	69.00 Cr.
30	T. Jones	429	10	1.50	11.50 Cr.
			94	14.10	108.10
			(Dr.)	(Dr.)	(Cr.)

G. Harrison's Sales Ledger:

Date	Particulars	Folio	Dr.	Cr.	Balance
J. Jones a/c					
June 1	Balance				156.
30	Returns In	RI 4		11.50	144.50 Dr
T. Smith a/c					
June 1	Balance				385. Dr.
15	Returns In	RI 4		27.60	357.40
T. Dooley a/c					
June 1	Balance				224. Dr.
23	Returns In	RI 4		69.	155.

ILLUSTRATED EXAMPLE

The Returns Outward Day Book

Creditor's balances in G. Harrison's Purchase Ledger on 1 June were:

	£	
Dunlop Sports	96.21	Cr.
Sondico	124.62	Cr.
Arena Sports	150.00	Cr.

The Returns Outward Day Book for the month of June:

					No. 2
Date	Supplier's a/c	C/N No.	Returns Outward a/c	VAT a/c	Total Creditor's a/c
			£	£	£
June 4	Dunlop Sports	142	16.82	2.42	19.24 Dr.
18	Sondico	234/C	10.86	1.60	12.46 Dr.
26	Arena	67	24.60	3.51	28.11 Dr.
			52.28	7.53	59.81
			(Cr.)	(Cr.)	(Dr.)

G. Harrison's Purchase Ledger:

Date	Particulars	Folio	Dr.	Cr.	Balance
Dunlop Sports a/c					
June 1	Balance				96.21 Cr.
4	Returns Out	RO 2	19.24		76.97
Sondico a/c					
June 1	Balance				124.62 Cr.
18	Returns Out	RO 2	12.46		112.16
Arena a/c					
June 1	Balance				150.00 Cr.
26	Returns Out	RO 2	28.11		121.89

G. Harrison's Nominal Ledger

Date	Particulars	Folio	Dr.	Cr.	Balance	
Returns Inward a/c						
June 1	Balance				—	
30	Debtors	RI 4	94.		94.	Dr.
VAT a/c						
June 1	Balance				—	
30	Debtors	RI 4	14.10		14.10	Dr.
30	Creditors	RO2		7.53	6.57	
Sales Ledger Control a/c						
June 1	Balance				765.	Dr.
30	Returns In + VAT	RI 4		108.10	656.90	
Returns Outward a/c						
June 1	Balance				—	
30	Creditors	RO2		52.28	52.28	Cr.
Purchase Ledger Control a/c						
June 1	Balance				942.50	Cr.
30	Returns Out + VAT	RO2	59.81		882.69	

The Statement

Statements are normally sent to customers once a month to remind them of their outstanding balance. In the example, T. Smith owes Harrison £164.40 at the end of June. This balance should cross-check with Smith's Sales Ledger account balance.

A Debit Note was sent on 25 June because Invoice No. 1156 was incorrectly valued by £23, because of an item which had been omitted.

STATEMENT

G. Harrison
214 The High Street
POOLE
DORSET

Telephone: 674221

T. Smith
56, 57 Ringwood Rd.
POOLE
Dorset

VAT Reg:
  42428422

All accounts are rendered on
a net basis and are due for
settlement within 30 days.

Account No. S 25

Date	Details	Debit £	Credit £	Balance £
1 June	Balance			385.00
15	C/n 427 Returns		27.60	357.40
21	Invoice 1156 Sales	160.		
	VAT	24.		541.40
24	Debit Note 46	20		
	VAT	3		564.40
28	Cash — thank you		400.00	164.40
30	Balance now due			164.40

CHECKING STATEMENTS WITH LEDGER ACCOUNTS

When statements are received from creditors they are checked with the
Purchases Ledger account to see if balances agree. If they do and all details
are correct, the statement is passed on to the Cashier for payment.

If statements do not agree with the ledger accounts, they must be checked
and reconciled before they are passed on for payment.

G. Harrison received a statement from Dunlop Sports Ltd. The balance
owing was £3.08. The date of the statement June 16.

On checking the ledger account, it was found that the Dunlop balance had been settled:

Purchases Ledger

Dunlop Sports a/c	Dr.	Cr.	Balance
June 1 Balance			96.21 Cr.
4 Returns	19.24		76.97
6 Bank	73.89		—
Discount	3.08		

Dunlop Sports Ltd. had not taken cash discount into account, whereas Harrison had deducted 4% for payment within 7 days. If the statement is believed to be in error it must be settled with the supplier in order to solve the problem. Either the discount is valid or it is not. Did Harrison pay on time or was it an error by the accounts section at Dunlops?

Dunlop confirm by telephone that the discount should have been deducted in Harrison's favour:

Reconciliation of Account:

	£
Balance as per Statement:	3.08
Less Cash Discount Received	3.08
Balance as per Purchases Ledger	—

Exercises

1. Debtor's balances on 1 June in the books of G. Harrison were:

   Sales Ledger: £

Arthur	100 Dr.
Brian	120 Dr.
Colin	150 Dr.

   Nominal Ledger:

Returns Inward a/c	257 Dr.
VAT a/c	125 Dr.
Sales Ledger Control a/c	370 Dr.

Harrison sent Credit Notes to customers who had returned goods during June:

			Credit Note
12/6	Brian	60 + VAT	261
20/6	Arthur	20 + VAT	262
24/6	Colin	50 + VAT	263

Required:

(a) The Returns Inward Day Book for June.
(b) Sales Ledger accounts of Arthur, Brian and Colin for June.
(c) Nominal Ledger accounts for June.

2. Creditor's balances on 1 June in the books of G. Harrison were:

Bought Ledger: £
    Dick   280 Cr.
    Eric   100 Cr.
    Fred   120 Cr.

Nominal Ledger:
Returns Outward a/c   352 Cr.
VAT a/c   125 Dr.
Bought Ledger Control   500 Cr.

Harrison received Credit Notes from suppliers for returns outward during June:

		£	Credit Note
13/6	Dick	80 + VAT	42
20/6	Eric	48 + VAT	215
26/6	Fred	60 + VAT	88

Required:

(a) The Returns Outward Day Book for June.
(b) Bought Ledger accounts of Dick, Eric and Fred for June.
(c) Nominal Ledger accounts for June.

3. The books of G. Harrison:

Suppliers' Summary of Invoices 31 May

Date		Supplier	Invoice No.	Quantity	Unit Price
					£
May	7	Dunlop Sports	3427	100	5.95
				250	4.50
	10	Sondico	84521	500	1.25
				100	3.25
				50	10.65
	15	Dunlop Sports	3692	200	4.50
	24	Metre Sports	895	100	6.75
				50	8.50
	27	Sondico	85971	150	3.25
				50	10.65
	31	Metre Sports	1052	125	6.50
				200	8.50
	31	Dunlop Sports	4573	100	4.50
				50	6.00

Terms:
>   Dunlop and Sondico allow Taylor a 10%
>   TRADE DISCOUNT.
>   Metre Sports allow a 20% TRADE.

On 31 May, Harrison returned goods, Dunlop Sports [invoice 3692] 100 units @ £4.50 and Sondico [invoice 85971] 150 units @ £3.25 and received credit notes for them.

Required:
(a) The appropriate journals to record the above information.
(b) The individual accounts of Dunlop and Sondico as on 31 May.

4. The balances in the Bought Ledger of *Freddy Smith* (outfitter) as on 1 June were:

	£	
Truman, F S	1,090	(cr.)
Statham, B	250	"
Tyson, F	975	"
Snow, J	340	"
Illingworth, R	420	"

Invoices were received during June from the following:–

	Invoice No.	Supplier	Amount	VAT
6/6	27481	Truman, F	£580	+15%
8/6	4278W	Snow, J	520	+15%
15/6	992	Illingworth, R	210 .	+15%
22/6	52833	Statham, B	330	NIL
25/6	888	Tyson, F	360	+15%
30/6	A998	Old, C	580	+15%

You are required to prepare:

(a) The Purchases Day Book of Smith, for the month of June.
(b) The individual suppliers accounts in the Bought Ledger.
(c) A separate Returns Outward Day Book (see returns below).
(d) The Purchase Ledger Control account for the month of June.

(e) *Credit notes were received from:*
   Illingworth   No. C447   29/6   £ 6.30 + VAT
   Tyson   No. 42/82 30/6   £90.00 + VAT

   Because of faulty goods.

5. M. Crooks has the following accounts in his ledgers on 1 May

Sales Ledger:
J. Hunt	£600	Dr.
R. Speedie	£240	
J. Milton	£400	

Bought Ledger:

R. Ball	£500	Cr.
J. Carlson	£400	Cr.
D. Smith	£150	Cr.

Invoices issued during May:

	£		
Hunt	130	+	VAT
Milton	200	+	VAT
Speedie	180	+	VAT

Invoices received during May:

	£		
Ball	250	+	VAT
Smith	120	+	VAT

Credit Note received during May:

Carlson	£200	+	VAT

Cheques received during May:

Hunt	£580	in settlement of account of 1st May
Milton	£390	in settlement of account of 1st May
Speedie	£200	on account

Cheques paid during May:
   Settled all creditors accounts due 1st May less $2\frac{1}{2}$% cash discount.

Required:
(a) Enter the opening personal accounts in the ledgers of M. Crooks.
(b) Post all the above transactions to these ledger accounts and balance off at the end of the month.

PART 6

Introducing the Cash Book

The cash book is used to record all receipts and payments of cash or cheques.

It has TWO sides. The left is the debit side for receipts.
The right is the credit side for payments.

It deals with cash and cheque transactions and therefore it is dealing with two ASSETS at the same time:

The debit side increases the asset
The credit side reduces the asset

The purpose of the Cash Book is

(a) To reduce the volume of transactions in the nominal ledger dealing with cash or cheques. In this way it is really an extension of the ledger itself.
(b) To find the cash and bank balances at regular intervals.

If there are numerous entries of cash and cheques, it may be better to make a subdivision of the cash book and have special separate books, one for cash receipts and one for cash payments.

Cash Discounts

Cash discount may be offered to customers if they pay their accounts promptly. A column is added to the cash book to record the totals of these. They are *not* however, part of the cash or bank balances.

(a) Discount Allowed: is entered on the *left side* of the cash book and is given to debtors for prompt payment by a reduction on the balance owing.

(b) Discount Received: is entered on the *right side* of the cash book and is received from creditors for prompt payment of debts reducing the balance owed.

In practice, cash books rarely look the same because they are adapted to suit the needs of the business. Some businesses may prefer multi-columns for receipts and payments because they may want to analyse various aspects of the business, such as different categories of sales, VAT, different types of expenses.

The Need to Record Cash Transactions in the Cash Book

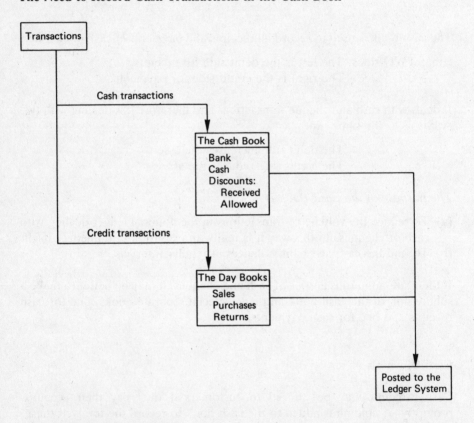

Cash and Credit transactions

Transactions basically fall into two categories: those for cash and those on credit. Cash transactions refer to actual cash or cheques received or given. Credit transactions refer to sales or purchases where a period of time is given for payment.

The business must therefore record a transaction on credit at two stages:

(a) A the point of sale or purchase.
(b) At the point of payment received or given.

Cash Book transactions for G. Harrison during the month of January:

January
1	Balances in Cash £25, Bank £900
4	Paid stationery by cash £20
5	Cash sales £72
13	Paid rates £125 by cheque
15	Cash sales £15
25	Paid cash to creditor James £115 on account
26	Cash sales £80
28	Paid Fox, another creditor, a cheque £76 in settlement of an £80 account (£4 discount received)
28	Received £57 cheque from Jones (debtor) in settlement of a £60 account (£3 discount allowed)
29	Received from Smith (debtor) cheque for £152 in settlement of £160 owing (£8 discount allowed)

Balancing G. Harrison's Cash Book [see over page]

(a) The cash balance   £

Total Cash In   (Dr. column)   192
less Total Cash Out (Cr. column)   135
                                    —————
                                     57

31/1 Balance c/d   £57   Cr.
 1/2 Balance b/d   £57   Dr. *[under totals on opposite side]*

(b) Bank Balance: £

Total Bank In   (Dr. Column)   1,109
less Total Bank Out (Cr. Column)   201
                                 —————
                                   908

31/1 Balance c/d   £908   Cr.
 1/2 Balance b/d   £908   Dr. *[under totals on opposite side]*

114 The Development, Purpose and Function of Accounting

Ledger posting from cash book:

To complete the double-entry, entries on the debit side of the cash book are posted to the credit side of the respective ledger account.

Entries on the credit side of the cash book are posted to the debit side of the respective ledger account.

When posting cash discounts to the nominal ledger, the totals posted remain on the *same* side.

Discount Allowed £11 Dr.
Discount Received £ 4 Cr.

Introduction to Cash Book — as a subsidiary ledger	Cash, Bank and Discounts in the Cash Book
	G. Harrison

DR. Page No. 42 CR.

Date	Particulars	Disc. All.	Cash	Bank		Particulars	Disc. Rec.	Cash	Bank
1 Jan.	Balance		25	900	4 Jan.	Stationery		20	
5. Jan	Sales		72		13 Jan.	Rates			125
15 Jan.	Sales		15		25 Jan.	James		115	
26 Jan.	Sales		80		28 Jan.	Fox	4		76
28 Jan.	Jones	3		57					
29 Jan.	Smith	8		152	31 Jan.	Balance c/d		57	908
		11	192	1,109			4	192	1,109
1 Feb.	Balance b/d		57	908					

(i)

DEBIT	*Increases* in Cash and Bank	+A
CREDIT	*Decreases* in Cash and Bank	−A

(ii) The double-entry is completed when entries in the cash book are posted to their corresponding accounts in the ledger.

For example: Cash Sales Dr. cash column as above (Asset +)
         Cr. Sales a/c in the ledger (Revenue +)

For example: Paid Rates Cr. bank column above (Asset −)
         Dr. Rates a/c in ledger (Expense +)

General Ledger: Harrison

Date	Particulars	Folio	Dr.	Cr.	Balance
			£	£	£
Sales a/c					
1/1	Balance				0
5/1	Cash	C 42		72	72 Cr.

				Dr.	Cr.	Balance
15/1	Cash	C 42			15	87
26/1	Cash	C 42			80	167

Stationery a/c

1/1	Balance					0
4/1	Cash	C 42		20		20 Dr.

Rates a/c

1/1	Balance					0
13/1	Bank	C 42		125		125 Dr.

Discount Allowed a/c

1/1	Balance					0
31/1	Sundries (total of)	C 42		11		11 Dr.

Discount Received a/c

1/1	Balance					0
31/1	Sundries	C 42			4	4 Cr.

Note:

(a) The folio C 42 refers to the Cash Book page number and is used as a cross-reference to the source of information.

(b) The double-entry with the first three accounts — that is, posted on the opposite side from the cash book entries.

(c) The discount accounts are not part of the double-entry and remain posted as the same side as the cash book. This is to facilitate the recording of discount totals for the year.

Sales Ledger: Harrison

Date	Particulars	Folio	Dr.	Cr.	Balance
			£	£	£
J. Jones a/c					
1/1	Balance				60 Dr.
28/1	Bank	C 42		57	
	Discount Allowed	C 42		3	0
R. Smith a/c					
1/1	Balance				160 Dr.
29/1	Bank	C 42		152	
	Discount Allowed	C 42		8	0

Bought Ledger: *Harrison*

Date	Particulars	Folio	Dr.	Cr.	Balance
			£	£	£
N. Fox a/c					
1/1	Balance				80 Cr.
28/1	Bank	C 42	76		
	Discount Received	C 42	4		0
R. James a/c					
1/1	Balance				115 Cr.
25/1	Cash	C 42	115		0

Note: The double-entry includes the discounts e.g.

J. Jones a/c 28/1   Bank £57 & Discount Alld. £3 Credit

N. Fox a/c 28/1   Bank £76   Discount Rcd. £4 Debit

A Revised Cash Book

Entries made in the Cash Book must have its sources of information in the same way as the Day Books and its sets of invoices and credit notes.

For example, if actual cash is received, this could be entered on something like a 'cash receipts abstract' form. The balances of the day's till-rolls could be entered on this type of document.

Cheques received could also be listed on the receipts abstract. Most sizable payments are normally made by writing out a cheque and there is always the cheque butt or a list of cheque counterfoils as the evidence of payment made.

If an organisation (for example, many of our retail outlets) makes numerous transactions by cash/cheques, the Cash Book may be modified in order to accommodate the posting procedure to the ledger system — basically to improve posting efficiency and information.

ABC Co. Receipts Abstract

	Customer's a/c	Dis. All.	Cheques	Cash Sales (Till-roll)	Day's Bank Totals
1 May				76.48 38.30	114.78
2				38.45 83.72	122.17
3				42.40 33.29	75.49
4	Jackson, P.	5.79	109.93	79.43 28.32	217.68
5	Thomson, J.	3.27	60.90	32.08 42.30	135.28
	WEEK'S SUMMARY £	9.06	170.83	494.57	665.40

ABC Co. Cash Payments Abstract

Date	Particulars	Cheque No.	Amount	Suppliers (creditors)	Dis. Rec.	Wages	Other Expenses
1 May	Wages	272348	186.48			186.48	
2	Light/Heat	349	44.54				44.54
2	Dunlop Co.	350	482.16	482.16	24.10		
3	Goldboro's	351	322.40	322.40	18.02		
4	Petty Cash	352	48.00				48.00
5	Slazenger Co.	353	82.00	82.00	—		
	WEEK'S SUMMARY £		1,165.58	886.56	42.12	186.48	92.54

Note: (a) Columns could be extended to facilitate further analysis of figures, such as a break-down of expenses.
  (b) The abstracts summarise the week's cash/bank transactions.
  (c) The abstracts facilitate transfer of entries to the cash book.

The use of a modified cash book showing extra columns for Debtors, Cash sales, Creditors, Wages and Miscellaneous expenses:

CASH BOOK ABC Co.

Date	Particulars	Dis. All.	Debtors	Cash Sales	BANK
1 May	Balance b/d				124.16
1	Sales			114.78	114.78
2	Sales			122.17	122.17
3	Sales			75.49	75.49
4	Jackson, P	5.79	109.93	107.75	217.68
5	Thomson, J	3.27	60.90	74.38	135.28
6	Balance c/d				376.02
		9.06	170.83	494.57	1,165.58

Date	Particulars	Dis. Rec.	Creditors	Wages	Misc. Expenses	BANK
1 May	Wages			186.48		186.48
2	Light and Heat				44.54	44.54
2	Dunlop Co.	24.10	482.16			482.16
3	Goldboro's	18.02	322.40			322.40
4	Petty Cash				48.00	48.00
5	Slazenger	—	82.00			82.00
		42.12	886.56	186.48	92.54	1,165.58

| 6 | Balance b/d (Overdraft) | | | | | 376.02 |

The advantages of using extra columns:

(1) Totals are available to show *where* the money is received and *where* it is paid out.

(2) They facilitate ledger posting in total; for example, sales £494.57 is posted to the Cr. side of Sales a/c in the Nominal ledger.

Personal Ledger of ABC COMPANY for Debtors and Creditors:

Sales Ledger (debtors)

Date	Particulars	Folio	Dr.	Cr.	Balance
Jackson, P. a/c					
1 May	Balance				364.86 Dr.
4	Bank			109.93	
	+ Dis. All.	CB 17		5.79	249.14 Dr.
Thomson, J. a/c					
1 May	Balance				64.17 Dr.
5	Bank			60.90	
	+ Dis. All.	CB 17		3.27	Nil

Purchase Ledger (creditors)

Date	Particulars	Folio	Dr.	Cr.	Balance
Dunlop and Co.					
1 May	Balance				846.82 Cr.
2	Bank		482.16		
	+ Dis. Rec.	CB 17	24.10		340.56 Cr.
Goldboro's					
1 May	Balance				340.42 Cr.
3	Bank		322.40		
	+ Dis. Rec.	CB 17	18.02		Nil
Slazenger					
1 May	Balance				482.00 Cr.
5	Bank	CB 17	82.00		400.00 Cr.

Nominal Ledger

Date	Particulars	Folio	Dr.	Cr.	Balance
Sales a/c					
1 May	Balance				8,424.10 Cr.
6	Cash	CB 17		494.57	9,418.67
Wages a/c					
1 May	Balance				511.22 Dr.
6	Bank	CB 17	186.48		697.70
Misc. Expenses a/c					
1 May	Balance				54.20 Dr.
6	Bank	CB 17	92.54		146.74
Discount a/c*					
1 May	Balance				26.50 Dr.
6	Sundries	CB 17	9.06	42.12	6.56 Cr.
S/L Control a/c [debtors]					
1 May	Balance				1,215.90 Dr.
6	Bank			170.83	1,045.07
	Dis. All.	CB 17		9.06	1,036.01
P/L Control a/c [creditors]					
1 May	Balance				2,927.75 Cr.
6	Bank		886.48		2,041.27
	Dis. Rec.	CB 17	42.12		1,999.15

*Using the same account for both discount allowed and received.
Discount allowed is regarded as an Expense   (Dr.).
Discount received is regarded as Revenue   (Cr.).

Using the Cash Book to Analyse Sales and VAT

ABC Co. want to analyse its sports sales into three distinct categories:

Sports Equipment	CODE	'A'
Clothing		'B'
Shoes		'C'

Goods will also be inclusive of VAT.

All goods will be coded and the cash registers will be set up to make such analysis, including appropriate VAT calculations.

The week's sales figures entered in the cash book were as follows:

CASH RECEIPTS

	Dis. All. £	Debtors £	SALES A £	B £	C £	Total £	VAT £	Bank £
8 May Sales			60		24	84	12.60	96.60
9 May Sales			42	12	22	76	11.40	87.40
10 May Smith	2.50	97.50	75	20	25	120	18.00	235.50
11 May Sales			47	25	22	94	14.10	108.10
12 May Sales			85	40	35	160	24.00	184.00
	2.50	97.50	309	97	128	534	80.10	711.60

Posting to Nominal Ledger:

SALES a/c

		A	B	C	Total £	
12/5	Bank	309	97	128	534	Cr.

VAT a/c

		£	
12/5	Bank	80.10	Cr.

S/L Control a/c

		£	
12/5	Bank	97.50	Cr.
	Dis. All.	2.50	Cr.

Exercises: Cash Book

1. Complete the following by entering the missing figures:

Cash Book — George Harrison

DR.

Date	Particulars	Disc. All.	Cash	Bank
1 May	Balances		41	300
7 May	Sales			162
16 May	Rogers	2		80
	Lee			9
24 May	Sales			60
30 May	Bank (contra)*		80	
31 May	Sales		79	40
	ICI PLC	15		285
1 June	Balance b/d			

CR.

Date	Particulars	Disc. Rec.	Cash	Bank
1 May	Johnstone and Smith	1		28
14 May	Crookes			50
15 May	Capel Stores		7	
29 May	Gibbs			10
30 May	Cash (contra)*			80
31 May	Wages		110	
	Southern Gas		33	
	Bank Charges			38
	Balance c/d			

Contra entry: Cash withdrawn from the bank
Bank Cr.
Cash Dr.

2. The following balances were brought down from the cash book of Harry Palmer on July 1 1988:

Cash   £747 Dr.   Bank   £1,022 Dr.

The transactions which took place during July were as follows:

			£
July	1	Paid rent by cheque	44
		General expenses by cheque	32
	3	Cash sales	156
	4	Paid a cheque of £95 to H. Smith, having been allowed £5 discount	
	6	Paid shop assistant's wages, cash	60
	10	Cash sales	188
	12	Paid for General expenses, cash	14
	15	Paid an advertising bill, cheque	35
	17	Cash sales	204
	18	Transferred to bank (Dr. bank, Cr. cash columns)	500
	20	Paid cheque to J. Jones £185, having been allowed a £15 discount	
	22	Received £98 cheque from A. Knott in settlement of £100	
		Received £296 from P. May in settlement of £300.	
	24	Cash sales £156 directly paid to bank	
	26	Paid shop assistant's wages, cash	60
	28	Received a cheque from C. Daley on a/c	140
	30	Paid rent by cheque	44
	31	Paid a cheque to J. Johnson of £180 in settlement of £200 owing.	

Required:

(a) Prepare the cash book of Harry Palmer for the month of July, bringing down the balances the next day.

(b) If Harry operated two personal ledgers and a nominal ledger, indicate how posting from the cash book to these would be done, using four of the above as examples.

3. On 1 July ABC Co. has the following balances in its Cash Book:

Cash in hand   £484
Bank   £276

During the month the transactions were as follows:

Cheques Received:		£	Discount Allowed:	£
2/7	Jackson and Son	186		14
3/7	Chappell Ltd	250		18.75
12/7	Clogg and Co.	100		—
28/7	Hughes, K.	358		17.90

Cheques Issued:			Discount Received:	
2/7	Mitre Sports	500		12.50
4/7	Arena	160		8.00
22/7	Dunlop	80.50		—
28/7	Slazenger Sport	172.50		7.50

Cash Received:

Week ending				
6/7	Shop takings	258.75	Paid £200 into Bank
13/7	Shop takings	196.80	Paid £150 into Bank
20/7	Shop takings	220.00	Paid £175 into Bank
27/7	Shop takings	187.75	Paid £150 into Bank

Cash Paid Out:

6, 13, 20, 27 July, Assistant salaries £56.75 (each date)

22/7	Advertising	£42.24
23/7	Delivery expenses	£14.75
25/7	Petty expenses	£ 8.50
29/7	Delivery expenses	£10.50

Required:

(a) Enter the above transactions in *date order* for the month of July. Balance as on 31 July and bring down the new balances.

(b) Ledger accounts required — for nominal accounts only. Assume balances Nil on 1 July.

4. The following personal accounts were in J. Loylands' ledger on 1 January 1988:

	£	
Smith, J.	220	Dr.
Jones, S.	84	Dr.
Bloggs, H.	280	Cr.

The following transactions took place during January:

			£	
Jan.	1	Balances b/d		
		Cash	25	
		Bank	381	Dr.
	2	Cash sales	140	
	3	General expenses — cash	15	
		— cheque	27	
	5	Personal drawings cheque	40	
	8	Cash sales	185	
	15	Salaries — cheque	85	
	16	Insurance premium — cheque	54	
	21	General expenses — cash	27	
	24	Cash sales	80	
	26	Smith pays a cheque to settle a/c		
		less 5% discount		
	28	Jones pays a cheque to settle a/c		
		less 5% discount		
	29	Cash sales paid directly into bank	285	
	31	Paid salaries — cheque	85	
		General expenses — cheque	54	
	31	Paid Bloggs sum owing and was		
		allowed $2\frac{1}{2}$ % discount		

Required:

(a) Prepare the cash book of J. Loyland for the month of January and balance on 31 January.
(b) Write up the personal accounts of J. Loyland using the running balance method, as they would appear in January.
(c) Write up the nominal accounts in J. Loyland's ledger as they would appear in January.

5. On 1 January 1988, D. Dawson had the following balances in his books:

	£	
Cash	142	(Dr.)
Bank (overdrawn)	150	(Cr.)
R. Smith	200	(Dr.)
J. Green	160	(Dr.)
D. Land	200	(Cr.)
A. Land	80	(Cr.)
J. Jones	300	(Cr.)

During the month of January, his cash/bank transactions were as follows:

Cheques paid

January	3	To D. Land £195 in settlement of his a/c
	9	To A. Land £76 in settlement of his a/c
	17	To Jones, £150 on account
	22	Withdrew from bank for personal use £100

Cheques received

January	16	From R. Smith £195 in settlement of a/c
	23	From J. Green £152 in settlement of a/c

Cash Received

January	5	Cash Sales for the week £125,	£100 in bank
	12	Cash Sales for the week £200,	£100 in bank
	19	Cash Sales for the week £150,	£125 in bank
	26	Cash Sales for the week £135,	£100 in bank

Cash Paid

January	5	Shop assistant's wages £45 per week for the month (to 26 January)
	22	To Southern Gas, cash £55
	27	General expenses £27
	29	Petty expenses £3

Required:

(a) Prepare the cash book for D. Dawson for the month of January, balancing on 31 January

(b) Show the personal accounts of D. Dawson in his ledger as they would appear on 31 January

6. Jack Jones used a modified cash book in his Music shop. All payments were made by cheque and shop takings were banked daily. On the receipts' side of his cash book he used columns for the following:

DISCOUNT ALLOWED	DEBTORS	RECORD SALES	OTHER SALES	BANK

On the payments' side:

DISCOUNT RECEIVED	CREDITORS	ASSISTANT'S WAGES	OTHER EXPENSES/ DRAWGS	BANK

Jack's bank balance on 1 May was £850.55 (dr.). During May the transactions were summarised as follows:

(a) *Cheques Issued*

2 May	To J. Brown £95 in settlement of £100 debt
2	To wages for assistant £56 per week to 30 May
4	To F. Smith £1,150 on account
8	To A. Jackson £190 in settlement of £200 debt
12	Delivery Expenses £27
15	Jack withdrew for personal use £150
22	To Wimborne D.C. for Rates £196
24	To British Telecom for Telephone £77
26	Delivery Expenses £42
28	Jack withdrew for personal use £125
30	Petty cash expenses £85

(b) *Cheques/Cash received*

		£
May 5	shop takings* for week ending amounted to	227.75
12	shop takings* for week ending amounted to	187.00
19	shop takings* for week ending amounted to	245.60
26	shop takings* for week ending amounted to	310.25
31	shop takings* for week ending amounted to	156.20

All banked the same day.

May 7	From G. Chappell £142.50 Discount Allowed £7.50
10	From D. Walters £50 on account
18	From R. Benaud £285 Discount Allowed £15
25	From D. Lillee £25 on account

*Shop takings: take 'record sales' to be 20% of week's takings.

Required:

Draw up the Cash Book of J. Jones for the month of May, balancing at the end of the month.

7. *Cash book analysis*

A wine shop owned by R. Lees kept an analysis cash book using columns for:
wine, beer & lager, spirits, other sales, total sales, VAT and bank
The daily takings are banked each day at the local branch. The cash register calculates the VAT separately when a sale goes through the till.

The takings over four days were as follows:

June	Wine £	Beer & Lager £	Spirits £	Other Sales £	Total Sales £	Bank £
2 Takings	200	250	80	30		
VAT	30	37.5	12	4.5		
3 Takings	150	200	50	20		
VAT	22.5	30	7.5	3		
4 Takings	180	240	60	24		
VAT	27	36	9	3.60		
5 Takings	300	340	100	60		
VAT	45	51	15	9		

Required:
(a) Prepare a suitable cash book using the above columns to analyse the different sale categories.
(b) Post the sales and VAT to the ledger.
(c) Why is it sometimes useful to make analysis columns?

PART 7

The Bank Reconciliation Statement

The Cash Book's bank balance needs to be confirmed with the bank statement at frequent intervals to check that its receipts and payments are in line with the bank's recording of these.

Bank reconciliation is a method of bringing together the bank balance as shown on the bank statement with the balance as shown in the Cash Book.

These balances may not agree at any specific time because:

(a) Items in the Cash Book may not yet have reached the bank in time for these to be entered in the bank statement.
(b) Items in the bank statement may not be in the Cash Book.

Some examples are as follows:

Items in the Cash Book not yet recorded in the Statement:

 (i) Cheque payments entered on the credit side of the Cash Book but not yet presented for payment at the bank — these are 'unpresented cheques'.
(ii) Cheques, cash entered on the debit side of the Cash Book, but not yet deposited at the bank — these are 'undeposited cheques, cash'.

Items in the Bank Statement not yet recorded in the Cash Book:

 (i) Payments and charges made by the bank and charged against the business:

       Standing orders
       Direct debits

Interest and bank charges
Cheques r/d (returned to drawer, insufficient funds)

These items will be entered on the CREDIT side of the Cash Book.

(ii) Receipts by the bank on the business's behalf and not yet recorded in the Cash Book:

Cheques from customers paid through the Bank Giro
Interest received on deposits at the bank
Dividends received from investments

These items will be entered on the DEBIT side of the Cash Book.

Procedure for Reconciliation

Checking must be made in some systematic order. Have the appropriate Cash Book pages ready to be compared with the latest batch of bank statements.

1. Tick those items which appear on *both* sets of records — for example, the receipt's side of the cash book with the receipts side of the statement. Check the payment's side of both records.
   If entries appear on both sets of records — no action is required.
   Also check the opening and closing balances for any differences.
2. If there are unticked items on the bank statement, such as bank charges, standing orders, interest received, these need to be first entered in the Cash Book.
   The Cash Book balance will then have been adjusted. Once the Cash Book has been adjusted the final stage is set for the reconciliation — that is, preparation of a simple bank reconciliation statement. This is composed of those items left unticked in the Cash Book.

3. *The Bank Reconciliation Statement*
   (a) Balance as per bank statement (end balance).
   (b) *Add* any UNDEPOSITED cheques.
   (c) *Deduct* any UNPRESENTED cheques.
   (d) This should equal the Balance as per Cash Book (adjusted).

Example Exercise: Bank Reconciliation

Cash, Bank and Discounts in the Cash Book
G. Harrison

DR.   Page No. 42   CR.

Date	Particulars	Disc. All.	Cash	Bank	Date	Particulars	Disc. Rec.	Cash	Bank
1 Jan.	Balance		25	900 ✓	4 Jan.	Stationery		20	125 ✓
5 Jan.	Sales		72		13 Jan.	Rates		115	
15 Jan.	Sales		15		25 Jan.	James			(76)
26 Jan.	Sales		80		28 Jan.	Fox	4		
27 Jan.	Jones	3		57 ✓	31 Jan.	Balance c/d		57	908
29 Jan.	Smith	8		(152) ✓					
		11	192	1,109			4	192	1,109
1 Feb.	Balance b/d		57	908		Bank charges			7
						Insurance			25
			57	908		Balance c/d		57	876
1 Feb.	Balance b/d		57	876				57	908

BARCLAYS BANK PLC

Account: G. Harrison

STATEMENT OF ACCOUNT
Account No.   44494410
31 January   ....

Details	Payments	Receipts	Date	Balance
	£	£		£
Balance forward			1 Jan.	900 ✓ Cr.
100111 (rates)	125 ✓		18 Jan.	775
Cornhill Insurance STO	㉕		20 Jan.	750
Credits (Jones)		57 ✓	27 Jan.	807
Charges	⑦		30 Jan.	800

Procedure so far:
After checking entries on both sets of records, the Cash Book was brought up to date by entering the bank charges and the standing order for Insurance on the credit side. The adjusted bank balance in the Cash Book is now £876.

The final stage is to prepare the reconciliation statement commencing with the final balance on the statement of £800, to be reconciled with the Cash Book balance of £876.

BANK RECONCILIATION as on 31 January:

	£	£
Balance per Bank Statement		800
Add		
Deposits not yet credited:		
Smith	152	152
		952
less		
Cheques not presented:		
Fox	76	76
Balance as per Cash Book		876

Exercises: Bank Reconciliation

1. From the information given below, prepare the bank reconciliation of John Lloyd for the month of January. Adjust the cash book with the appropriate entries first.

Cash Book — *John Lloyd* (Bank columns)

			£				£
Jan.	1	Balance	93	Jan.	1	Jack Jones	52
	4	Sales	88		8	Office Expenses	24
	7	Tom Jones	87		9	Harry Smith	141
	16	A. Knott	228		10	Gas, Electricity	34
	18	J. Snow	74		12	Freddy Smith	108
	21	Sales	255		17	Rates	46
	28	A. Clarke	54		21	Salaries	84
	31	R. Wilson	36		30	George Fame	116
						Balance c/d	?
			915				915

Bank Statement — John Lloyd — for month of December

			Debit	Credit	Balance
			£	£	£
Jan.	1	Balance			93 Cr.
	4	Sundries		88	181
	8	Sundries		87	268
	11	452	52		
		453	24		192
	12	SO	55		137
	14	DD	18		119
	16	Sundries		228	347
	17	455	34		313
	18	456	108		205
	19	Sundries		74	279
	21	Sundries		255	534
	22	457	46		488
	24	458	84		404
	29	Dividend		16	420

2. The following represents the Cash Book and Bank Statement figures of J.
    Jones (Sportsman/Businessman) for the month of June:

Cash Book (bank columns only)

		£			£
1/6	Balance b/d	469	6/6	Jones, F.	130
14/6	Doyle, C.	393	9/6	Singleton, S.	63
17/6	Cronin,A.	200	20/6	Jackson, J.	292
28/6	Smith, W.	205	27/6	Hemmings, R.	78
				Balance c/d	?

Bank of education   Statement of J. Jones — for the month of June

		DR.	CR.	BALANCE
		£	3	£
1/6	Balance			469 Cr.
5/6	Credit		393	862 Cr.
12/6	123971	130		732 Cr.
19/6	123972	63		669 Cr.
20/6	Credit		200	869 Cr.
26/6	Credit			
	Smith, R.		100	969 Cr.
28/6	S.O.			
	Leicester BSC	86		883 Cr.
29/6	Charges	19		864 Cr.

Required:

1. Bring down the balance of J. Jones' Cash Book and check both sets of
   records and action any unticked items.
2. Adjust the Cash Book.
3. Prepare the Bank Reconciliation Statement as at 30 June.

3. The Cash Book of P. Bentley in the 1st and 2nd weeks of May appeared as follows:

			£				£
May 1	Balance		2,300	May 2	Harrison		168
3	Smith	125		4	Rent, Rates		154
	Jones	217	342	8	Wages		218
				10	Jackson		517
6	Sales	115		12	Robson		26
	Jones	13	128		Balance	c/d	?
10							
	Fox	259					
12	Sales	175	434				
	Knott	189					
	Sales	215	404				

Bank statement to the 12th May was as follows:

		Dr.	Cr.	Balance
May 1	Balance			2,300 Cr.
1	Counter Credit		342	2,642
5	449	168		2,474
6	Credit transfer R. White		435	2,909
6	Counter Credit		128	3,037
7	450	218		2,819
9	S.O. (A.B. Soc.)	125		2,694
10	Counter Credit		434	3,128
12	Direct Debit (SEB)	44		3,084

Required:

(a) Adjust the Cash Book with the appropriate entries. Balance on 12 May.
(b) Prepare the Reconciliation Statement on 12 May.

4. The following information refers to the accounts of G. Fame:

Bank Statement received on 6 August

LLOYDS BANK P.L.C.

Account: G. Fame

STATEMENT OF ACCOUNT
Account No.   44244214
5 August   ....

Date	Details	Payments	Receipts	Balance
		£	£	£
Aug. 1	Balance			471.19 Dr.
2	CC		80.	391.19
3	DV B.D.H. PLC		4.28	386.91
4	CC		97.	289.91
5	465725	48.		337.91
5	DD Wimborne DC	41.49		379.40

Abbreviations:

CC   Cash or cheques deposited
DV   Dividends
DD   Direct Debit charges
SO   Standing Order charges
CH   Charges
Dr.   Balances Overdrawn on account

Required:

(a) Check the details of the above statement with the Cash Book of G.
   Fame overleaf. Tick the items which are the same on both sets of
   records. Bring the Cash Book up-to-date and balance on the 6
   August.
(b) Prepare the Bank Reconciliation Statement on 6 August.

No. 4

DR.   CR.

Cash Book —George Fame

Date	Particulars	Disc. All.	Cash	Bank	Date	Particulars	Disc. Rec.	Cash	Bank
1 Aug.	Balance		41.00		1 Aug.	Balance			471.19
	Sales		88.00		2 Aug.	Bank (contra)		80.00	
2 Aug.	Robertson Co.	3.00		97.00	3 Aug.	Jones	2.00		48.00
	Cash (contra)			80.00		General expenses		6.24	
4 Aug.	Jackson and Son			24.00	5 Aug.	Boston Bros			22.10
5 Aug.	Balance c/d				5 Aug.	Balance c/d			
		3.00	129.00				2.00	129.00	
6 Aug.	*				6 Aug.	Balance b/d (overdrawn)			

5. The Cash Book of J. Jones is as follows:

Dr.		Bank £			Bank £	Cr.
1/5	Balance b/d	850.55	2/5		95	
5/5		227.75			56	
7/5		142.50	4/5		1,150	
10/5		50	8/5		190	
12/5		187	9/5		56	
18/5		285	12/5		27	
19/5		245.60	15/5		150	
25/5		25	16/5		56	
26/5		310.25	22/5		196	
31/5		156.20	23/5		56	
					77	
			26/5		42	
			28/5		125	
			30/5		85	
					56	
					25	
			31/5	Balance c/d	37.85	
		2,479.85			2,479.85	

Required:

Check the cash book entries with Jones's bank statement below and bring it up to date. Prepare the reconciliation statement dated 31 May.

Details	Payments	Receipts	Balance	
	£	£	£	
Balance forward			850.55	Cr.
2741	56	227.75	795.55	
CC		142.50		
CC			1,164.80	
2742	95			
2743	1,150	50.	80.20	Dr.
CC			30.20	Dr.
2746	56		86.20	Dr.
CC		187.	100.80	Cr.
2744	150			
2745	27	285.	76.20	Dr.
CC		245.60		
CC		200.		
Bank Giro			654.40	Cr.
(R. Smith)		25.		
CC			679.40	
2747	56	310.25	623.40	
CC			933.65	
2748	56			
Charges	31.50			
Lillee R/D	25			
2749	196		625.15	Cr.

6. The following information refers to a summary of R. David's Cash Book as at the month ended, 31 May 1987:

Receipts		£	*Payments*	£
May	1 Balance b/d	2,706	General Expenses	7,225
	Cash Sales	11,142	Creditors	6,955
	Debtors	3,100	Wages	2,580
	Commission	2,152	Office Equipment	1,000

The Bank Statement dated 31 May 1987 received by R. David had an overdrawn balance of £893 (Dr.).

When checking with the cash book records the following facts were revealed:

(a) A payment of £420 to a supplier had been entered as a receipt.
(b) Bank commission of £19 and administrative charges and interest payment of £23 had not yet been entered in the cash book records.
(c) A cheque of £215 from a customer of R. David had been dishonoured by the bank and marked 'R/D'.
(d) A credit transfer of £426 from an R. David customer had been directly paid through the bank.
(e) Cheques of £375, £410, £72 and £95 had not yet been presented to the bank for payment.
(f) The opening cash book balance of £2,706 was b/d in error and should have read £2,607.
(g) A request to transfer £850 from deposit to current account, and entered in the cash book, had been misinterpreted by the bank and the transfer had been made the opposite way round. Cash book to be corrected.
(h) Cash sales of £11,142 were under-cast in error and should have read £11,642.
(i) The final paying-in-book deposit of £1,215 had not yet been credited by the bank.

Required:

1. Reconstruct the cash book incorporating the information above and bring down the balance on 31 May 1987.
2. Prepare the bank reconciliation statement for the month ended 31 May 1987.
3. Why is there a need to reconcile banking transactions?

7. *Situation:*

The following information relates to the Cash Ledger of A.D. Robert for the month of June, 1989:

		£		£
1/6	Balance b/f	2,870	General Expenses	2,420
	Debtors	8,755	Creditors	10,455
	Cash Sales	6,420	Salaries	2,815
	Other Receipts	895	Rental Charges	400

The Bank Statement received by the business on 30 June showed a balance of £1,935 (credit).

When the proprietor checked his records with those of the Statement, the following facts were revealed:

(a) The bank's commission and other charges amounted to a total of £79.

(b) A customer's cheque which had been sent to Robert, had been marked 'R/D' and dishonoured by the bank. The cheque was for £1,353.

(c) A receipt of £300 from a customer of Robert, had wrongly been entered as a payment in his cash ledger.

(d) The opening cash ledger balance of £2,870 was brought forward in error and should have been £2,780.

(e) Several cheques signed by Robert and presented for payment, had not yet been cleared by the bank. The cheques were for: £315, £455, £170 and £595.

(f) Wages of £200, had been undercast in error and had not been recorded in the cash ledger.

(g) A credit transfer of £420 from a Robert customer had been directly paid into the bank.

(h) Other entries in the Statement included £122 paid to Robert as a dividend from ACY Ltd. and a direct debit relating to an insurance premium for £70.

(i) The final paying-in-book deposit of £1,800 had not yet been credited by the bank.

Required:

Reconstruct the cash ledger for the month of June, 1989, bringing down the balance on the 30th June.

Prepare the bank reconciliation statement for the month ending, 30 June 1989.

PART 8

The Petty Cash Book

The main points which concern the petty cash book are:

(a) It is a subsidiary book of the cash book and is primarily used to record small payments of cash as an alternative to the credit side of the cash book. In this way, numerous small cash payments need not interfere with the main channels of cash entries.

(b) It uses a voucher system as evidence that cash payments have been made. These must be countersigned by an authorised person before money can be released.

(c) It is based on using a 'float' such as £100 per month from which these petty cash payments are made. When this sum is used up, it is reimbursed from further cash received through the cash book.

(d) Analysis columns can be used in the petty cash book to identify the different areas of payments.

The advantages of having a petty cash book include:

(a) The handling of work can be subdivided between a number of employees. The cashier who is responsible for the cash book may delegate petty cash control to a junior accounts clerk.

(b) It frees the cash book from too many smaller and less significant figures.

(c) The style of the petty cash book allows for the analysis columns to be totalled, which facilitates easier ledger posting.

The petty cash book is also known as the 'imprest system' because it uses a float or 'imprest'. A sum of money, transacted through the cash book, is used to make payments for minor expenses such as travel, office cleaning, office refreshments, stationery and so forth.

When the float or imprest is used up after a set period of time, it is reimbursed by further payment via the cash book. Reimbursements may be made weekly, monthly or whenever appropriate to the business.

Petty cash vouchers must be signed by any person who receives a cash payment and also by a person authorised to make the payments, such as the cashier or office manager. Vouchers are numbered and receipts are filed with vouchers because they will be required for audit purposes.

Control of Petty Cash

Each payment from the Petty Cash Book should be supported by a cash voucher. The voucher shows why the petty cash is required and who has authorised the payment. The petty cashier should always support the giving of petty cash by the signature of the person taking the cash.

An example of a petty cash voucher:

| PETTY CASH VOUCHER | No.: *1* | | |
	Date: *2 June*		
Description		**Amount**	
Office refreshments:			
Coffee		*1*	*12*
Buns			*38*
		1	*50*
Signature:			
Authorisation:			

The vouchers are numbered consecutively from the beginning of the month. They should be authorised by the person responsible for allowing petty cash to be paid. The person signing the petty cash is the person entitled to receive the money.

It is advisable that receipts for money spent on items of petty cash should be produced. On some items, VAT may be reclaimable if receipts are attached as evidence of spending.

Random checks can be made on the petty cashier. At any particular time, the total sum of the number of vouchers used in the month — thát is, their total value — added to the balance of petty cash should equal the petty cash float (or imprest). For example

Petty cash balance	£ 4.25
Vouchers used	£45.75
= Float	£50.00

Double-entry with Cash Book

When any sum for petty cash is to be withdrawn from the cash book and entered in the petty cash book, the double-entry is

Debit the Petty Cash Book
Credit the Cash Book

In the following example the petty cash float is £125 per month. During May, £87.25 was used for petty cash expenses leaving a balance brought down on 1 June of £37.75. A reimbursement of £87.25 is required to give the petty cash book its float of £125:

Dr. Petty Cash Book   £87.25
Cr. Cash Book   £87.25

Example Exercise

R. Taylor uses a petty cash book in his business. He uses small sums of cash frequently for items such as

Office refreshments, Packing materials, Travel expenses,
Postages and telegrams, Sundry expenses and VAT

Petty Cash float: £125 month
Balance brought forward from 31 May: £37.75
The entries for the month of June were as follows:

June		Amount £	VAT £	Voucher No.
1	Petty Cash reimbursement	87.25		
2	Office refreshments	1.50		1
5	Taxi fares	5.00		2
6	Packing materials	15.44	2.32	3
7	Petrol	5.45	0.82	4
12	Postages	8.50		5
14	Replacement glass	17.17	2.57	6
16	Telegrams	4.20		7
18	Office refreshments	2.12		8
21	Packing materials	14.43	2.17	9
22	Petrol	3.03	0.45	10
24	Miscellaneous expenses	16.21		11
28	Refreshments and taxi fares	15.50		12

Required:

(a) Enter the above details in the appropriate columns of R. Taylor's Petty Cash Book for the month of June.
(b) Balance the Petty Cash Book on 30 June and bring down the balance on 1 July.
(c) R. Taylor decided to increase the float to £150 per month. Show the appropriate reimbursement on 1 July.

See page 145, R. Taylor's Petty Cash Book for the month of June.
Note the balancing procedure is similar to that of the Cash Book.

PETTY CASH BOOK — R. Taylor   No. 42

Dr. £	Date	Details	No.	Cr. Total £	Office refresh. £	Packing material £	Travel expenses £	Post and telegrams £	Sundries £	VAT £
37 75	1/6	Balance b/d								
87 25	1	Cash Book (reimbursement)								
125										
	2	Office refreshments	1	1 50	1 50					
	5	Taxi fare	2	5 00			5 00			
	6	Packing materials	3	17 76		15 44				2 32
	7	Petrol and oil	4	6 27			5 45			0 82
	12	Postages	5	8 50				8 50		
	14	Replacement glass	6	19 74					17 17	2 57
	16	Telegrams	7	4 20				4 20		
	18	Office refreshments	8	2 12	2 12					
	21	Packing materials	9	16 60		14 43				2 17
	22	Petrol and oil	10	3 48			3 03			0 45
	24	Misc. costs	11	16 21			14 40	1 26	0 55	
	24	Office refresh., taxi	12	15 50	5 50		10 00			
				116 88	9 12	29 87	37 88	13 96	17 72	8 33
	30	Balance c/d		8 12						
				125 00						
-125-										
8 12	1/7	Balance b/d								
141 88	1	Cash Book (reimbursement)								
150										

Posting from the Petty Cash Book to the Nominal Ledger:

Nominal Ledger: G. Harrison

	Folio	Debit	Credit	Balance
		£	£	£
Office Refreshments a/c				
June 1 Balance				20.15 Dr.
30 Petty Cash	PC 42	9.12		29.27
Packing Materials a/c				
June 1 Balance				50.10 Dr.
30 Petty Cash	PC 42	29.87		79.87
Travel Expenses a/c				
June 1 Balance				40.06 Dr.
30 Petty Cash	PC 42	37.88		77.94
Postages and Telegrams a/c				
June 1 Balance				15.24 Dr.
30 Petty Cash	PC 42	13.96		29.20
Sundry Expenses a/c				
June 1 Balance				12.20 Dr.
30 Petty Cash	PC 42	17.72		29.92
VAT a/c				
June 1 Balance				12.15 Dr.
30 Petty Cash	PC 42	8.33		20.48

Note: each of the analysis columns identifying the petty cash expenses is posted from the credit side of the Petty Cash Book to the debit side of its respective ledger account.

Exercise No. 1

Petty Cash Book of J. Smith

£	Date	Details	Voucher No.	TOTAL £	VAT £	Postages £	Stationery £	Travel £	Cleaning £	Sundries £						
200	1/6	Balance b/d														
	4	Stamps	1	14 34												
	6	Bus fares	2	3 24												
	7	Taxi	3	8 50												
	10	Typing paper	4	20 70	2 70											
	12	Petrol	5	9 20	1 20											
	15	Envelopes, etc.	6	18 86	2 46											
	16	Window clean	7	11 50	1 50											
	20	Washing liquid etc.	8	1 80	0 24											
	22	Taxi	9	22 00												
	23	Stamps, telegrams	10	15 50												
	23	Crockery	11	9 48	1 23											
	24	Car repairs	12	31 05	4 05											
	26	Tea, coffee, etc.	13	4 83	0 63											
	28	Typing paper	14	2 60	0 34											
	30	Petrol, oil	15	14 29	1 85											
	30	Window clean	16	11 50	1 50											

Exercises:

1. On page 147 is an incomplete Petty Cash Book of Jack Smith for the month of June. Complete the analysis columns across the page. (VAT is deducted from the total, where applicable).

    Balance the Petty Cash Book on 30 June and include the appropriate reimbursement from the Cash Book after the balance has been brought down on 1 July.

2. Prepare a Petty Cash Book from the following information for the month of May and balance it at 31 May.

    Your analysis columns should be for:

      (i) Cleaning
     (ii) Stationery
    (iii) Postages
     (iv) Sundry Expenses

The agreed amount of the Imprest is £100.

Transactions during the month of May.

		£
1	Balance of Cash on hand	14.50
3	Cash received from Cashier to make up total of imprest	
3	Postages	2.85
4	Envelopes	1.40
5	Cleaner's wages	5.65
6	Bus fares	2.50
7	Gummed paper	1.30
10	Postage stamps	2.60
11	Cleaner's wages	5.65
12	Rail fares	4.82
13	Cleaning materials	1.85
14	Typing paper	12.26
18	Cleaner's wages	6.65
19	Paper clips, etc.	1.60
20	Postages	1.80
24	Typing paper	14.75
25	Cleaner's wages	5.65
28	Bus fares	2.28
31	Cleaning materials	2.14
31	Parcel Post	1.10
31	Received cash from cashier to make up total of imprest.	

Ledger entries:

Post the totals of the analysis columns to the nominal ledger and commence each petty cash expense with a 'nil' balance on 1 May.

3. Prepare a Petty Cash Book from the balance brought down in exercise 2. The imprest is £100. You will need to add *two* further columns: packing materials and VAT transactions for the month of June were as follows:

June		£
1	Typing paper, pencils	10.50
2	Taxi fares	5.75
3	Postages, telegrams	6.55
5	Cleaner's wages	5.65
7	Bus fares	2.25
10	Miscellaneous stationery	15.15
12	Packing materials	8.00
	VAT	1.20
16	Cleaner's wages	8.21
17	Taxi fares	11.50
18	Received a further £50 imprest to increase float to £150	
19	Packing materials	16.00
	VAT	2.40
20	Typing paper	12.00
21	Parcel post	4.50
23	Postages	6.75
25	Cleaner's wages	8.21
26	Packing materials	8.00
	VAT	1.20
28	Pens, pencils etc.	2.25

July
1   Received cash from cashier to make up imprest

Required:

1. Balance the petty cash book on 30 June. Bring down the balance and show the reimbursement entry on 1 July.

2. Ledger entries:
   Post the totals of the analysis columns to the same accounts in the nominal ledger. Add the two further accounts.

4. ABC Co. uses its bank for all significant receipts and payments of cash. All cash payments under £10 come out of the petty cash. The imprest is £100 and is reimbursed every month by a cheque payment from the cash book.

The headings used by ABC Co. are as follows:

Cleaning, Travelling expenses, Stationery, Post Office,
Refreshments, General and VAT

The balance of the petty cash on 30 June was £15.65. The firm uses the Voucher system and all vouchers begin from No. 1 on the first of the month.

The transactions for July were as follows:

July		£
2	Reimbursement from Cash Book	
2	Cleaning materials	1.50
	VAT	0.22
3	Stamps and parcel post	8.68
6	Window cleaning	6.00
	VAT	0.90
8	Pens, pencils, typing paper	10.00
	VAT	1.50
11	Newspapers	0.85
12	Tea, coffee, and sugar	3.76
15	Envelopes, ribbons	2.40
	VAT	0.36
19	Telegrams	4.60
20	Taxi fares	3.85
23	Charity donations	1.50
27	Bus fares	4.50
28	Window cleaning	6.00
	VAT	0.90
29	Floor polish and dusters	2.80
	VAT	0.42

Required:

(a) Draw up a petty cash book using the appropriate columns. Bring the imprest balance up to date on 2 July.

(b) Enter the above transactions and balance the book on the 31 July. Bring down the balance and make the appropriate reimbursement on 1 August.

(c) Post the analysis totals to the Nominal Ledger on 31 July, commencing with a 'nil' balance for each of the petty cash expenses on 1 July.

5. The following details refer to J. Smith's petty cash. He keeps the amount of imprest at £50 per month. The balance on hand, 1 January, is £8.42 and the necessary reimbursement is made.

Jan. 7	Voucher No. 1	Petrol and oil	8.05	(VAT inc.)
10	2	Stationery	4.50	(VAT inc.)
14	3	Cleaning materials	2.20	(VAT inc.)
25	4	Refreshment supplies	4.85	
26	5	Postage stamps	3.00	
27	6	Envelopes and typing paper	7.60	(VAT inc.)
29	7	Cleaning materials	2.80	(VAT inc.)
30	8	Petrol and oil	7.20	(VAT inc.)

Required:

(a) Because VAT is inclusive on some of these items (@ 15%) a method of calculating the amount before VAT is shown — by dividing the total by 1.15. For example, Voucher No. 1:

$$\frac{£8.05}{1.15} = £7.00 \qquad \text{Petrol and Oil}$$

Check:	Goods	£7.00
+15%	VAT	1.05
		8.05

(b) Balance the petty cash book on 31 January and bring down the appropriate reimbursement on the next day.

Note: VAT refers to value-added-tax. This is an indirect source of taxation which is charged or levied on many of our goods and services. Food is not charged however. The current rate of tax is 15%.

If tax is added to sales it is referred to as 'output tax' and is collected by the trader on behalf of the Customs and Excise Department. If tax is paid on purchases, it is referred to as 'input tax'.

If a business collects more in output than input tax, the difference between them is paid to the Customs and Excise. If more input tax is paid by the trader, then the Customs and Excise make up the difference by sending a cheque for the balance.

PART 9

The Use of Computer-based Accounts: the Sales and Purchase Ledger Programs

The Ledger programs have been operated on the Pegasus Accounting System. This system includes a wide range of accounting programs such as invoicing, stock control, payroll and job costing.

This section will concentrate on the two personal ledgers, that is, the sales and purchase ledger programs, for the purpose of drawing the student's attention to the reality of recording accounts by using a micro-computer, a system they are more likely to use in the business world.

The same principles of accounting apply whether data is entered via the use of a computer keyboard, or, manually in an accounting book. However, once data is entered into a computer, the facilities offered by the computer's memory for listing and analysing data are far easier and superior. At the press of a button on the computer's keyboard, instant analysis is possible of anything which has been previously entered, with the additional bonus of a printout if required.

The Pegasus Accounting Package is user-friendly in that it takes little time for students to become acquainted with what is called the 'Menu System'. This is a system which offers a menu of functions on screen, for the user to choose. One of the most frequent functions to be operated is 'Ledger Processing' which deals with the entry of day-to-day transactions.

Computer Programs

Computers in business have helped to modernise and speed up the whole system of financial reporting. In particular, repetitive, routine transactions can be recorded, classified, up-dated and recalled in an instant.

Accurate recording of financial information is regarded as one of the most important and fundamental functions in accounting and keeping a track of the business's accounts provides management with vital day–to–day information:

Is sufficient cash coming in?
Which products sell the best?
Is adequate stock available?
Which customers pay regularly?
Which customers are slow payers?
How much is owed to creditors?
How much has been spent on overheads?

These are the type of questions which need constant answers. Accounting provides management with vital information needed to make sound decisions. A good software program can help management by providing a means to quickly record and instantly display as much detailed information as required.

Software refers to the program disks which are designed for the computer to carry out precise instructions. A program disk contains the instructions which the computer carries out and some hold a number of different programs (or files) on the same disk, for example, files for sales, bought and nominal ledgers, on a single disk.

The program is loaded into the computer's memory and data can then be stored onto the disk. Data may be filed on the same program disk although much of the 'memory capacity' of the computer may be taken up by the program and therefore the amount of data which can be input might then be restricted. A separate data disk is required on some computer networks.

Loading Data

Data comes from the day–to–day financial transactions which occur in a business. The disk is fed into the computer and is then ready to receive the facts and figures from the source of documents like an invoice. Data is typed in from the computer's keyboard and the information is fed into the computer's memory system and relayed to the appropriate accounts.

The computer can be used to operate any account in a business. The computer's printer enables all kinds of information to be run off and can provide a whole range of important printouts such as customer statements, employee pay slips, bank payment notices, stock records, receipt slips, as well as the financial statements.

A computer program can provide a flow of information which helps a business make better, informed decisions. The key areas of a business must be carefully monitored for better control:

Sales	:	which products are moving?
Customer's	:	which customers are paying?
Supplier's	:	which suppliers need paying?
Stock	:	what level of stocks are carried?
Cash	:	is there adequate cash?

The right software can provide the right supply of information to a business at the time it is needed.

A Computer Network

The computer 'hardware' relates to the computer itself. In the diagram on p. 155 the basic parts of a system are illustrated:

1. The screen, which visually displays the program details and the information required from the program.
2. The keyboard, which is like that of a typewriter but with a greater number of keys to provide further functions.
3. The disk drive, where the disks are loaded into the computer.
4. The printer, which prints out the information, including business documents and financial statements.
5. The program disks. The compact floppy disk type which are fed into the disk drive and give the computer its precise instructions.

The Sales Ledger Program

An accounting program may either be part of a network system or mainframe where it may be conveniently called upon the screen when required, by simply pressing the appropriate command key, or, it may be necessary to load

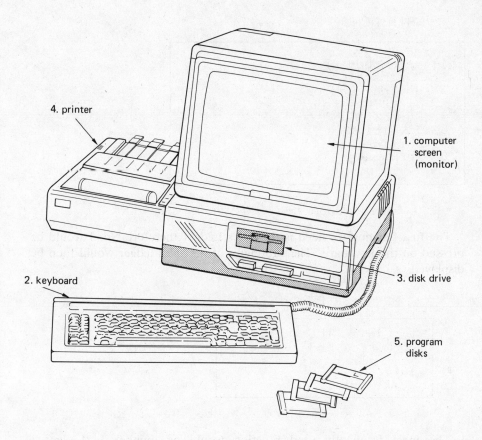

a program disk which has written on it, the program instructions to run a particular function such as the sales or purchase ledgers.

A data disk will be used to record the program and the information stored on it.

Once a disk is loaded onto the computer, the operator will choose which file or menu is required. There may be several files on an accounting package and the computer may require an identifying letter or number, for example '1' may be the code for the sales ledger program, '2' for the purchase ledger.

Programs in business usually operate on what is called a MENU system, that is, it gives the operator a number of choices or functions on which to use. The user will choose a particular function and press the relevant key in order to get started. For example, in the programs shown in this section, the Jenkins Jeans Company Ltd. displays the following main menu:

```
MAIN MENU
```

```
┌─────────────────────────────┐
│                             │
│  1. Sales Ledger            │
│  2. Purchase Ledger         │
│  3. Nominal Ledger          │
│  4. Stock Control           │
│  5. Payroll                 │
│  6. Invoicing               │
│  7. Costing                 │
│  8. Terminate               │
│                             │
│                             │
└─────────────────────────────┘
```

```
   Select and Press Number Required
```

The first function we need is the Sales Ledger therefore No. 1 would be pressed on the keyboard. The sub-menu of the sales ledger would then be displayed:

```
        MENU: SALES LEDGER
   ┌─────────────────────────────┐
   │                             │
   │  1. Ledger Transactions     │
   │  2. Period End              │
   │  3. Analysis of Sales       │
   │  4. Reports                 │
   │                             │
   └─────────────────────────────┘
```

```
     Select and Press Number Required
```

The most frequently used function would be number 1 'Ledger Transactions' which would give a list of further options to operate such as entering invoices, credit notes and receipts.

The function 'Period End' may be used to end a financial period and sales turnover may be zeroed to commence a new period. The customers' balances are not zeroed of course, the balance being brought forward.

The 'Analysis of Sales' function may be particularly useful to those types of businesses which want to know which stocks are moving and which may be slow. It may want an analysis of sales geographically, or by department, or by sales executives. Sales may easily be coded for this purpose.

The fourth function, 'Reports' may be used to indicate batches of sales over periods of time or any other statistical information provided by a particular program.

The general features of reasonable sales ledger program would include:

A facility to store a large number of accounts.
Details of each debtor's records.
Individual customer turnover to date.
Automatic processing to the nominal ledger, thereby completing the double-entry.
Sales Journal
VAT analysis.
Credit control limits for customers.
Aged debtors analysis.
Receipts analysis and details of discounts.
Customer statements.

Most of the above items would be available for printout and this gives computer-based accounting a further edge. Not only can this information be stored on a tiny-sized disk, it can be retrieved instantly when needed and a copy taken on the printer whenever the information is required. Unbeatable over a manual system any time! In large organisations the use of computerised information is essential for management and helps them in their daily decision-making.

If the user selected function No. 1 of the Sales Ledger Menu, Ledger Transactions, a further menu would appear, giving a further list of options:

```
MENU: LEDGER TRANSACTIONS
```

```
  1. Accounts Up-Date
  2. Ledger Postings
  3. Invoice & Credit Note Listing
  4. Receipts & Adjustments
  5. Customer Accounts
  6. Customer Statements
  7. Aged Debtors List
  8. List of Accounts
  9. Outstanding Debtors Total
 10. Terminate.
```

```
Select and Press Number Required
```

The Ledger Transactions function would be used on a daily basis to enter details relating to customers. What each of the options provide is summarised below:

1. *Accounts Up-Date*: The screen would show information such as:

```
* ACCOUNT                    NAME & ADDRESS
  NUMBER

┌─────────────────┐     ┌────────────────────────────┐
│ A001            │     │ Chappell Bros.             │
│                 │     │ 570 Alton Rd               │
└─────────────────┘     │ Lower Parkstone            │
                        │ Poole                      │
                        │ Dorset BH3 12YU            │
                        └────────────────────────────┘

COMMENT               CREDIT          CODE
                      LIMIT
┌─────────────────┐
│ Tele.           │
│ 730256          │   ┌──────────┐   ┌──────────┐
│                 │   │ 2,500    │   │ S        │
└─────────────────┘   └──────────┘   └──────────┘

* Cursor flashing
```

The cursor is awaiting an instruction from the user and in this case it is flashing over the Account No. and is waiting for the operator to enter the relevant number. If the account is new, the computer will state 'New Account' and await further input. If the account is an existing one, all other relevant information will be displayed on screen (as above).

2. *Ledger Posting:* The cursor on the screen would prompt which account was required and then automatically, the details of the customer would be displayed:

```
ACCOUNT    DATE    TYPE   REFERENCE   VALUE   VAT/    PERIOD
NUMBER                                        DISC.
A001       1/1/90   A    Open/Bal.    1025              1
```

Chappell Bros

In the above example, the opening balance of a customer, Chappell Bros. has been entered. Under 'TYPE', the letter 'A' signifies the appropriate code to enter an opening balance.
The letter 'I' could signify invoice, the letter 'C' credit note, and so forth. Once details of any transaction are entered, the sales ledger file is automatically up-dated and may be viewed when required.

Note: Printouts of functions 3, 4, 5, 7 and 8 are shown on pages 163–7 and relate to the illustrated example of Jenkins Jeans Co. Ltd.

3. *Invoice & Credit Note Listing:*
This function lists the invoice and credit notes for any given period, for example, a day, or a week, a month, or longer. In the printout, the month's invoices and credit notes are listed. This detail would be the same as given in the Sales Day Book:

Sales:	£3,130
VAT	£ 469.5
Total Debtors	£3,599.5

4. *Receipts & Adjustments Listing:*
This function allows the operator to list the receipts and adjustments for the period required as in the same case as the invoice and credit note listing. In the printout, the details would be taken from the Cash Book receipts:

Receipts:	£1,925
Discounts:	£ 40
Adjustments:	£2,575
(Open/Bal's)	

5. *Customer Accounts:*
This function is used to display either on screen or printout, the details of each customer's account. All transactions to the debtor are shown, including:

date of entries
invoice and credit note numbers
cheque numbers
discounts given
the age of the debt in months.

This function is used frequently to check records of individual customers and will be an important check on credit control.
How much does the customer owe?
When did he last pay his account?
Does he pay in reasonable time?
These are important questions which need answers in order to keep adequate control of customer accounts. The speed of debt collection is vital to a business's cash flow and working capital.

6. *Customer Statements:*
If a customer statement needs to be printed and sent, this function will give details of the account as found in option number 5, above.

7. *Aged Debtors List:*

This function may be viewed on screen or as a printout, as shown in the example. The balance of each customer is indicated and 'aged' according to how old the debt is.

In the printout, all the debts are listed as 'current', the total debt being £4,209.5. This figure should equal the Sales Ledger Control a/c as in the Nominal Ledger. The credit limit and telephone numbers of each customer are also printed for convenience.

8. *List of Accounts:*

This function gives a list of the customer accounts required. In the printout, the 5 accounts of Jenkins Jeans are listed, also indicating the turnover to date, credit limit and telephone number of each customer. Code 'S' can refer to the geographical area the customer comes from.

9. *Outstanding Debtors Total:*

This function will display on the computer screen the outstanding debt owed by the total of the business's customers.

It should equal the total sum in option 7 (the Aged Debtors List) and is used as a quick check on how much debtors owe.

The screen should display:

```
Total Debtors = £4,209.50
```

10. *Terminate:*

This function has nothing to do with liquidation! It is used to return the operator back to the main Sales Ledger menu.

Illustrated Example of a Software Program

The following information refers to the Sales and Purchase Ledgers of Jenkins Jeans Co. Ltd. The accounts have been fed into the micro-computer using the Pegasus Accounting Package.

On 1 January 1990 the balances of customers and suppliers were as follows:

SALES LEDGER

CUSTOMER	ACCOUNT NUMBER	BALANCE ON 1/1/90
		£
Chappell Bros.	A001	1,025
Lawrie & Sons	A002	200
Redpath & Edwards	A003	600
Walker Ltd.	A004	285
Walters & Co. Ltd.	A005	465

All balances are debit.

PURCHASE LEDGER

SUPPLIER	ACCOUNT NUMBER	BALANCE ON 1/1/90
		£
Illingworth & Edwards	B001	1,975
Milburn & Harries	B002	300
Snow Material Supplies	B003	1,215
Underwood Mills Ltd.	B004	2,150

All balances are credit.

Required:

(a) Set up the ledgers of the company using sales and purchase programs. Make up appropriate addresses for each customer and supplier and any further information which might prove useful (telephone numbers).

Credit Sales and Credit Purchases

The credit sales for January 1990 were as follows:

Date	Customer ac	Invoice No.	Net Sales	VAT	Total
Jan 5	Chappell Bros	4219	500		
8	Lawrie & Sons	4220	240		
12	Chappell Bros	4221	200		
17	Walker Ltd	4222	350		
18	Redpath & Edwards	4223	450		
24	Lawrie & Sons	4224	180		
25	Chappell Bros	4225	290		
27	Redpath & Edwards	4226	650		
30	Walters Ltd	4227	300		
31	Chappell Bros	cn 42	(30)		
			3130		

(b) Use this page to record your figures. Calculate VAT at 15% and total the columns. Post the transactions to the ledgers.

The credit purchases of stock for January 1990 were as follows:

Date	Supplier ac	Inv.No. Recd.	Gross Purchases	Net	VAT	Total
			£	£	£	£
Jan 5	Underwood Mills Ltd	3046	1,000	800	114.	
7	Illingworth & Edwards	29851	1,200	960	136.8	
10	Milburn & Harris Ltd	4367	500	425	60.56	
15	Underwood Mills Ltd	4768	380	304	43.32	
20	Illingworth & Edwards	34420	530	424	60.42	
25	Snow Material Supplies	2321	240	204	29.07	
			3,850	3,117		

(c) Use this page to record your findings. Check the accuracy of the invoices before totalling the columns. Underwood Mills Ltd and Illingworth & Edwards give 20% Trade and 5% Cash Discounts. Milburn & Harris and Snow Supplies give 15% Trade and 5% Cash Discounts. Post to the ledgers.

Receipts & Payments for January

Extract from Jenkins Jeans Cash Book:

Receipts

Date	Customer	Amount	Discount
		£	£
Jan. 5	Redpath & Edwards	290	10
10	Walker Ltd.	200	
15	Redpath & Edwards	290	10
17	Chappell Bros.	480	20
20	Lawrie & Son	200	
29	Walter Ltd.	465	

```
Payments

Date       Supplier                   Amount  Discount
                                        £        £
Jan.  5   Illingworth & Edwards       1,000     50
      8   Snow Material Supplies        500     12.5
     13   Underwood Mills Ltd.        1,500
     16   Milburn & Harries  ,         292.5   7.5
```

Required:

(d) Post the above receipts and payments to the relevant accounts in the Sales and Purchase Ledgers. Ensure that the totals of debtors and creditors cross-check with the control accounts in the Nominal Ledger.

The Sales Ledger Program

```
Printouts from Ledger Transactions

  Option 3:  Invoices & Credit Notes
  Option 4:  Receipts & Adjustments
  Option 5:  Customer Accounts
  Option 7:  Aged Debtors List
  Option 8:  List of Accounts
```

Option 3: *Invoices & Credit Notes*

```
                 Jenkins Jeans Co. Ltd.

01.01.90       SL Invoices & Credit Notes (To Date)   Page 1

Ac   Date    Type  Ref   Value   Goods   VAT

A001 05.01.90  Invce 4219   575.00  500.00   75.00 Chappell Bros.
A002 08.01.90  Invce 4220   276.00  240.00   36.00 Lawrie & Sons
A001 12.01.90  Invce 4221   230.00  200.00   30.00 Chappell Bros.
A004 17.01.90  Invce 4222   402.50  350.00   52.50 Walker Ltd
A003 18.01.90  Invce 4223   517.50  450.00   67.50 Redpath & Edwards
A002 24.01.90  Invce 4224   207.00  180.00   27.00 Lawrie & Sons
A001 25.01.90  Invce 4225   333.50  290.00   43.50 Chappell Bros.
A003 27.01.90  Invce 4226   747.50  650.00   97.50 Redpath & Edwards
A005 30.01.90  Invce 4227   345.00  300.00   45.00 Walters Co. Ltd
A001 31.01.90  Cnote cn     -34.50  -30.00   -4.50 Chappell Bros.
                     42

Total Invoices        3634.00 3160.00 474.00
Total Cr. Notes -      -34.50  -30.00  -4.50
Total                 3599.50 3130.00 469.50
```

Option 4: *Receipts & Adjustments*

```
                        Jenkins Jeans Co. Ltd.

01.01.90   SL Receipts & Adjusts (To Date)   Page 1

Ac   Date      Type    Reference   Value    Period

A001 01.01.90  Adjust  open bal    1025.00      1    Chappell Bros.
A002 01.01.90  Adjust  open bal     200.00      1    Lawrie & Sons
A003 01.01.90  Adjust  open bal     600.00      1    Redpath & Edwards
A004 01.01.90  Adjust  open bal     285.00      1    Walker Ltd
A005 01.01.90  Adjust  open bal     465.00      1    Walters Co. Ltd
A003 08.01.90  Recpt   chq 9809    -290.00      1    Redpath & Edwards
A003 08.01.90  Discnt  chq 9809     -10.00      1    Redpath & Edwards
A004 10.01.90  Recpt   chq 8908    -200.00      1    Walker Ltd
A003 15.01.90  Recpt   chq 6577    -290.00      1    Redpath & Edwards
A003 15.01.90  Discnt  chq 6577     -10.00      1.   Redpath & Edwards
A001 17.01.90  Recpt   chq 6754    -480.00      1    Chappell Bros.
A001 17.01.90  Discnt  chq 6754     -20.00      1    Chappell Bros.
A002 20.01.90  Recpt   chq 5645    -200.00      1    Lawrie & Sons
A005 29.01.90  Recpt   chq 5656    -465.00      1    Walters Co. Ltd


Total Discounts                 -40.00
Total Receipts                -1925.00
Total Refunds                     .00
Total Adj _ Contras               .00
Total Adj _ Bad Debts             .00
Total Adj _ Write Offs            .00
Total Adj _ Misposts              .00
Total Adj _ Discounts             .00
Total Adj _ Interest              .00
Total Adj _ Sundry             2575.00
Total                           610.00
```

Option 5: *Customer Accounts*

```
Chappell Bros.          Account A001          01 Jan 1990
570 Alton Road
Lower Parkstone
Poole                   TOver    960Jan   Cr.Lim 2500
DORSET                  Interest Rate 0.00%
BH3 12YU

Date      Type     Reference   Status   Debit    Credit Balance

01.01.90  Adjust   open bal    Jan      1025.00
05.01.90  Invoice  4219                  575.00
12.01.90  Invoice  4221                  230.00
25.01.90  Invoice  4225                  333.50
31.01.90  Cr. Note cn 42                          34.50
17.01.90  Receipt  chq 6754    Jan               480.00
17.01.90  Discnt   chq 6754    Jan                20.00

3 Months+ 2 Months  1 Month   Current              Total
   .00       .00       .00     1629.00             1629.00
```

```
Lawrie & Sons              Account A002         01 Jan 1990
1 Selfrige Close
Southbourne
Bournemouth
DORSET                     TOver   420Jan   Cr.Lim 1020
BH4 6LU                    Interest Rate 0.00%


Date       Type      Reference   Status   Debit     Credit Balance

01.01.90  Adjust    open bal    Jan      200.00
08.01.90  Invoice   4220                 276.00
24.01.90  Invoice   4224                 207.00
20.01.90  Receipt   chq 5645    Jan                 200.00


3 Months+ 2 Months  1 Month     Current                    Total
    .00       .00       .00     483.00                     483.00


Redpath & Edwards          Account A003         01 Jan 1990
120 Hintonwood Avenue
Highcliffe
Christchurch
DORSET                     TOver   1100Jan   Cr.Lim 2000
BH4 57W                    Interest Rate 0.00%

Date       Type      Reference   Status   Debit     Credit Balance

01.01.90  Adjust    open bal    Jan      600.00
18.01.90  Invoice   4223                 517.50
27.01.90  Invoice   4226                 747.50
08.01.90  Receipt   chq 9809    Jan                 290.00
08.01.90  Discnt    chq 9809    Jan                  10.00
15.01.90  Receipt   chq 6577    Jan                 290.00
15.01.90  Discnt    chq 6577    Jan                  10.00

3 Months+ 2 Months  1 Month     Current                    Total
    .00       .00       .00     1265.00                    1265.00


Walker Ltd                 Account A004         01 Jan 1990
Footloose Industrial
  Estate
Footloose Way
Highcliffe
DORSET
BH7 89Y


                           TOver   350Jan   Cr.Lim 1500
                           Interest Rate 0.00%

Date       Type      Reference   Status   Debit     Credit Balance

01.01.90  Adjust    open bal    Jan      285.00
17.01.90  Invoice   4222                 402.50
10.01.90  Receipt   chq 8908    Jan                 200.00

3 Months+ 2 Months  1 Month     Current                    Total
    .00       .00       .00     487.50                     487.50
```

```
Walters Co. Ltd          Account A005          01 Jan 1990
134 Jeremy Way
Charlie Industrial Estate
Christchurch
DORSET                   TOver   300Jan    Cr.Lim 1000
BH7 560                  Interest Rate 0.00%

Date      Type      Reference   Status    Debit    Credit Balance

01.01.90  Adjust    open bal    Jan       465.00
30.01.90  Invoice   4227                  345.00
29.01.90  Receipt   chq 5656    Jan                465.00


3 Months+2 Months  1 Month    Current                    Total
  .00      .00       .00      345.00                     345.00
```

Option 7: *Aged Debtors List*

```
                    Jenkins Jeans Co. Ltd.

01.01.90                  Aged Debtors List          Page 1


Ac   3 Mths+2 Mths 1 Mth   Current Total      Cr.
                                              Limit

A001 .00     .00    .00    1629.00 1629.00    2500  Chappell Bros.
                                                    000 Tel 730256
A002 .00     .00    .00     483.00  483.00    1020  Lawrie & Sons
                                                    000 Tel 465712
A003 .00     .00    .00    1265.00 1265.00    2000  Redpath &
                                                    Edwards
                                                    000 Tel 272713
A004 .00     .00    .00     487.50  487.50    1500  Walker Ltd
                                                    000 Tel 536765
A005 .00     .00    .00     345.00  345.00    1000  Walters Co. Ltd
                                                    000 Tel 478095

Total.00     .00    .00    4209.50 4209.50
```

Option 8: *List of Accounts*

```
A001    Chappell Bros.                 000 Tel 730256
        570 Alton Road                 Code S
        Lower Parkstone                Type B
        Poole                          Cr.Limit 2500
        DORSET                         TOver    960Jan
        BH3 12YU

A002    Lawrie & Sons                  000 Tel 465712
        1 Selfrige Close               Code S
        Southbourne                    Type B
        Bournemouth                    Cr.Limit 1020
        DORSET                         TOver    420Jan
        BH4 6LU

A003    Redpath & Edwards              000 Tel 272713
        120 Hintonwood Avenue          Code S
        Highcliffe                     Type B
        Christchurch                   Cr.Limit 2000
        DORSET                         TOver   1100Jan
        BH4 57W
```

```
A004    Walker Ltd                              000 Tel 536765
        Footloose Industrial Estate             Code S
        Footloose Way                           Type B
        Highcliffe                              Cr.Limit  1500
        Dorset                                  TOver    350Jan
        BH7 89Y

A005    Walters Co. Ltd                         000 Tel 478095
        134 Jeremy Way                          Code S
        Charlie Industrial Estate               Type B
        Christchurch                            Cr.Limit  1000
        DORSET                                  TOver    300Jan
        BH7 560
```

The Purchase Ledger Program

This program operates almost in an identical way as the Sales Ledger Program and is used to record the individual suppliers of a business, giving details of purchases, returns, payments, and any other information which relates to creditors.

The control of purchasing is a key management function. All purchases must be bought and paid for at the right time, at the right quantity and quality and at the right price. Management needs to have up-to-date information about all its suppliers. How long will they wait before payment? What discounts do they offer? Who is the person(s) to contact in the event of queries?

The amount of money a business spends on its stock can be a major expenditure and therefore affects its cash flow and working capital. Has the business sufficient cash resources to pay its creditors on time? A good computer program can provide up-to-the minute information management needs including:

A facility to store a large number of accounts.

Details of supplier's records.

Supplier turnover.

Printouts of the Purchase Journal.

VAT Analysis.

Automatic processing to the Nominal Ledger.

Analysis of purchases, payments, discounts.

Aged creditors analysis.

A link up to Stock Control.

The options available on the Purchase Ledger Program are virtually the same as those of the Sales Program and the sub-menu, 'Ledger Transactions' is the one most frequently in use:

```
MENU: LEDGER TRANSACTIONS

┌─────────────────────────────────────────┐
│ 1.  Accounts Up-date                     │
│ 2.  Ledger Postings                      │
│ 3.  Invoice & Credit Note Listing        │
│ 4.  Payments & Adjustments               │
│ 5.  Supplier Accounts                    │
│ 6.  Aged Creditors List                  │
│ 7.  List of Accounts                     │
│ 8.  Outstanding Creditors Total          │
│ 9.  Terminate                            │
└─────────────────────────────────────────┘

Select and Press Number Required
```

The Ledger Transactions function would be used on a daily basis to record details relating to suppliers' accounts.

Each of the options are summarised below:

1. *Accounts Up-Date:*
   The screen would display the following:

```
ACCOUNT                              NAME & ADDRESS
NUMBER

B001                                 Illingworth & Edwards
                                     The Albany
                                     Manor Road
                                     Bournemouth

SETTLEMENT       DISCOUNT       DAYS BEFORE     CREDIT        CODE
DAYS             RECEIVED       SETTLEMENT      LIMIT
────────         ────────       ──────────      ──────        ────
   30               5%              4            5000           S
```

In the above example, B001 refers to the supplier, Illingworth & Edwards. This creditor allows 5% cash discount if payment is made within 30 days and the cheque should be arranged to be paid within 4 days of the 30 day limit.

The supplier has allowed a credit limit of up to 5000 at present.

The Code 'S' signifies that the supplier is located in the south of England.

2. *Ledger Posting:*
   This function is used perhaps the most frequently, the cursor * flashing on screen would prompt the operator for the number of the account required.
   B001 would bring the details of Illingworth & Edwards on screen:

```
ACCOUNT    DATE    TYPE    REF     VALUE    VAT/DISC   PERIOD
 B001     1/1/90    1      2985    1096.8   136.8         1
```

In this example, Jenkins Jeans has purchased £1,096.80 of goods which included £136.80 VAT from Illingworth & Edwards.

Under 'Type' the letter 'I' signified that an invoice was to be entered, the invoice number also being entered under the heading 'Reference'.

Printouts of the Purchase Ledger Program include the following:

3. *Invoice & Credit Note Listing:*
   The details of this function would be the same as for the Purchase Day Book:

Purchases:	£3,117
VAT	£ 444.17
Total Creditors	£3,561.17

4. *Payments & Adjustments:*
   This function allows the operator to list all payments and adjustments for the period required. The details would be taken from the Cash Book payments:

Payments:	£3,292.5
Discounts:	£ 70.
Adjustments:	£5,640.
(Open/Bal's)	

5. *Supplier Accounts:*
   All transactions relating to the creditor are shown, including:

   date of entries
   purchase invoices and credit notes
   cheque numbers and payments
   discounts received
   the age of the amount due in months.

   This is a function used frequently to check that payments are made on time and valuable discounts taken if they are available. For example, Illingworth & Edwards are owed £2,506.22, all current month. If 30 days are allowed, then payment need not be made until February.

6. *Aged Creditors List:*
   The balance of each creditor is indicated and 'aged' according to how old the amount due is.

In the printout, the total due for payment is all under the current month, £5838.67.

This figure should also equal the balance of the Purchase Ledger.

Control a/c in the Nominal Ledger. The number of days on invoice (30), discount (5%): and the days before cheque payment (4) are also shown for each supplier's account.

7. *List of Accounts:*

This provides a list of the supplier accounts required. Jenkins have only 4 of them at present. Details of supplier turnover, credit limit, settlement terms and code are also indicated.

8. *Outstanding Creditors Total:*

This is not provided as a printout but the outstanding debt due to suppliers will be shown on screen and can also serve as a check with the Purchase Ledger Control a/c.

```
Total Creditors = £5,838.67
```

9. *Terminate:*

This terminates the sub-menu and returns the operator to the main Purchases Ledger menu.

The Purchase Ledger Program

Printouts from Ledger Transactions

```
Option 3:  Invoices & Credit Notes
Option 4:  Payments & Adjustments
Option 5:  Supplier Accounts
Option 6:  Aged Creditors List
Option 7:  List of Accounts
```

Option 3: *Invoices & Credit Notes*

```
                        Jenkins Jeans Company Ltd.

01.01.90             PL Invoices & Credit Notes (To Date)   Page 1


Ac    Date     Type    Ref.   Value    Goods    VAT

B004  05.01.90 Invce   3046    914.00   800.00  114.00 Underwood
                                                       Mills Ltd
B001  07.01.90 Invce   2985   1096.80   960.00  136.80 Illingworth &
                                                       Edwards
B002  10.01.90 Invce   4367    485.56   425.00   60.56 Milburn &
                                                       Harris Ltd
B004  15.01.90 Invce   4768    347.32   304.00   43.32 Underwood
                                                       Mills Ltd
B001  20.01.90 Invce  34420    484.42   424.00   60.42 Illingworth &
                                                       Edwards
B003  25.01.90 Invce   2321    233.07   204.00   29.07 Snow Material
                                                       Supplies

Total Invoices               3561.17  3117.00  444.17
Total Cr.Notes                  0.00     0.00    0.00
Total                        3561.17  3117.00  444.17
```

Option 4: *Payments & Adjustments*

```
                        Jenkins Jeans Co. Ltd.

01.01.90             PL Payments & Adjusts (To Date)   Page 1


Ac    Date     Type    Reference  Value   Period

B001  01.01.90 Adjust  open bal  1975.00  1    Illingworth & Edwards
B002  01.01.90 Adjust  open bal   300.00  1    Milburn & Harris Ltd
B003  01.01.90 Adjust  open bal  1215.00  1    Snow Material Supplies
B004  01.01.90 Adjust  open bal  2150.00  1    Underwood Mills Ltd
B001  05.01.90 Paymnt  CHQ 1234 -1000.00  1    Illingworth & Edwards
B001  05.01.90 Discnt  CHQ 1234   -50.00  1    Illingworth & Edwards
B003  08.01.90 Paymnt  CHQ 1235  -500.00  1    Snow Material Supplies
B003  08.01.90 Discnt  CHQ 1235   -12.50  1    Snow Material Supplies
B004  13.01.90 Paymnt  CHQ 1236 -1500.00  1    Underwood Mills Ltd
B002  16.01.90 Paymnt  CHQ 1237  -292.50  1    Milburn & Harris Ltd
B002  16.01.90 Discnt  CHQ 1237    -7.50  1    Milburn & Harris Ltd

Total Discounts            -70.00
Total Payments          -3292.50
Total Refunds               0.00
Total Adj _ Contras         0.00
Total Adj _ Write Offs      0.00
Total Adj _ Misposts        0.00
Total Adj _ Discounts       0.00
Total Adj _ Sundry       5640.00
Total                    2277.50
```

Option 5: *Supplier Accounts*

```
Illingworth & Edwards        Account B001        01 Jan 1990
The Albany
Manor Rd                     TOver   1384Jan    Cr.Lim 5000
Bournemouth

Date          Type        Reference    Status Debit    Credit Balance

01.01.90      Adjust      open bal     Jan                1975.00
07.01.90      Invoice     2985                            1096.80
20.01.90      Invoice     34420                            484.42
05.01.90      Payment     CHQ 1234     Jan    1000.00
05.01.90      Discnt      CHQ 1234     Jan      50.00

3 Months+    2 Months    1 Month     Current                 Total
   0.00        0.00        0.00      2506.22               2506.22


Milburn & Harris Ltd         Account B002        01 Jan 1990
10 Alton Road
Lower Parkstone              TOver    425Jan     Cr.Lim 3000
Poole
Dorset
BH3 12YU

Date          Type        Reference    Status Debit    Credit Balance

01.01.90      Adjust      open bal     Jan                 300.00
10.01.90      Invoice     4367                             485.56
16.01.90      Payment     CHQ 1237
16.01.90      Discnt      CHQ 1237     Jan     292.50
                                       Jan       7.50

3 Months+    2 Months    1 Month     Current                 Total
   0.00        0.00        0.00       485.56                485.56


Snow Material Supplies       Account B003        01 Jan 1990
999 Jeremy Way
Charlie Industrial Estate    TOver    204Jan     Cr.Lim 5000
Christchurch
Dorset
BH7 56U

Date          Type        Reference    Status Debit    Credit Balance

01.01.90      Adjust      open bal     Jan                1215.00
25.01.90      Invoice     2321                             233.07
08.01.90      Payment     CHQ 1235     Jan     500.00
08.01.90      Discnt      CHQ 1235     Jan      12.50

3 Months+    2 Months    1 Month     Current                 Total
   0.00        0.00        0.00       935.57                935.57


Underwood Mills Ltd          Account B004        01 Jan 1990
10 Keswick Road
Boscombe                     TOver   1104Jan     Cr.Lim 5000
Bournemouth
Dorset
B301 777S
```

```
Date            Type            Reference    Status Debit   Credit Balance

01.01.90        Adjust          open bal     Jan            2150.00
05.01.90        Invoice         3046                         914.00
15.01.90        Invoice         4768                         347.32
13.01.90        Payment         CHQ 1236     Jan    1500.00

3 Months+       2 Months        1 Month      Current                Total
   0.00            0.00            0.00       1911.32                1911.32
```

Option 6: *Aged Creditors List*

```
                     Jonkino Jeans Company Ltd.

01.01.90                          Aged Creditors List           Page 1

Ac    3 Mths+2 Mths  1 Mth  Current  Total    Cr.
                                              Limit

B001 0.00     0.00   0.00   2506.22  2506.22  5000   Illingworth &
                                                     Edwards
                                                     30 5.00%
                                                     4 Days
B002 0.00     0.00   0.00    485.56   485.56  3000   Milburn & Harris
                                                     Ltd
                                                     30 5.00%
                                                     4 Days
B003 0.00     0.00   0.00    935.57   935.57  5000   Snow Material
                                                     Supplies
                                                     30 5.00%
                                                     4 Days
B004 0.00     0.00   0.00   1911.32  1911.32  5000   Underwood Mills
                                                     Ltd
                                                     30 5.00%
                                                     4 Days

Total0.00     0.00   0.00   5838.67  5838.67
```

Option 7: *List of Accounts*

```
B001    Illingworth & Edwards        30 5.00%              4 Days
        The Albany                   Code S
        Manor Rd                     Type B
        Bournemouth                  Cr.Limit    5000
                                     TOver       1384Jan

B002    Milburn & Harris Ltd         30 5.00%              4 Days
        10 Alton Road                Code S
        Lower Parkstone              Type B
        Poole                        Cr.Limit    3000
        Dorset                       TOver       425Jan
        BH3 12YU

B003    Snow Material Supplies       30 5.00%              4 Days
        999 Jeremy Way               Code S
        Charlie Industrial           Type B
        Estate                       Cr.Limit    5000
        Christchurch                 TOver       204Jan
        Dorset
        BH7 560U
```

```
B004      Underwood Mills Ltd          30 5.00%                4 Days
          10 Keswick Road              Code S
          Boscombe                     Type B
          Bournemouth                  Cr.Limit    5000
          Dorset                       TOver       1104Jan
          B301 777S
```

Nominal Ledger

		Debit	Credit	Balance
Sales Ledger Control Account				
1190	Balance			2,575 Dr.
31190	Sales	3,130		
	VAT	469.5		6,174.5
31190	Bank		1925	
	Dis. Alld.		40	4,209.5
Purchase Ledger Control Account				
1190	Balance			5,640 Cr.
31190	Purchases		3,117	
	Vat		444.17	9,201.17
31190	Bank	3,292.5		
	Dis. Recd.	70		5,838.67

Note: Check both these accounts with the Aged Debtors and Aged Creditors List, Option 7 in the Sales Ledger and Option 6 in the Purchase Ledger. Make sure the balances cross-check.

Notes:

1. Computer-based accounts give immediate access to any section of information needed. The menu system of a program represents the various options (functions) which an operator may use.

2. The sales and purchase ledger programs may have many features including the aging of debtors and creditors, which helps a business to monitor and control its information more easily and assists management to make better decisions.

3. The sales and purchase ledger programs may be integrated with the nominal ledger. When information is entered in the personal ledgers, the double-entry may automatically be transferred to the appropriate nominal accounts.

Questions

1. What advantages do you think a computer program has to offer over a manual system of recording a relatively large number of personal accounts?

2. When data is typed into the computer, the appropriate menu is used. Use a specific example to explain what this means.

3. In a sales or purchase ledger program, which functions tend to be used most frequently?

4. In the printouts of both sales and purchase ledger programs, what functions does option 3 relate to when compared with a manual system of accounts?
   In option 5, check how the accounts of customers or suppliers compare with recording accounts in a manual system.

5. If it is possible for you to obtain and use a computer, why not try an exercise yourself by using a question from the sales or purchases day books?

The Construction of Financial Statements for Private, Public and Social Organisations

Objectives

The Private Sector:

To understand the meaning and construction of financial statements — the trading and profit and loss account and balance sheet.

To provide adjustments to financial statements for accruals, pre-payments, bad debts and depreciation.

To understand the meaning and construction of partnership accounts.

To understand the meaning and construction of company accounts.

To understand the purpose of a funds flow statement.

The Public Sector:

To appreciate the accounts found in the public sector — that is, revenue and expenditure statements.

Social Organisations:

To appreciate the accounts of clubs and societies.

Accounting reports or statements attempt to explain what has happened in an organisation's financial year. Reports are required for a number of reasons. An organisation wants to know how successful or otherwise it has been; whether it has earned profits or incurred losses. It wants to know how its money has been used, where it has come from and where it has gone. It wants to know the value of its resources and how these resources have been financed.

The Inland Revenue needs to have accounting reports in order to assess an organisation's tax liability. Creditors require reports to inform them about the reliability and financial stability of their clients. Potential investors also require accounting reports to help them investigate whether or not it is worth risking their capital.

Making a profit is one of the most significant objectives of an organisation in the Private Sector as distinct from the Public Sector. Not that the State is averse to making profits. The Government's guidance to the Nationalised Industries is to run them in the same way as commercial enterprises.

Profit is basically the difference between revenue and expenses. If revenue is more than expenses, then a profit is made. The Profit and Loss Account is a report which states an organisation's position of profit or loss.

The Balance Sheet is another financial report which identifies the value of an organisation's resources and the financing of them. Any profit which is retained by an organisation is reflected as an increase in its resources and also as an equivalent increase in its net worth (or capital). In this way the five groups of accounts are linked together. The difference between revenue and expenses equals profit or loss which is related to an equivalent increase or decrease in net assets.

A further financial report is the Sources and Application of Funds Statement which identifies the movement of resources — that is, where the money has come from and where it has gone. The statement attempts to link the movement of funds between one financial period and the next and helps to provide a further explanation of what has happened to an organisation's resources.

Public organisations prepare revenue and expenditure statements which identifies where a public authority spends its money and how it finances its spending. Central Government finance basically comes from taxation, whereas local authority finance is raised from a mix of community charge, grants from Government and borrowing. Local authority spending provides local regions with essential services including Education, Police, Housing, Roads and Health and Social Services.

'Social organisations' refers to clubs and societies which provide sporting and other recreational activities for members. These organisations are essentially non-profit motivated. The club or society usually prepares some basic financial reports which will show members the extent of their cash resources, what they have raised and spent during the year and their overall financial position.

PART 1

Profit Calculation

G. Harrison's accounting year runs from 1 January to 31 December. This represents his accounting period. To calculate whether or not he has made a profit in this period, he will need to match his revenue accounts with his expenses accounts.

This matching process must be done precisely and this means that all revenue earned within the period and all expenses paid or incurred within the period must be accounted for.

This may include expenses which have been used up in this period but are still unpaid (accrued expenses), or expenses paid which relate to the subsequent period (pre-paid expenses). Adjustments such as these will have to be made to the accounts in order to get a 'true and fair view' of them and of the profit or loss for the period under review. Other adjustments to the accounts include depreciation of fixed assets and provisions against debtors going bad. These will be dealt with in subsequent parts of this section.

Basically, Profit = Revenue *less* Expenses. There are two types of profit:

1. *Gross Profit*
    Gross profit is the difference between Sales *less* Cost of Sales. In other words selling price *less* cost price. For example

(a)	Sales	£11,000
	Purchases	£ 5,000
	Gross Profit	£ 6,000

However, the *stock* value both at the beginning and end of an accounting period affects the value of purchases.

(b)   If stock value on 1 January was £1,000 and the unsold stock value on 31 December was £1,500:

Cost of Sales =	Stock (1/1)	£1,000
	+ Purchases	5,000
		6,000
	− Stock (31/12)	1,500
		4,500

Gross Profit   =   Sales − Cost of Sales
 £6,500   £11,000 − £4,500

(c)   Returns: if there were Returns Inward of £250 (sales returns) and Returns Outward of £350 (purchases returns), these would be deducted from sales and purchases value respectively:

	£	£
Sales	11,000	
− Returns In	250	10,750
Less Cost of Sales		
Stock (1/1)	1,000	
+ Purchases	5,000	
	6,000	
− Returns Out	350	
	5,650	
− Stock (31/12)	1,500	4,150
Gross Profit		6,600

The *trading account* is the account where gross profit is calculated.

2.   *Net Profit*

The net profit is the difference between the gross profit and all other expenses, plus any other revenue earned (other than sales):

Net Profit = Gross Profit − Other Expenses + any other revenue

	£	£
Gross profit		6,600
less other Expenses:		
Salaries	850	
Light and Heat	300	
Printing and Stationery	100	
Telephone	155	
Delivery Expenses	125	

Advertising	300	
Packing materials	340	
Discount allowed	65	
Rates and Water	285	
Motor expenses	500	
Interest paid	140	3,160
		3,440
add other Revenue:		
Discount received	125	
Commission	85	210
Net Profit		3,650

The *profit and loss account* is the account where the net profit is calculated.

G. Harrison's Trial Balance as on 31 December

Account	£	£
Capital: G. Harrison		10,000
Drawings	2,600	
Premises	12,000	
Fixtures and Fittings	2,000	
Equipment	3,000	
Motor Van	1,250	
Building Society Mortgage		8,000
Bank Loan		1,000
Stock (1 January)	1,000	
Bank/cash	400	
Debtors	850	
Creditors		950
Sales		11,000
Returns Inward	250	
Purchases	5,000	
Returns Outward		350
Salaries	850	
Light and Heat	300	
Printing and Stationery	100	
Telephone	155	
Delivery Expenses	125	
Advertising	300	
Packing Materials	340	
Discount Allowed	65	
Rates and Water	285	
Motor Expenses	500	
Interest Paid	140	
Discount Received		125
Commission Received		85
	31,510	31,510

Note: Value of unsold stock
at cost 31 December   £1,500

Required:

(a) Prepare the Trading and Profit and Loss account of G. Harrison for the year ended 31 December.
(b) A Balance Sheet as at that date, 31 December.

G. Harrison

Trading and Profit and Loss Account
for the Year Ended 31 December

	£	£
Sales	11,000	
– Returns Inward	250	10,750
Less Cost of Sales		
Stock (1/1)	1,000	
+ Purchases	5,000	
	6,000	
– Returns Outward	350	
	5,650	
– Stock (31/12)	1,500	4,150
Gross Profit		6,600
Less other Expenses		
Salaries	850	
Printing and Stationery	100	
Telephone	155	
Delivery Expenses	125	
Advertising	300	
Packing Materials	340	
Discount Allowed	65	
Rates and Water	285	
Motor Expenses	500	
Interest Paid	140	
Light and heat	300	3,160
		3,440
Add other Revenue		
Discount Received	125	
Commission	85	210
Net Profit		3,650

(transferred to Capital a/c)

Note: The value of unsold stock on 31 December is entered in the balance sheet as a current asset.

The Net Profit is added to the Capital a/c in the balance sheet, increasing the owner's net worth in the business. The owner's drawings will be deducted from his net worth.

G. Harrison
Balance Sheet as at 31 December

	£	£	£
Fixed Assets (at cost)			
Premises	12,000		
Fixtures and Fittings	2,000		
Equipment	3,000		
Motor Van	1,250		18,250
Current Assets			
Stock (at cost) 31.12	1,500		
Debtors	850		
Bank/cash	400	2,750	
less Current Liabilities			
Creditors	950	950	
Working Capital			1,800
*Capital Employed			20,050
less Long-term Liabilities			
Mortgage (Building Society)	8,000		
Bank Loan	1,000		9,000
Net assets			11,050
Financed by:			
Capital: G. Harrison (1/1)	10,000		
+ Net Profit	3,650	13,650	
– Drawings		2,600	11,050

*Capital Employed: = Fixed Assets   +   Working Capital
    £20,050   =   £18,250   +   £1,800

Transfer of Nominal Ledger Accounts to Trading and Profit and Loss

All revenue and expense balances are transferred to the trading and profit and loss account at the end of an accounting period.

Once profit and loss has been calculated, revenue and expense accounts will start the new accounting period with new zero balances.

The stock account will also be transferred to trading and the unsold stock value at the end of the year will be entered in the stock account as the new stock value.

Nominal Ledger of G. Harrison after Trading and Profit and Loss account:

		Dr. £	Cr. £	Balance £
Sales a/c				
31 Dec.	Balance			11,000 Cr.
	Trading	11,000		Nil
*1 Jan.	Balance			—
Purchases a/c				
31 Dec.	Balance			5,000 Dr.
	Trading		5,000	Nil
*1 Jan.	Balance			—
Returns Inward a/c				
31 Dec.	Balance	250		250 Dr.
	Trading		250	Nil
*1 Jan.	Balance			—
Returns Outward				
31 Dec.	Balance			350 Cr.
	Trading	350		Nil
*1 Jan.	Balance			
Stock a/c				
1 Jan.	Balance			1,000 Dr.
31 Dec.	Trading		1,000	Nil
31 Dec.	Trading	1,500		1,500 Dr.
*1 Jan.	Balance			1,500 Dr.

*New accounting period. Note that the stock (end) £1,500 becomes stock (beg.) in the new period.

Nominal Ledger of G. Harrison

		Dr. £	Cr. £	Balance £
Salaries a/c				
31 Dec.	Balance			850 Dr.
	Profit and Loss		850	Nil
*1 Jan.	Balance			—
Printing and Stationery a/c				
31 Dec.	Balance			100 Dr.
	Profit and Loss		100	Nil
*1 Jan.	Balance			—
Telephone a/c				
31 Dec.	Balance			155 Dr.
	Profit and Loss		155	Nil
*1 Jan.	Balance			—
Delivery Expenses a/c				
31 Dec.	Balance			125 Dr.
	Profit and Loss		125	Nil
*1 Jan.	Balance			—
Advertising a/c				
31 Dec.	Balance			300 Dr.
	Profit and Loss		300	Nil
*1 Jan.	Balance			—
Packing Materials a/c				
31 Dec.	Balance			340 Dr.
	Profit and Loss		340	Nil
*1 Jan.	Balance			—

*New accounting period. The remaining revenue and expense accounts will also be transferred to Profit and Loss. All other accounts (that is, assets, liabilities and capital) are not affected in the same way and their balances are carried forward to the new accounting period.

Exercises

1. The following represents the Trial Balance of J. Wright on 30 June:

Account	Dr.	Cr.
	£	£
Capital: J. Wright		25,000
Premises	19,000	
Bank	1,250	
Equipment	4,075	
Motor Vehicle	2,250	
Drawings: J. Wright	1,750	
Stock (1/7) beg.	1,250	
Debtors	1,000	
Creditors		2,100
Sales		50,000
Returns Inward	200	
Returns Outward		550
Purchases	44,500	
General Expenses	650	
Salaries	1,125	
Administration Expenses	450	
Rates and Insurance	300	
Interest Received		150
	77,800	77,800

Note: At the year ended 30 June, the value of unsold stock was £3,750.

Required:

(a) A trading and profit and loss account for the year ended 30 June.
(b) A balance sheet as at that date. Show working capital.

2. The following represents the trial balance of Jack Armstrong as at 31 December 1988:

	Dr. £	Cr. £
Premises	27,000	
Motor Van	2,000	
Fixtures and Fittings	5,300	
Bank	4,250	
Cash	250	
Stock (1 Jan. 1988)	8,000	
Debtors	3,100	
Mortgage on Premises		20,000
Interest owing		1,000
Creditors		9,000
Capital: J. Armstrong		7,000
Sales		71,000
Discount		300
Returns Outward		1,000
Rates and Water	500	
Motor and Travel expenses	2,500	
Purchases	34,000	
Returns Inward	2,250	
Light and Heat	600	
Advertising	590	
Wages	16,500	
Insurance	360	
General expenses	2,100	
	109,300	109,300

Note: The ledger accounts are more or less listed in asset, liability, capital, revenue and expense order, making it a little easier to prepare the final accounts.

Required:

(a) Prepare the trading and profit and loss account of J. Armstrong for the period ended 31 December 1988. The value of stock on 31 December was £4,200.

(b) Prepare the balance sheet as at 31 December 1988, and clearly show working capital.

3. The following information relates to Freddy Smith, small retailer, as at year ended 31 December:

	DR. £	CR. £
Capital		2,000
Shop Premises	1,950	
Fixtures	750	
Stock 1 Jan.	320	
Debtors	1,020	
Creditors		1,245
Sales		6,950
Purchases	4,050	
Returns Inward	100	
Outward		150
Rent	250	
Wages and Salaries	600	
General Expenses	75	
Light and Heat	355	
Bank	875	
	10,345	10,345

Note: Closing stock at 31 December was £650.

Required:

(a) Enter all the above accounts in the Ledger of Freddy Smith as they would appear on 31 December. Transfer all revenue and expense accounts to the trading and profit and loss account. Adjust for stock end.

(b) Prepare the Trading and Profit and Loss Accounts for the year ending 31 December and a Balance Sheet as at that date.

4. The following balances were taken from the books of Freddy White as at 30 September 1988:

Trial Balance as on 30 September, 1988

	Dr. £	Cr. £
Capital: F. White		12,730
Drawings: F. White	1,200	
Purchases	8,400	
Sales		12,900
Stock (1 October 1987)	1,358	
Debtors	1,889	
Creditors		2,184
Commission		1,033
Water, Rates, Insurance	664	
Wages	3,173	
General expenses	125	
Equipment	1,500	
Motor Van	410	
Cash	528	
Overdraft at Bank		2,400
Premises	12,500	
Returns Inward	153	
Returns Outward		653
	31,900	31,900

Note: Stock value on 30 September 1988 was £2,415.

Required:

(a) Prepare the trading and profit and loss account of F. White for the year ended 30 September 1988 and a balance sheet as at that date.
(b) Why are some accounts transferred to the trading and profit and loss a/c and not others? Explain, giving examples.

5. James Robert has a small business enterprise. The following accounts were extracted from his ledgers at the financial year end 30 April:

Trial Balance as on 30 April

	Dr. £	Cr. £
Capital: J. Robert		18,000
Drawings	2,800	
Bank Overdraft		725
Premises	15,700	
Motor Van	1,000	
Equipment	1,400	
Debtors	2,900	
Creditors		3,850
Stock (beg.)	3,500	
Purchases	28.400	
Sales		42,650
Rent Received		750
Wages	8,500	
Rates and Insurance	270	
Light and Heat	195	
Administrative Expenses	325	
Selling and Distribution Costs	500	
VAT	275	
Returns Inward	400	
Returns Outward		190
	66,165	66,165

Note: Stock unsold on 30 April was valued £5,280.

The VAT is not an expense. Customs and Excise owe the money to J. Robert.

Required:

(a) The trading and profit and loss account for the year ended 30 April.
(b) A balance sheet as at this date.

6. The Trial Balance of G. Chappell on 31 March 1990:

	Dr. £	Cr. £
Bank Loan (2 Years)		402.77
Cash	48	
Bank	1,532.8	
Stock (1 Apr. 89)	700	
Fixtures & fittings	200	
Motor Van	1,025	
Sales Ledger Control	941.5	
Purchase Ledger Control		1,580.23
VAT	145.41	
Capital		4,050
Drawings	600	
Sales		1,867
Purchases	1,562.12	
Discount	42.15	
Overheads	546.25	
Wages	154	
Motor Expenses	303.77	
Petty Cash Expenses	99	
	7,900	7,900

Note: Stock on 31 March 1990, still unsold, £1300.

Required:
(a) The trading & profit & loss account for the year ended 31 March 1990.
(b) A Balance Sheet as at that date, showing working capital.

PART 2

The Accounting Period: Adjustments for Accruals, Pre-payments and Provisions

It has been previously mentioned that Mr G. Harrison's accounting period runs from 1 January to 31 December. Other organisations may not have the same financial year. Some businesses run from 1 April to 31 March, others from 1 June, and so forth. The important thing is, that once an accounting period is recognised and accepted, that period of time is consistently applied as to when the final accounts are prepared. In G. Harrison's case the final accounts are prepared at the end of the financial year, 31 December.

The accruals concept in accounting recognises that any transaction, part or whole, which relates to a specific accounting period, must be brought to account. In this way, a true and fair assessment of the accounting year is more likely to be made.

It may be necessary to make adjustments to the accounts at the end of an accounting period in order to achieve a true and fair position of the financial affairs of the business. The three major adjustments are:

(a) Accrued Expenses

These refer to expenses still outstanding at the end of the accounting period, which relate to the accounting period. Even though they are unpaid, they must still be brought into account.

For example, in G. Harrison's trial balance as on 31 December, he paid for a number of expenses. Suppose a gas bill was outstanding for £54 and there was £34 owing to salaries, both these related to the current year's expenses. What effect have they on the final accounts?

Profit & Loss a/c:	£	£
Light and Heat	300	
+ accrued expense	54	354
Salaries	850	
+ accrued expense	34	884

Balance Sheet:

Current Liabilities	
Accrued Expenses	88

Note: (a) An accrued expense increases the expenses during the accounting period and therefore reduces the profit for the year.
(b) Because the expense is still owing for the period, it is treated as a current liability, until the payment is paid.

Accrued Expenses as shown in the Nominal Ledger:

		Dr. £	Cr. £	Balance £
Light and Heat a/c				
31 Dec.	Balance			300 Dr.
	Accrued Expense	54		354
	Profit and Loss		354	Nil
1 Jan.	Accrued Expense		54	54 Cr.
7 Jan.	Bank	54		Nil

Note: (a) The accrued expense is brought down as a credit in the new financial period because £54 is still owing.
(b) When the bill was paid on the 7 Jan. it clears the bill. Any subsequent payments for gas or electricity will then be related to the new financial year.

(b) Pre-payments

These refer to expenses paid within a specific period of which part or whole of the expense belongs to the next period. They are expenses paid in advance of the current financial year, and are also referred to as 'pre-paid expenses'.

For example, in Harrison's trial balance as on 31 December he paid rates and water expenses of £285. If £160 was paid for rates for the year ended 31 March, 3 months ($\frac{1}{4}$) has been paid in advance because it is related to the next financial period. £40 is therefore pre-paid.

Profit and Loss a/c:

	£	£
Rates and Water	285	
– Pre-paid Expense	40	245

Balance Sheet:

Current Assets		
Pre-paid Expenses	40	

Note: A pre-payment decreases the current year's expenses, having the effect of increasing current profit.

Because some value of the expense is still to be used in the next accounting period, the pre-paid expense is regarded as a current asset in the balance sheet as on 31 December.

Pre-paid Expenses as shown in the Nominal Ledger

		Dr. £	Cr. £	Balance £
Rates and Water a/c				
31 Dec.	Balance			285 Dr.
	Pre-paid Expenses		40	245
	Profit and Loss		245	Nil
1 Jan.	Pre-paid Expenses	40		40 Dr.

Note: (a) The pre-paid expense is brought down as a debit entry in the new financial period 1 Jan.
(b) This indicates that £40 of rates already paid belongs to the new accounting period.

Other Pre-payments of G. Harrison

On 31 December, Harrison still had £20 stationery unused and £60 of packing materials. Because the unused stock of these can be used in the next accounting period, they are both treated as pre-paid expenses.

The total pre-paid expenses on 31 December = £120.

*The Trading and Profit and Loss a/c of Harrison for the period ended
31 December would now appear*:

	£	£	£
Gross Profit			6,600

Less other Expenses

	£	£	£
Salaries	850		
+ Accrued expense	34	884	
Light and Heat	300		
+ Accrued expense	54	354	
Rates and Water	285		
− Pre-paid expense	40	245	
Printing and Stationery	100		
− Pre-paid expense	20	80	
Packing Materials	340		
− Pre-paid expense	60	280	
Other Expenses		1,285	3,128
			3,472
Add other Revenue			210
Net Profit			3,682

How the Adjustments Affect Profit

Before the accrued and pre-paid expenses were taken into account,
Harrison's net profit was £3,650 for the year ended 31 December.

With adjustments taken into account, the profit has increased by £32 to
£3,682. This is the result of:

	£
Expenses + (accrued)	88
Expenses − (pre-paid)	120
Extra profit	32

The balance sheet would still balance:

Capital + Profit (extra)	=	Assets	−	Liabilities
		Pre-payments		Accruals
£32		£120		£88

(c) Provisions

These refer to amounts retained from the profits of the business to provide for items such as bad debts (debtors who default on their debts), or depreciation where fixed assets lose their value over accounting periods. Provisions for bad debts will be dealt with first.

Provisions for Bad and Doubtful Debts

Businesses tend to be conservative by nature in that if any asset is likely to be reduced in value, the accounting convention is to provide for the loss in advance. On 31 December 1989, Harrison had £850 owing to him from debtors. Looking through his Sales Ledger, he may decide that one or more accounts look 'a little doubtful' and therefore makes a 10% provision against his debtors.

What is the effect of a 10% Provision for Bad or Doubtful Debts in the final accounts?

	£	£
Profit and Loss a/c		
Provision for Bad and		
Doubtful Debts	85	
Balance Sheet:		
Current Assets		
Debtors	850	
less Provision for		
Bad and Doubtful Debts	85	765

Note: (a) The opening of a provision account for bad debts allows a sum to be set aside from profits, and is treated as an expense.
(b) The debts in the balance sheet are shown as net, the provision reducing their value to a sum the debtors are expected to pay.

Provision for Bad and Doubtful Debts in the Nominal Ledger

		Dr. £	Cr. £	Balance £
Provision for Bad and				
Doubtful Debts a/c				
31 Dec. 1989	Profit and Loss		85	85 Cr.
1 Jan. 1990	Balance			85 Cr.

Note: In the new accounting period, 1 January, the Provision account has £85 in credit. This account can be used to 'catch' the bad debts as they occur. Any bad debts written off can be debited against the Provision account.

In June of the new accounting period, Harrison writes off J. Hunt's account of £75 as a bad debt. This will be debited in the Provision account.

Harrison's debtors at the end of the year totalled £1,550 and again he uses a 10% provision against debtors going bad. How would these appear in Harrison's ledgers and final accounts?

Harrison's Sales Ledger:

		Dr.	Cr.	Balance
		£	£	£
J. Hunt a/c				
30 June	Balance			75 Dr.
	Provision for		75	Nil
	Bad Debts			

ACCOUNT WRITTEN OFF AS BAD DEBT

Nominal Ledger:

Provision for Bad and
Doubtful Debts a/c

		Dr.	Cr.	Balance
1 Jan. 1990	Balance			85 Cr.
30 June	J. Hunt	75		10
31 Dec.	Profit and Loss		145	155 Cr.

Note:　(a)　Writing off the bad debt:

> Debit the Provision for Bad Debts a/c　£75
> Credit J. Hunt's a/c　£75.

(b)　This leaves £10 Cr. in the Provision a/c.
Harrison wants a 10% provision against debtors £1,550 = £155.

Because of the £10 Cr. in the Provision a/c, only £145 is required to be set against the Profit and Loss account as an expense, at the end of the next accounting period.

Profit and Loss a/c:	£	£
Provision for Bad and		
Doubtful Debts	145	

Balance Sheet:		
Current Assets		
Debtors	1,550	
less Provision for Bad and		
Doubtful Debts	155	1,395

Provision for Depreciation of Fixed Assets

Assets lose their value over periods of time. Car owners will understand that as their vehicles become older, they lose their value. This is the case with most fixed assets. As the assets age, they lose their value because of wear and tear, damage, obsolescence and any other reason which may diminish their value.

G. Harrison has £18,250 of fixed assets valued at cost:

	£
Premises	12,000
Fixtures	2,000
Equipment	3,000
Motor vehicle	1,250

Premises are unlikely to depreciate; in fact the property may well appreciate in value rather than reduce in price. The other fixed assets will lose their value over time.

Purchasing an asset is really like buying an expense which will be divided over the accounting periods it is expected to last. The loss in value of an asset will be charged as an expense in each accounting period it is used. As the asset diminishes in value, the balance sheet will show the cost, the depreciation to date and the net value of the asset. For example

Equipment £3,000. Harrison expects to replace it in 5 years and he expects to receive an estimated £400 on its disposal.

How much depreciation should be charged each year?

Cost: £3,000
− Residual
value £ 400   £2,600/5 years = £520 per annum

In each accounting period, Harrison will depreciate the Equipment £520, charged as an expense in the profit and loss account.

This method of depreciation where the *same* amount is depreciated each year is known as the fixed instalment method (or straight line).

The balance sheet will show the Equipment's net value each year over its estimated 'life' of 5 years:

	Cost £	Depreciation £	Net Value [Net Book Value] £
Year 1	3,000	520	2,480
2	3,000	1,040	1,960
3	3,000	1,560	1,440
4	3,000	2,080	920
5	3,000	2,600	400 (residual value)

Formula for fixed instalment method:

$$\frac{\text{Cost of fixed asset} - \text{Residual value}}{\text{Life of asset}}$$

Harrison decides to depreciate his Fixtures by 25% on cost:

Fixtures £2,000 @ 25% = £500 depreciation

He revalues his Motor Vehicle to £1,000 in line with its market value on 31 December:

Motor Vehicle	£1,250		
Market Value	£1,000	=	£250 depreciation

What effect have these in the final accounts of Harrison on 31 December?

Profit and Loss account, year ended 31 December:

	£	£
Depreciation:		
Equipment	520	
Fixtures	500	
Motor vehicle	250	1,270

A total of £1,270 is charged as expenses and written off against profits for the year.

Balance Sheet as at 31 December:

	Cost £	Depreciation £	Net £
Fixed Assets			
Premises	12,000	—	12,000
Fixtures	2,000	500	1,500
Equipment	3,000	520	2,480
Motor vehicle	1,250	250	1,000
	18,250	1,270	16,980

Depreciation on Cost or Net Value

Harrison depreciated his fixtures 25% on cost = £500. If he chose, Harrison could apply a fixed rate percentage based on the net value of the asset each year. This would mean that the depreciation charge each year would be reduced over the life of the asset. Using this method, the asset would lose more of its value in the earlier years and less in the later years.

The reducing balance method of depreciation. If Harrison used this method on his Fixtures, what rate percentage would he apply for depreciation if:

	£
Cost	2,000
Estimated Residual Value	400
Estimated 'life'	4 years

Formula:

$$\text{Rate \%} = 1 - \sqrt[n]{\frac{\text{Residual Value}}{\text{Cost of Asset}}} \qquad (n = \text{no. of years})$$

$$1 - \sqrt[4]{\frac{400}{2,000}} = 33\% \text{ depreciation per year on the net value of the asset}$$

If the reduced balance method was applied, an estimated 33% depreciation would be deducted each year:

Year	Reduced Value	Depreciation @ 33%	Net Value
	£	£	£
1	2,000	660	1,340
2	1,340	442	898
3	898	296	602
4	602	199	403 (residual value)

$Check$: Residual Value of asset $=$ Cost of asset $(1 - \text{Rate \%})^n$

$$= £2,000 \ (1 - 33\%)^{4 \text{ years}}$$

$$= £2,000 \ (0.67)^4$$

$$= £403$$

Nominal Ledger Recording of Depreciation

The double-entry for depreciation is:

Dr. Profit and Loss a/c with the Expense
Cr. Provision for Depreciation of Asset a/c

In the above example, Fixtures and fittings a/c would be depreciated each year by 33% on reduced balance. This would mean that £660 would be debited to Profit and Loss in Year 1 and £199 debited in Year 4.

	Dr. £	Cr. £	Balance £
Fixtures and Fittings a/c			
Year 1			
1 Jan. Bank			2,000 Dr.
Provision for Depreciation of			
Fixtures and Fittings a/c			
Year 1			
31 Dec. Profit and Loss		660	660 Cr.
Year 2			
31 Dec. Profit and Loss		442	1,102 Cr.
Year 3			
31 Dec. Profit and Loss		296	1,398 Cr.
Year 4			
31 Dec. Profit and Loss		199	1,597 Cr.

The balance sheet in Year 4 would then read:

	Cost £	Depreciation £	Net £
Fixed Assets			
Fixtures and Fittings	2,000	1,597	403

At this point, Harrison estimated he would replace the Fixtures at a residual value of about £400. Whether he gets £400 depends on what the market will give.

Disposal of an Asset Account

When an asset is disposed of it can be transferred to a 'disposal of asset' account. Any depreciation to date associated with the asset is also transferred to the disposal account. If the asset is sold under its net value (or book value), a loss on the sale is charged against the year's profit and loss account. If the asset is sold for more than its net value, the gain is transferred to profit and loss. If Harrison disposed of the fixtures after Year 4 for £350, he would have made a loss on the net value of £53.

Nominal Ledger entries

		Dr. £	Cr. £	Balance £
Fixtures and Fittings a/c				
Year 4				
31 Dec.	Balance			2,000 Dr.
	Disposal a/c		2,000	—
Provision for Depreciation				
Fixtures and Fittings a/c				
Year 4				
31 Dec.	Balance			1,597 Cr.
	Disposal a/c	1,597		—
Disposal of Asset a/c				
Year 4				
31 Dec.	Fixtures and Fittings	2,000		2,000 Dr.
	Provision for Depreciation		1,597	403
	Bank		350	53
	Profit and Loss		53	—

By selling the Fixtures for £350, Harrison has lost £53 on the book value of the asset. This is charged as an expense loss in the profit and loss account.

Profit and Loss a/c G. Harrison,
(Year 4) ended 31 December

	£
Depreciation Fixtures	199
Loss on sale of asset	53

If the Fixtures had been sold for *more* than the book value of £403, for example, if Harrison received £450, he would have made a gain of £47 on the book value. This would have been entered as a gain in the profit and loss account and included under 'any other Revenue'.

A Summary of Major Adjustments Used in Final Accounts

Type of Adjustment   Effect on Final Accounts

	Trading & Profit & Loss	Balance Sheet
1. Accrued Expense	Increase Expense	Current Liability
2. Prepayment	Reduce Expense	Current Asset
3. Accrued Revenue	Increase Revenue	Current Asset
4. Provision for Bad Debts (increase)	Increase Expense	Reduce Debtors
5. Personal stock Drawings	Reduce Cost of Sales	Reduce Capital
6. Provision for Depreciation	Increase Expense	Reduced Fixed Asset

Model Exercise

Situation
You work for a firm of accountants and are asked to prepare the end of year accounts for a client, R. Horden.

Information

The following trial balance was extracted from the accounts of R. Horden on 31st October, 1990.

	Dr. £	Cr. £
Cash at bank/in hand	6,500	
Purchases/Sales	26,000	75,100
Motor vehicles	12,500	
Provision for Depreciation (Motor Vehicles)		5,000
Rent & Rates	1,400	
Light and Heat	700	
Carriage Inwards*	500	
Carriage Outwards	400	
Opening Stock	18,300	
Commissions Received		1,500
Drawings	9,000	
Returns	1,800	1,400
Office Salaries	26,000	
Debtors/Creditors	24,000	6,000
Provision for bad debts		2,000
Fixtures and Fittings	8,000	
Provision for Depreciations (Fixtures & Fittings)		2,400
Land and Buildings	50,000	
Bank Loan (repayable 1993)		10,000
Interest on Loan (10% p.a.)	1,000	
Capital		82,700
	186,100	186,100

Notes: 31 October 1990

(a) Closing stock £21,000
(b) Revenue accrued: £420 still to be received on Commission.
(c) Rates had been paid £200 in advance
(d) £120 is owed for electricity (heating and lighting)
(e) Provision for bad debts is to be increased to 10% of the debtors
(f) Provision for depreciation of 10% p.a. on cost is to be made on fixtures and fittings
(g) Provision for depreciation of 20% p.a. on book value of motor vehicles.
(h) During the financial year, R. Horden took goods for own use from the business which cost £800.

* Carriage Inwards – a trading a/c expense.

Required:

Prepare the Trading & Profit & Loss a/c of R. Horden for the year ended 31 October 1990 and a Balance Sheet as at that date.

R. Horden Trading and Profit & Loss Account for Year Ending 31/10/90

	£	£	£
Sales			75,100
Less returns inwards			1,800
			73,300
Less Cost of Sales:			
Opening Stock		18,300	
Purchases	26,000		
add carriage inwards	500		
less returns outwards	1,400		
less goods for own use	800	24,300	
		42,600	
Closing Stock		21,000	21,600
	Gross Profit		51,700
Rent and rates paid	1,400		
Rent and rates in advance	200	1,200	
Light and heat paid	700		
Light and heat owing	120	820	
Carriage outwards		400	
Office salaries paid		26,000	
Interest on loan		1,000	
Increase in provisions for bad debts		400	
Provision for depreciation – fix & fitt.		800	
Provision for depreciation – vehicles		1,500	32,120
			19,580
Add other revenue – Commissions received	1,500		
Add other revenue – Accrued	420		1,920
	Net Profit		21,500

R. Horden Balance Sheet as at 31/10/90

	£ (Cost)	£ (Cum. depn).	£ (Net)
Fixed Assets			
Land and buildings	50,000	–	50,000
Fixtures & Fittings	8,000	3,200	4,800
Motor vehicles	12,500	6,500	6,000
	70,500	9,700	60,800
Current Assets			
Stock		21,000	
Debtors	24,000		
Less prov. for bad debts	2,400	21,600	
Prepayments		200	
Bank/Cash		6,500	
Revenue Accrued		420	49,720
Current Liabilities			
Trade Creditors			
Accruals		6,000	
		120	6,120
Working capital			43,600
Long Term Liabilities Capital employed			104,400
Bank Loan			
			10,000
Capital employed			94,400
Financed by:			
Capital		82,700	
Add Net Profit		21,500	104,200
Less Drawings (9000 + 800)			9,800
			94,400

Exercises

1. The following accounts were taken from the books of Harry Wright for the financial year ended 31 December 1988:

	Dr. £	Cr. £
Capital: H. Wright		16,000
Drawings	4,200	
Stock (1 Jan. 1988)	12,890	
Purchases	22,430	
Sales		32,300
Premises	12,000	
Equipment	760	
Motor Van	2,250	
Debtors	23,220	
Creditors		33,600
Returns Inward	250	
Returns Outward		540
Rates and Water	850	
Wages	4,480	
Advertising	250	
Office expenses	280	
Discount received		350
General expenses	820	
Bank overdraft		1,890
	84,680	84,680

Note: At 31 December, 1988
  (a) The value of stock £10,500.
  (b) Wages owing £42.
  (c) Rates pre-paid £30.
  (d) An invoice for office stationery still unpaid £55.

Required:

Prepare the trading and profit and loss a/c of H. Wright for the year ended 31 December 1988 and a balance sheet as at that date. (Show working capital.)

2. The following informations represent the accounts of James Hunt on 31 December:

Account	£
Capital: J. Hunt	8,000
Drawings	2,500
Cash	100
Bank	400
Equipment	400
Motor Vehicle	1,500
Stock (1/1)	4,800
Debtors	2,500
Creditors	3,130
Sales	12,200
Purchases	7,000
Returns Outward	250
Rent	160
Discount Received	20
Stationery	90
Wages	3,000
General Expenses	1,000
Rates	150

Adjustments: *31 December*
(a) Stock unsold £4,300.
(b) Rates pre-paid £38.
(c) A provision for bad debts is to be made to equal 5% of debtors.
(d) Wages outstanding £120.
(e) Stationery unused £40.

Required:

(a) A trading and profit and loss account for the year ended 31 December.
(b) A balance sheet as at that date.

3. The following represents the Trial Balance of G. Chappell as at year ending 30 June

	DR.	CR.
Capital		9,950
Drawings	540	
Furniture and Fittings	100	
Motor Vans	4,450	
Bank	105	
Debtors	440	
Plant	6,600	
Creditors		180
General Expenses	390	
Salaries	665	
Purchases	1,800	
Sales		5,060
Stock (beg.)	100	
	£15,190	£15,190

(a) Stock (end) estimated £125 (30 June)
(b) Depreciate: Motor vans valued at £3,900
        Plant $33\frac{1}{3}\%$
        Furniture and fittings   25%

Required:

Prepare G. Chappell's Trading and Profit and Loss Account for the year ending 30 June and a Balance Sheet as at that date.

4. The following is a trial balance of John Lloyd, Sports Shop proprietor, as at year ended 31 December 1988.

Before commencing the final accounting report, calculate his capital and enter the trial balance totals.

	Dr. £	Cr. £
Capital (1 January)		170,350
Drawings	14,240	
Stock (1 January)	12,890	
Purchases and Sales	122,430	132,370
Returns	5,210	2,470
Premises	110,000	
Fixtures and Fittings (at cost)	12,760	
Van (at cost)	7,200	
Trade Debtors and Creditors	23,270	33,690
Rent	7,850	
Wages and Salaries	24,480	
Advertising	1,350	
Discount	450	1,260
Office Expenses	1,160	
Cash	1,020	
Bank Overdraft		4,170
	344,310	344,310

You are required to prepare a Trading and Profit and Loss Account for the year 31 December and a Balance Sheet as at that date, taking the following items into consideration:

(i) Stock at 31 December was valued at £15,477.
   Depreciation: at 31 December
(ii) Fixtures and fittings 25% of cost. Vans have a market value of £5,750.

5. Prepare a Trial Balance from the following Ledger account of Tom Dooley as at year ending 31 December 1988.

    Prepare Trading, Profit and Loss accounts and Balance Sheet taking into consideration the adjustments at the foot of the accounts.

a/c	£	DR. £	CR. £
Capital	9,048		
Debtors	1,780		
Creditors	4,369		
Cash	125		
Bank	7,235		
Plant and Machinery	2,800		
Motor Vehicles	2,200		
Prov. for Depreciation. (Plant and Machinery)	560		
Prov. for Depreciation. (Motor vehicles)	330		
Prov. for Bad Debts	60		
Rent Received	1,160		
Wages and Salaries	3,850		
Rent	830		
Rates, Insurances	785		
Light and Heat	325		
Carriage Out	84		
Returns Inwards	27		
Returns Outwards	140		
Stock (1 Jan.)	2,362		
Purchases	5,990		
Sales	12,726		

Notes: (31 December)
1. Stock-taking figure £2950.
2. Bad Debts provision increased to £90.
3. Provide for Depreciation on Plant and machinery 10% of cost.
4. Provide for Depreciation on Motor Vehicles 20% on book valuation.

6. The following accounts relate to Arthur Jones, a local businessman as at
   year ended 31 December 1988.

   Prepare Trading, Profit and Loss accounts and Balance Sheet from the
   information below:

Trial Balance as on 31 December

	Dr.	Cr.
Capital — A. S. Jones		71,000
Premises	57,500	
Equipment	23,000	
Provision for Depreciation of Equipment		6,000
Motor Van	8,000	
Provision for Depreciation of Motor Van		2,000
Stock (Jan. 1)	8,300	
Purchases and Sales	30,800	66,600
Returns Inward	700	
Returns Outward		900
Wages	16,500	
Carriage Inwards*	500	
Carriage Outwards	400	
Commission Received		500
Bank interest	350	
Lighting and Heating	1,650	
Postage and Stationery	600	
Insurance	1,200	
Telephone	500	
Rent Receivable		750
Debtors, Creditors	7,000	11,750
Bank	1,950	
Discount	100	
Bad Debts	450	
	159,500	159,500

Adjustments to be taken into account 31 December:

(a) Unsold stock valued at cost £9,500.
(b) Wages due to be paid £550.
(c) Jones, the proprietor, takes goods for own use valued at cost £800.
(d) Pre-paid stationery — unused stock valued £95.
(e) Rent receivable still outstanding £180.
(f) Depreciation: Motor Van revalued to £4,500.
                    Equipment depreciated 20% on net value.
(g) Provision for bad and doubtful debts to equal 10% of debtors.

* Trading account.

7. The trial balance of ABC Co. as on 31 December was as follows:

Account	Debit	Credit
	£	£
Premises (cost)	24,000	
Fixtures and fittings (cost)	4,000	
Motor Vehicle (cost)	5,000	
Bank	3,305	
Stock	5,750	
Debtors	20,500	
Creditors		24,220
Loan (3 years) 10% p.a.		15,500
Capital: ABC Co.		18,000
Sales		21,274
Commission Received		485
Discount		557
Salaries	2,864	
Light and Heat	122	
Petty cash expenses	44	
General expenses	268	
Purchases	14,090	
Returns Outward		484
Returns Inward	577	
	78,520	78,520

The following information is to be taken into account as on 31 December:

(a) The value of unsold stock £6,259.
(b) Gas bill still outstanding £42.
(c) Under general expenses, stationery unused was £70.
(d) The owner took stock for his own use £2,100.
(e) Depreciation: Furniture and fittings 10% on cost.
    Motor Vehicle revalued to £3,750.
(f) Provision for bad debts 5% of debtors.
(g) 6 months' interest on loan unpaid.

Required:

(a) Prepare the trading and profit and loss account of ABC Co. for the year ended 31 December.
(b) A balance sheet as at that date, showing working capital and capital employed.
(c) Calculate the working capital ratio (current assets/current liabilities). Is it adequate?

8. The following trial balance was extracted from the accounts of Jack Jones, 31 December 1988.

Prepare trading and profit and loss accounts for the year and a balance sheet as at that date.

a/c	Debit	Credit
Premises	14,600	
Motor Vehicles	1,250	
Provision for Depn (MV)		500
Cash	125	
Bank	1,625	
Fixtures, Fittings	800	
Provision for Depn (F+F)		240
Debtors	2,360	
Provision for Bad Debts		186
Bank Loan		12,100
Creditors		565
Sales		7,260
Purchases	2,350	
Rent, Rates	125	
Light and Heat	60	
Carriage In*	50	
Carriage Out	35	
Stock (1 Jan.)	1,825	
Commission		135
Returns	165	160
Wages (Warehouse)*	1,520	
Office Salaries	980	
Capital		7,574
Drawings	850	
	28,720	28,720

Notes:
1. Stock (end) £1,950.
2. Warehouse wages due £20.
3. Pre-paid rates £15.
4. Invoice of £5 electricity unpaid.
5. Depn of Fixtures and fittings by 10% of cost.
6. Motor vehicles revalued £500 (net).
7. Provision for Bad Debts adjusted to equal 10% of debtors.

*Trading account

9. On 31 December 1990, D. Lewis decided to set aside a provision for bad debts to equal 5% of his total debtors.

    Debtors, as on 31/12/90: £12,000

    During the following year, 1991, D. Lewis had written off £550 of customers as 'bad'. These bad debts were transferred to the provision for bad debts account.

    On 31 December 1991, D. Lewis had debtors owing a total of £14,200 and he decided to maintain his 5% provision.

    Required:

    (a) Prepare the Provision for Bad Debts account as would be found in Lewis's Ledger for the period to 31 December 1991.
    (b) Show the effect of the above entries on the final accounts for the period to 31 December 1990, 1991.

10. The following information relates to the fixed assets of Rockbourne Company Limited on 1 January 1987:

	Cost	Depreciation to 31/12/86
	£	£
Premises	1,200,000	–
Plant & Machinery	950,000	413,500
	2,150,000	413,500

The company depreciates Plant and Machinery at the rate of 10% p.a. straight line basis. A full year's depreciation being provided in the year of purchase, but none in the year of sale.
   During the year ending 31 December 1987 the following took place:

   (i) The Directors decided to revalue the premises to £1,500,000.
   (ii) Plant and Machinery purchased in 1983 for £200,000 was sold in October 1987 for £130,000.
   (iii) New plant was purchased in July 1987 for £150,000.

Required:
(a) Provide relevant ledger accounts including an asset disposal account as they would appear on 31 December 1987.

(b) Prepare a schedule of fixed assets for inclusion in the accounts to be published for the year ended 31 December 1987.

(c) Provide any details you think are relevant to accompany the accounts to be published for the year ended 31 December 1987.

Note: Zero scrap value is assumed for plant.

11. The following figures have been extracted from the ledgers of Frank Mitchell:

Trial Balance as at 30th June 1987

	Dr. £	Cr. £
Sales		276,156
Purchases	164,700	
Carriage Inwards	4,422	
Carriage Outwards	5,866	
Drawings	15,600	
Rent and Rates	9,933	
Insurance	3,311	
Postage and Stationery	3,001	
Advertising	5,661	
Salaries and Wages	52,840	
Bad Debts	1,754	
Debtors	24,240	
Creditors		25,600
Return Outwards		131
Cash	354	
Bank	2,004	
Stock (1 July, 1986)	23,854	
Equipment	116,000	
Capital, F. Mitchell		131,653
	433,540	433,540

The following additional information was available on 30th June, 1987:

(a) Wages are accrued by £420.

(b) Rates have been prepaid by £1,400.

(c) Stock of unused Stationery valued £250.

(d) A provision for Bad Debts is to be created to equal 5% of Debtors.

(e) Unsold stock at the close of business valued at £27,304.

(f) Equipment to be depreciated by 10%.

Required:

(a) Prepare the Trading & Profit & Loss account for the year ended 30th June 1987 and a Balance Sheet as at that date.

(b) Advise Mr Mitchell on the position of the working capital of the business.

12. The following information is taken from the accounts of Mike Walker, a businessman selling science equipment to colleges:

Trial Balance of M. Walker
as on 30th June 1990

	£	£
Stock (1/7/89)	6,855	
Motor Vehicle (cost)	8,750	
Premises (cost)	36,900	
Accumulated Depreciation of Vehicle		1,750
Purchases	55,725	
Sales		120,344
Discounts	855	1,044
Returns	548	738
Salaries (assistants)	18,346	
Overheads	14,385	
Creditors		6,755
Debtors	7,400	
Bank		2,045
Cash	400	
Drawings	10,420	
Capital		?

On 30th June, the following additional information was also available:
(a) Stock in hand valued £7,455
(b) The motor vehicle is depreciated on straight line and is now 3 years old.
(c) Of the overheads, £240 is prepaid and £600 is accrued.
(d) A provision for bad debts of 5% is to be created.
(e) Interest on bank charges of £55 has not yet been accounted for.

Required:
Prepare Mr Walker's Trading and Profit and Loss account for the year ended 30th June, 1990 and a Balance Sheet as on that date.

PART 3

An Introduction to Partnership Accounts

A partnership is defined as two or more persons in business with a view to making a profit. There is little legal constraint and most partnerships can be formed without complex documentation or procedure. As far as the law is concerned, the *1890 Partnership Act* and *1907 Partnership Act* apply — the former to all partners and the latter to limited partners. A limited partner is one who has limited liability and has no control in the partnership because he is not involved in any decision-making in the business. Only general partners have the right to control the partnership. However, general partners do not have the advantage of limited liability and are therefore liable to the debts of the enterprise, even up to the extent of their personal wealth.

It is advisable that a *written agreement* should exist between partners (rather than merely a verbal arrangement) so that if disagreements arise between the partners, the written agreement can be referred to in a court of law. A 'Deeds of Partnership' is such an agreement, where a contract is signed by each partner and witnessed by a member of the legal profession, outlining the proposed agreements by the partners. Agreements between partners usually include the following important items:

(a) The amount of capital to be contributed by each partner.
(b) How profits and losses are to be shared (for example, equally, or by some specific ratio).
(c) Whether salaries are to be paid.
(d) Whether interest is to be paid on capital or charged on partners' drawings from the business.
(e) Whether loans by partners to the business are to be paid interest and at what rate of interest.
(f) The level of control entitled to each partner.
(g) The length of time the partnership is to exist.

(h) The procedure to be followed in the event of a new partner admitted or an existing partner leaving.
(i) The procedure to be followed in the event of the partnership being dissolved (wound up).

In the event of non-agreement between partners, where a Deeds of Partnership does not exist, the *1890 Partnership Act* applies. Under Section 24, the Act states:

(a) Profit or Loss is to be borne *equally* between partners.
(b) No interest is to be paid on capital or charged on drawings.
(c) No partnership salaries are to be paid.
(d) Loans by partners are to be paid interest at 5% per annum.

Partnership Final Accounts

The final accounts of a partnership are prepared identically to those of other business units as far as the calculation of profit and the preparation of a balance sheet are concerned.

The partnership does have, however, an 'appropriation account' to show how profits (or losses) are shared between partners. This account is prepared after profit/loss is calculated.

Profit & Loss Appropriation a/c of A & B Partners
Year ended 31 December . . . . .

		£	£	£
Net Profit				7,500
deduct:				
Salary:	A	1,500		
	B	1,500	3,000	
Interest on Capital (5%):				
	A	250		
	B	250	500	3,500
				4,000
Add:				
Interest charged on Drawings:				
	A	200		
	B	150		350
				4,350
Share of Profits:				
	A	2,175		
	B	2,175		4,350

Partners A & B agreed to share profits equally. Other items such as salaries, interest paid on capital and interest charged on drawings are accounted for leaving a residue of £4,350 to be divided equally.

Partners' Current Accounts

A current account is a record of a partner's personal finances in the business. Items recorded in this account include additions such as partner's share of profits, interest paid on capital, salary paid and any other money deposited by the partner. Deductions from the current account is mainly drawings of cash or stock and the interest charged on drawings.

The appropriation account at the end of the accounting period acts as a source of entry to the current account, in effect, being part of the double-entry:

Nominal Ledger

Current Account: 'A'		Dr. £	Cr. £	Balance £
Dec. 31	Balance			200 Cr.
	Salary		1,500	1,700
	Interest on Capital		250	1,950
	Profit		2,175	4,125
	Drawings	2,000		2,125
	Interest charged	200		1,925

Current Account: 'B'		Dr. £	Cr. £	Balance £
Dec. 31	Balance			500 Dr.
	Salary		1,500	1,000 Cr.
	Interest on Capital		250	1,250
	Profit		2,175	3,425
	Drawings	1,500		1,925
	Interest charged	150		1,775

Note: A debit balance in the partner's current account above indicates that the partner has overdrawn on his account.

The Balance Sheet

In the balance sheet, each of the partners' capital and current account balances are recorded under the section 'financed by'.

Balance Sheet (extract) of A & B Partners as at 31 December . . .

	£	£	£
Net Assets			13,700
Financed by:			
Capital accounts:			
A	5,000		
B	5,000	10,000	
Current accounts:			
A	1,925		
B	1,775	3,700	13,700

Example Exercise

A, B and C are in partnership, sharing profit and losses in the ratio of 2:2:1 respectively. During the financial year ended 31 December . . . the net profit was £16,810. The partners' drawings for the year were:

A	£3,150
B	£3,000
C	£1,800

Interest charged:

A	£320
B	£300
C	£275

These charges were based on average drawings over the year. Interest is to be paid on partners' capital accounts at the rate of 5% per annum. Only partner B is entitled to a salary of £1,500 per annum because of his extra duties. The balances of the partners' other accounts were:

	Capital accounts	*Current accounts*
A	£10,000	£700 Cr.
B	£10,000	£450 Dr.
C	£ 5,000	£350 Dr.

Required:

(a) Prepare the partners' Profit and loss appropriation account and partners' Current accounts for year ended 31 December . . .

(b) Prepare an extract of the 'financed by' section of the partners' balance sheet as at 31 December . . .

(c) What is the difference between a General Partner and a Limited Partner?

(a) The P & L Appropriation Account of A, B and C for year ended 31 December . . .

	£	£	£
Net Profit:			16,810
Salary: B		1,500	
− Interest on Capital:			
A	500		
B	500		
C	250	1,250	2,750
			14,060
+ Interest charged on Drawings:			
A	320		
B	300		
C	275		895
			14,955
Share of Capital:			
A		5,982	
B		5,982	
C		2,991	14,955

Note: After contingencies of salary, interest paid and interest charged, the residue was £14,955. This was divided in the ratio agreed by the partners of 2:2:1 respectively.

Partners' Current Accounts:

Nominal Ledger:

Current a/c 'A'	Dr. £	Cr. £	Balance £
Dec. 31 Balance			700 Cr.
Interest on Capital		500	1,200
Profit		5,982	7,182
Drawings	3,150		4,032
Interest charged	320		3,712

Current a/c 'B'			
Dec. 31 Balance			450 Dr.
Interest on Capital		500	50 Cr.
Salary		1,500	1,550
Profit		5,982	7,532
Drawings	3,000		4,532
Interest charged	300		4,232

Current a/c 'C'

Dec. 31	Balance		350 Dr.
	Interest on Capital	250	100 Dr.
	Profit	2,991	2,891 Cr.
	Drawings	1,800	1,091
	Interest charged	275	816

(b) Extract from partners' balance sheet:

Balance Sheet of A, B and C as at 31 December . . .

	£	£	£
Net Assets			33,760
Financed by:			
Capital: A	10,000		
B	10,000		
C	5,000	25,000	
Current a/c's:			
A	3,712		
B	4,232		
C	816	8,760	33,760

(c) A general partner has a right to share in the decisions which affect the partnership and therefore shares in the control of the business. He is not protected by limited liability and therein he is liable for the debts of the business, even up to his own personal wealth.

A limited partner is one who has registered as a limited partner with the Registrar and is protected with limited liability. This means that, in the event of bankruptcy and debt, he is only liable to the extent of his capital contributed to the business and not his personal wealth. However, he must never be part of partnership decisions and holds no control or active part in the business. Retired partners sometimes wish to be part of the partnerships, at the same time relinquishing control, and hence apply to become limited partners.

Goodwill

The term 'goodwill' may arise in a business because it may have earned itself a good name or reputation built up over a period of time through its business activities. The value of goodwill can be calculated on certain factors like average sales over a period of time, or profits earned over a number of accounting periods.

When a business is sold, the net value of the assets is assessed and a value may then be paid towards goodwill. If, for example, a business has an average turnover (sales) of £30,000 per annum based on the last three year's sales, the vendor (the seller) may want something in the region of 10 to 20% goodwill. The buyer and seller may agree on anything between £3,000 to £6,000 depending on how much the buyer wants to buy and how much he can afford.

If a new partner is admitted to the partnership, he may well have to pay the existing partners a sum for goodwill. In the opening example of A and B Partners, the two partners decided to admit partner C to help expand the business and also to inject new capital. The three of them mutually agree to the proposal that C is to pay £2,000 as goodwill and that this should be credited to the partners' A and B capital accounts:

Double-entry:	Dr.	Bank a/c	£2,000
	Cr.	Partner A	£1,000
		Partner B	£1,000

Partner C is to introduce £3,000 of capital into the business which will also be debited to the Bank a/c:

| Double-entry: | Dr. | Bank a/c | £3,000 |
| | Cr. | Partner C | £3,000 |

Alternatively, if partner C had insufficient money to pay the £2,000 goodwill, a goodwill account may have been debited and partners A and B still credited with the £1,000 to their capital:

Double-entry:	Dr.	Goodwill a/c	£2,000
		(Asset)	
	Cr.	Partner A	£1,000
		Partner B	£1,000

The partners then agree to share profits and losses in the ratio of 2:2:1 respectively.

		£
Capital accounts:	A	6,000
	B	6,000
	C	3,000

Exercises

1. A and B are in partnership and agree to sharing profits and losses equally. During the year to 31 December . . . the Net Profit of the firm was £14,680.

The partners' drawings for the year were:

	£
Partner A	4,950
B	4,565

Interest charged on drawings is at 10% per annum based on average drawings for the year:

Average balance of	A:	£2,500
	B:	£2,100

Interest is paid on capital of 5% per annum
The balances on the partners' accounts were:

	Capital a/c (1/1)	*Current a/c* (1/12)
	£	£
Partner A	12,000	600 Cr.
B	12,000	50 Dr.

Partners' salaries:

A	3,500
B	2,500

Required:

(a) Prepare the partnership profit and loss appropriation account and the partners' current accounts for the year ended 31 December . . .
(b) An extract of the partners' balance sheet as at 31 December . . .
(c) A and B decide to admit a new partner, admittedly named 'C'. Goodwill is agreed at a value of £6,000. This account is to be debited on 1 January, the new financial period. Partners A and B are to be credited equally with the value of goodwill.

Partner C will inject £10,000 of his own capital which will be debited to the business's bank account. If profits and losses are then to be shared on a capital input ratio, what will be the profit sharing ratio? How would the balance sheet be affected on 1 January?

2. Smith and Jones are in partnership, sharing profits and losses in a ratio to their capital accounts. The trial balance as on 31 December was as follows:

		Dr. £	Cr. £
Premises		23,500	
Furniture and Fittings		2,750	
Motor Van		2,000	
Provision for Bad Debts			115
Carriage In		142	
Returns		288	343
Purchases		11,665	
Sales			21,429
Discounts		199	146
Stock (1/1)		3,865	
Debtors, Creditors		2,355	3,569
Salaries		5,055	
Rates and Insurance		645	
Light and Heat		162	
Bank		522	
Capital:	Smith		18,000
	Jones		12,000
Current accounts:	Smith	625	
	Jones	540	
Drawings accounts:	Smith	2,303	
	Jones	1,500	
Rent Received			2,514
		58,116	58,116

Notes: 31 December . . .

(a) The value of unsold stock £4,200.
(b) Gas bill due for payment £65.
(c) Rates paid in advance £30.
(d) Provision for bad debts to be increased to £250.
(e) Depreciation: Furniture and Fittings by 20%
                  Motor Van revalued £1,800.
(f) Jones is paid a salary of £1,000 for extra responsibilities.
(g) Interest charged on Drawings: Smith £209
                                 Jones £160.

Required:

(a) Prepare the trading, profit and loss and appropriation accounts for the year ended 31 December . . . and balance sheet as at that date.
(b) Show the current accounts as they would appear in the ledger.

3. Lee and Crooks are partners sharing profits and losses equally. At the end of the financial year, the trial balance extracted from the books was:

at 31 December		£	£
Premises		15,000	
Equipment (cost)		3,600	
Provision for Depreciation of			
Equipment a/c			360
Motor Vehicle		3,500	
Stock (1/1)		3,742	
Debtors		5,188	
Creditors			3,165
Bank			850
Cash		255	
Provision for Bad Debts			70
Rates and Insurance		450	
General overheads		600	
Wages		6,342	
Carriage In		450	
Carriage Out		156	
Discount			440
Bank charges		235	
Advertising		350	
Printing, Stationery		285	
Sales			24,565
Returns Inward		350	
Purchases		13,080	
Returns Outward			2,052
VAT			340
Current accounts:	Lee		300
	Crooks	155	
Drawings:	Lee	3,700	
	Crooks	2,704	
Capital accounts:	Lee		14,000
	Crooks		14,000
		60,142	60,142

Notes: at 31 December . . .
(a) The value of unsold stock (at cost) £5,150.
(b) Crooks took goods for his own use £420.
(c) Provision for Bad Debts increased to £500.
(d) Depreciation: Equipment 10% on Cost. Motor Vehicle 20%.
(e) Partners' charge on Drawings: Lee   £300
                                   Crooks £249
(f) Partners' Salaries: Lee   £1,500.
                                   Crooks £1,000.

Required:

Prepare the trading, profit and loss and appropriation accounts for the year ended 31 December . . . and a balance sheet as at that date.

4. May and Cowdrey are in partnership in a small business. They share profits (losses) three-quarters and one-quarter respectively. The Trial Balance of the business is indicated below. Prepare the Trading and Profit and Loss Account(s) for the year ending 31 December, and the Balance Sheet at that date after making all necessary adjustments.

Trial Balance at 31 December

	DR	CR
Capital Accounts — 1 January		
MAY		10,000.00
COWDREY		4,000.00
Drawings		
MAY	1,750.00	
COWDREY	1,250.00	
Current Accounts — 1 January		
MAY		500.00
COWDREY		300.00
Debtors and creditors	4,520.00	5,420.25
Warehouse Wages*	3,200.00	
Office Salaries	1,500.00	
Stock 1 January	6,334.00	
Purchases and Sales	10,472.00	22,232.75
Returns In and Out	361.00	547.25
Bank	2,641.00	
Cash	142.25	
Light and Heat	470.00	
Warehouse $\frac{4}{5}$, Office $\frac{1}{5}$*		
Rates	248.00	
Warehouse $\frac{3}{4}$, Office $\frac{1}{4}$*		
Freehold Premises	6,500.00	
Fixtures and fittings	1,440.00	
Vehicles	1,600.00	
Stationery	156.75	
Sundry Expenses	64.00	
Postage and Telephone	136.00	
Insurance	60.50	
Discounts	248.00	426.75
Provision for Bad Debts		125.00
Bad Debts	72.00	
Vehicle Expenses	386.50	
	£43,552.00	£43,552.00

Make provision for the following items:

1. Stock at 31 December — £4,400.00.
2. Depreciation Fixtures and Fittings by 15% and vehicles by 10%.

*Any warehousing costs to be attributed to the Trading a/c.

3. Rates pre-paid amount to £64.00.
4. Unexpired Insurance amounts to £10.00
5. Provision for Bad Debts at 31 December is to be 5% of debtors' total.
6. 5% interest is allowed on partners' capital and a salary of £1,046.00 is paid to Cowdrey.

5. *Partnerships*

Situation:

Jones, Smith and Brown are partners in a wholesaling enterprise. They have a warehouse and a small section of offices. Expenses attributed to the warehouse are to be listed under 'Distribution Costs' in the P & L a/c. All other expenses in the P & L a/c are to be listed under Administration Expenses'. The accounts extracted for the trial balance at the year ended 31 December were:

Trial Balance of Jones, Smith and Brown as on 31 December . . .

	£	£
Premises (at Cost)	35,000	
Fixtures (at Cost)	18,500	
Motor Vans (at Cost)	12,750	
Bank		2,460
Cash	100	
Equipment (at Cost)	11,000	
Stock (1 Jan.)	77,450	
Debtors	18,142	
Creditors		64,800
Purchases/Sales	86,257	142,000
Returns	4,150	4,400
Provision for Bad Debts		180
Rates ($\frac{3}{4}$ Warehouse)	840	
Wages ($\frac{1}{4}$ Warehouse)	16,424	
General Expenses ($\frac{1}{4}$ Warehouse)	1,764	
Insurance	283	
Loan (5 years)		27,000
Capital accounts, Balances 1 Jan.		
Jones		25,000
Smith		20,000
Brown		5,000
Current accounts, Balances 1 Jan.		
Jones		1,242
Smith		1,615
Brown	37	
Drawings for the year:		
Jones	6,000	
Smith	4,000	
Brown	1,000	
	293,697	293,697

The following additional information is to be taken into account, 31 December . . .

(a) Unsold stock valued at cost or Net Realisable value whichever is the lower, £82,427.
(b) Rates unpaid £120.
(c) Invoice due on stationery £125 (Administration Expense).
(d) Depreciation: Motor Vans revalued to £11,250 (Distribution Cost)
  Equipment and Fixtures 10% on cost
  (Administration Expense).
(e) Insurance pre-paid £37.
(f) Smith was awarded a salary of £2,750.
  Drawings by partners to be charged 5% interest.
  Interest on Capital to be paid 6%.
  Profits are shared according to their capital ratio on 1 January.

TASK A

Prepare the partners Trading, Profit & Loss a/c and Appropriation a/c for the year ended 31 December . . .
What is meant by the term 'lower of cost or net realisable value'?
[See later chapter on stock valuation].

TASK B

Prepare the partners' current accounts as they would appear in the Ledger.

TASK C

Prepare the partners Balance Sheet as at 31 December. Show working capital.

6. The following information refers to the accounts of Smith, Jones and Rogers who are in partnership and according to their Deeds, share profits and losses in the ratio of 2 : 2 : 1 respectively.
    During the financial period ended 31 May 1987, the net profit of the business was £7,300 and the partners' drawings for the year were:

	£
Smith	2,000
Jones	1,900
Rogers	1,500

Interest on partners' drawings has been calculated as follows:

	£
Smith	65
Jones	55
Rogers	45

As far as the partners' capital accounts are concerned, the agreement states that 6% will be allowed as interest payment. The partners had agreed that Smith should withdraw £1,000 from his capital account on 1 December 1986 and that Rogers should contribute the same amount on that date. Jones is awarded a salary of £900 for extra responsibilities. The balances on the partners' accounts on 1 June, 1986 were:

	Capital a/c's £	Current a/c's £	
Smith	9,000	600	Cr.
Jones	8,000	400	Dr.
Rogers	7,000	300	Dr.

Other balances on 31 May 1987 were as follows:

	£
Fixed assets (net)	30,700
Stocks	12,750
Debtors	4,655
Cash	500
Bank (Cr.)	2,995
Creditors	14,560
Accruals	300
Bank Loan (5 years)	4,950

Required:

1. Prepare the partnership profit and loss appropriation account and the partners' current accounts for the year ended 31 May 1987.
2. Prepare the partners' balance sheet as at 31 May 1987 and show net current assets as part of its construction.
3. Make a brief comment on the partners' financial position as at 31 May 1987.

7. Situation:

French and Saunders run a business consultancy and have the following account balances in their books on 31 March 1990:

Capital Accounts:	
French	20,000
Saunders	25,000
Current Accounts:	
French	4,200 Cr.
Saunders	2,060 Dr.
Drawings for the Year:	
French	12,000
Saunders	15,000
Premises	60,000
Vehicles	6,000
Depreciation of Vehicles	5,000
Bank	3,800
Debtors	3,210
Creditors	6,970
Bank Loan 11% 1995	20,000
Net Trading Profit for Year	19,800
Interest Accrued on Loan	
6 months	

Notes:

1. The partners have agreed on equal sharing of profits/losses.
2. The partners have agreed 8% interest on capital accounts.
3. Interest charges on Drawings amount to: French £200, Saunders £600.

As an assistant to a group of accountants who have French and Saunders as one of their clients, you have been asked to prepare in draft form:

TASK A

The Profit & Loss Appropriation Account of French & Saunders for the year ended, 31 March 1990 and the Current Accounts of each partner.

TASK B

The Balance Sheet of the partnership as on 31 March 1990.

TASK C

A brief memorandum, addressed to the partners, commenting on the partnership liquidity and suggesting how it could be improved.

TASK D

French has used his own premises for the business partnership and £500 has been agreed for running costs. No entries have been made. What effect would this have on the preparation of the above accounts?

8. Situation:

You work as Accountant for Wooldridge and James, a partnership, and have to prepare their final accounts for the year ended 31/5/87.

Data

		£ DR.	£ CR.
Capital A/C balances: 1/6/86			
Wooldridge			50,000
James			30,000
Current A/C balances: 1/6/86			
Wooldridge			1,000
James			2,000
Drawings on 30/11/86		5,000	
Wooldridge		8,000	
James			
Drawings on 31/6/87			
Wooldridge		8,000	
James		10,000	
Fixed Assets (Net)	31/5/87	114,000	
Current Assets	31/5/87	80,650	
Deferred Liabilities	31/5/87		29,000
Current Liabilities	31/5/87		75,000
Profit for the year			38,650
		225,650	225,650

The Partnership agreement between Wooldridge and James stipulates:

(i) Profits and Losses to be shared 60% Wooldridge and 40% James.
(ii) Salaries to be received Wooldridge £9,000, James £12,000.

(iii) Interest to be paid on Capital and Current account balances as on 1/6/86 at 10% per annum.

(iv) Drawings also to be subject to interest at a rate of 10% per annum calculated on their half-yearly balances.

TASK A

Prepare the partnership Profit and Loss Appropriation account for the year ending 31/5/87.

Prepare the partners' Current accounts after completion of the Profit and Loss and Appropriation account.

TASK B

Prepare the partnership Balance Sheet in its abbreviated form as on 31/5/87.

TASK C

Write a memorandum to the partners explaining the situation under Section 24 of the Partnership Act 1890 if no Partnership Agreement existed.

TASK D

Prepare a statement, to be sent with the above memorandum, showing how the profits would be divided if Section 24 of the Partnership Act 1890 applied.

PART 4

Introducing Company Accounts

Company accounts are regulated by the *Companies Acts 1948*, *1967*, *1976* and *1981*, recently consolidated under the *1985 Act*.

The formation of a limited company needs only a minimum of two founder members who are willing to subscribe share capital. There is no maximum limit.

Basically, there are two distinct types of limited company:

(a) The Private Limited Company.
(b) The Public Limited Company (PLC).

A PLC must bear these letters after its name on all correspondence to distinguish it from a private company (for example, Barclays Bank PLC). The word 'limited' means that shareholders' liabilities are limited to the nominal capital of their shares, in the same way a limited partner is limited to the amount of capital he has subscribed.

The private company can only sell its shares privately. It cannot issue a prospectus inviting the public to buy its shares. This privilege is only permitted to the PLC. A private company, therefore, is restricted in the amount of share capital it can raise because it cannot, by Statute, advertise to sell its shares. It is likely to sell its shares to family and friends interested in financing a business venture.

Unlike the private company, the PLC has the potential to raise large sums of capital by offering its shares for public sale. A merchant bank or issuing house can arrange for the issue of shares and, indeed, could buy the shares outright, then offer them to the public for sale via the prospectus.

Most private companies are small business ventures with a limited number of members and rarely employ more than twenty people. On the other hand, PLCs like the commercial banks, large retail chains and manufacturing enterprises are big business concerns which have thousands of members and employees.

PLC shares may be listed on the Stock Exchange once they have been vetted and accepted by the Stock Exchange Council. Private company shares cannot be listed.

The procedure to form a limited company is a little more involved than forming other business units. The sole-trader has virtually no legal constraint and partnerships are advised to prepare a 'Deeds of Partnership' before starting up business. A limited company must prepare two important documents which are sent to the Registrar at Companies House (London) for English companies to obtain approval before it can proceed. These documents are the Memorandum and Articles of Association.

The Memorandum gives the 'external' view of the company to the public, including details of its name, address, registered office, share capital and, most important, its objectives (that is, what it proposes to do).

The Articles give the 'internal' view of the company which relates to the rules and regulations governing the internal organisation of the company, such as voting rights, conduct at meetings, power of directors and so forth.

Once approval is given by the Registrar, a limited company is issued a Certificate of Incorporation which gives it the status of being a *separate legal entity* from the owners of the business (the shareholders). The company has then the right of its own identity and can proceed under its own name, acting under its own name in the course of its business.

A Board of Directors is elected by the shareholders to take control of the company on their behalf. The directors control, the shareholders own.

A private company, on receipt of its Certificate of Incorporation, can commence trading. A PLC must issue its prospectus to sell its shares before it can begin. The directors of the company must state, in the prospectus, the minimum amount of share capital it requires in order to start business and that the share issue has been underwritten (guaranteed) to ensure that the minimum capital is raised. Once this minimum capital is raised, the Registrar can issue the PLC its Certificate of Trading — its right to commence business operations.

The Preparation of Company accounts

The *1985 Companies Act* gives guidance as to the preparation of final accounts relating to companies.

The Trading and Profit and Loss a/c. The Act illustrates a choice of four formats of presentation. The first, Format 1 will be used because it is in the same style already used in the text. Expenses are subdivided into categories like distribution costs and administration expenses. The net profit is shown before and after taxation.

The Appropriation a/c. This shows the division of profits before tax. Basically, profits are distributed by:
(a) provision for taxation
(b) dividends to shareholders on the basis of the number of shares issued and paid up on the value of nominal capital.
(c) Transfer of profit to the company reserves (profits retained in the company helping it to expand and grow).

There are two classes which may be issued to shareholders:

Ordinary Shares.   These are the most common type and represent the 'true' shares, taking the greater risks. The rate of dividend depends on how much profit is made and how much is to be distributed. They are also referred to as 'Equity' shares and are given voting rights — one share, one vote. These votes may be used at annual general meetings but rarely are they exercised in PLCs because very few shareholders actually attend.

Preference Shares.   These are paid at a *fixed* rate of dividend and are entitled to be paid first before ordinary shares. The shares do not hold voting rights and are suitable for the less adventurous type of shareholder who wants a more reliable and consistent rate of dividend.

Debentures.   These represent loan capital and not share capital. They are paid at a fixed rate of interest over the specified period of the loan. The interest paid is an expense entered in the profit and loss account, not the appropriation account.

The 1985 Companies Act

Under Part VII of the *1985 Companies Act* and particularly, sections 221 and 222, the main points state:

1. Every limited company must keep accounting records, with reasonable accuracy, to disclose the financial position of the company.
2. Financial records must be kept daily including receipts and payments of money, the assets and liabilities of the company, including stocktaking at the year end. These records must be kept for a period of 3 years for a private company and 6 years for a public company.
3. The final accounts of the company must be kept in accordance with the formats laid down in Schedule 4 of the Act. This must include:

   A Profit & Loss account.
   A Balance Sheet, as at the same period.
   An Auditors' Report.
   A Directors' Report.

Public companies must have at least two directors and a private company, one. Every company must have a secretary. The directors of a company must make a report as part of the annual accounts and must present a fair view of the business's development in its financial year. The directors must also indicate the dividend they wish to recommend and also the amount they propose to withhold as reserves.

Annual reports must be filed with the Registrar, Companies House. For companies registered in England and Wales, there is an address in London and Cardiff. For companies registered in Scotland, there is an address in Edinburgh.

A company must show its accounts to its members for each accounting period at its annual general meeting. It must ensure that a copy of its accounts is sent to the Registrar within a period of 10 months following the end of the financial period for a private company and 7 months for a public company.

The 1989 Companies Act

The new *Companies Act, 1989*, is a supplementary Act and does not replace the *1985 Companies Act*, which in effect, consolidated all previous Acts from 1948 – 1981.

The 1989 Act amends and adds to the existing legislation of the 1985 Act. It is expected that the accounting provisions relating to Part I are likely to be effective in respect to accounting periods beginning on or after 1 January, 1990.

The necessity of the new Act comes about as a result of the United Kingdom's obligation to implement the European Community's 7th Directive on consolidated accounts and its 8th Directive on the regulation of company auditors. At the same time, the Government had an opportunity to take stock of its company law and to bring in desired amendments such as the power to investigate and obtain information, to make provision for the safeguarding of certain financial markets and to amend the Financial Services Act, 1986 and the Company Securities Act, 1985 (Insider Dealing).

As far as company accounts go, the provisions of the Act under sections 221 and 222 (Part VII), emphasise the duty of all companies to keep accounting records.

Some of the 1989 Act's interesting sections are outlined below:

221 Every company shall keep accounting records, sufficient to show and
(1): explain the company's transactions with reasonable accuracy at any time, the financial position of the company and to enable the directors to ensure that the balance sheet and profit and loss account complies with the requirements of the Companies Act.

A company's accounts shall be kept at its registered office or such other place where the directors think fit and shall at all times be open to inspection by the company's officers.

221   Accounting entries shall contain day to day records of all sums of
(2):   money received and spent as well as a record of its assets and liabilities.

221   If a company deals with goods for resale, the accounts must contain
(3):   statements of the value of stock held at end of the financial year and to
      show sufficient details of buyers and sellers, except by way of ordinary
      retail trade.

226:   It is the duty of the directors to have individual, as well as group
      company accounts prepared for each financial period, a balance sheet
      as at the last day of that period and a profit and loss account for that
      period. Both these financial reports must give a "true and fair" view of
      the state of affairs of the company for the financial period under review.

227:   Where a company acts as a parent company and has subsidiary
      companies, the directors must prepare individual accounts for each
      company and also consolidated accounts for the group, as whole.

238:   The persons entitled to receive copies of the annual accounts and
      director's and auditors' reports are:
      (a) Every member of the company.
      (b) Every holder of the company's debentures.
      (c) Every person entitled to receive notice of general meetings and not
          less than 21 days before the meeting is held.

242:   Copies to the Registrar, Companies House.
      Directors must send to the Registrar a copy of the company's annual
      accounts and also a copy of the director's and auditor's reports.
      Penalties for not complying within the stated specified time (within 7
      months of the financial period end for a public company and 10 months
      for a private company) will be fined according to the length of time the
      accounts are delayed.
      For a public company, the fine will range between £500 and £5000 and
      for a private company, the fine will range between £100 and £1000.

   Other sections of the 1989 Companies Act deal with aspects largely outside
the scope of this text. These include matters relating to the following:
   (a) Investigations and power to obtain information.
   (b) The eligibility for the appointment of company auditors.
   (c) Various amendments to company law.
   (d) Mergers and related matters.
   (e) Financial markets and insolvency.

(f) The Financial Services Act 1986 – amendments.
(g) The transfer of securities.

Presentation of Trading and Profit and Loss a/c and Appropriation a/c —
Format 1 y/e 31/12
(Accounts for internal use)

	£	£	£
Turnover (net sales)			100,000
less			
Cost of Sales			
Stock (1/1)	4,000		
+ Purchases	66,000		
	70,000		
− Stock (31/12)	10,000		60,000
Gross Profit			40,000
less			
Distribution Costs			
Salesmen's salaries	8,500		
Distribution expenses	1,500		
Advertising	2,500		
Motor expenses	1,500		
Depreciation of Motors	500		
Depreciation of Equipment (sales)	2,000	16,500	
Administration Expenses			
Office salaries	7,350		
General office expenses	1,400		
Discount	250		
Bad debts provision	350		
Rates and Insurance	500		
Miscellaneous costs	1,200		
Light and Heat	150		
Depreciation of Equipment (office)	1,300	12,500	29,000
			11,000
add			
Other Income			
Discount	450		
Bank interest	350		800
			11,800
Income from Shares			
Dividends from other companies			800
			12,600

less
Interest Payable

Bank loan interest accrued			250
Net Profit (before Tax)			12,350
Corporation Tax			3,150
Net Profit (after Tax)			9,200
+ Profit and Loss balance (1/1)			400
			9,600
Provision for Dividends:			
8% Preference shares	1,600		
Ordinary shares	3,000	4,600	
Transfer to Reserve		4,000	8,600
Profit and Loss balance (31/12)			1,000
(transferred to shareholders' funds)			

Note: The Profit and loss balance is the residue of profit after appropriations to dividends and reserves. The balance at the end of one accounting period becomes the opening balance in the next.

The 8% dividend to preference shares was based on the issued and paid up nominal capital of £20,000. The ordinary share dividend was based on a 6% share-out on £50,000 of issued and paid up nominal capital.

Accounts for internal use are those used for internal purposes of the company, in the main for management use. When accounts are for publication only, the sub-totals of each heading needs to be shown. A copy of the published version needs to be sent to the Registrar.

The Company Balance Sheet. The Act lays down a choice of two formats. The first will be used because it is shown in the vertical form as used in the text. The alternative is represented in the horizontal form, showing assets on the left and liabilities and capital on the right. A full version of the balance sheet is required both for internal and publication use. Again, a copy of the balance sheet is sent to the Registrar.

Balance Sheet as at y/e 31/12

	£ Cost	£ Depn.	£ Net
Fixed Assets			
Premises	50,000		50,000
Equipment	35,000	8,000	27,000
Motor Vehicles	4,000	1,000	3,000
Investments	10,000		10,000
	99,000	9,000	90,000
Current Assets			
Stock	10,000		
Debtors	17,500		
Bank	3,500		
Pre-payments	1,000	32,000	
less			
Current Liabilities			
Creditors	16,000		
Accruals	250		
Provision for Dividends	4,600		
Provision for taxation	3,150	24,000	
Working Capital			8,000
Capital Employed			98,000
less			
Long-term Liabilities			
Bank Loan (5 years)			6,000
Net Assets			92,000

Financed by		
Shareholders Funds:	*Authorised Capital*	*Issued and Paid Up Capital*
Ordinary Shares @ £1	100,000	50,000
8% Preference Shares @ £1	20,000	20,000
		70,000
Share Premium Account		5,000
General Reserves		16,000
Profit and Loss balance		1,000
		92,000

Note: The share premium account is the amount received in excess of the nominal value of shares when issued. In the above case, they sold at £1.10 each (50,000 × 10p).

Authorised capital is the amount stated in the Memorandum of Association and also in the Prospectus. A PLC must have a minimum of £50,000 registered in its Memorandum.

Issued and Paid Up capital is the amount issued and paid up by shareholders. A PLC must have at least £12,500 of shares issued and paid up.

Reserves refer to the profits retained in the company. When reserves are built up over the years, they may be capitalised by converting them into bonus shares for existing shareholders. In the above accounts, £4,000 was transferred to reserves in the appropriation account, indicating that £12,000 was already in the reserve account.

Example Exercise: Company Accounts

The following information relates to an electrical components manufacturing company. Its cost of production (factory cost) is transferred to the cost of sales in the profit and loss statement. The figures are for the financial year end of Hardcastle Co. Ltd. 31 December 1989:

	£	£
Turnover		327,000
Stock (1/1/89)	58,750	
Cost of Production	201,500	
Sales & Distribution	44,800	
Administration Exps.	38,700	
Interest Charges	5,500	
Fixed Assets (net)	135,100	
Debtors & Creditors	76,750	89,400
Bank Overdraft		19,800
Accruals		4,900
Prepayments	500	
Loans (15 years)		52,000
Issued & Paid Up		
Ordinary Shares (£1)		50,000
Share Premium a/c		10,000
Reserves		17,500
	561,600	561,600

Note: as on 31 December 1989

1. Stock Value £68,750.
2. A proposed dividend of 5p per share.
3. To provide £14,500 for Corporation Tax.
4. To transfer £25,000 to Reserves.

Required:

Prepare the Profit & Loss Account of the Company for the period ending 31 December 1989 and a Balance Sheet as on that date. Use Format 1 of the 1985 Act. The accounts are for *external* purposes only.

Trading and Profit & Loss Account Hardcastle Ltd Year Ending 31/12/89

	£	£	£
Turnover			327,000
Cost of sales:			191,500
GROSS PROFIT			135,500
Sales and Distribution Costs		44,800	
Administration Expenses		38,700	83,500
			52,000
Interest Payable			5,500
NET PROFIT [before tax]			46,500
Provision for Corporation Tax			14,500
NET PROFIT [after tax]			32,000
Dividends Proposed		2,500	
Transfer to Reserves		25,000	27,500
Profit and Loss			
Balance c/f [31/12/89]			4,500

Balance Sheet Hardcastle Ltd as at 31/12/89

	£	£	£
Fixed Assets [net value]			135,100
Current Assets			
Stock	68,750		
Debtors	76,750		
Prepayments	500	146,000	
Creditors Falling			
Due < 12 months			
Creditors	89,400		
Accruals	4,900		
Taxation Provision	14,500		
Dividends Proposed	2,500		
Bank/Cash	10,800	122,100	

Net Current Assets		23,900
Total Assets – Current Liabilities		159,000
Creditors Falling Due > 12 Months		
Loans		52,000
		107,000

Capital and Reserves		
Issued & Paid Up Capital:		
Ordinary Shares@ £1	50,000	
Share Premium A/c	10,000	
Revenue Reserves	42,500	
Profit & Loss Balance	4,500	107,000
[31/12/89] b/f		

Exercises

1. XYZ Co. Limited had an authorised capital of £200,000 divided into 100,000 ordinary shares of £1 each and 100,000 $7\frac{1}{2}$% preference shares of £1 each. The following balances remained in the accounts of the company after the Trading and Profit and Loss accounts had been prepared for the year ended 31 December 1988:

	Debit £	Credit £
Ordinary share capital: fully paid		80,000
$7\frac{1}{2}$% preference shares: fully paid		50,000
Machinery and plant at cost	95,000	
Provision for depreciation on machinery and plant		19,000
Premises at cost	68,000	
Profit and loss account balance (1 January 1988)		5,000
Net profit (for year ended 31 Dec. 1988)		15,500
Accruals		2,150
Bank		395
Stock	9,750	
Debtors and Creditors	3,100	3,955
Pre-payments	150	
	176,000	176,000

(a) The directors have recommended an ordinary dividend of 10% and wish to provide for payment of the year's preference share dividend.
(b) A Revenue Reserve is to be created of £2,000.
(c) Taxation of £3,760 to be provided for.

Required:

(i) The profit and loss appropriation account for the year ended 31 December 1988.
(ii) Prepare the balance sheet at 31 December 1988 to show clearly the working capital.
(iii) Make brief comments with reference to the company's working capital.

2. The following balances remain on the books of ABC Co. Ltd after the preparation of Trading and Profit and Loss accounts for the year ended 31 December 1988:

	£	£
60,000 Ordinary Shares of £1 each fully paid		60,000
Machinery and plant (at cost)	52,500	
Motor vehicles (at cost)	4,000	
Furniture and fittings (at cost)	5,750	
General reserve		30,000
Premises (at cost)	45,000	
Profit and Loss		
balance brought forward (1/1/88)		5,460
Net profit for year		18,750
Accrued Expenses		2,810
Provision for depreciation:		
Machinery and plant		10,500
Motor vehicles		1,500
Furniture and fittings		1,000
Provision for Bad and Doubtful Debts		650
Sundry debtors	10,855	
Sundry creditors		4,900
Stocks	11,985	
Cash in hand	500	
Bank	4,980	
	135,570	135,570

You are required to prepare a Profit and Loss appropriation account for the year ended 31 December, and a balance sheet at that date. The following information is available:

(a) The directors decided to transfer £10,000 to reserve and to recommend a dividend of £15% on the ordinary shares.

(b) The Authorised Capital of ABC Co. Ltd is 100,000 Ordinary Shares of £1 each.

(c) The provision for taxation payable next year is £1,500.

(d) Briefly comment on the adequacy of the Company's working capital.

3. Bournemouth Trading Company Limited has extracted the following trial balance from its books at the end of the accounting period, 31 December 1988:

	£	£
Issued Share Capital:		
60,000 @ £1 shares fully paid		60,000
6% Debentures		5,000
Share Premium Account		6,000
Stock (1/1)	20,600	
Purchases	118,940	
Debtors	12,460	
Wages, Salaries	10,768	
Directors' fees	2,500	
Debenture Interest	150	
Furniture and Fittings (cost)	4,000	
General Expenses	1,820	
Insurances	42	
Provision for Bad Debts		750
Creditors		4,860
Bank Overdraft		940
Freehold Premises (cost)	52,000	
Sales		149,500
Maintenance and Power	5,840	
Provision for Depreciation of Furniture and Fittings		1,500
Returns Inward	650	
Cash	80	
P & L balance (1/1)		1,300
	229,850	229,850

You are to take the following into account on 31 December:

(a) Unsold stock valued at £22,000.

(b) Provision of 15% is to be made for ordinary shares. The outstanding debenture interest is also to be accounted for.

(c) Under Maintenance and Power, there is £76 due to Rates and £14 insurance relates to the next financial period.

(d) Furniture and Fittings to be depreciated 15% on cost.

(e) The provision for bad debts is to be adjusted to 5% of the Debtors.

(f) The figure of £600 is to be transferred to General Reserve.

(g) For taxation, £500 is to be provided for.

Required:

Prepare the company's Trading and Profit and Loss account and Appropriation account for the year ended 31 December and a Balance sheet as at that date (show full set of figures as for internal use).

4. The accounts of Robertson and David Co. Ltd were extracted from the books on 30 June 1988:

Trial Balance as on 30 June 1988

	Dr. £	Cr. £
Issued and Paid Up Capital:		
160,000 Ordinary Shares @ £1		160,000
40,000 8% Preference Shares @ £2		80,000
P & L a/c (1 July 1987)		7,780
General Reserve		25,000
7% Debentures		40,000
Premises (cost)	287,910	
Motor Vehicles (cost)	32,000	
Plant, Equipment (cost)	16,880	
Provision for Depreciation of Motor Vehicles		4,800
Stock (1 July 1987)	49,600	
Bank		11,752
Cash	1,558	
Purchases	535,600	
Sales		696,500
Returns	500	1,600
Wages	65,460	
Rates, Water, Insurance	3,600	
General Expenses	22,536	
Preference Dividend Paid		
(31 December 1987)	3,200	
Debtors, Creditors	63,380	53,944
Bad Debts	2,150	
Provision for Bad Debts		3,120
Discount Allowed	122	
	1,084,496	1,084,496

Note: Additional details, 30 June 1988

(a) Stock value £39,400.
(b) Rates pre-paid £1,000, Wages still outstanding £3,360.
(c) Invoice unpaid for general expenses £30.
(d) Depreciation: Motor Vehicles 20% on book valuation
                    Plant and Equipment 25% on cost.
(e) Adjust the provision for bad debts to equal 5% of debtors.
(f) The Directors of the company propose a dividend of 10% for ordinary shares.
    Preference shares to receive their final dividend.

(g) No interest has been paid on the Debentures.
(h) A transfer of £4,000 is to be made to General Reserve.
(i)   A provision of £19,200 is to be made for taxation.

Required:

Prepare the Trading, Profit and Loss Appropriation accounts for the year
ended 30 June 1988, and a Balance sheet as at that date.

5.   The following trial balance represent the accounts of G. Chappell & Sons
     Ltd as on 31 December 1988:

	£	£
Authorised and Paid Up Capital		
125,000 @ £1 shares (Equity)		125,000
Share Premium		2,500
Premises	110,000	
Furniture and Fittings (cost)	4,200	
P & L a/c (1/1)		1,170
Discounts	422	329
Salaries	7,537	
Rates and Insurance	2,333	
Rent Received		825
Purchases	90,450	
Returns	782	1,789
Sales		105,411
Stock (1/1)	9,142	
General Overheads	2,197	
Provision for Bad Debts		108
Dividend Paid (30/6)	1,000	
Provision for Depreciation of Furniture and Fittings		200
Debtors	9,920	
Creditors		5,226
Bank	6,575	
General Reserve		2,000
	244,558	244,558

You are to take the following into account on 31 December 1988:

(a) Value of unsold stock £12,498.
(b) Rates paid in advance £70.
(c) Salaries accrued: £263. Apportion 25% to Distribution.
(d) Overheads: a bill for gas £103 was still outstanding. Apportion 50% of
     overheads to Distribution.
(e) Depreciation of Furniture and Fittings 25% on book value.
(f) Provision for bad debts to be adjusted to equal 5% of debtors.
(g) The Directors propose to provide for a final dividend of 2.5% and to
     transfer £2,000 to Reserve.

(h) Taxation: a sum of £1,250 is to be provided for.

Required:

Prepare Trading, Profit and Loss and Appropriation accounts for the period ended 31 December, and a Balance Sheet as on that date.

6. *Company Accounts*

Situation:

Harrison's is a small private company producing electrical components. It is a relatively new business and the Board are anxious to do well and hope that the year's final accounts will look promising.

The following information has been extracted from the books:

Trial Balance of Harrison Co. Ltd. on 31 December 1988

	£	£
Stock (Jan. 1)	5,760	
Purchases	82,500	
Premises (at Cost)	60,500	
Plant and Equipment (at Cost)	60,000	
Provision for Depreciation of Plant		18,000
Office Equipment (at Cost)	15,000	
Provision for Depreciation of Office Equipment		6,000
Bank		2,400
Debtors, Creditors	48,750	45,100
Cash	440	
*Summary of Expenses	66,550	
Sales		176,000
Finance Loan $12\frac{1}{2}$% (5 years)		40,000
General Reserve		2,000
Authorised and Paid Up Capital:		
50,000 £1 Ordinary Shares		50,000
	339,500	339,500

*Divided into Distribution Costs 60%
        Administration Expenses 40%.

Additional information was available on 31 December:

(a) The value of unsold stocks (at cost) £6,485.
(b) Administration Expenses: Stationery of stock unused valued £1,250.
                              Rates pre-paid £110.
                              Office Salaries outstanding £260.
(c) Distribution Costs: Salesmen's Salaries outstanding £484.
(d) A provision for bad debts is to be created to equal 10% of Debtors (enter under (b) above).

(e) Depreciation: both Plant and Office Equipment is depreciated by reduced balance method, 20% on net value (enter under (b) above).

(f) The Directors have proposed a Dividend of $7\frac{1}{2}$% on ordinary shares. Taxation of £3,750 is to be provided.

(g) There was no P & L balance on January 1.

(h) The interest on the Loan has not yet been paid.

TASK A

Prepare the Company's Trading and Profit and Loss a/c, and Appropriation a/c for the year ended 31 December 1988.

TASK B

A Balance Sheet as at that date showing clearly working capital.

TASK C

Prepare a brief report for the directors of the company with regard to working capital.

7. You work as an assistant to the Accountant for Jason Limited which has a registered capital of £500,000, divided into 800,000 ordinary shares of 50p each and 200,000 8% preference shares of 50p each. The following balances remained in the accounts of the company after the trading and profit and loss accounts had been prepared for the year ended 30 November 1987.

	Debit £	Credit £
General Reserve		5,000
Ordinary share capital: fully paid		100,000
8% preference shares: fully paid		30,000
Premises at cost	140,000	
Light and heat owing		880
Profit and loss account balance (1 Dec. 1986)		19,200
Bank		8,200
Debtors and Creditors	5,800	1,120
Net Profit (for year ended 30 Nov. 1987)		40,600
Machinery and plant at cost	50,000	
Provision for depreciation on machinery & plant		30,000
Stock	38,340	
Insurance prepaid	820	
Cash	40	
	235,000	235,000

Information as on 30 November 1987

The directors of Jason Ltd. have recommended:

(i) To provide payment of the year's preference dividend.
(ii) To provide for corporation tax of £8,400.
(iii) A maximum dividend which would maintain a working capital ratio of 1.5 : 1. The balance remaining from profits to be transferred to General Reserve.

Required.

(a) The profit and loss appropriation account for the year ended 30 November 1987.
(b) The balance sheet as at 30 November 1987.
(c) State the number of ordinary and preference shares which can still be issued by the company. Briefly explain the difference between these classes of shares.

8. Situation:

You work as Assistant to the Financial Accountant of COMPTON LTD, manufacturers of cosmetics, and are working on the annual accounts.

Information

The following balances remain in the ledger of COMPTON LTD after the preparation of the Profit and Loss account for the year ended 31 March, 1988.

	£
Stocks and W.I.P.	98,000
Debtors	87,000
Provision for Bad Debts	4,000
£1 Ordinary Shares	400,000
[Authorised £600,000]	
16% Preference Shares of £1 each	100,000
[Authorised £200,000]	
Creditors	74,000
Balance at Bank	4,000
Accruals	3,500
Prepayment	2,500
General Reserve Account	14,000
Share Premium Account	20,000
Net Profit for the year ended 31/3/88	108,000
Profit and Loss Account Balance 1/4/87	22,000
Premises (at cost)	300,000
Plant and Equipment (at cost)	310,000
Vehicles (at cost)	200,000

The Directors propose the following:

(i) To transfer £20,000 to Reserve.
(ii) To propose an ordinary dividend of 12% and to pay the preference dividend.
(iii) To provide for corporation tax of £30,000, payable in October, 1988.

Depreciation of fixed assets has been calculated as follows:

(i) Plant and Equipment has a residual value of £30,000 and a 'life' estimated at 10 years. It is five years old and depreciation is based on the straight-line method.
(ii) The Vehicles are valued at current market value of £84,000.
(iii) There is no depreciation on Premises.

Required:

Draw up a Profit & Loss Appropriation A/c for the year ended 31 March 1988 and a Balance Sheet as at that date.

9. Situation:

You are an assistant to the accountant at J. P. Davies plc, which has been in business for several years. The trial balance on 30 June 1990 was as follows:

Trial Balance – J. P. Davies PLC as on 30 June 1990

	DEBIT £	CREDIT £
£1 Preference Shares (15%) (Authorised £200,000)		100,000
£1 Ordinary Shares (Authorised £500,000)		200,000
Revenue Reserves		45,000
Debenture Stock (12.5%), 1995		100,000
Profit for Year Ending, 30/6/1990 (before Debenture Interest)		80,000
Profit & Loss Balance (1/7/89)		40,000
Stocks	200,000	
Premises	200,000	
Plant & Machinery	180,000	
Vehicles	50,000	
Office Equipment	90,000	

Provisions for Depreciation:

Premises		10,000
Plant & Machinery		70,000
Vehicles		30,000
Office Equipment		55,000
Debtors	220,000	
Creditors		190,000
Cash	500	
Provision for Bad Debts		11,000
Prepayments	9,500	
Accruals		21,000
Bank Overdraft		5,500
Interim Preference Dividend paid	7,500	
	957,500	957,500

Note:

1. A full year's Debenture interest is still to be charged.
2. Corporation Tax is to be provided, payable in March, 1991, £20,000.
3. The final dividend on Preference Shares is to be provided for.
4. To propose an Ordinary dividend of 20%.
5. To transfer £25,000 to Revenue Reserves.

TASK

Draw up the company's Profit and Loss Appropriation A/c for the year ended 30 June 1990 and a Balance Sheet as on that date.

PART 5

The Statement of Sources and Application of Funds

In the final accounts of business enterprises, the Trading and Profit and Loss account shows the profit or loss earned during the financial year by matching revenue with expenses and the Balance Sheet lists the business's resources (assets) and who has financed them (capital and liabilities).

The statement of sources and application of funds, or simply, the funds flow statement, is an attempt to give a *fuller* view of the accounting reports by trying to identify the movement of resources during the accounting period. In other words

Where did the finance come from during the year?

and

Where did it go?

Where got?   Where gone?   The funds flow is the *link* between

(a) Two Balance Sheets in the financial period. One at the beginning of the year, the other at the end.
(b) The Profit and Loss account for the year.

Because the funds flow links these together, it becomes easier to recognise where new finances have come from during the year and where the money has been spent during the same period. The surplus or deficit resulting from this should equal the business's change in working capital. One basic function of funds flow is to emphasize this change for purposes of evaluation.

The funds flow is in four sections:

1. *Sources of Funds*
    (a) Net profit *before* tax. This often represents the main source of income from the business's trading.
    (b) Depreciation charged against profit is *added* back on to net profit because it relates to a book entry only. Depreciation is not paid to anyone.
    (c) New sources of money. For example, issues of shares or debentures, loans procured from financial institutions.
    (d) Sale of fixed assets — that is, the proceeds of the sale. (Any profit or loss resulting from the sale requires the net profit to be adjusted.)

2. *Application of Funds*
    (a) The purchase of fixed assets.
    (b) Taxation paid during the year.
    (c) Dividends — ordinary or preference — paid during the year.
    (d) Repayment of loans or debentures.

The difference between the source of funds (1) and the application of funds (2) equals the surplus or deficit in resources for the year.

3. *Changes in Working Capital*
    This relates to either increases or decreases in working capital during the year and specifically to

    Stocks
    Debtors (include pre-payments)
    Creditors (include accruals)

4. *Movement in Net Liquid Funds*
    This refers to bank and cash movement during the year. The net change to bank and cash balances.

The net result of 3 and 4 should equal the change in working capital, either in surplus or deficit, which must also represent the net result of 1 and 2.
Note: the provision for taxation and dividends is not to be included as part of the creditors. The actual payment of these relating to the current year is entered in section 2 — application of funds.

Presentation

Funds Flow Statement of J. Jones Ltd. Year ended 31 December 19 . . .

		£ 000's	£ 000's
1.	*Sources of Funds*		
	Net Profit (*before* tax)	1,430	
	Add Depreciation charged	380	
		1,810	
	Less profit on sale of fixed asset	5	1,805
	Other Sources		
	Issue of shares (ordinary)	80	
	Loan from Bank	8	
	Sale of fixed asset	12	100
			1,905
2.	*Application of Funds*		
	Dividends paid during year:	250	
	Preference	150	
	Ordinary		
		400	
	Taxation paid during year	690	
	Purchase of fixed assets	455	1,545
			360
3.	*Changes in Working Capital*		
	Increase in Stocks	+310	
	Increase in Debtors, Pre-payments	+120	
	Increase in Creditors, Accruals	−115	315
4.	*Movement in Net Liquid Funds*		
	Increase in Bank	48	
	Decrease in Cash	3	45
			360

A Worked Example

ABC Co. Ltd. Funds Flow Statement Year ended 31 December...

	Year 2	Year 1
Balance Sheet	£	£
Fixed Assets (cost)	4,000	2,500
Depreciation	1,000	800
	3,000	1,700
Current Assets:		
Stock	2,500	2,000
Debtors	1,000	800
Bank	—	500
Cash	50	50
	3,550	3,350
— Current Liabilities:		
Creditors	1,000	700
Bank (overdraft)	250	
Tax provision	300	250
Dividends provision	50	100
	1,600	1,050
Working Capital	1,950	2,300
Capital Employed	4,950	4,000
— Loan Capital	500	
	4,450	4,000
Financed by:		
Issued and Paid Up Capital	3,000	2,800
P & L balance (31/12)	1,450	1,200
	4,450	4,000

Profit & Loss a/c. Year ended 31 December, Year 2	£
Net Trading Profit	
(after £200 depreciation charges)	600
Provision for Tax	300
	300
Provision for Dividend	50
	250
P & L balance (1/1)	1,200
P & L balance (31/12)	1,450

Required:

Prepare a sources and application of funds statement for the year ended 31 December, Year 2 showing the change of working capital over the financial period.

Funds Flow Statement of ABC Co. Ltd.
Year ended 31 December, Year 2

	£	£
Sources of Funds		
Net Trading Profit (before tax)	600	
+ Depreciation charges	200	800
Other Sources:		
Issued share capital	200	
Loan	500	700
		1,500
Application of Funds		
Purchase of fixed assets	1,500	
Dividends paid	100	
Taxation paid	250	1,850
		(350)
Changes in Working Capital		
+ Stock	500	
+ Debtors	200	
+ Creditors	−300	400
Movement in Net Liquid Funds		
− Bank		(750)
		(350)

Exercises

1. The final accounts of J. Jones Ltd for the year ended 31 December 19. . . are listed below:

Balance Sheet as at 31 December . . .	1990	1989
	£	£
Fixed Assets (cost)	20,970	16,650
Depreciation	1,570	1,070
	19,400	15,580

	1990	1989
Current Assets		
Stock	3,500	1,950
Debtors	3,055	2,139
Bank	1,870	1,625
Cash	300	125
	8,725	5,839
− Current Liabilities		
Creditors	2,096	400
Provision for Taxation	400	165
Provision for Dividends	50	25
	2,546	590
Working Capital	6,179	5,249
− Loan	5,000	600
	20,579	20,229

Profit and Loss Account *Year ended 31 December, Year 2*	£	£
Net Trading Profit		
(after £500 Depreciation charges)		800
P & L Balance (1/1)		229
		1,029
Provision for Taxation	400	
Provision for Dividend	50	450
		579
General Reserve		500
P & L Balance (31/12)		79

Note: There was no change to issued capital during the year

Required:

A statement of source and application of funds for the year ended 31 December, 1990.

2. The final accounts of ABC Co. Ltd for year ended 31 March were as follows:

Balance Sheet of ABC Co. Ltd as at 31 March; 1990

	1990 £	1989 £
Assets		
Fixed (net)	195,000	140,000
Stocks	21,550	23,500
Debtors	18,450	14,725
Bank	2,925	4,150
Cash	500	500
	238,425	182,875
Liabilities		
Creditors	26,450	19,550
Provision for Taxation	15,000	12,500
Provision for Dividends (ordinary)	6,500	6,000
Debenture Stock	50,000	35,000
	97,950	73,050
Net Assets:	140,475	109,825
Shareholders Funds:		
Issued and Paid Up Capital:		
Ordinary Shares	75,000	75,000
Preference Shares	25,000	15,000
Reserves	33,725	15,725
P & L Balance (31/3)	6,750	4,100
	140,475	109,825

Profit and Loss Account of ABC Co. Ltd
Year ended 31 March . . ., 1990

Net Trading Profit		
(Depreciation charges £8,000)		44,150
Corporation Tax		15,000
		29,150
P & L Balance (1/4, Year 1989)		4,100
		33,250
Preference Dividends *paid*	2,000	
Provision for Ordinary	6,500	
Reserves	18,000	26,500
P + L Balance (31/3, 1990)		6,750

Required:

(a) A sources and application of funds statement for year ended 31 March, 1990.

(b) Comment on the change of working capital.

3. The following information refers to the accounts of P. Jackson & Co. Ltd:

	31 Dec. 1987 £	31 Dec. 1988 £
Assets		
Premises (cost)	35,000	45,000
Machinery*	20,000	21,500
Stock	15,000	20,580
Debtors	8,450	12,375
Bank/Cash	2,255	1,835
	80,705	101,290
Liabilities		
Creditors	10,150	12,755
Accruals	1,125	955
Taxation due	5,100	6,530
	16,375	20,240
Capital		
Issued @ £1 Ordinary Shares	50,000	60,000
P & L a/c	14,330	21,050
	64,330	81,050

*Machinery**

	Cost £	Depreciation £	Net £
Balance (31 Dec. 1987)	25,000	5,000	20,000
Additions 1988	6,000		
	31,000		
Sale of Old stock	(3,000)	(2,000)	
Depreciation 1988		3,500	
Balance (31 Dec. 1988)	28,000	6,500	21,500

Profit & Loss a/c Year Ended 31 December, 1988

Net Trading Profit	12,750
+ Gain on Sale of Machinery	500
	13,250
Corporation Tax	6,530
Retained to P & L a/c	6,720

Note:
Any gain or loss on the sale of a fixed asset *is not* included in the 'source of funds' as net profit although the actual sum received *IS* included.

Required:

(a) A statement of Source and Application of Funds for the year ended 31 December 1988.

(b) Comment on the change of working capital over the two periods.

4.   Study the following Balance Sheets of Jones & Rogers PLC, and Profit and Loss account for the year ended 31 May 1988.

Jones & Rogers PLC
Balance Sheets as at 31 May

	1987		1988	
	£	£	£	£
Ordinary Shares	170,000		200,000	
Share Premium a/c	17,000		20,000	
P & L a/c	8,000	195,000	10,000	230,000
Fixed Assets (cost)	180,000		260,000	
Depreciation	40,000	140,000	60,000	200,000
Investment (cost)		10,000		5,000
Current Assets:				
Stock	50,000		60,000	
Debtors	30,000		47,000	
Bank	10,000	90,000	18,000	125,000
Current Liabilities:				
Creditors	17,000		18,000	
Provision for Tax	16,000		18,000	
Provision for Dividends	12,000	(45,000)	14,000	(50,000)
Deferred Liability:				
9% Debentures	—			(50,000)
		195,000		230,000

Jones & Rogers PLC Profit & Loss a/c Year ended 31 May 1988

Net Trading Profit	30,000
+ Profit on Investment	4,000
	34,000
− Provision for Taxation	18,000
	16,000
+ P & L balance (1/6/87)	8,000
	24,000
− Provision for Dividends	14,000
P & L a/c	10,000

Required:

(a) Calculate the working capital ratio over the two years and briefly comment on the business's liquidity.

(b) Prepare a statement of Sources and Application of Funds for the year ended 31 May 1988.

5. *Company Accounts*: Funds Flow Statement, Accounting Ratios and Evaluation of Trading Performance.

Situation

The following final accounts relate to Harry Fox Co. Ltd for the year ending 31 December, Years 1 and 2. Study the figures carefully from the point of view of analysing the firm's performance between the two financial periods.

Profit & Loss a/c Harry Fox Co. Ltd. Years ended 31 December . . .

	1989 £	1990 £
Retail Sales	128,640	196,480
Net Profit (before Tax)	12,850	21,590
Corporation Tax (provision for year)	5,100	9,250
Net Profit (after Tax)	7,750	12,340
Dividends: Ordinary Shares	6,500	9,000
Retained Profits	1,250	3,340

Note: Depreciation charges for the year were £4,500.

Balance Sheet, Harry Fox Co. Ltd, as at year ended 31 December . . .

	1989	1990
	£	£
Fixed Assets (net)	28,904	38,244
Current Assets		
Stock	7,288	10,338
Debtors	4,942	8,358
Bank	3,750	1,674
Cash	100	50
Current Liabilities		
Creditors	1,930	2,670
Accruals	550	1,000
Taxation	5,100	9,250
Dividends	6,500	9,000
Deferred		
Bank Loan	5,000	2,500
Shareholders Funds		
Authorised Capital		
50,000 @ £1 Ordinary Shares	50,000	50,000
Issued and Paid Up Capital		
@ £1 Ordinary Shares	20,000	25,000
Reserves	5,904	9,244

TASK A

Prepare two separate balance sheets at the year ended 31 December 1989 and 1990 for Harry Fox Co. Ltd, showing clearly working capital and capital employed.

TASK B

Prepare a Funds Flow Statement for the year ended 31 December, 1990

6. *Situation*

You work in the accounts office of XYZ Ltd. and the Accountant has provided you with the following information at the end of the financial period, 31 March 1987:

Balance Sheets of XYZ Ltd. at 31 March 1986 and 31 March 1987

	31 March 1986 £	1987 £		31 March 1986 £	1987 £
Freehold property at cost	25,000	25,000	Issued Share Capital	30,000	30,000
Equipment (see Note)	18,000	22,200	Profit & Loss a/c	27,000	33,000
Stock in trade	16,400	17,800	Corporation Tax due:		
Debtors	13,600	14,000	1 January 1986	6,000	–
Bank	2,000	1,000	1 January 1987	–	4,000
			Creditors	12,000	13,000
	75,000	80,000		75,000	80,000

Note: Equipment movements during the year ended 31 March 1987 were:

	Cost £	Depreciation £	Net £
Balance at 31 March 1986	30,000	12,000	18,000
Additions during year	9,000		
Depreciation provided during year		3,800	
	39,000	15,800	
Disposals during year	4,000	3,000	
Balance at 31 March 1987	35,000	12,800	22,200

The company's summarised profit calculation for the year ended 31 March 1987, revealed:

	1986 £	1987 £
Sales	95,000	100,000
Gain on sale of Equipment		2,500
		102,500
Less Cost of sales and other expenses	84,800	92,500
Net profit	10,200	10,000
Corporation tax on profits of the year	6,000	4,000
Retained profit of the year (after tax)	4,200	6,000

Required: Prepare a Funds Flow Statement for the year ended 31 March 1987.

7. *Situation/Information*

You work for a small limited company and are assisting in the preparation of the annual accounts for year ending 30/5/88.

Details:

ASPEN LIMITED BALANCE SHEET AS AT 30TH MAY

	1987				1988	
	£	£	£	£	£	£
Fixed Assets at Cost		173,000			243,400	
Less Depreciation		57,800	115,200		78,100	165,300
Current Assets:						
Stock		74,400			72,080	
Debtors		97,920			100,020	
Bank		10,880			–	
		183,200			172,100	
Current Liabilities:						
Creditors	41,440			37,080		
Overdraft	–			2,320		
Provision for Tax	17,120			12,400		
Proposed Dividend	10,000	68,560	114,640	12,000	63,800	108,300
			£229,840			£273,600
Financed by:						
£1 Ordinary Shares			200,000			220,000
Reserves			29,840			53,600
			£229,840			£273,600

ASPEN LIMITED PROFIT & LOSS ACCOUNT FOR YEAR ENDED 30/5/88

	£
Profit for the year	48,160
Provision for Tax	12,400
	35,760
Undistributed Profits from last year	29,840
	65,600
Proposed Dividend	12,000
Undistributed Profits carried to next year	53,600

TASK A
Prepare the Sources & Application of Funds Statement of Aspen Limited for the year ended 30/5/88.

TASK B
Compute the Current Ratio for both years.

TASK C
Compute the Return on Capital Employed for the year ended 30/5/88.

TASK D
Comment on Aspen's Liquidity position over both years.

Note: See later chapter on accounting ratios to assist you in Tasks B,C and D.

8. The Balance Sheets of RADS Ltd on 31st December 1987 and 31st December 1988 were as follows:

	1987		1988	
Tangible Assets				
Land and Buildings (at cost)	250,000		430,000	
Plant and Machinery (NBV)	150,000		185,000	
		400,000		615,000
Current Assets				
Stock	185,000		250,000	
Debtors	97,000		71,900	
Bank	103,000		63,000	
Cash	18,000		26,100	
	403,000		411,000	
Less: Current Liabilities				
Creditors	41,000		84,000	
Proposed dividends	20,000			
	61,000	342,000	84,000	327,000
		742,000		942,000
Share Capital		500,000		600,000
Share Premium		200,000		200,000
P & L A/C Balance		42,000		142,000
		742,000		942,000

The Profit and Loss summary for the year is as follows:

Net Profit for the year	155,000
Interim dividend (paid)	55,000
Profit & Loss a/c	100,000

Plant and Machinery which originally cost £140,000 and which had a written down value of £60,000 at 31st December 1987, was sold during the year for £80,000. A depreciation provision of £25,000 was made during 1988.

TASK A
Draw up a Statement of Sources and Applications of Funds for the year ended 31st December 1988.

TASK B
Write a brief report based on the figures you have prepared, assessing in particular whether in your opinion the additional capital expenditure was financed in a suitable manner.

PART 6

Public Sector Accounts: Central Government and Local Authorities

Central Government

The State is responsible for providing the public with a wide range of essential needs and services which will cost in the region of £160–170 billion for the financial year ending 30 April 1987. This is likely to increase to approximately £180 billion for the year ending 1990–1991 and rising to £203 billion for 1992–1993.

Central Government is responsible for providing social security benefits, pensions, health and personal social services and education, which take up about half of public spending. The bulk of the remaining half goes to finance local authorities, defence and debt interest payments.

Public expenditure is a rather complex affair and some items like education, the police and health services are paid for by a combination of both Central and local Government.

To finance the public expenditure programme, the bulk of the money comes from a variety of sources. Taxes, either direct or indirect and National Insurance contributions account for about 70%. The rest is made up of rates, borrowing and various other sources.

Below is the revenue and expenditure programme forecast for the 1986–87 financial year.

Central Government Finance Public Money 1990–1991 Forecast

Expenditure	£ Billions	Revenue	£ Billions
DHSS		Income Taxes	42
Health & Social Security	68	Corporation Tax	18
Defence	18	National Insurance	
Environment & Transport	13	and other contributions	31
Home Office	7	VAT	25
Education & Science	18	Local Authority Rates	18
Other Depts.	14	Custom & Excise duties –	
Interest Payments	18	road fuel, alcohol, tobacco	20
Scotland, Wales and NI	18	North Sea revenues	2
Other expenditure	6	Expenditure Taxes	10
		Miscellaneous sources	9
		Capital Taxes	5
	180		180

Local Authority Finance

Local government expenditure was financed by the rates which was a local tax paid by the occupiers of land and property to meet part of the cost of local services. It was supported by the Government in the form of the Rate Support Grant (RSG) and also specific grants to help finance capital projects like roads, schools and hospitals.

Local authority finance has now been reformed and the domestic rates have been replaced by a community charge. Each authority sets a sum payable by every resident of adult age and a grant system provided by the Government is intended to offset or compensate for differences in the individual needs of local authorities.

The new system has created a great deal of conflict between local authorities and local residents because it was seen to be unfair, particularly when the community charge raised in one region may have been so different from another. The Government took a great deal of criticism for its introduction.

The Community Charge was introduced in April, 1990 in England and Wales, and a year earlier in Scotland, by the Government. Its introduction caused a great deal of controversy and much public unrest. According to the calculations of the Department of Environment, no one should have been called upon to pay more than about £150 in community charge than in rates. If the bill was greater than this, a resident would be entitled to claim some transitional relief. However, almost every council had set its community charges far greater than the Government's calculations. It estimated that the average charge per adult head would be in the region of £280 in England and Wales. In fact, the average was something approaching £400 and this meant that most community charge payers were requiring relief on a sum far in excess of £150 (above their last rate bill).

Restrictions by the Department of the Environment kept the cost of relief down which inevitably meant that many people would suffer, particularly those living in overcrowded homes and poor tenants in rented housing, crammed bedsits in the cities and also pensioners and the disabled. If the right amount of poll tax relief is given to such groups of people, only then could it be a more acceptable form of local tax.

The pattern of local authority spending is a complex mixture between:

(a) County Council services.
(b) District Council services.
(c) Parish Council services.

Because the County Councils provide the majority of services and, in particular, finance the heavy costs of education, police, transport and highways for the whole county, the bulk of local authority money is spent by the County Councils.

The District Councils also provide services for their own localities, including council housing, environmental health (sewerage, drainage, refuse collection, food inspection), recreation and leisure amenities, and special projects such as development and maintenance of parks, buildings, roads and other features unique to the district.

The Parish Councils spend a relatively small proportion of the finances available and grants may be allocated by the District Councils for parish projects such as a sports pavilion or a girl guides' hall.

During the financial year ending 30 April 1986, the income from Rates in a District Council of Dorset amounted to £17 million (excluding block grants) of which

£15.2 million was allocated for the County Council
£ 1.5 million was allocated for the District Council
£ 0.3 million was allocated for the Parish Council

Local authority spending falls into two distinct categories: Current Expenditure and Capital Expenditure.

Current Expenditure refers to the day-to-day running expenses of the authority, described as 'Revenue Expenditure' for private sector businesses. Capital Expenditure refers to capital projects on housing, schools, roads and general development of the region.

The capital building projects of Dorset for 1986–87 is estimated to be approximately £22 million, including allotted money for phase II of Bournemouth and Poole College, stage III of the Wessex Motor Way and almost £10 million for the Dorchester Town Centre relief road.

Below is the forecast of County Council spending for 1986–87:

Dorset County Council
Forecast of Public Spending 1986–87

Expenditure	£ (millions)	Revenue	£ (millions)
Education	124	Rates	127
Personal Social Services	26	RSG	
Police, Courts, Fire		Domestic Grant	28
Services	25	Block Grant	52
Highways and Transport	24	Other Sources	5
Libraries	4		
Other Services	9		
	212		212

Dorset District Council's
Forecast of Public Spending 1986–87

Expenditure	£ (millions)	Revenue	£ (millions)
Health & Housing	0.28	Rates	1.55
Technical Services:		RSG	1.25
(refuse collection,			
recreation, drainage etc.)	1.76		
Planning (building control)	0.51		
Policy & Resources			
(district administration)	0.25		
	2.8		2.8

Spending by a Parish Council in the District Council's precept given below was approximately £0.25 million, financed by about 3p in the rates.

The rates payable by the local ratepayers in the District Council is likely to be 170p in the £ for 1986–1987, a rise of about 10%, largely due to the reduction in Government Support Grant. A domestic property therefore, in the District Council, with a rateable value of say £285 would pay

$$285 \times 170p = £484.50 \text{ in rates for the year}$$

The following represents the balance sheet of a District Council in Dorset. The format is identical to other business organisations, although some of the items included are peculiar to public authority accounting.

Balance Sheet of a District Council — forecast. Year ended 31 March 1987

	£	£	£
Fixed Assets			
Buildings, Equipment (Net)			26,500,000
Current Assets			
Stocks	68,000		
Debtors (Mortgagors and others)	3,400,000		
Investments	37,000		
Cash	5,500		
Debtors (from assets sold)	2,199,500	5,710,000	
Less			
Current Liabilities			
Temporary Loans	3,200,000		
Creditors	760,000		
Overdraft	580,000		
Provisions	830,000	5,370,000	
Net Current Assets			340,000
			26,840,000
Less			
Long-term Borrowing			
Public Works Loan Board			
(Exchequer Loan)	8,100,000		
Mortgages and Negotiable Bonds	2,400,000		10,500,000
			16,340,000
Financing			
Capital Funds	9,700,000		
Funds from Capital Receipts			
(Repayment of Advances and			
revenues from land, buildings)	4,455,000		
Capital Grants	545,000		
Revenue a/c Surplus	920,000		
Other a/c Surplus	720,000		16,340,000

The Source and Application of Funds Statement for the District Council again follows the identical format to that of other business organisations, with some of the items peculiar to public authorities.

Source and Application of Funds Statement. Forecast of District Council Year ended 31 March 1987

	£	£
Source of Funds		
Revenue		
Ratepayers and Tenants	17,500,000	
Government Grant	7,200,000	
Sales, Fees, Charges for Public Services	1,450,000	
	26,150,000	
Less		
Expenditure for Authority Services	10,480,000	15,670,000
Add		
Internal Interest Receipts	1,122,000	
Adjustments for internal transfers	815,000	1,937,000
		17,607,000
Other Sources		
Capital Receipts	2,623,500	
Long-term Borrowing:		
Public Works Loan Board	675,500	
Other Loans	300,200	3,599,200
Total Source of Funds		21,206,200
Application of Funds		
Capital Payments on Fixed Assets	5,252,000	
Repayment of Loans	1,350,000	
County Precept	16,210,000	
Parish Precept	355,000	23,167,000
Net Funds Movement		(1,960,000)
Changes in Working Capital		
Stocks	215,400	
Debtors	(327,800)	
Creditors	(152,300)	
Temporary Borrowing	1,541,200	
	(1,805,900)	
Net Movement in Liquid Funds		
Cash	(154,900)	(1,960,800)

Exercises

1. What is the difference between Central and Local Government expenditure?
   How does Central Government raise most of its finance?
   Why are local authorities dependent on Central Government?

2. How might revenue be raised to meet local authority spending?
   What is the difference between current and capital expenditure?

3. How might the balance sheet of a local authority differ from a company balance sheet? What are the similarities?

4. The following figures refer to the revenue and expenditure of Dorset County Council for the year ended 31 March 1988:

	£ (000's)
Public Amenity Services	4,798
Education	118,290
Transport and Planning	48,360
Police	26,365
Social Services	21,882
Fire and other	6,245
Other projects	340

Resources:

Domestic Government Grant	34,180
Block Grant	60,200
Other Sources	100
Rates (to calculate)	?

Required:

(a) Calculate the amount required by the County to be raised from local Rates.
(b) Prepare a statement to show the County's Income and Expenditure for the year ended 31 March 1988.
(c) The Government introduced its Community Charge in England & Wales in April 1990, and a year earlier in Scotland. What is this charge?

5. The following information refers to the Balance Sheet of a local authority as on 31 March . . .

	£ 000's	£ 000's
Assets		
Land, Buildings and Works	63,530	
Loans to other authorities and to individual persons	4,045	
Investments	5	
Deferred interest owed and other outstanding debts	5,190	
Stocks, Stores, Work in Progress	600	
Debtors	2,215	
Bank	3	75,578
Liabilities		
Loans Outstanding:		
Short term	7,975	
Creditors	3,600	
Bank Overdrawn	1,555	
	13,130	
Long Term (Mortgages, Local Bonds)	18,560	31,690
		43,888
Financing		
Capital Discharged		
Capital Receipts, Funds	31,560	
Capital Receipts in Hand	10,450	
Deferred Capital Receipts (sale of property)	1,358	
Reserve Funds	520	43,888

Required:

(a) How does the balance sheet of a public authority differ from that of a limited company? List items which are different.

(b) Calculate the working capital, taking the first 3 of the assets listed as 'fixed'.

(c) Why is working capital adequacy not as critical to a local authority?

Accounting for Social Organisations

Most private sector businesses are profit motivated. Goods and services are produced and distributed for the purpose of making money. However, there are non-profit organisations which are not primarily set up to make profits. These are the clubs and societies which are organised for specific purposes — for example, social, sporting, political and other organisations.

In many regions up and down the country, there are local tennis, cricket, football and rugby clubs. There are also amateur dramatic and choral societies as well as political and other associations.

Finance is raised by the members of these social organisations in a number of ways. Members' subscriptions provide a major source of income, while donations from various bodies and fund-raising activities are ways of raising extra finance. The sources of finance are used to pay for the running and up-keep of the club or society.

Money which comes in and goes out of a social organisation should be properly accounted for in order to safeguard the members' interests. It is therefore necessary to keep some basic records of the accounts in order to know what funds are available at what time.

Most of the social organisations elect honorary members who take on specific responsibilities. The club chairman is usually the spokesman and figure-head of the organisation. The club secretary will have the responsibility of taking care of the essential paper work such as letters to members, agendas, minutes of meetings, reports of activities and so forth. The club treasurer will have the responsibility of looking after the accounts.

The Treasurer's Accounting Reports

Formal accounting methods tend to be uncommon because the treasurer may lack time or expertise or both when it comes to keeping the accounts of the club or society. However, he should be expected to keep a tight control of cash and be in a position to prepare for members the following financial reports at the end of the club or society's social year:

(a) A receipts and payments account.
(b) An income and expenditure account.
(c) A balance sheet showing the organisation's state of affairs.

The Receipts and Payments Account

This statement is a summary of all cash receipts and payments of the organisation for the year and is, in effect, a simplified cash book. The purpose of it is to show members where the cash has come from and where it has gone and, significantly, how much is left in balance at the end of the year under review.

The Income and Expenditure Account

This is a statement which is the equivalent of the business's trading and profit and loss account where expenses are matched against income. Adjustments such as accruals, pre-payments and depreciation are also accounted for because they affect the profit or loss for the year. A social organisation uses the words 'surplus' or 'deficit' to indicate its profit or loss. Some clubs and societies operate a bar or refreshment counter for the benefit of its members. The treasurer can prepare a special bar or refreshment account to indicate whether or not such an activity has made a surplus or deficit.

The Balance Sheet

This statement may be prepared in the same way as any other organisation. The net resources of the club or society are financed by the 'accumulated funds' — that is, the capital or net worth of the social organisation. Accumulated funds represent assets less liabilities in the same way as capital. Any surplus from the income and expenditure account is added to the funds. Any deficit is deducted.

Example

Poole Tennis Club begins its social year on 1 April 1987. Its accumulated funds at this date were £17,704 made up of:

	£
Bank balance	304
Equipment	400
Club House	15,000
Investment	2,000
	17,704

At the end of the social year, 31 March 1988, the treasurer listed the following receipts and payments for the year and prepared the club's receipts and payments account:

Receipts and payments Account for the period ended 31 March 1988

Poole Tennis Club Receipts and Payments Account for the period ended 31 March 1988

Receipts	£	Payments	£
Bank balance (1 Apr. 1987)	304	Sports equipment	108
Subscriptions	400	Tennis balls	30
Subscriptions in advance	55	Hire of courts	230
Refreshment sales	91	Light and Heat	35
Dance tickets	25	General expenses	140
Tournament fees	72	Refreshment purchases	60
Donations	30	Club house improvement	350
		Bank balance (31 Mar. 1988)	24
	977		977

Note: on 31 March 1988 the following were to be taken into consideration before preparing the Club's Income and Expenditure account for the period ended:

	£
(a) stock of refreshments	27
(b) subscriptions owing for current year	150
(c) Electricity bill owing	35
(d) sports equipment to be depreciated by	58
(e) bill for refreshment purchases due	12

Preparing a Refreshment or Bar account

It may be useful to prepare a separate account to deal with these to show whether a surplus or deficit is made. A surplus or deficit may then be transferred to the Income and Expenditure account.

Refreshment Account
Poole Tennis Club

	£	£
Sales		91
Less Cost of Sales:		
Stock (1 Apr. 1987)	–	
+ Purchases	60	
+ Purchases due	12	
	72	
	27	
– Stock (31 Mar. 1988)		45
*Surplus		46

*Transferred to the Income side of the Income and Expenditure account.

Poole Tennis Club

Income and Expenditure Account for the period ended 31 March 1988

Expenditure		£	Income		£
Tennis balls		30	Subscriptions	400	
Hire of courts		230	+ owing	150	550
Light and Heat	35				
+ owing	35	70	Refreshment surplus		46
	—		Dance tickets		25
General expenses		140	Tournament fees		72
Depreciation of			Donations		30
equipment		58			
Surplus		195			
(income greater than					
expenditure)					
		723			723

Note: The subscriptions owing £150 belong to the current period ending 31 March 1988 and are therefore added to income. The subscriptions in advance are not included because they belong to the next period ending 31 March 1989.
The last statement is the balance sheet showing the Club's resources and the financing of them via the Accumulated Funds.

Poole Tennis Club Balance Sheet at 31 March 1988.

	£	£	£
Fixed Assets			
Club House	15,000		
+ Improvements	350		15,350
Equipment	400		
+ New Purchases	108	508	
– Depreciation		58	450
Investment			2,000
			17,800
Current Assets			
Stock of refreshment	27		
Bank	24		
Subscriptions due	150	201	
– *Current Liabilities*			
Subcription in advance	55		
Accrued expenses	47	102	99
			17,899
Financed by			
Accumulated Funds	17,704		
+ Surplus	195		17,899

Exercises

1. The following statement has been submitted to you by the Corfe Mullen Social Club whose year ends 31 March 1988.

   Receipts and Payments Account

	£		£
Bank balance		Insurance & rates	480
(1 Apr. 1987)	2,000	Wages	5,650
Subscriptions	5,575	Light and Heat	480
Surplus from Bingo	850	Bar purchases	6,500
Bar takings	10,225	General expenses	275
		New furniture	500
		Maintenance and	
		repairs to Club	1,275
		Bank balance	
		(31 Mar. 1988)	3,490
	18,650		18,650

Other information

		£
1 April 1987	Club premises valued	25,000
	Furniture and equipment	2,000
	Bar stock	1,600
	Bank balance (as above)	
31 March 1988	Bar stock	850
	Subscriptions in arrear	480
	in advance	50
	Furniture and Equipment valued	1,950
	Bar purchases still due	500
	Insurance pre-paid	35

Required:

(a) The Club's Bar account for the period ended 31 March 1988.
(b) The Club's Income and Expenditure account for the period ended 31 March 1988.
(c) A Balance Sheet as at 31 March 1988.

2. From the following Receipts and Payments Account of the Parkstone Golf Club and the further particulars provided below prepare an Income and Expenditure Account for the year ended 31 March 1988 and a Balance Sheet as at that date.

Receipts and Payments Account for the year ended 31 March 1988

Receipts	£	Payments	£
Balance from last year	1,600	Wages	4,800
Entrance fees	8,400	Payment for new Equipt.	3,500
Subscriptions:		Printing & Stationery	200
Current year	4,800	Postages	175
In advance	500	Lighting and Heating	575
Profits and refreshments	1,160	Insurances	250
Equipment rented to		General Expenses	1,850
members	750	Balance (bank)	5,860
	17,210		17,210
Balance b/d	5,860		

Additional Information (31 March 1988)

(i)   £50 is owing for subscriptions for the year.
(ii) £15 is owing by members for equipment rentals.
(iii) Printing and Stationery, value £28, is still unpaid.
(iv) The Club House and equipment appear in the Books on 1 April 1987 at a value of £10,000.

3. The Sandal Rugby Club was started on 1 April 1988 with a Bank balance of £3,300 which was provided by its members. After its first season, the receipts and payments for the year ended 31 March, 1989 was as follows:

	£
Pavilion and other buildings, land	8,150
Equipment	500
Gate money	3,500
Collections at matches	1,642
Donations from members and other	1,585
Refreshment expenses	756
Receipts from refreshments	1,100
Loan from local Bank secured on land and buildings (@ 12% per annum)	5,000
Rates, water	185
Light, heat	75
Wages of groundsman (part-time)	800
Match expenses paid	115
Printing and other expenses	125
Advertising	176
General expenses	80
Transport costs	1,050

Note: 31 March 1989

(a) Rates pre-paid £45.
(b) The interest on loan has not yet been accounted for and was taken out on 1 July 1988.
(c) Wages owing to groundsman £40.
(d) Stocks of catering amounted to £65.
(e) The equipment was to be depreciated by £100.

Required:

(a) Prepare the income and expenditure account for the year ended 31 March 1989.
(b) A balance sheet as at that date.

4. The following is the Trial Balance of the Broadwent Rugby Club on
    31 December 1988:

	£	£
Accumulated Fund at 1 January		10,500
Club House	18,560	
Club-room Equipment	755	
Sports Equipment	150	
Sale of Refreshments		3,765
Purchase of Refreshments	2,400	
Interest accrued		50
Subscriptions received for		
Current Year		2,800
Subscriptions in advance		55
Receipts from Club-house Games		200
Maintenance of Games		
Equipment	500	
Postage	150	
Insurance	850	
Sundry Expenses	275	
Printing and Stationery	105	
Wages	1,450	
Bank		1,870
Loan from Building Society		5,955
	25,195	25,195

Prepare:

(a) An account to show the profit or loss on sale of refreshments and
(b) the Income and Expenditure Account for the year ended 31
    December, and a Balance Sheet at that date.

Take into consideration the following:
(a) Sports equipment is to be depreciated at 10% per annum and
    club-room equipment at 20% per annum.
(b) £75 subscriptions are due for the current year.
(c) £95 is owing for the purchase of refreshments.
(d) Stock of refreshments on hand at 31 December was £370.

5. The following information relates to Broadstone Tennis Club at the
    beginning of their season 1 April 1987:

	£
Club House	15,000
Equipment	800
Bank	500
Stock (refreshments)	250

A summary of receipts for the year:

Subscriptions	1,500
Subs. in Advance	150
Refreshments	1,855
Dances	550
Fees for Tournaments	360
Donations from members	100
Members' Loan (5% p.a.)	2,000
Sales of Lottery	875

A summary of payments for the year:

Sports equipment	450
Tennis balls (expense)	50
Lottery tickets, prizes	565
Light & Heat	80
General expenses	240
Refreshment purchases	1,255
Club House re-building	1,850
Maintenance of grounds	200
Insurance, Rates, Water	375

At the end of the season, 31 March 1988, the following information was available to the Club Treasurer:

(a) The sports equipment (including additions) was valued at £900.
(b) Stock of refreshments valued at cost £165.
(c) Subscriptions owing by members £80.
(d) A gas bill was still to be paid £18.
(e) Insurance was pre-paid £25.
(f) Club House rebuilding is classified as a capital expense, not revenue expense.
(g) Members' interest on loan had not been paid. (From 1 April, 1987)

Required:

(a) Prepare a receipts and payments account for the year ended 31 March 1988.
(b) Prepare the club's income and expenditure account for the year ended 31 March 1988 and a balance sheet as at that date.

6(a). From the following details and the notes attached relating to the Wiltshire Tennis Club prepare the Final Accounts of the Club for the year ended December 31 1989.

On January 1 1989, the club's assets were: freehold club-house, £1,000.00, equipment £70.00; club subscriptions in arrear £8.00; balance at bank £76.00. The club owed £40.00 to Caterer's Ltd for Christmas dance catering.

Summary of Receipts and Payments for 1989

RECEIPTS	£	PAYMENTS	£
Subscriptions	164.00	Catering-Christmas Dance	
Locker Rents	10.00	(Caterer's Ltd)	40.00
Receipts from Dances		This Year's Dances and	
and Social	139.00	Socials	95.00
Sales of Used Match		Band Fees-Dances	25.00
Tennis Balls	15.00	New Lawn Mower	53.00
Sale of old Lawn Mower	8.00	Repairs to Tennis Nets	19.00
		Match Tennis Balls	31.00
		Match Expenses	17.00
		Repair and Decoration of	
		Club-house	65.00

Note: (a) The book value on January 1 1989 of the old lawn mower sold during the year was £15.

(b) The club has 40 members and the subscription is £4.00 per annum. The subscriptions received in 1989 included those in arrear for the previous year.

(c) On December 31 1989 £11.00 was owed to James Ltd for tennis balls supplied.

(d) Equipment as at December 31 1989, is to be depreciated by 15 per cent.

(e) Tennis balls are regarded as revenue expenditure, not capital expenditure.

6(b). Why is it important to clearly distinguish between capital and revenue expenditure?

The Interpretation of Financial Information

Objectives

To calculate accounting ratios concerning an organisation's profitability, liquidity and efficiency.

To measure the performance of organisations in absolute or relative terms and to give some interpretation of an organisation's performance.

To understand the uses and limitations of accounting information.

To understand the distinction between revenue and capital expenditure and how this distinction affects financial information.

To understand the concepts (or conventions) used in accounting.

To be aware of the importance of finance in organisational decision making.

PART 1

Accounting Ratios

Analysis and Interpretation of Financial Information

All business enterprises need to calculate their profit or loss at least once in the accounting period. For taxation purposes alone, the business must prepare its final accounts because the Inland Revenue needs to assess the taxation liability of the business.

Profit and Loss can be calculated as frequently as the business requires. In large organisations, this may be on a monthly basis in order to give management as much information as possible to assist it in making better decisions in running the business. Monthly trends may then be analysed and compared with previous performances and against forecasts made by management.

Accounting ratios can assist management when comparing trading performances in one period with another. Ratios can help relate figures over periods of time and can identify the trends of business performance.

Key questions which need answers are:

(a) Is the business profitable?
(b) Is the business financially stable? Has it adequate liquidity to meet its creditors?

The following information will be used as an example for the calculation of accounting ratios. The company, Allied Components, Plc, is a small public company, recently quoted on the stock exchange. Ratios to test for profitability, liquidity, efficiency, structure and investment, will be calculated, including a brief evaluation of the results.

Allied Components PLC Profit & Loss Account Year Ended, 31 December 1990

	£ [00's]	£ [00's]
Turnover		9,000
Cost of Sales		
Stock (1/1)	500	
Purchases	5,650	
Stock (31/12)	(150)	6,000
Gross Profit		3,000
Distribution Costs	550	
Administration Expenses	850	
Interest Payable	400	1,800
Net Profit (before tax)		1,200
Provision for Tax		300
Net Profit (after tax)		900
Profit & Loss Balance (1/1)		0
		900
Provision for Dividends:		
8% Preference Shares	160	
Ordinary Shares	300	460
Retailed Profits (to Reserve)		440

Allied Components PLC Balance Sheet as at Year Ended, 31 December 1990

	£[00's]	£[00's]
Fixed Assets (net value)		20,000
Current Assets:		
Stock (31/12)	150	
Debtors	2,400	
Bank Cash	850	
Prepayments	100	
	3,500	
Creditors falling within 12 months:		
Trade Creditors	700	
Accruals	40	
Provision for Tax	300	
Provision for Divis.	460	
No. 2 Bank	500	
	2,000	
Net Current Assets		1,500
Capital Employed		21,500
Creditors falling after 12 months:		
Debenture Stock		6,500
		15,000
Capital & Reserves		
Ordinary Share Capital	3,000	
8% Preference Shares	2,000	
Reserves 9,560		
+ Retained Profits 440	10,000	15,000

1. Profitability Ratios

These ratios are used to measure the trading performance of a business in terms of profit to sales or profit to capital. The ratios in themselves may have little meaning unless they are compared to past performances or with businesses in the same category, for example, supermarkets or electrical appliances. Allowing for factors such as inflation or other economic indicators which may influence demand, ratio analysis can be useful in detecting trends and the reasons behind them.

The ratios used are not the whole category available but they are amongst the most common:

(a) The Gross Profit % $= \dfrac{\text{Gross Profit} \times 100}{\text{Net Sales}}$

(b) The Net Profit % $= \dfrac{\text{Net Profit} \times 100}{\text{Net Sales}}$

(c) Return on Capital Employed $= \dfrac{\text{Net Profit} \times 100}{\text{Capital Employed}}$

(d) Return on Net Worth $= \dfrac{\text{Net Profit} \times 100}{\text{Net Worth (Owner's Equity)}}$

(e) Return on Total Assets $= \dfrac{\text{Net Profit} \times 100}{\text{Total Assets}}$

The Net Profit returns may be shown (for a company) as before or after tax, or both. When comparing ratios with other periods, it is important to be consistent. Compare like with like, otherwise distortions will occur and negate the usefulness of any comparison.

(a) Gross Profit % $= \dfrac{\pounds3,000 \times 100}{\pounds9,000}$

$= 33.33\%$

(b) Net Profit % $= \dfrac{\pounds1,200 \times 100}{\pounds9,000}$

$= 13.33\%$

(c) Return on Capital Employed $= \dfrac{\pounds1,200 \times 100}{\pounds21,500}$

$= 5.58\%$

(d) Return on Net Worth $= \dfrac{£1,200 \times 100}{£15,000}$

$= 8\%$

(e) Return on Total Assets $= \dfrac{£1,200 \times 100}{£23,500}$

$= 5.1\%$

Note: The net profit has been taken *before tax* in the above figures.

Are these profit returns reasonable? With no comparative figures to guide our analysis, it is difficult to make useful comment. However, if the 'norm' for Allied Components, within its own industry was for example, within 35% – 40% gross and between 14% and 18% net, then we could assume that the company's profitability was marginally lower than was expected.

Is the company satisfied receiving around £33 gross per £100 sales and £13 net per £100 sales (before tax)? Could it do any better? Is it buying its materials at optimum prices? Is its production as efficient as it could be if it manufactured its products?

Is its return on capital a reasonable figure? How does it measure up to interest rates? All Allied's profits to the balance sheet figures are between 5% and 8%. The return on capital employed, seen by the majority of organisations as *one of the most significant* returns on capital, is only a low 5.58%. With base interest rates high, the return on capital is very mediocre. This measures profit to the business resources as a whole and the directors of the company would need to seek improvement on a miserable 5%.

Is the sales department doing its job effectively? Could an improvement in marketing be the answer? Could some of the expenses be cut without affecting the quality of the product?
These are some of the questions management could be asking, to seek ways of improving profits.

2. Liquidity Ratios

These ratios indicate the business's ability to have sufficient cash resources to meet current debts. The two most significant ratios are:

(a) Working Capital ratio (or Current Ratio).
(b) Quick-asset ratio (or Acid Test).

Calculation of ratios:

$$\text{Working Capital ratio} = \frac{\text{Current Assets}}{\text{Current Liabilities}}$$

$$= \frac{£3,500}{£2,000} = 1.75$$

$$\text{Quick-Asset ratio} = \frac{\text{Current Assets (less Stock)}}{\text{Current Liabilities}}$$

$$= \frac{£3,500 - £150}{£2,000}\ 1.68$$

Working Capital needs to be adequate to enable the business to trade with reasonable 'comfort'. It should be enough to finance short-term debts (those which are due within the financial period). If creditors demand payment, the business should be in a sound enough financial position to meet the demands.

The working capital ratio should not fall below 1:1 because then there would be insufficient liquid resources to meet debts. A ratio falling below 1:1 means the business is 'insolvent' — that is, it has insufficient liquidity to meet current debt.

Liquidity is as important as profit-earning, if not more so. A business could be in an attractive profit earning position and and yet still fail because it has disregarded its liquidity. Creditors can force a business to pay its debts by taking them to court. If the court ruled that the business must pay up within a specific time, it may well mean that it must be 'liquidated' to pay off its outstanding debts.

The quick-asset ratio is an immediate test of liquidity because the value of stock is deducted from the total of current assets. Can a business, without relying on its stock, meet its immediate debts? However, the importance of this ratio is also related to the business's rate of stock turnover — the speed by which a business sells its stock. The faster stock is sold, the less important is the quick-asset ratio. A supermarket like Sainsbury's, for example, has such a high rate of stock turnover, that stock is almost like cash anyway. On the other hand, a manufacturing business making motor vehicles could have a much lower rate of turnover, therefore taking longer to produce and sell its goods and receive its cash.

Comparisons need to be made with previous years to check the business's liquidity trend. Expected ratios, depending on the type of business should be

Working Capital ratio   2.5:1 to 1.5:1
Quick-Asset ratio   1.5:1 to 0.75:1

Ideally, the working capital and quick-asset ratios should fall somewhere between these ratios, 2:1 and 1:1 respectively, although this depends on the size and nature of the business. As long as there is adequate liquidity to satisfy creditors, that is what is important.

3. Efficiency Ratios

These ratios are used to try and identify the strengths and weaknesses of a business using a variety of different ratios including the money incurred on relative expenses, stock turnover, debt collection, the investment of assets to turnover and productivity. This list is by no means exhaustive but it is emphasised that past figures and norms for similar industries are needed in order to give a better and more in-depth analysis.

(a) *Expense %'s*

Each type of expense may be analysed in relation to sales for the purpose of evaluating in absolute or relative terms the significance of different types of expense and how they affect profit.

Expense type

$$\text{Cost of Sales \%} = \frac{\text{Cost of Sales} \times 100}{\text{Sales}}$$

$$= \frac{£6,000 \times 100}{£9,000} \quad 66.66\%$$

$$\text{Distribution Expenses \%} = \frac{\text{Distribution Expenses} \times 100}{\text{Sales}}$$

$$= \frac{£550 \times 100}{£9,000} \quad 6.11\%$$

$$\text{Administration Expenses \%} = \frac{\text{Administration Expense} \times 100}{\text{Sales}}$$

$$= \frac{£850 \times 100}{£9,000} \quad 9.44\%$$

$$\text{Financial Expenses \%} \quad = \quad \frac{\text{Financial Expenses} \times 100}{\text{Sales}}$$

[interest]

$$= \quad \frac{£400 \times 100}{£9,000} \qquad \underline{4.44\%}$$

Total Expenses %	=	86.65%
Therefore Net Profit %	=	13.35%
		$\underline{100\%}$

These expenses may be related to pence in the £ to indicate an easy break-down of expenses to the number of pence profit in the £:

Pence/£

Cost of Sales	67 p
Distribution Expenses	6 p
Administration Expenses	$9\frac{1}{2}$p
Financial Expenses	$4\frac{1}{2}$p
	$\overline{87\ \text{p}}$ total
	$\underline{13\ \text{p}}$ in the £ profit

Is 13p in the £ an adequate return? How does it compare with previous trading performances? How does it compare with similar organisations trading in similar goods or services?

If 13p is regarded as an insufficient return, investigation is needed in order to find out why the return is low. Is 67p/£ for cost of sales too high? — is the firm inefficient in buying or producing its goods? How do the other expenses compare with previous years? Is the selling price too low? These points need to be analysed and are important in assisting management and owners in making decisions.

(b) *The Rate of Stock Turnover*

This ratio refers to the number of times the stock is sold within an accounting period. It gives an indication of the business's selling efficiency.

Calculation: $\text{Rate of Stock Turnover} = \dfrac{\text{Cost of Sales}}{\text{Average Stock}}$

$$= \frac{£6,000}{£325} = 18.5 \text{ times per year}$$

A high rate of stock turnover   = Stock sold every 2.8 weeks

The speed of stock turnover depends on the nature of goods sold. A large supermarket will have a high turnover rate because it sells goods required every day. For goods required less frequently, such as furniture, the stock rate will be less. Because turnover of stock measures the business's selling efficiency, the trend should be carefully checked and deviations from the normal patterns investigated.

If the rate of stock is sold every 2.8 weeks, it is seen as relatively fast compared with another organisation whose rate is, say, every 16 weeks and which sells goods like jewellery or furniture and not supermarket goods.

The stock turnover should be compared with the gross profit percentage (33.3%) to see the effect of selling prices on turnover figures. For example, if the rate of turnover gains, it may indicate a policy by the firm of reducing its selling prices in order to increase turnover and sales. If the gross profit percentage falls but actual gross profit increases, the policy will be seen as successful. On the other hand, if selling prices are forced down because of intense competition, the gross profit percentage may fall without either an increase in actual gross profit or stock turnover.

The actual calculation of stock turnover also needs a little caution. If stock taking is only carried out at the end of a financial year, the average stock is computed on the basis of adding stock beginning with stock end and dividing by 2:

Stock (1 Jan.)	£500	
Stock (31 Dec.)	£150	£650/2 = £325

If stock levels at the end of the financial period are not an average indication of stock, because of seasonal changes, the turnover ratio is likely to be a false representation of the business's true selling efficiency.

(c) *The Collection of Debt*

This ratio is an indication of the period of credit taken by debtors. In other words, how long it takes them to pay their debts. The ratio has a significant bearing on both the efficiency of credit control and the accuracy of liquidity. If credit control is doing its job properly, the period of credit taken by debtors should be satisfactory. If debtors are paying their bills regularly, the liquidity ratio is more reliable.

$$\text{Average Credit taken by debtors} = \frac{\text{Debtors} \times 365}{\text{Credit Sales}}$$

(assume all sales in ABC's accounts are credit sales)

$$= \frac{£1,080 \times 365}{£9,000}$$

= approximately 44 days to collect debts

In general, a monthly invoice is paid within about 45 days.

Some manufacturing organisations which produce and sell highly expensive goods like motor vehicles, machinery and equipment, may need to give distributors a far longer period of time in which to settle debts, such as 3 to 12 months. The method of payment may also be far more complex, involving time-payments calculated to suit both buyer and seller. The important thing to remember is that credit control should be constantly checking the reliability of individual debtors rather than merely observing an average collection period as a whole.

(d) *Trading Assets to £1,000 Sales*

This ratio identifies the sum invested in current assets to produce a turnover of £1,000.

$$\text{Trading Assets}/£1{,}000\ \text{Sales} = \frac{\text{Current Assets}}{\text{Sales ('1000's)}}$$

$$= \frac{£3{,}500}{£9\ (000's)}$$

$$= £388.9$$

This indicates that it takes an investment of about £400 by Allied to produce a turnover of £1,000. Is this a satisfactory figure in terms of the resources used to buy stock, incur debtors and spend cash? If the norm for the industry was say, £350, we could assume that the business was less efficient at utilising these resources to produce its sales. If the norm was more than £400, the reverse could be true and Allied may be more efficient in the use of its trading assets.

(e) *Productivity*

Two ratios may be used to identify productivity in terms of the number employed. If we assume that Allied has a workforce of 20, two ratios may be calculated:

$$\text{(i) Sales/Employees} = \frac{£900{,}000}{20}$$

$$= £45{,}000\ \text{turnover/employee}$$

(ii) Profit (b/tax)/Employee. $= \dfrac{£120,000}{20}$

$= £6,000$ profit/employee

Productivity has always been seen to be an important contributory factor to efficiency in business because the greater the productivity, the greater the profit and more resources are available for distribution.

A business can afford to pay its workforce more if productivity increases, without it being inflationary. If productivity falls, the business is seen to be less efficient and employees produce less in terms of units to man-hours.

This could be caused by a number of factors such as the inefficient use of manpower, plant and machinery, or, technology may need up-dating. Are the figures for Allied adequate enough to satisfy the demand of management and shareholders?

4. Structure Ratios

There are a number of ratios which may be used to identify the relationship between the members' capital and the extent of liabilities. In this sense, the structure only refers to how the business is financed, that is, internally by its owners, or, externally by the extent of its liabilities. Capital gearing is one of these and is explained separately later in this section. Two ratios are used here:

(a) The Owner's Stake $= \dfrac{\text{Capital (Net Worth)}}{\text{Assets (Total Assets)}}$

$= \dfrac{£15,000}{£23,000}$

$= 63.8\%$

(b) The Liability Ratio $= \dfrac{\text{Liabilities (Total Liab)}}{\text{Capital (Net Worth)}}$

$= \dfrac{£8,500}{£15,000}$

$= 56.6\%$

The owner's stake identifies how much the owners are worth in the business. In this case, 63.8% is in the hands of the shareholders.

The liability ratio looks at how the business is financed. A ratio of 100% indicates that there is equal financing between the owners and the liabilities. Allied's 56.6% infers that liabilities only finance about half of the shareholders' investment (total funds). The majority of the financing is therefore in the hands of the business's shareholders.

5. Investment Ratios

The shares of public limited companies can be bought and sold on the Stock Exchange and these may be listed if the shares or debentures have obtained an official quotation from the Stock Exchange Council. It is these stocks and shares which are published in the daily national newspapers. Some public companies do not necessarily want official listing and may seek to be listed on the USM (the Unlisted Securities Market). This 'second division' of listing still permits the buying and selling of securities (stocks and shares) but is not under the same strict code of practice demanded of an official listing.

The shares of private limited companies do not appear on any listing of the Stock Exchange simply because securities of private companies must be dealt with privately and not publicly.

The major newspapers and particularly the *Financial Times*, list the securities each day, giving information about share prices, their change in value, dividends, yield, cover and price-earnings ratio and other significant information about the fluctuating fortunes of the stock market.

The *Financial Times Index* (FTI) is the barometer of the Exchange and its rise or fall each day, indicates how the market responds to the demand for stocks and shares. If the market believes there is confidence in the economy, demand for shares could pick up and the market is said to be 'bullish' and share prices are likely to rise. On the other hand, if confidence falls, demand can dry up and investors may rush out and sell, causing share prices to fall. This is a 'bear' market.

The investment ratios all concern ordinary shares (equities) rather than preference shares which are on a fixed rate of dividend. The following ratios are considered to be of significance:

(a) Earnings per Share (Eps)

$$= \frac{\text{Net Profit (after tax)} - \text{Preference Dividend}}{\text{No. of Ordinary Shares}}$$

$$= \frac{£900 - £160}{3,000 \text{ shares}} = 25\text{p per share}$$

(b) Percentage Dividend

$$= \frac{\text{Sum to Ordinary Shares} \times 100}{\text{Issued \& Paid Up Capital}}$$

$$= \frac{£300 \times 100}{3,000} = \frac{\text{10p per share}}{(10\%)}$$

(c) Yield Percentage

$$= \frac{\text{Dividend per Share} \times 100}{\text{* Market Value per Share}}$$

$$= \frac{\text{10p} \times 100}{125} = 8\% \text{ yield}$$

* Market Value as listed on Exchange for Allied Components, £1.25 (125p per share).

(d) Cover

$$\frac{\text{Net Profit (after tax)} - \text{Preference Dividend}}{\text{Dividend on Ordinary Shares}}$$

$$= \frac{£900 - £160}{£300} = 2.5 \text{ times}$$

(e) Price/Earnings Ratio

$$= \frac{\text{Market Price per Share}}{\text{Earnings per Share (Eps)}}$$

$$= \frac{\text{125p}}{\text{25p}} = 5 \text{ times}$$

The Eps (earnings per share) is one of the most publicised ratios when companies report their half-yearly or yearly results. It indicates the earning potential of each ordinary share. Allied has an Eps of 25p per share which may look very attractive to some shareholders, each share literally earning 25p in profit. This does not mean that the dividend is 25p per share, it simply indicates that each share has earned 25p.

The dividend per share is the dividend recommended by the board to its ordinary shareholders. Allied are recommending 10% or 10p per share. This links with the cover. Ordinary shares could have been paid 2.5 times what has been offered. The higher the cover, the greater the sum retained by the company, rather than paid as dividends. If the cover is low, it indicates that the board is offering the shareholders most of the available profit, less being retained by the company as reserves.

The price to earnings ratio indicates the market value of a share in relation to the number of years' profits it represents. In other words, a P/E of 5 means that the current market price of £1.25 equals approximately 5 years of current profit earned. Generally speaking, the higher the P/E ratio, the better the share prospectus. It indicates what the market is prepared to pay for them.

The investment ratios concerning Allied PLC may then be analysed and compared with other stocks and shares on the Exchange.

Earnings per share	25p/share
Dividend to Ordinaries	10p/share or 10%
Yield	8%
Cover	2.47 times
P/E ratio	5 times

The figures appear far from spectacular but the market value of the shares is only 25p above the nominal value and it may be, given time, with more profits retained for expansion purposes, the market value of the shares could increase. The dividends to ordinary shareholders may remain relatively small. What does the investor want? Income from dividends or Capital income derived from the increase in the market value of the shares?

A good investment or not? Retain or Sell? It is difficult to say. The Stock Exchange is a reliable source as far as the reporting of figures is concerned, yet nothing is certain as to which shares will be successful.

Capital Gearing

Gearing refers to the relationship between Ordinary shares and fixed interest payable shares plus fixed interest payable long-term liabilities, often in the shape of debentures. Gearing may be high or low, depending on the level of borrowed capital and preference capital.

The company which is high-geared has a high proportion of borrowed and preference capital relative to Ordinary shares. If Ordinary share capital predominates then the company is said to be low-geared.

Gearing plays an influential part in the payout of ordinary share dividends. If profits are good, the high-geared company can benefit its ordinary shareholders by paying higher dividends.

For example, if borrowing at fixed interest rates is $8\frac{1}{2}\%$ and return on investment is $14\frac{1}{2}\%$, the ordinary shareholders will obviously be delighted because they earn 6% above the fixed interest borrowed. Conversely, if returns are the opposite way around and fixed interest payments are greater than investment, the result may not only be disappointing but also financially precarious because fixed interest must be paid, regardless of profits. If creditors hold the balance of financial power they can soon call in their loans and precipitate the collapse of the company.

$$\text{Capital Gearing} = \frac{\text{Debt}}{\text{Equity}}$$

$$= \frac{\text{Long-term Borrowing} + \text{Preference Share Capital}}{\text{Shareholders Funds (less Preference Shares)}}$$

Capital Gearing
of Allied Components: $\dfrac{\text{£8,500}}{\text{£13,000}}$

$$= 65\% \text{ (moderately low)}$$

An Example of Capital Gearing

Company A   Low-gearing — a high proportion of ordinary share capital
       B   High-gearing — a low proportion of ordinary share capital

Company:	A	B
	£	£

Capital Employed:

	A	B
Issued £1 ordinary shares and paid up	100,000	25,000
11% Debenture Stock	25,000	100,000
	125,000	125,000
Ratio:	25%	400%
GEARING	LOW	HIGH

Profit and Loss Statement	A	B
Trading Profit (before interest paid to Debentures)	20,000	20,000
11% Debenture Interest	2,750	11,000
Profit before Tax	17,250	9,000
Corporation Tax (50%)	8,625	4,500
Profit after Tax	8,625	4,500

$$\text{\% Dividend available to Equities:} \qquad \frac{8{,}625 \times 100}{100{,}000 \quad 1} \qquad \frac{4{,}500 \times 100}{25{,}000 \quad 1}$$

$$= 8.6\% \qquad\qquad = 17\%$$

Note: Company A Returns are not so high as Co. B.
Company B rewards it shareholders more even with the same level of profits. When times are good, high returns will be expected but when profits decline (or losses are made) interest must still be paid and a high-geared business may then be in a precarious financial position, vulnerable to its creditors. Debenture interest has also reduced the profit before Tax of Company B and therefore their tax liability is less, a distinct advantage.

The Limitations of Accounting Ratios and Parties interested in Financial Information

Accounting ratios need to be analysed and interpreted and not merely listed as a set of figures. They need to be compared with previous year's performances and, where possible, with other similar organisations to investigate and evaluate what the figures indicate.

There have been a number of cases where accounting ratios have indicated a sound financial position but on closer inspection of the accounts, evidence has revealed that the 'apparent soundness' of the figures is merely an empty shell and the organisation is far from sound.

For example, a liquidity ratio may indicate an 'ideal' situation of 2:1, yet this may be entirely because of a heavy stock position which is old or obsolete and although measured at cost, in real terms is worth far less and would be difficult to off-load to the market.

It may be that a preponderance of debtors who are at best unreliable, is responsible for achieving an unrealistic liquidity ratio which looks very sound on paper but in actual terms is precarious because a certain proportion of debtors should have been written down or written off. What of the 'ideal' 2:1 ratio when the business goes bankrupt or a company is liquidated a few months later?

Not only are owners and management interested in the performance of their organisations. Bankers and creditors who may be asked to lend money to the business need to know if their investment is going to be sound. Accounting ratios may help them to decide whether or not to go ahead. They will also need to be cautious about the reliability of the accounts and the ratios calculated and may wish to make more enquiries to organisations like Dunn and Brad street who specialise in assessing the 'credit rating' of different business organisations.

Employees may also be interested in the financial performance of their organisations from the point of view of productivity and profits. If the business is successful and productivity is improving, the trade unions have a solid platform when negotiating new pay awards and conditions.

Shareholders of companies and potential shareholders who may not be in a position to know the reliability of firms, need investment advice from a bank or other financial institution. The *Financial Times* share section can also give current information concerning dividends and yields, etc. but professional help is still needed to guide shareholders through the maze of security (shares) dealings.

The Inland Revenue is also an interested party because it needs to assess the level of taxation to be charged against profits and against dividends paid to shareholders.

Example Exercise

Accounting Ratios & Evaluation

The following represents the accounts of XYZ Co. for the Year ended 31 December ....

Trading & Profit & Loss a/c year ended 31 December ....

	Year 1 £	Year 2 £
Sales	50,000	60,000
Cost of Sales	30,000	40,000
Gross Profit	20,000	20,000
Distribution Costs & Selling Expenses	5,000	7,000
Administration Expenses	4,000	5,000
Net Profit	11,000	8,000

Balance Sheet as at 31 December

Fixed Assets	37,000	45,700
Current Assets	20,900	24,000
	57,900	69,700
Current Liabilities	9,900	18,500
Long-term Liabilities	6,000	3,700
	42,000	47,500

Financed by:

Capital: 40,000 @ £1 Ord. Shares	40,000	40,000
Reserves	2,000	7,500
	42,000	47,500
Note: Average Stock	7,500	8,500

Required:
(a) Use appropriate accounting ratios to evaluate both Year 1 and 2.
(b) Compare the performance of the firm over the two years.

(a) *Accounting Ratios*

	Year 1	Year 2
1. *Profitability:*		
Gross Profit %	40%	33.33%
Net Profit %	22%	13.33%
Return on Capital Employed	22.9%	15.6%
Earnings per Share (E.P.S.)	27.5p	20.0p
2. *Liquidity:*		
Current Ratio (WC ratio)	2 : 1	1.3 : 1
Acid Test	1.35 : 1	0.75: 1
3. *Efficiency:*		
Stock Turnover	4. times	4.7 times
COS %	60. %	67.%
D & S Expenses	10. %	11.%
Administrative Expenses	8. %	8.3%
4. *Ownership Structure:*		
Shareholder's Stake	72.5%	68.1%
(Proprietorship Ratio)		
Liability Ratio	39.9%	46.7%

(b) *Evaluation of Performance*

The Year 1 profit ratios are all superior to Year 2. The basis reason why this is the case lies in the cost of sales which increased from 60% to 67% in the year, thereby reducing the gross % by 7%. Why was this?

Sales had expanded by £10,000 in Year 2 and stock turnover had also increased marginally but the actual gross profit remained the same at £20,000 in both years. Perhaps sales prices were marked too low (to generate greater sales) but sales did not respond sharply enough to gain more gross profit. It could also mean that insufficient savings were made when buying stocks.

The extra profit & loss expenses ensured that the net profit fell by £3,000, thereby reducing returns. The company has expanded (not only its sales but also in its fixed assets) but it has not yet generated greater profit returns.

Liquidity has also suffered with both current and acid test ratios declining markedly. From an 'ideal' 2 : 1, the current ratio has slipped to a more marginal 1.3. Creditors have doubled in the year due to expansion and this has weakened the company's ability to meet its short-term debts. Expanding the business has required greater credit and the purchase of fixed assets (£8,700) has also added to the pressure.

However, the expansion scheme may show improved results in the following years depending on whether or not the company can increase its share of the market. It may take time for expansion schemes to develop towards full potential.

The shareholder's ownership in the business has declined marginally due to the extra burden of liabilities. Even so, the net worth has increased by £5,500 over the year.

Limitations:

One must recognise the fact that figures alone cannot tell the full tale! What else is known about this company? Very little.

What does it produce/buy/sell? How do these figures compare with similar enterprises in terms of size and nature of business? What style of management exists? Is the workforce relatively stable? Are the figures realistic in terms of valuation? (Stock, premises, equipment etc.) Are provisions adequate?

In summary, we may say that the company has expanded its operations and in terms of accounting ratios, the results are virtually all inferior in Year 2. However, it may take some time for improvements to channel through and benefits to materialise. If it does, then financial performance will improve. It all rests with customers. They alone create the demand for goods or services and are the arbiters of fortune. Success or failure depends on them.

Exercises

1. The following trading results refer to the accounts of P. Jackson & Co. during the last 3 years, year ending 31 December.

	Year 1 £	Year 2 £	Year 3 £
Trading & Profit & Loss			
Sales:			
Cash	5,000	6,000	8,000
Credit	25,000	30,000	37,000
Cost of Sales	20,000	24,000	31,950
Distribution Costs	3,000	3,200	4,100
Administration Expenses	3,150	3,750	4,275
Stock:			
1 Jan.	1,950	2,050	2,950
31 Dec.	2,050	2,950	5,050
Balance Sheet (extract)			
Debtors	5,000	6,000	9,000
Capital Invested (1 Jan.)	26,500	30,000	31,750

Required:

(a) The trading and profit and loss account of P. Jackson & Co. for each of the 3 years ending 31 December.
(b) Accounting ratios to indicate:

Gross Profit %
Net Profit %
Expense %'s

Rate of stock turnover
Credit taken by debtors

Return on Capital Invested

(c) Brief comments using the accounting ratios to give some indication of the firm's performance over the 3 years.
What limitations do the ratios impose?

2. Study the following information regarding companies A and B then answer the following questions below.

Profit & Loss Account	Company A £	Company B £
Turnover	9,000	24,000
Cost of Goods	5,000	10,500
Other Expenses		
Selling	500	4,750
Administration	750	2,250
Financial	300	500
Balance Sheet		
Fixed Assets	7,000	10,000
Current Assets	4,275	6,750
Current Liabilities	2,000	3,500

Required:

1. Preparation of profit & loss accounts for the year ended 31 December and balance sheets as at that date.
2. Profitability: Gross Profit %
     Net Profit %
     Return on Capital
3. Working Capital and Working Capital Ratio.
4. A brief comment on the results comparing the two firms.

3. Below are shown the summarised balance sheets of Harry Smith at the end of three consecutive years:

	Year 1 £	Year 2 £	Year 3 £
Creditors	6,480	9,740	12,565
Bank	—	—	1,500
Loan (long-term)	12,500	10,500	10,000
Capital	24,100	24,180	26,220
	43,080	44,420	50,285
Cash in Hand	100	100	250
Bank	1,450	1,750	—
Debtors	8,455	7,940	9,165
Stock	4,575	6,230	10,120
Shop Fittings	3,500	3,400	5,750
Premises	25,000	25,000	25,000
	43,080	44,420	50,285

From these balances you are required:

(i) to calculate the amount of the working capital at the end of each year;
(ii) to calculate the ratio of current assets to current liabilities correct to one decimal place at the end of each year;
(iii) to calculate the acid test correct to one decimal place at the end of each year;
(iv) which year do you consider has been the 'safest' as far as Harry's ability to repay debts?

4. The following represents the accounts of XYZ Co. for the Year ended 31 December . . .

Trading & Profit & Loss a/c year ended 31 December . . .

	Year 1 £	Year 2 £	Year 3 £
Sales	50,000	60,000	80,000
Cost of Sales	30,000	40,000	48,000
Gross Profit	20,000	20,000	32,000
Distribution Costs & Selling Expenses	5,000	7,000	12,000
Administration Expenses	4,000	5,000	6,000
Net Profit	11,000	8,000	14,000

Balance Sheet as at 31 December

	Year 1	Year 2	Year 3
Fixed Assets	37,000	45,700	55,000
Current Assets	20,900	24,000	30,000
	57,900	69,700	85,000
Current Liabilities	9,900	18,500	24,000
Long-term Liabilities	6,000	3,700	5,500
Net Assets	42,000	47,500	55,500
Financed by:			
Capital	31,000	42,000	47,500
Net Profit	11,000	8,000	14,000
Drawings		(2,500)	(6,000)
	42,000	47,500	55,500

Required:

(a) Use appropriate accounting ratios to evaluate Year 1, Year 2 and Year 3.
(b) Compare the performance of the firm over the three years.

5. Rocco Bank Ltd and Ball Bearings Ltd are two independent companies in the type of business activity their names suggest.

As a young financial adviser, you are asked to assess the situation of both companies, by studying the figures given below:

	Ball Bearings Ltd £ 000's		Rocco Bank Ltd £ 000's	
Fixed Assets (Net)	39,000		4,000	
Intangibles	4,000		—	
Investments (long-term)	2,000	45,000	9,000	13,000
Stocks	27,000			
Debtors	25,000			
Advances			21,000	
Cash, liquid assets	—		59,000	
Investments	3,000	55,000	7,000	87,000
		100,000		100,000
Creditors	48,000			
Taxation	1,000		1,000	
Current and Deposit accounts			91,000	
Bank	7,000	56,000		92,000
10% Debenture Stock		33,000		500
Shareholder's Funds				
Ordinary Shares @ £1	10,000		2,000	
Reserves	1,000	11,000	5,500	7,500
		100,000		100,000
Net Profit (before tax)		2,500		2,600
Proposed ordinary dividends		700		400

Required:

Choose accounting ratios which you consider will reveal the differences between the two companies. Discuss your calculations from the point of view of profitability and financial stability.

6. *Situation*:

ABC Co. Ltd is a small private company in the rag trade. Its first four years trading annually to 31 December were made up as follows:

Year	Sales	Purchases	Increase or Decrease of material stocks during Year	Selling & Distribution Costs	Rent	General Admin. Expenses
	£	£	£	£	£	£
1	36,000	39,000	+ 12,000	900	3,000	4,500
2	54,000	37,500	− 3,000	1,250	3,000	5,250
3	78,000	63,000	+ 4,500	2,500	3,000	6,000
4	120,000	108,000	+ 12,000	4,000	3,500	11,500

Tasks:

A Trading and profit and loss accounts in columnar form for each of the four years ending 31 December 1984.
B Two accounting ratios for each of the four years.
C A brief discussion of the implication of these figures and the inferences drawn from them.

7. *Situation:*

The following figures relate to a retailing organisation which has expanded its business operations. Its premises were converted into a 'self-service' style during the year 1987:

	1986	1987	1988
	£	£	£
Net sales	120,000	150,000	200,000
Gross Profit %	30%	33⅓%	35%
Fixed Expenses:	20,000	25,000	30,000
Variable Expenses: (12% of Sales)	?	?	?
Average Stock held (cost):	8,000	8,500	10,000
Capital Employed:	60,000	105,000	160,000

TASK A

Prepare the trading and profit and loss accounts for each trading year, preferably in columnar format.

TASK B

In tabular form, prepare the appropriate business profit returns and also the rate of stock turnover for each of the above years.

TASK C

Briefly evaluate the business's progress over the three years in terms of its efficiency and profits.

8. *Situation:*

Andrew Rob-David p.l.c. intends to expand its business activities and the Board of Directors are in agreement that an extra £500,000 will be required to meet their plans.

The schemes which have been put forward are:

Scheme A
To issue £500,000 10% Preference Shares @ £1 per share at par.

Scheme B
To issue £500,000 Ordinary Shares @ £1 per share at par.

Scheme C
To issue £500,000 10% Redeemable Debenture Stock 1990/1995 at par.

The company's current share capital consists of 3,000,000 @ £1 ordinary shares, issued and paid up.
Next year, it is estimated that a dividend of 12% will be declared by the board.

The accountant of the company has estimated that the profit for the budget year ended 31 December 1989, will be £700,000, *before* the payment of interest or taxation.
This year's interest payments on the company's overdraft is £5,000 and it is estimated that the same payment will be made in 1989.

Corporation tax on the company's profits is at a rate of 35%.

As the assistant to the accountant, you have been asked to prepare the following:

TASK A

An estimated Profit & Loss Appropriation Account for each of the three schemes, in tabular form, relating to next year's figures. Commence your account with Net Profit *before* interest payments and taxation.

TASK B

Calculate for each of the three schemes, the earnings per share and capital gearing and state which scheme, in your view, is likely to be the most appropriate.

TASK C

As an information leaflet is to be sent to existing shareholders, draft a suitable section to be included which will clearly differentiate between:
  (a) equity shares
  (b) preference shares
  (c) redeemable debentures.

PART 2

The Distinction between Capital and Revenue Expenditure

Capital Expenditure

This is expenditure associated with the purchase of fixed assets or with the improvement of them.

The items of purchase are part of a firm's asset structure and therefore belong to the balance sheet when financial reports are presented. For example, improvements or extensions to premises, purchasing of new plant, machinery, equipment, office machines and so forth, which are expected to have some *permanency* in their use and extend over a number of accounting periods.

Revenue Expenditure

This is expenditure concerned with the running expenses of a firm which are 'used up' *within* an accounting period (for example, within 12 months). These expenses are deducted against the firm's revenue and appear as trading and Profit and Loss expenses, reducing profits. For example

gas and electricity
rent, rates, insurance
wages, salaries
purchases for resale
administration, selling and financial expenses

It is important to make this division of expenditure because if capital expenditure, for example, was to be treated as revenue expenditure, the value of assets and chargeable expenses will be miscalculated. For example

> Purchase of office machinery £500 wrongly treated as revenue expenditure and entered under purchases. This would have the effect of *understating the value of assets* and *overstating the value of chargeable expenses*.

> This would result in reducing the value of assets and reducing the year's profits.

Check the following table.

	Transaction		Revenue	Capital
			£	£
1.	Purchase of new computer	£2,500		2,500
2.	Paid rates and insurances	£ 500	500	
3.	Paid advertising programme to last 18 months	£1,500	1,000	500
4.	Modernised the premises	£6,500		6,500
5.	Painted the offices (to last 5 years)	£4,000	800	3,200
6.	Paid salaries	£1,250	1,250	
7.	The warehouse had additional shelving	£3,500		3,500

Note: Some expense items like painting may all be written off during the year incurred irrespective of how long it is expected to last. Advertising could also have been treated in a similar way.

Exercises

1. Classify the following items in the accounts of G. Harrison as to whether they are capital or revenue expenditure:

    (a) Purchased recording equipment for use on premises £400.
    (b) Refitting of stock room with new shelving and cupboards £600.
    (c) Paid gas bill £47.
    (d) Paid for purchases of goods for resale £300.
    (e) Paid for taxi fares from petty cash £18.
    (f) Bought new cash-till on credit from CRS Suppliers £321.
    (g) Made an extension of premises £1,560.
    (h) Discounts allowed £88.
    (i) General Repairs to motor vehicle £106.
    (j) An advertising campaign to cost £150.

(k) Running expenses on the motor vehicle £160.

(l) The purchase of an accounting machine £500.

Why is it important to distinguish between capital and revenue expenditure?

2. G. Harrison bought a motor vehicle for use in the business. Classify the following under capital or revenue expenditure:

	£
Cost of basic vehicle	800
Additional fittings	300
Motor tax (6 months)	55
Insurance premium	42
Petrol and oil	20
Initial running repairs	30
Additional lighting	50
New car seat & cover	100
Additional new tyre	55

Give what you consider would be entered in the Nominal Ledger as the total value of the motor vehicle under 'Motor Vehicle' account.

PART 3

Concepts used in Accounting

All final accounts involve some element of judgement on the part of the Accountant who has prepared them. Accountants could easily prepare different final accounts from the same data, and each would conform with fundamental principles. The accounting profession recognises four basic concepts which are assumed to be followed in preparing final accounts — unless otherwise stated. The four fundamental concepts are:

    (a) Going concern concept
    (b) Accruals concept
    (c) Consistency concept
    (d) Prudence concept

Going Concern Concept

The value of an organisation's assets are based on the assumption that the firm will continue trading. Businesses tend to value their assets at cost less estimated depreciation. If for any reason (such as lack of working capital) there is a probability of closure because of bankruptcy or liquidation, then the balance sheet would have to reflect the situation — that is, assets would have to be valued at a realistic market valuation and other liabilities may arise, such as redundancy payments.

Accruals Concept (or Matching Concept)

It is taken for granted that a set of final accounts includes *all* expenses incurred and *all* income earned, not merely the payment date; for example, if

319

an organisation owed its employees £50,000 in wages at the end of the financial year it would have to include this figure as an accrued expense, otherwise the profits of the firm would appear overstated. In this concept, the matching of revenue with expenses must include all items pertinent to the period, paid or unpaid.

Consistency Concept

There are a number of bases of dealing with accounting data, such as the different methods of valuing stock or the different methods of depreciation. Organisations are expected to adopt consistent accounting policies in order to prevent profit distortions. Thus, if an organisation changed its method of depreciation from straight-line to market valuation, it must clearly state in the accounting reports the effect on the profit for the year.

Prudence Concept (or the Concept of Conservatism)

Accountants are expected to take a pessimistic view when preparing the final accounts. Thus, the accountant should provide in full for any expected loss (such as provisions for bad debts) but not to take profit if there is any doubt regarding its realisation. Where, for instance, there may be two or more values relating to an asset, the lower value would tend to be chosen.

In addition to the above fundamental concepts there are a number of other accounting concepts which include:

Cost Concept
Materiality Concept
Realisation Concept
Money Measurement Concept
The Dual-Aspect Concept

Cost Concept

The common standard practice is for ALL items of either capital or revenue expenditure, to be valued at cost. Therefore, the purchase of assets, including stock, and the payment of expenses, are at their cost price. Stock may be valued lower than cost if it has lost its value for reasons such as damage, obsolescence, etc.

Materiality Concept

The view that small, insignificant items may be excluded from the normal accounting policy. The *size* of the business enterprise will dictate what is materially relevant. A large organisation may consider a valuation of a fixed asset under £500 insignificant. It will be treated as an expense item and written off in the year it was bought, irrespective of how long it will last. A smaller organisation may consider £500 as significant and depreciate the asset over a number of accounting periods.

Realisation Concept

This concept is part of the matching process between income and expenditure. Only when a definite sale has been made can it be realised as income — for example the date of issue of the sales invoice rather than the date of receipt of the order contract.

Money Measurement Concept

Essentially this concept recognises that a set of final accounts will only be the outcome of financial transactions. A profit and loss account or balance sheet cannot possibly measure the value to an organisation of intangibles like the morale or skill of its employees — even a football club cannot include the value (or fees paid) for its players in the balance sheet, although Tottenham Hotspur PLC have included players like Lineker and Gascoigne on their balance sheet.

The Dual-Aspect Concept (the Accounting Equation)

The basic accounting equation recognises the fact that the assets represent the business. These assets are claimed by proprietor(s) and liabilities according to the value of their ownership:

Assets	=	capital + liabilities
(The business)	=	(proprietor's claim) + (external liabilities claim)
or A	=	C
or A	=	L

In a large organisation's final accounts, the statement of accounting policies followed (for example, regarding depreciation) will often take at least one full page to declare, as the application of accounting policies is of prime importance to all those concerned about the enterprise.

"Fixed assets are stated at cost less government grants or at valuation. No depreciation is provided on the book cost attributed to the site values of freehold property. Other fixed assets are depreciated over their estimated economic life by equal annual instalments."

The Importance of Finance on Organisational Decision-making

In this section we have shown how important it is for an organisation to have adequate financial resources and that it obtains an adequate return on those resources.

A 'young' business may find itself in a poor liquidity position — as in an expanding situation the business will need to increase the amount invested in stock, also its debtors will probably be higher and more fixed assets will be required. Therefore, if the management does not consider the effect on working capital of taking on extra business then a position of insolvency may be the result. Thus if acquiring more fixed assets, the drain on capital can be greatly reduced if the assets are leased rather than purchased outright. Each potential major order must be subject to the scrutiny of the accountant in order that the effect on cash flow can be assessed and extra finance obtained if necessary, such as by obtaining an overdraft or possibly by obtaining some payment in advance from customers (as long as this is done at the time of the contractual negotiations).

If an organisation does not carefully monitor its working capital position then, even though it has a profitable product/service, it may find itself in an insolvent position. In such a case it may end up being wound up through the court action of a creditor or become the subject of a takeover by a more stable organisation. Obviously, in the latter situation, the takeover organisation is in a very strong position and can drive a very hard bargain for itself — all through the financial laxity of the smaller organisation. Thus adequacy of finance is vital for survival. Financial control is exercised by the use of budgetary control, professional stock management, capital appraisal techniques and other cost and management controls — all dealt with in this book.

As far as profit is concerned, what is considered adequate for one type of organisation may not be adequate for another. The general rule though is that the higher the element of risk involved then the higher the rate of return would need to be. The major financial indicator for profit is that of return on capital employed. Most industrial and commercial organisations aim to achieve a return on investment in excess of 20% p.a. An objective of anything less would seem to be a waste of effort — as capital can usually be safely invested with blue chip financial institutions at rates of interest of around 10% p.a. (for example, Government and Local Authority bonds). Thus an entrepreneur with capital invested in a business would want to achieve considerably above safe interest rates as a reward for the extra risks.

Throughout the text we stress the importance of profitability on business decision-making but would acknowledge that in arriving at key policy decisions, management should consider other aspects. Peter Drucker, author of many books on management, suggests there are eight key areas vital to the continual existence of any business organisation:

Profitability
Market Standing
Productivity
Product Leadership
Personal Development
Employee Attitudes
Public Responsibility
Maintaining a balance between short- and long-term objectives

Earlier in the text we examined the Public Sector where for the large part commercial profit objectives cannot be applied. Central and Local Government place a lot of emphasis on providing services on a Value For Money (v.f.m.) basis — that is, constantly examining the methods employed in providing services with a view to providing the same level of service at a lower cost or a higher level of service at the same cost. In some instances, a public sector authority has carried out a v.f.m. analysis and concluded that privatisation of parts of the service is the best option — for example, private contractor employed for household refuse collection, outside caterers used in schools, hospitals, etc.

However, the objective of all organisations must clearly be to utilise the factors of production in the most efficient manner for the benefit of the owners, employees and customers. Therefore, ensuring adequacy of finance and control of costs is of paramount importance in operating an organisation.

Exercises

1. The following is an extract from the Chairman's financial report:

   "The Company adopts the accruals concept in the preparation of its accounts with the exception of items where in the opinion of the directors the inclusion would have no material effect on the profits of the organisation."

   "The Company has a policy where it capitalises the cost of additions and major alterations to premises and records at cost."

   "The Company adopts a 'straight-line' basis when providing for depreciation of machinery, equipment and furniture. Market value is adopted for the depreciation of the Company's motor vehicles. These policies will continue until the disposal of the assets."

   "Stock is to be valued at the 'lower of cost and net realisable value', computed on the basis of selling price after deducting appropriate overheads."

   "Land and buildings will be recorded at the cost valuation."

Required:

(a) Identify the fundamental concepts in the Chairman's report.
(b) Can you identify any other concepts?
    If certain assets are valued at cost rather than current value, how might this affect the accounting reports?

2. In the private sector of business, organisations are primarily motivated by making profits. What other considerations are thought to be relevant?

3. Explain and illustrate with examples, the four fundamental concepts of accounting:

    (i) Going Concern
    (ii) Accruals
    (iii) Consistency
    (iv) Prudence

4. *Accounting Policies for the year ended 31 December 1989*

    The financial statements have been prepared under the historical cost convention.

    The principal accounting policies have remained unchanged from the previous year and are set out below.

    a) *Turnover*

    Turnover is the total amount receivable by the company in the ordinary course of business with outside customers for goods supplied as a principal and for services provided, excluding VAT, recorded on invoice.

    b) *Depreciation*

    Depreciation is calculated to write down the cost of all tangible fixed assets over their expected useful lives.

    Depreciation is by equal annual instalments in the case of leasehold premises, fixtures and fittings, and plant and machinery and is calculated on the reducing balance method in the case of motor vehicles.

The periods generally applicable are:

Leasehold premises	Period of lease
Plant and equipment	5 years
Motor vehicles	5 years
Fixtures and fittings	5 years

c) *Stock and work in progress*

Stock and work in progress is stated at the lower cost and net realisable value.

In the case of raw materials and consumable stores, cost means purchase price less trade discounts, calculated on a first in first out basis. In the case of work in progress and finished goods, cost consists of direct materials, direct labour and attributable production and other overheads. The amount of work in progress has been reduced by progress payments.

Net realisable value means estimated selling price (less trade discounts) less all further costs to completion and all costs to be incurred in marketing, selling and distribution.

Required:

a) Identify the accounting concepts which may be apparent in the above accounting policies.
b) Check terminology such as raw materials, work in progress, direct labour and net realisable value in later sections of the text.

Personal Finance

Objectives

To recognise the sources of personal finance.

To be aware of personal taxation and other deductions from pay.

To understand the need for saving and borrowing.

To be aware of the various organisations to save and borrow.

To understand the need for personal cash budgeting, cash planning and cash flow.

PART 1

Sources of Personal Finance and Personal Taxation

Most of an individual's expenditure is financed out of current income — that is, out of earnings. The majority of people work for organisations and are not self-employed. For an organisation, the design of pay systems is one of the most important of management decisions and must take into account a wide range of human and material factors. There are two major bases on which remuneration is calculated.

(a) Time rates
(b) Payment by results

Time Rates

This is the most common method and quite simply means that the employer agrees to pay and the worker to accept a fixed amount of money for a specified unit time, such as per hour, per week, per month.

Payment by Results (PBR)

The purpose of a payment by results system is to overcome, where possible, the major drawback of time rates — that of lack of incentive. A PBR system is often used where an organisations's output is fairly standard and repetitive. PBR may be associated with work study, where a given task will be given a time allowance for that task and a bonus paid on any time saved. For example

Time allowed for a task 8 hours
Time taken by an employee = 6 hours
Basic hourly rate of pay = £3.00
Bonus is paid at the rate of half the time saved

Therefore, the employee will earn £21 for the 6 hours work — calculated as follows:

Time allowed	8 hours	
Time taken	6 hours	
Time saved	2	
Bonus hours $= \frac{1}{2} \times 2$ hours $= 1$ hour		
Basic time taken	6 hours	
Gross Pay	7 hours $\times$ £3 $=$ £21.00	

Another form of PBR is the Piecework system whereby the employee is paid an agreed rate per unit produced; for instance, if the rate if 50p per 100 units then an employee who makes 24,000 units will earn gross pay of £120.

Now let us consider the systems involved in recording and paying wages.

The Recording of Wages

Wages Procedure

Documents	*Accounts Department*
Clock cards	Wages — Gross Pay
Salary cards	Deductions
Tax tables	Bank — Cash, Cheques
Pension records	Giro payments
National Insurance	Inland Revenue
Pay roll	
Pay slips	

Two of the largest payments involving expenses in business are the purchasing of stock and the payment of wages and salaries. Wages are normally paid weekly to non-office staff, whereas salaries may be paid monthly through the banking or post office systems, or by cheque.

It is becoming more frequent, however, to pay *ALL* employees through a bank or post office system as a matter of greater efficiency and, of course, better security.

The system of recording either wages or salaries is the same.

To record wages a clock card is often used to time workers in and out of work. From the card it is then possible to calculate the number of hours worked, including any overtime or loss of hours worked. The cards then provide the information needed to write up the wages account.

NAME					WKS No.	
DEPT					WK ENDING / /8	

DAY	IN	OUT	IN	OUT	BASIC TIME	OVER TIME
MON	07.00	12.00	13.00	16.00	8	0
TUE	07.00	12.00	13.00	17.30	8	1.5
WED	07.00	12.00	13.00	16.00	8	0
THU	07.00	12.00	13.00	17.30	8	1.5
FRI	07.00	12.00	13.00	16.00	8	0
SAT	08.00	10.00			0	2
SUN						

NUMBER OF HOURS WORKED

BASIC TIME 40	OVERTIME 5	TOTAL 45

RATE OF PAY £ 2.50 PER HOUR

40 Hours @ £2.50 per hour   £100.00

5 Overtime Hours @ £3.75 per hour   £ 18.75

======

GROSS PAY £ 118.75

======

Deductions

Income Tax. The common broad band of tax paid by most employees in 1990–91 was levied at 25%. This is the basic tax.
National Insurance contributions, levied at a certain percentage rate, is paid by both employee and employer.

The above deductions are statutory and are demanded by law to be paid to the Inland Revenue. The rates tend to get changed from time to time by the Chancellor of the Exchequer in his Budget Statement.

Tax tables and National Contribution tables are available to payroll clerks to enable them to make the appropriate deductions. These deductions are variable because they depend on each employee's personal allowances.

Other deductions such as pension scheme contributions, social fund, trade union fund and so on, may be voluntary. The example below is based on a tax rate of 27% and National Insurance 9% of gross.

Recording

		£
(a)	The Gross Pay is calculated	118.75
(b)	If a pension or superannuation scheme is paid this is deducted from gross before tax is charged. Say	12.50
		106.25
(c)	Income tax payable*:	
	From tax tables. 'Free pay' is allowed to the employee before tax is deducted. Free pay is taken from the employee's tax code and represents allowances which reduces his taxable pay.	
	Tax payable (27% rate) 15.12	
(d)	National Insurance contribution (9% rate) 10.69	
(e)	Other deductions:	
	Works Social Fund 1.00 Trade Union Fund 0.45	
	Total Deductions	27.26
	Net Pay	78.99

*Free pay £50.25, leaving £56 as taxable pay (£106.25 − £50.25)
27% tax on £56 = £15.12

Pay Roll

Once gross pay is calculated from all the clock cards and salary cards or sheets, and the appropriate deductions have been made from work sheets, the total of the employees pay is entered on a pay roll. The pay roll lists all employees and shows their:

(a) Gross rates of pay
(b) Superannuation or Pension deductions
(c) Statutory deductions

> Income Tax
> National Insurance Contributions
> both employee and employers

(d) Amount of tax free pay (taken from employees Tax Code)
(e) Other deductions

> Trade Union funds
> Social funds
> Savings

(f) Total deductions
(g) The net amount payable

The pay roll is used to transfer details in total, of gross pay, National Insurance Contributions, Income Tax and other deductions to the accounting records.

Pay Slip (or Pay Advice)

The Pay Slip is an individual employee's pay details informing him of the amount of pay he has earned over a given period of time. Gross pay, deductions of tax and National Insurance and other details are shown, advising the employee of his net pay and also his earnings to date in the current tax year. The pay slip details are simply taken from the pay roll.

Below is an example of an employee's pay slip (or pay advice).

Personal Tax

Everybody in full-time employment is liable to pay income tax through the PAYE (Pay As You Earn) system — that is, where employers deduct the amount due from their employees' gross wages. The amount of tax an

```
                    P A Y     A D V I C E

Description       Code       Hours       Rate      Amount          Total

  000 334578      BR         18.50       1190.     220.15
                              2.00        850.      17.00          237.15
Deductions
National Insurance    :    11.60
Taxation              :    64.52
Superannuation        :     3.50                                    79.62

                                             Amount Payable:       157.53
                                                                  _____

------------------------------------------------------------------------
Accumulations
Taxable Pay            Income Tax          Nat. Ins.
  508.73                 147.32              30.97

------------------------------------------------------------------------

National Insurance Number       Tax Code          Period Ending / No.
  WL 03 7542 B                    0442 H             30.04.88         16

Works Number     44842
                 CHQ
Name             D. ROGERS
```

employee has to pay is based on the size of income and on what allowances and reliefs are claimed. Everybody is allowed a personal allowance — the allowances we are mainly concerned with are:

1990–1991 Tax Rates

	£
Single person's allowance	3,005
Married couples	1,720
Personal & Married Couples	4,725

This means that the amount of tax paid will be gross pay less allowances. For example:

    a.   A married man earning £12,000 p.a. will pay tax on (12,000 – 4,725) = £7,275.

    b.   A single person earning £12,000 p.a. will pay tax on (12,000 – 3,005) = £8,995.

In addition to personal allowances you may be entitled to further reliefs, these would include:

   i. Interest paid on mortgages
  ii. Pension fund contributions
 iii. Subscriptions to professional bodies

Types of mortgage

There are two main types of mortgage:

  Endowment Mortgage and
  Capital and Interest Mortgage (sometimes called repayment mortgage)

With an Endowment Mortgage the monthly payment falls into two parts. Firstly there is the interest payment on the whole of the mortgage, paid to the lender over the full term. The second payment is to an insurance company for an Endowment Policy, with payments again being made throughout the term of the loan. Should the Borrower die during the mortgage term, the Endowment policy guarantees payment of the loan. At the end of the mortgage term, it will usually mature with a value sufficient to repay the full loan, often with a cash surplus as well, although this is not guaranteed.

With a Capital and Interest Mortgage the monthly payment is made up of partly interest on the outstanding loan and partly capital repayment of the loan itself. In the early years the majority of the monthly payment is used to pay the interest, with only a small part being used as capital repayment. Then, as the outstanding loan is gradually repaid, the interest charges reduce so that, eventually the major part of the monthly payment is used to repay capital.

Interest Paid on Mortgages

To encourage house ownership, the policy of successive governments has been to allow relief from interest paid on mortgages.

There is a 'ceiling' to the amount of mortgage on which relief of interest can be claimed (currently £30,000). To make administration easier the Inland Revenue introduced the MIRAS (Mortgage Interest Relief At Source) scheme. Under MIRAS most people with a mortgage obtain their tax relief through the lender, rather than have it added to their allowances. Their repayments to the lender are paid on a net basis — that is, tax relief already deducted. Some people with mortgages exceeding the relief of interest ceiling still get their tax relief via their tax coding numbers.

Pension Fund Allowances

To encourage people to make financial provisions for their old age, pension fund contributions are free from tax. How this works is that a person's taxable pay is his gross pay less pension contribution. For example

Gross Salary £15,000
Pension Fund Contribution 5% of Salary

Taxable Pay will be: 15,000
                                                750
                                         ─────
                                        £14,250
                                         ─────

Note: Any personal allowances' etc. would further reduce taxable pay.

Subscription to Professional Bodies

Subscriptions paid to many professional bodies can be 'set off' against tax. This means that a person's tax code will be increased by the amount of the subscription.

Taxable Income and National Insurance

Each year everyone in work should receive from their local tax inspectors office an annual return to complete — in practice, because of the volume of work, many people do not get one every year. On this form the employee gives various information including employment details, subscriptions paid and mortgage interest paid. From this information your tax code is established by the inspector of taxes and notified to employer and employee.

   The tax code allocated determines the amount of 'free pay'. For example a married man on a salary of £15,000 paying mortgage interest on a loan of £32,000 at 10% and an annual subscription to the Chartered Association of Certified Accountants of £65 will have the following allowances:

	Tax Year 1990–1991 £
Personal & Married couples	4,725
Mortgage Interest Relief 10% of £30,000	3,000
Annual Subscription	65
	7,790

The tax code allocated will be 779H, which means that he will pay tax at 25% on £7,210 (that is, £15,000 − £7,790). Tax to pay = £1,802.50

Tax Tables

There are two books of Tables: Table 'A' gives the amount of free pay and Table 'B' gives the amount of tax payable. A full description of the payroll routine is not necessary for the Finance Unit, therefore it has been omitted from this text.

Tax Rates

Income tax is a progressive tax — that is, the higher a persons income the more tax is paid. Not only is the taxable income higher but the rate of tax also increases — the intention is that the better off contribute proportionately more than the not so well off. Income tax has, therefore, been arranged in 'bands of taxable income'. In 1990–91 the rates were:

1–20,700	at	25%
20,701 & above	at	40%

National Insurance

An employee's National Insurance contribution is not officially regarded as personal tax but as contributions cannot be avoided then effectively National Insurance can be regarded as a tax on income.

National Insurance contributions normally have to be paid if an employee earns more than a certain amount – the lower earnings limit in 1990–91 was £46 with an upper limit of £350.

As with Income Tax, these rates are subject to periodic revision by the Chancellor of the Exchequer and the DHSS provides employers with contribution tables to enable them to make the appropriate deduction. In 1990–91 the rates were:

Up to £46 per week	2% rate
£46.01 to £350	9% rate

Examples of Pay Using 1990–1991 rates for tax and NIC

1. A married person earning £100 per week. What would he receive as net pay?

National Insurance (NIC):

	£
1st £46 × 2%	.92p
(46 – 100) £54 × 9%	4.86
	5.78

Taxation:
Personal & Married Couple's
Allowance £4,725 p.a.

= £90.87 per week tax free

Taxable income = (100 – 90.87)
$\qquad\qquad\quad$ = £9.13 × 25%
$\qquad\qquad\quad$ = £2.28 tax

		£
Gross Pay:		100

Deductions:

NIC	£5.78	
Tax	£2.28	
		8.06
Net Pay		91.94

2. A married person earning £17,160 per year. What would he receive as net pay per week?

Gross pay per week: £17,160/52
$\qquad\qquad\qquad\qquad$ £330 per week

National Insurance (NIC):

	£
1st £46 × 2%	.92p
(46 – 330) £284 × 9%	25.56
	26.48

Pension: 6% of gross = £19.80 per week.

Taxation:

Personal & Married Couple's
Allowance £4,725 p.a.

   =   £90.87 per week tax free
+ pension £19.80 per week tax free

Taxable income = (330 − 110.67)
               = £219.33 × 25%
               = £54.83 tax

	£
Gross Pay:	330

Deductions:

NIC	£26.48	
Tax	£54.83	
Pension	£19.80	101.11
Net Pay		228.89

3. A single person earning £150 per week and overtime of 8 hours at £4.75
    per hour. What would he receive as net pay per week?

Gross pay per week:	£150
+ overtime	£ 38
	188

National Insurance (NIC):

	£
1st £46 × 2%	.92p
(46 − 188) £142 × 9%	12.78
	13.70

Taxation:

Single person's allowance £3,005 p.a.
  = £57.79 per week tax free

Taxable income = (188 − 57.79)
               = £130.21 × 25%
               = £32.55 tax

	£
Gross Pay:	188

Deductions:

NIC	£13.70
Tax	£32.55

46.25

Net Pay	141.75

Exercises

1. Calculate the net pay of Harry Smith from the following:

No. of Hours	39
Basic Week:	36 hours @ £4.00 per hour
Overtime:	Paid @ $1\frac{1}{2}$ rate per hour

Deductions	
National Insurance:	@ 9% of gross pay.
Taxable income:	
Harry is allowed	£42.30 tax free pay
	Assume Basic rate of tax at 30%

Other:	
Trade Union	0.85
Social fund	1.25
Pension	2.50

2. Calculate the gross pay for the following employees:

Jack	46 hours
Fred	43 hours
Harry	51 hours

The basic working week is 38 hours @ £2.80 hour.
Overtime pay over 38 hours is at time and a quarter.

3. Calculate the gross pay of an employee who is paid a basic rate for attendance and piece-rate according to how much he produces:

    Attendance money: £1.25 per hour

    Production (piece-rates)
    (a) from 500 to 1,000 units   2p per unit
    (b) from 1,001 to 1,500 units   3p per unit
    (c) over 1,500   2.5p per unit

How much will he earn on a 40 hour week if he produces 1,650 units?

4. Calculate the gross pay of S. Robbins from the following:

    A bonus system operates where the employee is paid a bonus of half-time saved.

	Time Allowed	Time Taken
Monday	12	8
Tuesday	10	8
Wednesday	11	8
Thursday	11	8
Friday	10	7

    S. Robbin's basic hourly rate is £3 per hour for a 39 hour week.

5. The following is a clock card for B. Balderstone who works a 38 hour basic week, and all additional hours are counted as overtime, at time-and-a-half. His basic rate of pay is £2.40 per hour. As far as clocking in or out is concerned employees are allowed, a 2 minute tolerance either way (this means that arriving at 8.02 counts as 8.00 and leaving at 18.32 counts as 18.30).
    From the above information calculate the gross pay, clearly showing the overtime amount. (You may use the blank sections on the clock card if you wish.)

    For the purpose of exercises 6, 7 and 8 assume the following:

Single Person's Allowance	£2,335
Married Allowance	3,655
Wife's earned income allowance	2,335
Standard Rate of Tax	25%

```
┌─────────────────────────────────────────────────────────────┐
│  NAME    B BALDERSTONE          WKS No. 807                  │
│                                                              │
│  DEPT    ASSEMBLY          WK ENDING  9/ 8 /86               │
├───────┬─────────────────────────────┬───────────────────────┤
│ DAY   │ IN    OUT    IN    OUT      │ BASIC      OVER        │
│       │                             │ TIME       TIME        │
├───────┼─────────────────────────────┼───────────────────────┤
│ MON   │ 8.00   12.01  13.00  18.32  │                       │
├───────┼─────────────────────────────┼───────────────────────┤
│ TUE   │ 7.59   12.02  13.00  17.31  │                       │
├───────┼─────────────────────────────┼───────────────────────┤
│ WED   │ 8.01   12.00  13.01  18.33  │                       │
├───────┼─────────────────────────────┼───────────────────────┤
│ THU   │ 7.58   12.00  13.00  18.02  │                       │
├───────┼─────────────────────────────┼───────────────────────┤
│ FRI   │ 8.00   12.01  13.01  17.00  │                       │
├───────┼─────────────────────────────┼───────────────────────┤
│ SAT   │                             │                       │
├───────┼─────────────────────────────┼───────────────────────┤
│ SUN   │                             │                       │
├───────┴─────────────────────────────┴───────────────────────┤
│                                                              │
│              NUMBER OF HOURS WORKED                          │
├─────────────────┬────────────────────┬───────────────────────┤
│ BASIC TIME      │ OVERTIME           │ TOTAL                 │
├─────────────────┴────────────────────┴───────────────────────┤
│         RATE OF PAY £      PER HOUR                          │
├──────────────────────────────────────────────────────────────┤
│ ____Hours @ £_____  per hour      £                        │
│ ____Overtime                                                 │
│     Hours @ £_____  per hour      £                        │
│                                     ======                   │
│                    GROSS PAY £                               │
│                                     ======                   │
└──────────────────────────────────────────────────────────────┘
```

6. Alfie Biggs is a married man and his wife does not work. Their financial circumstances are as follows:

a. Alfie's gross salary is £14,000 p.a.
b. Alfie's contribution to his company's pension scheme is 6% of his gross salary.
c. Interest on the couple's mortgage during the year will be £2,100. (Mortgage amount = £24,000.)

Calculate Alfie's tax liability for the year.

7. Harold Jarman is a single person. His financial circumstances are as follows:

   a. Harold's gross salary is £17,000.
   b. Harold's contribution to his company's pension scheme is 5% of his gross salary.
   c. Interest on his mortgage during the year will be £2,500. (Mortgage amount = £29,000.)
   d. Allowed professional subscriptions amount to £120.

   Calculate Harold's tax liability for the year.

8. Pamela Hale is a single person. Her financial circumstances are as follows:

   a. Pamela's gross salary is £15,000 p.a.
   b. Pamela's contribution to her company's pension scheme is 6% of her gross salary.
   c. Interest on her mortgage during the year will be £2,200 (Mortgage amount = £26,000.)
   d. Allowed professional subscriptions amount to £70.

   Calculate Pamela's tax liability for the year.

9. A single person works a basic 36 hour week and earns £180. All overtime is paid at one and a quarter. In a week where he works 43 hours, calculate his net pay, using 1990–1991 rates for tax and NIC.

10. A married couple earn the following rates of pay:

    One earns a salary of £14,820 per annum and pays 4% of the salary towards a pension fund.

    The other person earns £120 per week. Calculate their separate net incomes per week, using the 1990 – 1991 rates for tax and NIC.
    Assume the married couple's allowance to be taken on the annual salary.

PART 2

Saving and Borrowing

What is Saving?

Saving is refraining from spending all of your income and setting money aside for future use.

Reasons for Saving

People save for many reasons:

    (a) as a protection against inflation
    (b) as a way of achieving capital growth
    (c) as a form of security, especially for retirement
    (d) as a way of achieving an asset, such as saving for a specific item like a motor bike
    (e) as a source of income

In this part of the text we are mainly concerned with savings as a source of income.

The small saver can invest money in several different ways, the principal agencies concerned being:

    (a) The National Savings Movement
    (b) The Building Societies
    (c) The Commercial Banks
    (d) Investments in stocks and shares either directly or through unit trusts and investment trusts

Investing Money

(a) The National Savings Movement

The Movement offers the following:

    (a) Ordinary savings account
    (b) Investment account
    (c) Savings certificates
    (d) Index-linked savings certificates
    (e) Premium Bonds

The Ordinary savings account pays the first 'slice' of interest tax free. The Investment account pays interest at a much higher rate but is taxable and one month's notice of withdrawal is required. One of the main advantages of the Ordinary NSB account is that of convenience — there is always an NSB somewhere near and they are open $5\frac{1}{2}$ days per week. However, with the increasing provision of electronic cash dispensers by banks and building societies, this is not the competitive factor it used to be. National Savings certificates offer a fixed return over a fixed period — the saver will lose interest if the certificate is cashed before the period expires. During the mid-1970s, Index-linked savings certificates were introduced to preserve the capital value of peoples savings during periods of high inflation. Premium bonds are not really a form of saving but in effect are a 'coward's form of gambling'.

(b) The Building Societies

Building societies are now administered under the terms of the 1986 Building Society Act for the purpose of assisting the objective of home ownership. In order to attract funds, the Societies offer a wide range of saving schemes:

    (a) Paid up shares
    (b) SAYE Schemes
    (c) 'High Interest' Accounts

An important feature about building society interest is that it is paid to the investor net of tax. What this means is that if you pay tax at the standard rate you are not liable for further tax on the interest. Building society interest is not tax free as the tax is paid direct to the Inland Revenue by the Society. This is called Composite Rate Tax and it cannot be reclaimed by non-tax payers.

Paid Up Shares

Each £1 invested purchases a fully paid-up share on which interest is earned. Withdrawals can be paid on demand up to certain limits (say £1,000) but for larger sums a short period of notice may be required. Unlike company shares, building society shares cannot be traded on the Stock Exchange.

SAYE Schemes

For investors who are prepared to save on a regular basis, a higher rate of interest is paid. The investor agrees to save a fixed sum each month, often by having the agreed sum deducted from gross wages by his employer on behalf of the Building Society.

Higher Interest Accounts

Most Societies have some form of 'Higher Interest' scheme usually with a minimum investment, say £500, which requires notice of withdrawal — often one month or 91 days. But, because of increased competition, the notice of withdrawal aspect is now often waived if there is a minimum limit to the account.

Like the NSB (Post Office), most Building Societies are open on Saturday mornings and some such as the Halifax Building Society now have electronic cashpoints for both depositing and withdrawing cash.

(c) The Commercial Banks

In essence there are two main types of account that a private individual will tend to use:

(1) Current Account
(2) Deposit Account

Interest is paid on a deposit account but not on a current account. Seven days' notice is required for withdrawals from a deposit account but most banks waive this period of notice. With a current account, cash is repayable on demand and a cheque book is issued. Most banks currently make no bank charges as long as the current account remains in surplus.

Increasingly in the 1980s the Clearing Banks have introduced high interest accounts, which compete against the Building Societies. There are high interest current accounts and high interest deposit accounts — the latter usually requiring a minimum deposit of £1,000 and paying 2–2½% above the normal deposit account rate; more interest is paid on larger sums deposited.

(d) Investments in Stocks and Shares

Earlier, describing sources of business finance, we dealt with types of shares. During the 1980s more private individuals have invested in shares with a view to receiving a regular income (dividends) and some capital appreciation. A popular way to invest in stocks and shares has been through unit trusts, many of which are run by banks. The trust uses people's savings and invests their money in a wide range of equities and gilts, so spreading the risk. Specialised unit trusts also exist. One of the major influences in the trend towards wider share ownership has been the privatisation of former public sector institutions — in financial terms, British Telecom and British Gas were the largest issues and were responsible for several million small investors.

Buying on Credit

Most of the expenditure of a private individual, such as rent, rates, light, heat, petrol, entertainment costs, etc., is paid for out of current income. In accountancy terms this is called *Revenue Expenditure*.

But there are occasions when an individual wishes to purchase a major item, such as a TV, Motor Car or Freezer, and wishes to borrow in order to make the purchase. In accountancy terms this is called *Capital Expenditure* — that is, the item purchased will give several years of useful life.

The major sources of loan finance include:

(a) Commercial Banks — personal loan or overdraft
(b) Hire Purchase Finance Companies
(c) Credit Card Companies

(a) Commercial Banks

The procedure for obtaining either a personal loan or an overdraft is a little different. If an overdraft is required, say for 3 months, a simple letter of application to the bank manager will usually suffice. The Manager will arrange to mark the account with an overdraft limit — usually a few hundred pounds — for the pre-set period. With an overdraft, interest is only paid when one is overdrawn, on a daily basis, and is linked to the Bank's base rate.

A major company may be charged 1% over base rate, whereas a smaller company may be charged 3 or 4% over base and a personal borrower may pay

6 or 7% over base rate. The deciding factor is the degree of risk — that is, the safer the loan the lower the interest rate.

For a personal loan, most banks do not require to interview the applicant unless there is some problem. The customer will complete an application form giving full details of his income from all sources, and his outgoings (expenses). The customer has to state on his application form:

How much he wishes to borrow
For what purpose he wishes to borrow the money
How he intends to repay it — his income source
How long he wants the loan for
What contribution he is making from his own savings towards the cost of the item.

This then introduces cash budgets; the preparation of such a cash budget would be essential in this instance. If the borrower is not a well-known customer the bank will make general status enquiries as to his job, salary, dependants and other financial commitments. Essentially, if the Manager or Loans Officer is satisfied that a customer is creditworthy, then a loan can be arranged — after all, this is why banks exist and how they make much of their profits. For a large loan the bank may require some form of collateral (security) such as property or life assurance policy.

One of the main advantages of bank finance is that the borrower has the freedom to purchase the actual goods wherever he prefers — which means that the best discount price can be obtained. Furthermore, the title to the goods moves to the buyer immediately, whereas in a Hire Purchase situation this is not the case until the final payment is made.

Example of a Personal Loan

	£
Amount of loan required	600
Interest at 10% for 24 months	120

$$720 \div 24 = £30$$

that is, 24 monthly instalments of £30

Note: The true rate of interest (APR) is approximately 19.85% p.a. (that is, nearly double the flat rate).

In addition, the bank may charge an arrangement fee in the above case; this may be in the region of £10.

(b) Hire Purchase Companies

Many retail stores offer HP facilities — sometimes through their own 'inhouse' company or by using an outside HP company. In most circumstances the rate of interest charged is much higher than that charged by the banks. The advantage to the customer is that obtaining HP at the point of purchase is convenient; that is, you do not have to apply to or visit the bank, just complete the appropriate agreement form.

A major drawback of buying on HP is that the buyer does not own the goods until the final instalment has been paid. The contract that exists is that the customer will hire the goods for the duration of the contract, paying rent for their use, and will complete the purchase at the end of the period. Until the final payment, the supplier has certain rights about regaining possession. Therefore, an individual would be well advised to look very seriously at the alternatives before purchasing on hire purchase.

(c) Credit Card Companies

A credit card enables the holder to buy goods or services up to individual limits at shops, restaurants, garages, etc. which belong to the scheme, without paying at the time of purchase. The card-holder presents the card and the supplier completes a voucher in triplicate at the same time, imprinting the number of the card on the vouchers, which are then signed by the card holder.

The main types of Credit Card available are

(1) Barclaycard
(2) Access Card
(3) American Express   These are really charge cards, as the
(4) Diners Card   balance *has* to be paid each month

Although these are mainly backed by different banks, cards are available to any suitable applicant, regardless of the bank to which he belongs. Note that retail companies such as Debenhams, Tesco, Comet and Marks & Spencer, now operate their own in-house credit card schemes.

Advantages to card-holder:

(1) Large sums of money do not have to be carried about.
(2) Cash, up to a certain sum, can be withdrawn from any bank (interest is charged immediately on such transactions).
(3) One cheque only is written each month to cover all transactions.
(4) If used sensibly to time purchases carefully, a credit card can be economical (55/59 days credit can be obtained).
(5) Barclaycard also doubles as a cheque guarantee card for cheques drawn on Barclays Bank only.

Disadvantages to card-holder:

(1) There is always the temptation to spend more than one can afford.
(2) Interest rates on accounts not paid in full are much higher than overdraft or personal loan rates — it is an expensive way to borrow!

Advantages to dealers:

(1) Higher sales result.
(2) Payment is assured (as against cheques which may be returned after goods are taken)

Disadvantages to dealers:

(1) Vouchers have to be completed, distributed to card organisations and checked against payments from card organisations.
(2) A small charge is raised by the card organisations on every transaction, usually $1\frac{1}{2}$–2% of the cost of the sales.

PART 3

Cash Budgeting

"Annual income twenty pounds — annual expenditure nineteen pounds nineteen and six, result happiness.

Annual income twenty pounds — annual expenditure twenty pounds and six pence —result misery"

(Mr McCawber — Charles Dickens' famous character)

It is just as important for an individual to consider cash flow as it is for a business. For an individual or a business to be unable to meet commitments is at least embarrassing, will certainly cause anxiety and can lead to bankruptcy.

It is recommended that an individual compiles a budget on a regular basis. The mechanics of drawing up a budget are very simple, the skill lies in forecasting income and expenditure. Certain expenditure is more or less known and can be regarded as fixed in nature; for example, mortgage payments, rent, rates, insurance premiums, car licence, HP commitments, etc. — in all these cases we know when the amount is due and often how much. Other expenditure such as food and drink, entertainment, petrol and oil, holidays, clothing, etc. is much more variable and much more in the control of the individual.

Example of a Personal Cash Budget

Phillip, a single person, has the following regular income and commitments.

Income
Net monthly salary £550.
Income from investments received at three-monthly intervals commencing in March of £40 (net of tax).

Known expenditure (fixed)
Rent £140 monthly; rates £20 monthly; car tax £100 due in February; gas bill due in March estimated at £80; electricity bill due in February estimated at

£70; annual life assurance premium of £50 due in January; instalment on the car of £60 per month.

Unknown expenditure (variable)

Food and drink, say £20 per week; entertainment, say £25 per week; clothing £15 per week.

Other information

Assume Phillip has £100 on 1 January and wishes to prepare a cash budget to cover 3 months. Note that the expenditure in the 'unknown' category can be tailored to what can be afforded — the cash budget would indicate how much (if anything) can be saved for the future.

First of all it is probably best to make a schedule of payments:

Schedule of Payments

	Jan.	Feb.	March
Weeks in month	(4)	(4)	(5)
	£	£	£
Rent	140	140	140
Rates	20	20	20
Car Tax	—	100	—
Gas	—	—	80
Electricity	—	70	—
Life Assurance	50	—	—
HP	60	60	60
Food and Drink	80	80	100
Entertainment	100	100	125
Clothing	60	60	75
	510	630	600*

*These totals can now be transferred to the expenditure line of the cash budget.

Now we can show the cash budget:

Cash Budget

	Jan.	Feb.	March
	£	£	£
Balance brought forward	100	140	60
Income	+ 550	550	590
	650	690	650
Expenditure	− 510	630	600
Balance carried forward	140	60	50

Thus Phillip can tell from the above projected cash flow that he must be very careful during this period as his cash in hand will reduce from £140 to £50. In addition he would have problems coping with an unexpected event, such as a car repair bill. Phillip should, therefore, be as prudent as possible with his spending on entertainment and clothing during this period.

By preparing a cash budget it will be known in advance if any surplus or deficit is likely to occur. This will mean that one can decide the most advantageous means of investing any surplus and can make proper plans to fund any deficit. A short-term deficit of a month or two might best be coped with on a credit card, but for longer periods bank finance may be the solution. The fact that one has prepared a cash flow plan, showing when one expects to be back in surplus, will impress a bank manager, and assist in convincing him that one is a 'good risk'.

Exercises

1. Margaret, a single person, has the following regular income and commitments:

   Income
   Net monthly salary of £500

   'Known' expenditure (fixed)
   Housekeeping contribution to parents £20 per week; driving lesson £10 per week; HP payment £25 per month; monthly rail ticket £35; life assurance payment due in July £60.

   'Unknown' expenditure (variable)
   Margaret plans to spend around £40 per week on entertainment, clothing, LPs etc.

   Other information
   On 1 June Margaret has £80 in her current account and maintains a building society account.

   Required:

   (a) Draw up a personal cash flow budget for June to August inclusive, clearly showing the balance in her current account at each month end. Assume 4 weeks in June and July and 5 in August.
   (b) Make recommendations as to what Margaret can do with any resulting surplus/deficit. You may assume no bank charges will occur as long as her current account is not overdrawn.

2. Cyril and Cecelia are a married couple with no children and have the following commitments:

Income
Cyril has a net monthly salary of £600 per month (payable on last day of month).
Cecelia has a net monthly salary of £450 per month (payable on the 10th day of each month).

'Known' expenditure (fixed)
Rent £200 per month; regular building society savings subscription of £150 per month; HP payment of £30 per month; gas bill of £70 due in February; electricity bill of £80 due in January; credit card statement balance of £90 due on 12 January; car insurance of £90 due in March; petrol and oil £10 per week.

'Unknown' expenditure (variable)
Food and drink, say £30 per week; entertainment, say £30 per week; clothing £20 per week.

Other information
On 1 January their joint current account has £200 in it.

Required:

(a) Draw up a cash budget for the couple for January to March inclusive. Assume 4 weeks in January and February and 5 weeks in March.
(b) Assuming that Cyril and Cecelia like to keep about £200 in their joint current account, will they be able to save any more than they already do during the period? If so, how much in each month?

3. Jack, a single person, has just had to leave a well-paid job and take up a lower paid job. His 'new' income and existing commitments are:

Income
Net monthly salary of £450.

'Known' expenditure
Rent £150 monthly 3 weeks' notice of termination is required, and the rent is payable in advance; rates £25 monthly; electricity bill £50 due in May; HP payments of £40 monthly; gas bill £40 due in June.

'Unknown' expenditure
Jack has only been used to opening the odd pack of cornflakes and making tea and coffee, etc. at a cost of about £5 per week. He has been eating out a lot up until now, at a cost of about £60 per week. Jack has also been spending about £50 per week on clothes and entertainment.

Other information

On 1 April Jack starts his new job and has £250 in a current account and £600 in a building society account. His parents live nearby and have always maintained a room for his use.

Required:

(a) Assuming Jack maintains his existing style of living, draw up a personal cash flow budget for the period April to June inclusive. Start with an opening balance figure of £850 (£250 + £600). Assume each month consists of 4 weeks.
(b) Clearly Jack will be forced to alter his existing style of living — you are asked to make suggestions as to what he should do and to prepare a cash flow budget taking account of your suggestions.

4. *Situation*

Robert Cambell, a single person, has worked as a clerk for a large insurance company for three years. Robert left school at 18 with two 'A' levels, and is currently part way through the examinations of the Institute of Insurance. Roger has had one promotion since joining the Company and can expect to gain further promotions in the future. Robert shares a flat with a colleague. Robert is also hoping to purchase a car, and his parents will pay any deposit.

Information

  (i) Robert's current gross salary is £8,000 p.a., payable weekly.
 (ii) The single person's personal tax allowance is £2,400.
(iii) Robert pays 5% of his salary as pension contribution.
 (iv) Robert is not entitled to any other tax allowances.
  (v) Robert has to pay National Insurance at the rate of £12.30 per week.
 (vi) Robert has no other deductions from his salary.
(vii) Income Tax is 30% (standard rate).
(viii) Robert's known weekly personal expenditure is:
       Rent £25 per week and food and drink £20 per week.
       Bus fares £5 per week.
 (ix) In addition to the above weekly expenditure Robert is aware of the following bills to pay:
       January — pay off credit card balance £80.
       February — Life Assurance premium due £70.
       March — snooker club subscription £20.
  (x) On 1 January, Robert has £40 in his current account.
 (xi) Current interest charged on personal loans = 10% flat rate.

Tasks

A Compute Robert's net *weekly* salary.
B Using the above information, prepare a personal cash flow budget for January to March inclusive. (Assume 4 weeks in January, 4 in February and 5 in March.)
C How much on average could Robert spend per month during the period January – March inclusive on entertainment and clothing.
D Robert has now seen a car he likes and needs to obtain a loan of £1,800.
  (i) Calculate the monthly repayments over 2 years.
  (ii) Calculate the monthly repayments over 3 years.
E Robert has written to you, his uncle, and asked for your advice on how he should go about financing the purchase. You, therefore, have to write a letter to Robert giving him general advice on how to obtain finance, what sources are available, and specific advice regarding Robert's circumstances. You should also advise Robert on whether to borrow for 2 or 3 years.

Note: You may assume knowledge of all the preceding information.

Financial Planning for Decision-making

Objectives

To prepare the Manufacturing Account and to identify and classify the different areas of cost.

To understand marginal costing and its use in business situations.

To understand the importance of 'contribution'.

To calculate break-even and the preparation of a break-even chart.

To understand the need for budgeting and cash planning and its importance to business in terms of forecasting results.

To appreciate the significance of alternative investments concerning expenditure on capital projects.

There is a wide range of different business organisations in our economic environment which require financial reports. The larger the organisation, the more important it is to provide it with essential information so that management can make objective and sound decisions.

A manufacturing organisation which makes its own products wants to know, among other things, how much it costs to produce its goods and how these costs are divided in terms of costs directly or indirectly related to production. From these figures it is possible to analyse cost types and their effect on production levels and price.

A business needs to know its total costs of production for the purpose of setting its selling price. Given a certain production capacity (for example, 10,000 units) and a total cost (absorption cost) of say £100,000, the cost per unit is £10. From this, a selling price can be determined by adding a sum to the cost, a margin considered from what the market will pay.

357

Marginal costing is the area of cost which considers price in relation to varying levels of production and, in particular, it takes account of variable costs (costs sensitive to production levels) as distinct from fixed costs (costs insensitive to production levels). Once fixed costs have been covered, only variable costs affect the cost of output and any extra capacity produced generally means more profit.

Marginal costing also relates to what is known as 'break-even' — that is, the point where all costs are covered and any further sales mean profit. Break-even point is an important facet of information for management because there is then an awareness of when profit is made.

Organisations are very concerned about profits; management not only needs to calculate current results but to plan and estimate future profits in order to compare estimates with actual figures when they are available. Usually firms budget (or plan) 12 months ahead and try to forecast their expected revenues and expenditures as a basis for sound planning. This provides a framework for 'thinking ahead' in terms of expectations, targets and planned profits. Actual results may then be compared, analysed and debated. Forward planning gives management a platform on which to base their decisions:

Were results as planned?
Were results not as planned?
If not, why not?!
And so forth.

Capital appraisal looks at alternative methods of investment for the purpose of finding the most profitable returns on capital expenditure. Whether to invest in new equipment or machinery or simply lease it. Whether to invest in project A rather than project B or project C. Whether to extend the premises or buy a share in another business, and so forth. Estimations will be made to see which investment looks the most promising in terms of profit and length of time invested. Whether the estimations are reliable and accurate depends on time itself. In business, financial information is essential to guide the decisions made by management and owners of business, but it does have its limitations. Nothing is really certain, is it?

PART 1

The Manufacturing Account

The purpose of preparing a manufacturing account is to calculate the cost of production — that is, the factory cost as distinct from distribution costs and administration expenses.

The cost of manufacturing a product or a specific quantity of units over a specific period of time is basically composed of three parts:

(a) *Direct Costs*. These are directly involved with the making of the product, including the labour, the materials and any direct expense directly related to production.

  (i) Direct Labour. The factory wages related to the workers making the product.

 (ii) Direct Materials. The raw materials and components specifically used to make the product, such as the tube, frame, stand and electrical/electronic parts of a television set.

(iii) Direct Expenses. There are few of these because most of them tend to be indirect and related to factory overheads. Direct expenses include direct power, the hiring or leasing of special equipment or plant for production, or the payment of royalties for patents or trade marks used in production.

  The total of direct costs = the PRIME COST

(b) *Indirect Costs*. These refer to the factory overheads and include indirect labour, materials and expenses.

  (i) Indirect Labour. This relates to the factory employees but excludes direct wages. Factory storemen, cleaners, progress chasers, production controllers, engineers, draftsmen are some examples.

 (ii) Indirect Materials. These may relate to factory lubricants, fluids, stationery, safety clothing and any other materials used in the factory, but excluding direct materials.

(iii) Indirect Expenses. These relate to any factory overhead but exclude indirect labour and materials. Factory rates, insurance, light and heat, power (if not direct), rent, depreciation of factory equipment and any general factory expenses are examples.

(c) *Work-in-Progress.* This relates to the stock of partly finished goods both at the beginning and end of a financial period, such as TVs partly completed on the assembly line.

In the preparation of the manufacturing account, the direct costs (prime cost) and indirect costs (factory overheads) are added to give the sub-total of direct and indirect costs.

The work-in-progress stock at the beginning is added to the total of direct and indirect costs.

The work-in-progress stock at the end is deducted from the aggregate addition of direct and indirect cost and stock of work-in-progress at the beginning. Some factories (such as those concerned with food) may not have work-in-progress stock, because no assembly or process requiring valuation is involved.

Presentation of Manufacturing Account

	£	£	£
Direct Costs			
Stock of raw materials (Jan. 1)	2,000		
+ Purchases of raw materials	25,000		
	27,000		
− Stock of raw materials (Dec. 31)	3,000	24,000	
Direct Manufacturing Wages	19,000		
+ Accrued Wages	1,000	20,000	
Hire of Special Equipment		1,000	
Prime Cost			45,000
Indirect Costs			
Safety clothing		1,000	
Indirect factory wages		12,000	
Depreciation of plant	500		
Factory rates, insurance	2,500		
Factory maintenance	4,000		
Factory general expenses	1.000	8,000	
Factory Overheads			21,000
			66,000

Work-in-Progress
  + Stock (Jan. 1)   1,500
                                                                ───────
                                                                67,500
  − Stock (Dec. 31)   2,500
                                                                ───────
            Cost of Production   65,000
            (Transferred to Trading a/c)   ───────

The Cost of Production per Unit

If 20,000 units were produced by the factory in the financial year:

(a) Production cost per Unit $= \dfrac{£65,000}{20,000} \quad \dfrac{\text{Cost of Production}}{\text{No. of Units}}$

  $= £3.25$ per Unit

(b) Prime Cost per Unit $= \dfrac{£45,000}{20,000} \quad \dfrac{\text{Prime Cost of Production}}{\text{No. of Units}}$

  $= £2.25$ per Unit

(c) Factory Overheads per Unit $= \dfrac{£21,000}{20,000} \quad \dfrac{\text{Factory OH Cost}}{\text{No. of Units}}$

  less adjustment for $= £1.05$ per Unit
  Work-in-Progress Stock $\dfrac{0.05}{£1.00}$ per Unit

The factory's production cost per unit is £3.25 made up of prime cost and factory overheads. It does not include the firm's profit and loss expenses per unit such as distribution costs and administration expenses.

  The production cost per unit is a guide to the factory to indicate whether the firm is cost effective in the production of its goods.

Transfer of Cost of Production to the Trading Account

	£	£	£
Sales			100,000
less			
Cost of Sales			
Stock: Finished Goods (Jan. 1)	5,500		
+ Cost of Production	65,000		
	70,500		
− Stock: Finished Goods (Dec. 31)	3,500		67,000
Gross profit			33,000

Example Exercise

The following figures relate to the accounts of ABC Company Limited, TV manufacturing business, for the year ended 31 December:

	£
Stocks of raw materials 1 January	3,186
Stocks of raw materials 31 December	4,479
Stocks of finished goods 1 January	4,264
Stocks of finished goods 31 December	9,651
Purchases of raw materials	23,766
Sales of finished goods net	79,695
Rent and rates	3,292
Manufacturing wages	23,463
Manufacturing power	765
Manufacturing heat and light	237
Manufacturing expenses and maintenance	819
Salaries and wages	13,870
Advertising	2,217
Office expenses	786
Depreciation of plant and machinery	745
Hiring of plant	504

One-half of the salaries and wages and three-quarters of the rent and rates are to be treated as a manufacturing charge.

	£
Work-in-Progress (1 January)	1,156
Work-in-Progress (31 December)	1,066

Required:

Manufacturing, trading and profit and loss accounts for the year to show clearly:

(a) The cost of raw materials used. (i)
(b) Prime cost. (ii)
(c) Cost of factory overheads. (iii)
(d) Factory cost of goods completed. (iv)
(e) Cost of goods sold. (v)
(f) Gross profit for the year. (vi)
(g) Total of administrative and selling expenses. (vii)
(h) Net profit for the year. (viii)

The Manufacturing Account of ABC Company Limited for the period ending 31 December:

		£	£	£
Direct Costs				
Stocks of raw materials (1/1)		3,186		
Purchases of raw materials		23,766		
		26,952		
Less stocks of raw materials (31/12)		4,479		
	(i)	22,473		
Direct wages		23,463		
Direct expenses		504		
	(ii)			46,440
Indirect Costs				
Indirect wages and salaries			6,935	
Indirect Expenses:				
Depreciation: plant		745		
Manufacturing heat and light		237		
Expenses and Maintenance		819		
+ power		765		
+ rent and rates		2,469	5,035	
	(iii)			11,970
				58,410
Add				
Work-in-Progress (1/1)				1,156
				59,566
less				
Work-in-Progress (31/12)				1,066
Cost of Production				
(transferred to Trading a/c)	(iv)			58,500

Trading and Profit and Loss Account of ABC Company Limited for the period ending 31 December:

	£	£	
Sales		79,695	
– *Cost of Sales*			
Stocks of finished goods (1/1)	4,264		
+ Cost of Production	58,500		
	62,764		
– Stocks of finished goods (31/12)	9,651	53,113	(v)
Gross Profit		26,582	(vi)
–*Other Expenses*			
Rent and Rates	823		
Wages and salaries	6,935		
Advertising	2,217		
Office Expenses	786	10,761	(vii)
Net profit		15,821	(viii)

SUMMARY
(1) Manufacturing Account:

	£
Prime Cost	46,440
Factory Overheads	11,970
	58,410
Adjustment for Work-in-Progress	90
Cost of Production	58,500

(2) Trading & Profit & Loss Account:

	£
Sales	79,695
less Cost of Sales	53,113
Gross profit	26,582
less other expenses	10,761
Net Profit	15,821

Costs per Unit

If 260 TV sets had been produced by ABC Company Limited for the period to 31 December, then

If we were to include *total costs* of running the firm (that is, production and office costs):

	£
Cost of Production	
Profit and Loss Expenses	58,500
Total Costs	10,761
	69,261

$$\text{Total Cost per Unit} = \frac{69{,}261}{260} = £266.38$$

The cost of production would show the amount it costs to run the factory — as separate from running the office.

$$\text{Factory Cost per Unit} = \frac{58{,}500}{260} = £225.00$$

This would be a check to see if the manufacturing side of the business was producing goods cost effectively. Could the firm 'buy out' (that is, from other manufacturers) at less than £225 per unit?

Prime Cost is a guide to show the *minimum* possible to produce a TV in terms of direct labour and materials:

$$\text{Prime Cost per Unit} \quad \frac{46{,}440}{260} = £178.60$$

The Valuation of Stock

The Unsold Stock of finished goods at the end of the financial year may be valued in a number of different methods:

(a) at prime cost per unit,
(b) at production cost per unit,
(c) at total cost per unit,
(d) at lower of cost or net realisable value.

Whichever method is used, it must be applied consistently when preparing the final accounts of the business, otherwise the accounting reports may be misrepresented. The value of unsold stock affects the calculation of gross profit because the greater the value of stock, the greater the value of gross profit.

Calculation:

No. of Units in stock (Jan. 1)   43
No. of Units produced in Year   260
                              303
No. of Units sold   260

Unsold Stock   (Dec. 31)   43 Units

(a) Valued at Prime Cost   £178.6 $\times$ 43 = £7,679.80
(b) Valued at Production Cost £225 $\times$ 43 = £9,675.00
(c) Valued at Total Cost   £266.38 $\times$ 43 = £11,454.34
(d) Valued at Lower of Cost or
     Net Realisable Value (net sales value)

If some stock was old, obsolete or damaged, it may be valued at less than, say, prime cost. Suppose 3 units were old stock and would only sell at £150 and the other 40 units were valued at production cost:

£225 $\times$ 40 = £9,000
£150 $\times$ 3 = £   450

Unsold stock at (d) = £9,450

If prime cost has been selected for stock valuation, the gross profit would have been reduced by £1,872:

Stock (Dec. 31) in Trading a/c £9,651
Valued at prime cost   7,679

Stock value reduced by   1,872

If total cost had been used, what affect would it have on gross profit?

The Calculation of 'Profit' in the Manufacturing Account

An assessment of profit may be determined in the manufacturing side of the business. This may be calculated if a *market value* of the goods manufactured can be given. In the previous exercise, 260 TVs were produced by ABC Company Limited at a production cost of £58,500. If the TVs could have been purchased from *other manufacturers* at, say £280 each, it is possible to calculate whether it is worth ABC producing the TVs in the first place! For example

Number produced

260
@ £280 Market value =	£72,800
ABC's production cost	£58,500
Profit on Manufacturing side	£14,300

It seems it *is* worth it. ABC can make £14,300 by manufacturing the TVs themselves. The Trading Account showed a gross profit of £26,582:

Manufacturing Profit	=	£14,300
Trading Profit	=	£12,282
		£26,582

If a manufacturer wanted to emphasise the profit made by the production side of the factory, the manufacturing account must include the market valuation of those goods manufactured:

Manufacturing Account of ABC Company Limited
31 December (extract)

	£
Cost of Production	58,500
Manufacturing Profit	14,300
Being Market Value	72,800
260 @ £280	

Trading Account of ABC Company Limited
31 December

	£	£
Sales		79,695
Stocks of finished goods (1/1)	4,264	
Market Value of Production	72,800	
	77,064	
− Stock of finished goods (31/12)	9,651	67,413
Trading Profit		12,282
Manufacturing Profit		14,300
		26,582

From this method of presentation, the manufacturer has an assessment of:

(a) the actual manufacturing profit   £14,300
(b) the trading profit   £12,282

        Gross Profit   £26,582

Thus, the profit figure is the same as before and the net profit is unaffected by this method of presentation

Mark-up and Margins of Profit

The 'Mark-up' is usually expressed as a percentage and is *added* to the cost price of goods to give the selling price.

ABC company produced and sold 260 Units earning revenue of £79,695:

$$\text{Selling Price per Unit} = \frac{£79,695}{260} = £306.5 \text{ per unit}$$

$$\text{Cost Price per Unit} = \frac{£69,261}{260} = £266.38 \text{ per unit}$$

$$\textit{Profit} \text{ per Unit} = £40.12 \text{ per unit}$$

Mark-up Percentage

This is always based on the *cost price*

$$= \frac{\text{Profit} \times 100}{\text{Cost}}$$

$$= \frac{£40.12 \times 100}{£266.38} = 15\% \text{ mark-up}$$

The percentage mark-up on cost is the guideline to selling price. How much to mark-up may be a problem. How much will the market be prepared to pay? What are the prices of the firm's competitors? What will be the cost of 'follow-up' services? ABC Co. has marked up its stock by 15% at present prices. Will competition in the market place become more intense and force the company to review its mark-up?

Margin Percentage

This is always based on the *selling price*

$$= \frac{\text{Profit} \times 100}{\text{Selling Price}}$$

$$= \frac{£40.12 \times 100}{£306.50} = 13\% \text{ Margin}$$

The margin percentage is a guideline to profit based on sales. In this case, every £100 sales will produce a profit of £13. Sales of £1,000 produces a profit of £130 and so forth. The margin percentage is a useful indicator of profit based on the volume of sales and may be compared with previous trading performances and with other businesses in the same field in order to evaluate profitability.

Example Exercise: Manufacturing A/c to Balance Sheet

ABC Co. Ltd is a small manufacturing concern producing component parts for various industries. It has a production capacity of 12,000 units per annum. The company commenced business last year and was fortunate barely to break even, because of initial lack of business experience.

This year, however, the company policy was to streamline its operations in an effort to increase productivity and profit. You are in the position of the firm's assistant to the accountant and have been asked to prepare a draft copy of the financial accounts.

The following represents the trial balance for year ended 31 December 1988.

Trial Balance ABC Co. Ltd, year Ended 31/12/88

	£	£
Premises	20,000	
Plant and Equipment at cost	75,000	
Motor Vehicles at cost	4,000	
Provision for depreciation of plant and equipment		20,000
Provision for depreciation of Motor Vehicles		2,200
Stock of raw materials 1 January	8,000	
Stock of finished goods 1 Jan. 500 units	6,000	
Purchases of raw materials	75,600	
Direct Wages	42,000	

Manufacturing Expenses	28,500	
Selling and Distribution costs	35,750	
Administrative Expenses	13,825	
Discount		430
General Expenses	6,600	
Debtors, Creditors	2,570	16,650
Bank	3,805	
VAT	2,630	
Sales 11,250 units		225,000
Capital:		
60,000 @ £1 ordinary		60,000
	324,280	324,280

Additional further information 31 December 1988

(a) Stock of raw materials £10,600.
   Stock of finished goods: unsold stock is to be valued at production cost. The firm's capacity of 12,000 units was produced in the year.

(b) Depreciation:
   Plant and equipment 10% of book value
   Motor Vehicle (Sales and Distribution) 20% of cost.

(c) Accruals:
   Direct Wages £2,800
   Administrative expenses £250.

(d) General expenses of £4,200 attributed to factory.
   The remainder to be allocated as Administrative expenses.

(e) Pre-payments:
   Sales and Distribution cost £345.

(f) It is proposed to provide a dividend of 5% to shareholders. A provision of £8,000 is to be made for taxation purposes and a General Reserve of £6,000 is to be created.

TASK A

Prepare the firm's manufacturing account, trading and profit and loss and appropriation accounts for the period ended 31 December 1988.

TASK B

Prepare the firm's balance sheet as at 31 December 1988, including in its presentation, the working capital.

Manufacturing Account
ABC Company year ended 31 December 1989

	£	£	£
Direct Materials:			
Stock rm (1/1)	8,000		
Add Purchases	75,600		
Less Stock rm (31/12)	(10,600)	73,000	
Direct Labour:			
Direct Wages	42,000		
Add Accrued	2,800	44,800	
		prime cost = 117,800	
Indirect Costs:			
Manufacturing Expenses	28,500		
Factory Expenses	4,200		
Depreciation			
(Plant & Equipment)	5,500		
		factory overheads	38,200
		factory cost =	156,000

Factory Cost/Unit:

$$\frac{\text{Factory Cost}}{\text{Output}} = \frac{156,000}{12,000} = £13 \text{ per unit}$$

Value of Finished Goods 31/12:

Output × Factory Cost   = 1,250 × £13 = £16,250

Trading and Profit and Loss account
ABC Company year ended 31 December 1989

	£	£	£
Sales			225,000
Less Cost of Sales			
Stock fg (1/1)	6,000		
Add Factory Cost	156,000		
Less Stock fg (31/12)	(16,250)		145,750
Gross Profit			79,250
Distribution Costs:			
S and D costs	35,750		
Less Prepayments	345	35,405	
Depreciation MV		800	
		36,205	
Administration Expenses:			
Administration	13,825		
Add Accrued	250	14,075	
General Expenses		2,400	
		16,475	52,680
			26,570
Add other income			430
Net Profit (b/t)			27,000
Tax			8,000
Net Profit (a/t)			19,000
Dividends		3,000	
Reserves		6,000	9,000
Profit and Loss (31/12)			10,000

Balance Sheet
ABC Company year ended 31 December 1989

	£	£	£
Fixed Assets:			
Tangibles:	Cost	Depn	Net Value
Premises	20,000	–	20,000
Plant and Equipment	75,000	25,500	49,500
Motor Vehicles	4,000	3,000	1,000
	99,000	28,500	70,500

Current Assets

Stocks: raw materials	10,600	
finished goods	16,250	
Debtors	2,570	
Bank	3,805	
Vat	2,630	
Prepayments	345	36,200

Current Liabilities

Creditors	16,650	
Tax and Dividends	11,000	
Accruals	3,050	30,700

Net Current Assets	5,500
	76,000

Capital and Reserves

Issued and P/U Capital:

Ordinary Shares	60,000	
Reserves	6,000	
Profit and Loss (31/12)	10,000	76,000

Exercises

1. From the following information, prepare Freddy Smith's Manufacturing Account, Trading and Profit and Loss Account for the year ended 31 December:

	£
Stocks (January 1)	
Raw Materials	5,675
Work-in-Progress	2,225
Finished Goods	7,550
Purchases of Raw Materials	40,850
Sales	101,255
Returns (Dr.)	7,235
Factory	
Wages (Direct)	18,600
Power	2,675
Depreciation of Plant	3,765
Rent and Rates	3,720
Insurances	500
Office	
Light and Heat	846
Insurances	245
General Expenses	170
Wages	6,750
Rent and Rates	975
Stocks (December 31)	
Raw Materials	6,200
Work-in-Progress	2,135
Finished Goods	8,225

At 31 December

(a) Wages owing: £854 (Office).
(b) Depreciation of office equipment (£2,500) by 20%.
(c) Rent and Rates pre-paid: 15% of both factory and office.

2. From the following information, prepare Jack Jones's Manufacturing Account, Trading Account, and Profit and Loss Account for the year ended December 31:

	£
Sales	155,000
Stocks (January 1)	
Raw Materials	5,856

Work-in-Progress	1,500
Finished Goods	10,575
Purchase of Raw Materials	85,424

Stocks (December 31)	
Raw Materials	6,255
Work-in-Progress	1,480
Finished Goods	12,555

Factory	
Wages (Direct)	22,575
Wages accrued (Direct)	425
Factory and Machinery Maintenance	2,550
Depreciation on Plant and Machinery	4,500
Factory Power	875
Factory Salaries	6,500

Factory Expenses	
Rent, Rates, and Insurance	2,142
Lighting and Heating	532

Office Expenses	
Rent, Rates, and Insurance	1,150
Lighting and Heating	350
Administrative Expenses	2,335

At 31 December

(a) Rates were pre-paid: £125 for factory and £60 for office.
(b) £70 for factory salaries was owing.
(c) A bill of £65 was due to the Gas Board for office heating.

3. Harry is a manufacturer. From the following details relating to his business, prepare separate accounts to show:

   (i) the factory cost of goods
  (ii) the manufacturing profit
 (iii) the trading profit
 (iv) the net profit

for the year ended 31 December.

	£
Stocks (1 January)	
Raw materials	6,757
Finished goods	10,560

Stocks (31 December)

Raw materials	5,583
Finished goods	12,565

Wages: factory (Direct)	15,500
office	12,765

Rent, rates and insurance	4,580
(factory four-fifths; office one-fifth)	
Sales of finished goods	101,500
Purchases of raw materials	40,875
Manufacturing expenses	5,945
Selling expenses	12,855
Administrative expenses	7,400
Depreciation: machinery	2,150
office furniture	500
accounting machines (office)	150

Other Information

(a) (1/1) Stocks of Work-in-Progress. (NIL)
   (31/12) Stocks of Work-in-Progress. (NIL)

(b) The market valuation of the cost of production is £78,000.

(c) Calculate: on the basis of 2,000 units produced in the year:
   (i) Direct Labour cost per unit.
   (ii) Direct Material cost per unit.
   (iii) Factory Overheads per unit.
   (iv) Production costs per unit.

(d) Was manufacturing cost-effective?
   Compare the market value per unit cost with production cost per unit.

4. ABC Co. Ltd is a manufacturer. From the following details relating to his business prepare separate accounts to show:
   (i) the factory cost of goods
   (ii) the gross profit
   (iii) the net profit

for the year ended 31 December.

	£
Stocks (1 January)	
Raw materials at cost	4,200
Finished goods at factory cost	7,525
Work-in-Progress	5,450
Stocks (31 December)	
Raw materials at cost	4,875
Finished goods at factory cost	9,674

Wages: factory (Direct)	27,855
office	15,640
Rent, rates and insurance	3,600
(factory four-fifths; office one-fifth)	
Sales of finished goods	121,565
Purchases of raw materials	45,750
Manufacturing expenses	4,380
Selling expenses	3,895
Administrative expenses	1,675
Depreciation: machinery	4,500
office furniture	1,500
office equipment	350

At 31 December	
Work-in-Progress	5,980
Factory wages accrued	255

Based on 10,500 units produced by ABC Co. during the year, calculate:

(i) The prime cost per unit.
(ii) The overhead factory cost per unit.
(iii) Production costs per unit.
(iv) Total costs per unit.
(v) Assuming that 10,000 units were sold during the year, calculate both the mark-up % and margin % applied by the Company.

5. Prepare the Manufacturing, Trading and Profit and Loss accounts of Fred's Co. Ltd for the year ended 31 December. Production output: 10,000 Units in year.

	£
Stocks (1 January)	
Raw Materials	4,250
Work-in-Progress	—
Finished Goods (2,050 Units)	10,250
Stocks (31 December)	
Raw Materials	5,150
Finished Goods: Units in balance	
valued at Production Cost	
Work-in-Progress	—
Purchases of Raw Materials	32,600
Sales (10,800 Units)	86,500
Factory	
Direct wages	15,255
Power (direct)	1,650
Indirect salaries	4,780
Factory maintenance	1,585

Rates, Insurance & General Expenses	750
Indirect Materials	1,480
Depreciation of Plant	1,875

Office

Rates, Insurance & General Expenses	455
Selling and Distribution Costs	2,875
Bad Debts	450
Administration Expenses	3,450
Discount (Dr.)	375
Depreciation of office equipment	500
Commission Received	1,750

At 31 December

(a) Direct wages owing £250.

  Rates in advance (office) £50.

(b) A provision for bad debts to be created to equal 5% of debtors (Debtors £7,850).

(c) £150 was still due for factory power.

6. The following information is taken from the accounts of Peter Jackson, a businessman producing science equipment to colleges:

Trial Balance of P. Jackson as on 30th June 1990

	£	£
Stocks (1/7/89)		
raw materials	6,885	
finished goods	3,500	
Motor Vehicle (cost)	8,750	
Premises (cost)	36,900	
Accumulated Depreciation		
of Vehicle (2 years)		1,750
Purchases		
(raw materials)	55,725	
Direct Wages	45,780	
Sales		180,344
Discounts	855	1,044
Returns	548	
Salaries (assistants)	18,346	
Overheads (factory)	14,385	
Overheads (office)	7,044	
Creditors		6,755
Debtors	7,400	
Bank		2,045
Cash	400	
Drawings	10,420	
Capital		?

On 30th June, the following additional information was also available:
(a) Stocks in hand were valued:
Raw Materials   £7,432
Finished Goods   £4,200
(b) The motor vehicle is depreciated on straight line and is now 3 years old.
(c) Of the factory overheads, £240 is prepaid and £600 is accrued.

Required:

Prepare the Manufacturing Account, Trading and Profit and Loss account for the year ended 30th June 1990 and a Balance Sheet as on that date.

7. *Manufacturing Account to Balance Sheet*
XYZ Co. Ltd is a company which manufactures electrical components for the car industry. Production is planned for 50,000 Units in the financial year ended 31 December.

The trial balance extracted from the ledgers on 31 December:

	£	£
Authorised and Issued Share Capital:		
70,000 @ £1 Ordinary Shares		70,000
Share Premium		7,000
Premises (cost)	86,000	
Plant (cost)	12,000	
Provision for depreciation of Plant		6,000
Debtors	10,498	
Creditors		58,409
Stock (Jan. 1):		
Raw Materials	5,892	
Finished Goods (2,500 Units)	8,500	
Provision for Bad Debts		200
Bad Debts	528	
Bank/Cash	2,910	
Direct Wages	56,804	
Raw Materials Purchases of	156,820	
Sales (48,000 Units)		204,000
General Expenses ($\frac{1}{2}$ factory)	2,944	
Profit & Loss Balance (1 Jan.)		5,830
Rates and Insurance ($\frac{1}{2}$ factory)	610	
Office Wages	5,220	
Delivery charges	2,400	
Discount	313	
	351,439	351,439

Further information at 31 December

(a) Stocks: Raw Materials unused £20,893.
              50,000 Units of finished goods were produced.
              The unsold stock to be valued at Production Cost/unit.
(a) The provision for Bad Debts to be increased to £750.
(c) The Plant is to be depreciated 10% on Net Value.
(d) A taxation provision of £750 is to be made.
(e) The directors have recommended a 5% Dividend on the share capital.
    A General Reserve is to be created by a transfer of £2,000 in the
    appropriation account.

Required:

(a) Prepare the Company's Manufacturing, Trading, Profit & Loss and
    Appropriation account for the period ended 31 December, and a
    Balance Sheet as at that date.
(b) Calculate on the basis of the number of units produced, the Direct
    Labour, Direct Materials and Total Overheads per Unit.

Cost Classification

After viewing the presentation of the manufacturing account, it was seen that
costs were broken down into different areas of the business:

Production Costs

   Prime Cost
   Factory Overheads

These were costs met by the factory, distinct from those of the office.

Office Costs

   Sales and Distribution expenses
   Administration
   Rent, Rates, Insurances
   Financial expenses
   Salaries
   Miscellaneous expenses

These are the general office expenses found in the profit and loss account.
There are cases where a certain type of expense, such as Rent, Rates and
Insurance, ought to be divided into the *area of the business* where such an
expense is used.

	£	
Total Rent and Rates	20,000	
75% Factory proportion	15,000	Factory Overheads
20% Sales Office	4,000	Sales and Distribution
5% Administration Office	1,000	Administrative Expenses

Example

Using the cost classification sheet, break down the following into their appropriate sections of cost:

		£
(a) Wages:	60% direct to production	
	30% to sales staff,	70,000
	10% to Administration	
(b) Purchasing:	75% direct materials	
	15% factory overheads	80,000
	10% office stationery	
(c) Rent, rates:	(as below in (e))	20,000
(d) Depreciation:	80% factory machines	5,000
	20% office machines	
(e) Power:	75% factory	
	20% sales office	2,000
	5% administration office	
(f) Sales representatives motor expenses		4,800
(g) Telephone charges:		
	25% factory	
	50% sales office	1,500
	25% administration office	
(h) Financial expenses		420
(i) Interest charges on overdraft		280

The above costs relate to T.J. Freeze Ltd which manufactures 2000 Units per annum. Further information for the financial year:

		£
Stocks (1 January)		
Raw Materials		8,755
Finished Goods (100 Units)		6,700
Work-in-Progress		—
Stocks (31 December)		
Raw Materials		6,215
Finished Goods in Stock		
valued at Prime Cost/unit		
Work-in-Progress		—
Sales (1,800 Units)		198,000

Required:

(a) Using the information from the cost sheet and from above, prepare T.J. Freeze Ltd's Manufacturing and Trading and Profit and Loss accounts for the year ended 31 December.

(b) Calculate:

      Prime Cost/unit
      Production Cost/unit
      Total Cost/unit

based on the production of 2,000 units in the year.

COST CLASSIFICATION SHEET

COSTS:	Wages, Salaries	Purchasing	Rent, Rates	Telephone	Motor Expenses	General Expenses	Stationery	POWER	Interest Charges	Depreciation	Transfer to:
Direct Labour	42,000										42,000 (Manufacturing a/c)
Direct Materials		60,000									60,000
Direct Expenses											
Indirect Labour											
Indirect Materials		12,000									12,000
Indirect Expenses			15,000	375				1,500		4,000	20,875
Distribution Costs	21,000		4,000	750	4,800			400			30,950 (Profit and Loss/Account)
Administration Expenses	7,000		1,000	375		420	8,000	100	280	1,000	18,175
Total Cost	70,000	72,000	20,000	1,500	4,800	420	8,000	2,000	280	5,000	184,000

COST CLASSIFICATION SHEET

Transfer to:		Depreciation	Interest Charges	POWER	Stationery	General Expenses			Rent, rates	Purchasing	Wages, Salaries	Total Expenses
Manufacturing Account	COSTS:											
	Direct Labour											
	Direct Materials											
	Direct Expenses											
	Indirect Labour											
	Indirect Materials											
	Indirect Expenses											
Profit and Loss Account	Distribution Costs											
	Administration Expenses											
	Total Cost											

Manufacturing a/c
T.J. Freeze Ltd, Year Ended 31 December

	£	£	£
DIRECT COSTS			
Stock of Raw Materials (1/1)	8,755		
Purchases of Raw Materials	60,000		
	68,755		
– Stock of Raw materials (31/12)	6,215	62,540	
Direct Wages		42,000	
Prime cost			104,540
INDIRECT COSTS			
Indirect Materials	12,000		
Indirect Expenses	20,875		
Factory Overheads			32,875
Work-in-Progress			137,415
Stocks			—
Cost of Production			137,415

$$\text{Prime Cost/Unit} = \frac{£104,540}{2,000} = £52.27$$

No. of Units in Stock (31/12) = 300 (2,100 – 1,800 units)

Value of finished goods (31/12) = 300 × £52.27

= £15,681

Trading & Profit & Loss a/c
T.J. Freeze Ltd, Year Ended 31 December

	£	£	£
Sales			198,000
–Cost of Sales:			
Stock of Finished Goods (1/1)	6,700		
+ Cost of Production	137,415		
	144,115		
– Stock of Finished Goods (31/12)	15,681		128,434
Gross Profit			69,566
Less			
Distribution Costs	30,950		
Administration Expenses	18,175		49,125
Net Profit			20,441

Exercises

1. The following information relates to ABC Co. Ltd for the year ended 31 December:

   ABC Co. Ltd make TV products and its trading figures were

	£
Sales (1,550 units)	215,000
Rent, Rates, Insurances	10,000
Power	12,000
Depreciation	18,000
Motor Expenses	16,000
Telephone, Postages	2,500
Stationery	4,200
Advertising	7,500
Wages, Salaries	42,000
Purchases	68,000
Administration	5,700

   (a) Wages: 50% direct, 20% indirect, sales office 15%, administration office 15%.
   (b) Factory rent is 75%. The rest is divided equally between sales and administration offices.
   (c) Purchases are 70% direct materials, 20% indirect materials, the rest being equally divided between sales and administration offices.
   (d) The factory heating was £9,000 power. The rest is equally divided between sales and administration.
   (e) Motoring expenses: 75% sales office, 25% administration.
   (f) Telephone, postages: 80% used by the sales office, 15% by administration; 5% by the factory.
   (g) Stationery: the finance section uses 60%, the factory uses 30% for its clock cards. The remainder is used by the sales office.
   (h) Depreciation: £15,000 to factory plant and machinery. Of the rest, two-thirds is machines in administration, one-third in the sales office.

   Other information relating to ABC Co. Ltd:
   The Company produces 1,500 units in the financial year. Unsold stock of finished goods are valued at Production Cost/unit.

Stocks (January 1)	£
Raw Materials	4,200
Finished Goods	
(200 Units)	14,950

Stock (December 31)

Raw Materials	5,100
Finished Goods —	
Valued at Production Cost	

There were no significant stocks
of work-in-progress.

Required:

(a) A Cost Sheet classifying the costs into their appropriate categories.
(b) A Manufacturing, Trading and Profit and Loss account of ABC Co.
   Ltd for the year ended 31 December.

2. The following information refers to the accounts of J. Jones, manufacturer, for the financial year ended 31 December. Production for the year
    was 5,000 Units.

	£
Wages	
Direct factory	19,450
Indirect factory	12,145
Sales Office	15,615
Administration	8,500
Purchases	
Raw Materials	15,575
Indirect Materials	1,450
Sales Office stationery	850
Administration	1,955
Factory Power (direct)	675
Factory Maintenance	1,800
Factory Rent, Rates	2,560
Depreciation of Plant	1,500
Office Rent, Rates	957
($\frac{1}{3}$ Sales Office)	
Office Light, Heat	366
($\frac{1}{3}$ Sales Office)	
Sales (4,800 Units)	86,400
Administrative Expenses	475
Discount (Dr.)	155
Depreciation of Office	
Machinery and Equipment	900
($\frac{1}{3}$ Sales Office)	

Stocks (1 January)

Raw Materials	2,375
Work-in-Progress	1,975
Finished Goods (550 Units)	4,750

Stocks (31 December)

Raw Materials	2,485
Work-in-Progress	1,900
Finished Goods:	
Unsold stock to be valued at	
Production Cost	

Other information on 31 December

(a) Accrued Direct wages £850.
(b) An unpaid invoice for Office Light & Heat £42.
(c) A provision for bad debts to equal 5% of debtors (Debtors £5,500) to be charged to Administration Office.

Required:

(a) Prepare a Cost Sheet to record the appropriate costs as above.
(b) Prepare the firm's Manufacturing account for the year ended 31 December, transferring sub-totals from the cost sheet.
(c) Prepare the firm's Trading and Profit and Loss account for the year ended 31 December, transferring sub-totals for distribution costs and administration expenses.

PART 2

The Nature of Costs

Absorption costing identifies all the business costs which 'absorp' a product in terms of its labour, materials and overheads.

Absorption cost would include all the direct and indirect costs of production including the indirect office overheads in the profit and loss account. Direct costs, as noted in the manufacturing account, are traceable to the unit cost of the product whereas for indirect costs, it is far more difficult to actually allocate the cost to the unit. For example, materials are easily identified and traceable in the unit cost but rates would be more difficult to apportion.

Marginal costing is related to those costs which are traceable (direct) to a particular unit. These costs are sensitive to changes in output. If output increases by one, the marginal cost will also increase by one.

For marginal costing to take place, it is necessary to divide costs into 2 categories: fixed and variable.

Fixed costs are those costs insensitive to output change, whereas variable costs are sensitive to changes in production levels. Therefore, direct costs like materials are variable and indirect costs like rent and rates are likely to be fixed. If output levels change, how does this affect costs?

Marginal costing changes directly with output and is particularly useful when finding how unit costs respond. If output changes, the variable costs will directly change relative to the output. However, fixed costs will not change in the same proportional way, being more insensitive to output change. This means that if output increases, fixed costs will be 'diluted' and the overall unit cost will fall. On the other hand, if output falls, the unit cost will increase because it will have to carry a greater proportion of fixed cost.

The Manufacturing Account gave a break-down of production costs; for example

Direct Costs	£	£	
Direct Labour	20,000		
Direct Materials	25,000	45,000	Prime Cost
Indirect Costs			
Indirect Labour	4,500		
Indirect Materials	—		
Indirect Expenses	10,000	14,500	Factory Overheads
Work-in-Progress			
Stock (beg.)	+ 2,000		
Stock (end)	− 1,500	500	
		60,000	Production Cost

The production cost allowed the product cost per unit to be calculated. If 1,000 units was the output:

$$\text{Product Cost per Unit} = \frac{£60,000}{1,000} = £60$$

To calculate the total cost of the product, the profit and loss expenses must also be included. These may be referred to as 'period costs' or 'office overheads'.

Profit & Loss Expenses	£	
Sales & Distribution Costs	3,500	
Administration Expenses	6,000	
Interest Payable	500	
	10,000	Office Overheads

Total Cost per Product:		
Production Cost	60,000	
Office Overheads	10,000	
	70,000/1000 units = £70 per unit	

In costing terms:	£	
Direct Labour	20,000	
Direct Materials	25,000	
Overheads (factory, office)	25,000	
	70,000/1000 units = £70 per unit	

In the above example, if all the direct costs were variable and the rest were relatively fixed, calculate:

(a) the variable cost per unit
(b) the total cost per unit (absorption cost) based on an output of 1,000 units and 2,000 units.

Output: 1,000 units

(a) Variable Costs per Unit $= \dfrac{£45,000}{1,000}$

$= £45$ per unit

(b) Total Cost per Unit $\quad = \dfrac{£70,000}{1,000}$

$= £70$ per unit

Output: 2,000 units

(a) Variable Cost per Unit $= \dfrac{£90,000}{2,000}$

$= £45$ per unit

(b) Total Cost per Unit $\quad = \dfrac{£115,000 \ (90,000 + 25,000)}{2,000}$

$= £57.50$ per unit

Note: the absorption cost has been reduced from £70 to £57.50 per unit on the basis that the fixed costs have been 'diluted' over 2,000 units rather than 1,000. Fixed costs, being insensitive to output, have remained the same. This is not to say that fixed costs do not increase. They do increase, but not in direct proportion to output.

In the previous exercise, ABC Company produced 260 TVs during the trading period. We could use the 260 figure as the normal output of ABC Company.

		£	£
1.	Direct Labour		23,463
2.	Direct Materials		22,473
3.	Overheads:		
	Factory	12,564	
	Office	10,761	23,325
			69,261

Production Capacity: 260 TVs

Absorption Cost $\dfrac{69,261}{260}$ = £266.39 per TV

As a management guideline the minimum selling price should be above the absorption cost, given this capacity of production.

Once the absorption cost is known, a firm can then estimate a mark-up on cost price. For example

	£
Absorption Cost based on 260 TVs	266.39
+ Mark-up 20%	53.28
Possible selling price	319.67 per TV

If the public chose to buy something more competitive elsewhere, then the 20% mark-up will have to be reconsidered.

Marginal (Variable) Costs

This refers to the *extra* costs involved in producing one or more units over and above the projected forecast of production (or one or more units fewer).

Marginal cost may be required in order to find out the effect on expenses when producing more or fewer items.

If ABC Company had produced 275 TVs within the production capacity, how much *extra* did the 15 TVs cost?

Consider:

(a) All Direct Materials are extra.
(b) Direct Labour earns £2.50 bonus for each TV produced.
(c) Power to produce one TV costs 30p.
(d) Other overheads are an extra 20p per TV.

How much is the marginal cost per TV?

Marginal Cost per TV

		£	£
(a) Direct Materials	$= \dfrac{22{,}473}{260} =$	86.43	
(b) Direct labour: (bonus)			2.50
(c) Extra overheads			
Power			30
Other			20
			89.43

Total Marginal Cost to produce
15 extra TVs   × 15 £1,342

Variable costs are costs as above, which are sensitive to changes in production levels. The more units produced, the greater the variable (or marginal) cost.

Fixed Costs

Those costs which are deemed not so sensitive and must be paid regardless of production levels are known as *fixed costs*.

Fixed costs do not change even if one extra or one less is produced. Factory overheads and office overheads tend to remain relatively fixed.

These cost types may now be broken down into their fixed and variable categories. Figures are based on a 260 unit capacity of production.

Capacity: 260 TVs	Total Cost	Fixed Cost	Variable Cost	Notes
	£	£	£	
Direct Labour	23,463	22,813	650	(£2.50 bonus)
Direct Materials	22,473	—	22,473	
Overheads	23,325	23,195	130	(50p per TV)
	69,261	46,008	23,253	

Summary

(a) Total Absorption Cost: $\dfrac{69{,}261}{260} = $ £266.39

(b) Marginal Cost: $\dfrac{23,253}{260} = £89.43$

To produce *extra* TVs, therefore, will *not* incur the full absorption cost because some costs are relatively fixed for a certain capacity of production.
  The above example shows that extra TVs produced will incur 100% of the costs of the materials directly, but extra costs involved are relatively low.
  It is very useful for management to *know* these extra costs because this will help them to determine at what price to charge extra orders to the relevant capacity.

The Importance of Contribution

If an order for an extra 50 TVs was received asking for a special mark-down price of, say, £140 per TV, management could accept the order knowing that marginal costs were around £90. That is, of course, if the extra 50 TVs could be produced within the normal production capacity. If more labour was to be hired, then direct labour costs would have to be added to marginal costs.

Calculate:

(a) The estimated profit if 260 units were produced and sold at £320 per unit.
(b) The *extra* profit is 275 units were produced and sold.

Profit Calculation using Marginal Costing

(a) Estimated Profit on 260 Units:

	£
Revenue:	
260 Units @ £320	83,200
Deduct	
Variable Costs:	
260 Unit @ £89.43	23,252
*CONTRIBUTION	59,948
Deduct	
Fixed Costs:	46,008
Profit	13,940

*The Importance of Contribution

Contribution = Revenue − Variable Costs

The more contribution, the more profit is available before fixed costs are deducted.

When production levels change, contribution will move proportionately so that any extra contribution as a result of higher production levels produces more profit. Conversely, if production levels are less than those forecasted (or budgeted), less contribution results in less profit.

Contribution plays a very significant part in marginal costing.

(b) *Estimated Profit on 275 Units*:

Revenue:	£
275 Units @ £320	88,000
Deduct	
Variable Costs:	
275 @ £89.43	24,594
CONTRIBUTION	63,406
Deduct	
Fixed Costs	46,008
Profit	17,398

The EXTRA PROFIT on 15 more Units? £3,458 (£17,398 − £13,940)
The EXTRA CONTRIBUTION? £3,458 (£63,406 − £59,948)

Check on Profit
To produce an extra 15 Units, the variable or marginal cost was

$$£89.43 \times 15 = £1,342$$

Revenue earned:

$$£320 \times 15 = £4,800$$

Extra Profit: = £3,458 *Note*: No change in Fixed Costs

The Use of 'Contribution per Unit'

The contribution per unit can be used to make quick calculations in marginal costing:

	£
Revenue:	320.00
− Variable Cost	89.43
Contribution per Unit	230.57

Extra profit on an Extra 15 Units?

> Contribution per Unit × 15
> £230.57   × 15
>   = £3,458 extra profit

Total profit on 275 Units?

> Profit on forecasted 260 Units = £13,940
>   +   15 Units =   3,458
>   275 Units   17,398

If only 250 Units were produced, what effect would it have on profit?

> Contribution per Unit × 10
> £230.57   × 10   = £2,306 *less* Profit
> Profit on 260 Units   = £13,940
>   on   10 Units fewer   =   2,306
>   250 Units   11,634

Check:

> Contribution × 250 Units
> £230.57   × 250   = £57,642   Contribution
> − Fixed Costs   = £46,008
>   11,634

Break-Even

Management need to know at what point in production the firm has 'broken-even'. This refers to the point at which the business has earned sufficient revenue to cover all costs. Any further revenue earned after this point will be a contribution towards profit.

Revenue less than the break-even point means losses. This is an important calculation for management because it needs to know at what point its costs are covered in terms of production units and revenue earned, and when this has been achieved.

The recently produced newspaper *Today* needed something like a circulation of 330,000 newspapers to break-even. Some of the major airlines need to have 60% of their seats sold to break-even. A number of manufacturers need to produce to at least 70% of their capacity to break-even, while others can manage on about half capacity.

The calculation of break-even in production units:

$$\text{Break-even (in Units)} = \frac{\text{FIXED COSTS}}{\text{Contribution/Unit}}$$

$$= \frac{£46,008}{£230.57}$$

$$= 199.54 \text{ Units (200 rounded up)}$$

Check:
Contribution/Unit × 200

            = £46,114 (Contribution)

less Fixed Cost   £46,008

(profit)   + 106 (because of rounding up to 200)

Profit on 201 produced?
Contribution/Unit × 1

            = £230.57
             +106.00

               336.57 Profit

Check:
Contribution/Unit × 201

            = £46,344.57

less Fixed Cost   46,008

               336.57 Profit

The Contribution to Sales Ratio [or Profit/Volume (PV) Ratio]

To find the break-even revenue is simply a matter of multiplying the number of units produced by the revenue per unit:

No. of Units to Break-Even = 200
Selling price per Unit   = £320
Break-Even revenue   = £64,000

If the contribution to sales ratio is used, break-even revenue may be calculated more directly.

$$\text{Contribution to Sales Ratio} = \frac{\text{Contribution/Unit}}{\text{Sales/Unit}}$$

$$= \frac{£230.57}{£320.00}$$

$$= 0.721 \quad (0.7205)$$

$$\text{Calculation of Break-Even Revenue} = \frac{\text{FIXED COSTS}}{\text{Contribution/sales}}$$

$$= \frac{£46,008}{0.721}$$

$$= £63,811 \quad \begin{array}{l}\text{Revenue needed} \\ \text{to Break-Even}\end{array}$$

The contribution to sales ratio may also be used to estimate profit on the sales revenue. If, in the financial year, £76,800 had been earned to date, what profit is estimated on this revenue?

Revenue × Construction/Sales Ratio (C/S ratio)
£76,800 × 0.7205   = £55,334

less Fixed Costs: 46,008

                      9,326 (profit)

Check:
No. of Units to earn £76,800 revenue?

$$= \frac{\text{Sales}}{\text{Unit Price}} = \frac{£76,800}{£320}$$

$$= 240 \text{ Units sold}$$

Can you take it from there?

240 Units sold × Contribution/Unit (£230.57 = £55,336 (Contribution)

Less Fixed Costs: 46,008

                      9,328 (profit)

Calculate estimated profit on £89,600 Sales Revenue . . .
Calculate estimated profit/loss on £62,400 Revenue . . .

The Break-Even Chart

The break-even chart is a graphic illustration showing the point at which revenue covers total costs — that is, the break-even point. In business it is rarely used because prices constantly change, making it difficult to use the chart effectively. However, the chart is useful because it does show the estimated point at which break-even takes place, both in units and revenue. In practice, it can be a guide to show a band of break-even rather than a point; for example, instead of 200 units representing break-even, it may be a band between 190 and 210 units.

The construction of the chart is shown below.

Fixed Costs for the financial period: £2,000

Variable Costs per Unit: £6.00
Sales Price per Unit: £10.00

Contribution: £4.00 per Unit (£10 − £6)

Break-Even point: $$\frac{\text{Fixed Costs}}{\text{Contribution/Unit}}$$

$$\frac{£2,000}{£4} = 500 \text{ Units}$$

Break-Even Revenue: 500 × £10 Unit

= £5,000

The Cost Chart (Fig. A)

Total Costs = Fixed + Variable Costs and *start at £2,000* because, irrespective of production levels, fixed costs of £2,000 are incurred.

From the chart:

What is the variable cost on 600 Units?
What is the total cost on 600 Units?

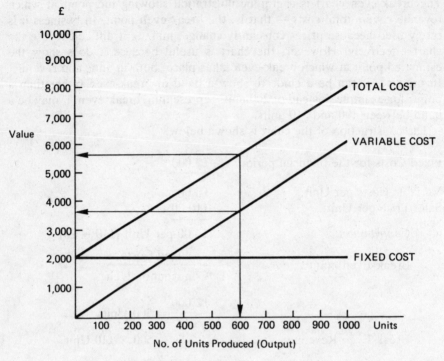

FIG. A

Chart showing Costs only

Variable Cost: 600 units = £3,600
Total Cost: 600 units = £5,600

The Break-Even Chart (Fig. B)

The break-even chart shows the additional line of revenue. Revenue commences at zero because it is dependent on the number of units sold and produced.

From the chart:

What sum of revenue is earned on 600 units?

600 × £10 = £6,000

The break-even point is the point where the revenue line crosses the total cost line — that is, at 500 Units. Revenue at this point is £5,000. Any point beyond 500 units means profit. Any point below 500 units means loss.

FIG. B

Chart showing Break-Even Point

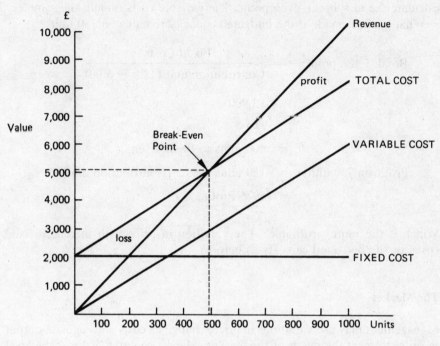

No. of Units Produced (Output)

From the chart:

What is the loss on 450 units?   Check: £200 loss
What is the profit on 610 units?   Check: £440 profit

If revenue was £6,250, what profit?   Check: £500 profit
If revenue fell to £4,200, what loss?   Check: £320 loss

If the budgeted capacity was 750 Units, what is the estimated profit for the year?

Use both the chart and costing figures for your answer.

Variations in Price

If the sales price increased by 25% and Fixed Costs increased to £3,900, calculate the new break-even point. The variable costs remain the same.
   What profit is made if the budgeted capacity remains on 750 units?

$$\text{Break-Even point:} \quad = \quad \frac{\text{Fixed Costs}}{\text{Contribution/unit } (12.5 - 6.00)}$$

$$= \quad \frac{£3,900}{£6.5}$$

$$= \quad 600 \text{ units to break-even}$$

$$\text{Profit on 750 units} \quad = \quad 150 \text{ units} \times £6.5 \text{ (Contribution/unit)}$$

$$= \quad £975 \text{ Profit}$$

Which is the more profitable? The variation in price with increased fixed costs, or the budgeted capacity as before?

The Market

Management may use variations in price, change its costs and regulate output in order to meet the needs of the market. Market research assesses the level and nature of demand in the market and if there is likely to be changes in consumer buying; management need to change its strategy (or planning) in order to maintain its share of the market, or indeed increase its share.

Which is the best plan?

Using the figures based on an output of 750 units as before and

Variable Cost/Unit	£6
Fixed Costs	£2,000
Sales Price	£12 per Unit

determine which of (a), (b), (c) or (d) below is the best course of action.

(a) Base the estimated profit on the above budgeted plan.
(b) Reduce the price by £1.00 per unit, research having indicated a 20% sales increase.
(c) Launch an advertising campaign costing £400, which produces a sales increase of 10%.

(d) Reduce the price by 15%, giving a market increase of 30%.

To give you a start:

> (a) Estimated profit on 750 Units
> Contribution/unit = £6.00 × 750 units
> Contribution   = £4,500
> *less* Fixed Costs = £2,000
> Profit   £2,500

Can the proposals in (b), (c) and (d) better £2,500 profit?

> (b) Reduced the price £1
> Sales increaes 20%
>
> Contribution/unit = £5.00 × 900 units
>
> Contribution   = £4,500
>
> *less* Fixed Costs = £2,000
>
> Profit   £2,500
>
> No change!
>
> Try (c) and (d)?

Example Exercise

As a costing assistant for a manufacturing company, you are asked to make a number of calculations. The company has a plant capacity of 10,000 units per annum, but at present is working only to about 90% capacity. The pricing policy of the enterprise is to add a 20% mark-up to cost.

The information you are given is listed below:

Costs based on a budget of 10,000 units per annum:

	£	
Direct Labour	100,000	100% variable
Direct Materials	200,000	100% variable
Factory Overheads	80,000	£2 per unit variable
Administrative Overheads	120,000	
Total Estimated Costs:	500,000	

Required:

(a) Prepare a table to show total, fixed and variable costs based on a planned output of 10,000 units per annum.

(b) Calculate the contribution per unit.

(c) What is the estimated profit on the planned output? If sales were only 9,000 units, calculate the estimated profit or loss.

(d) Calculate the break-even point.
What is the loss on 10 units below break-even?
What is the profit on 10 units above break-even?

(e) Calculate the contribution/sales ratio (profit/volume ratio).
Calculate the profit or loss on sales of £425,000.

(f) If the selling price was reduced by 10% and advertising costs were £20,000, to gain an estimated extra 1500 units sold, would it be worth going ahead with the project?

(g) An improved model is to be launched. Variable costs will increase by £8 per unit. Fixed costs will increase by an estimated £50,000. The selling price to launch the new model is £65.
What extra sales are required to cover these costs?

(a) Table of costs:

	Total	Output: 10,000 units Fixed	Variable
	£	£	£
Direct Labour	100,000	—	100,000
Direct Materials	200,000	—	200,000
Factory Overheads	80,000	60,000	20,000
Administrative Overheads	120,000	120,000	—
	500,000	180,000	320,000

(b) Contribution per Unit:

Selling Price £60 — Variable Cost/Unit £32
Contribution: £28

(c) Estimated profit on planned output:

	£
Revenue: 10,000 × £60 per unit	600,000
Costs:	500,000
Estimated Profit	100,000

Profit on 9,000 units:

	£
1,000 units × Contribution/Unit	1,000 × £28
	= 28,000 *less* profit
Estimated Profit	= 72,000

(d) Break-Even Point:

	£
Fixed Costs	180,000
Contribution/Unit	= 28
	= 6,429 units (rounded up)

Check

Revenue:	6,429 × £60 =	385,740
− Variable costs	6,429 × £32 =	205,728
Contribution:		180,012
− Fixed Costs		180,000
		12

Loss on 10 units below:

10 × Contribution/Unit	=	10 × £28
	=	£280 (loss £268)

Profit on 10 units above:

10 × Contribution/Unit	=	10 × £28
	=	£280 (profit £292)

(e) Contribution/Sales ratio:

$$\frac{\text{Contribution/Unit}}{\text{Sales/Unit}} \quad \frac{£28}{£60}$$

$$= 0.4666$$

Profit/Loss on Sales of £425,000:

Sales × C/S ratio	=	£425,000 × 0.4666
Contribution	=	£198,330
− Fixed Cost		£180,000
Estimated Profit		£ 18,330

(f) Is the project worth going ahead?   YES
New Selling price: £60 − 10% = £54
New Contribution/Unit: £22 × 1,500 extra units sold:

	= £33,000
less costs for advertising	£20,000
Estimated Profit	£13,000

(g) Extra Sales required:
Selling Price £65 − Variable Costs £40
New Contribution/Unit = £25
To cover an extra £50,000 fixed costs:

$$\frac{\text{Fixed Costs}}{\text{Contribution/Unit}} = \frac{£50,000}{£25}$$

$$\textit{Extra Sales required} = 2,000 \text{ units}$$

Exercises

1. The following costs relate to an output of 2,000 units:

	£	£
Direct Labour	25,000	
Direct Materials	40,000	
Overheads	35,000	100,000

Variable Costs

Direct Materials	100%
Direct Labour	£1.50 per unit.
Power (part of Overheads)	0.50 per unit.

Revenue
Sales per unit   20% above cost price.

Required:

(a) A table to show total, fixed and variable costs based on an output of 2,000 units.
(b) The contribution per unit.
(c) The estimated profit based on 2,000 units.
(d) The estimated profit on 2,100 units
                          on 1,950 units.

(e)   The Break-Even point.
      The profit on 1 above break-even.
      The loss on 1 below break-even.

(f)   *Variation.* If sales price per unit were to decrease by 10% and output
      was to increase by 10%, what is the estimated profit (or loss)?

2.   Mr Baldwin's small factory produces jeans. Output per month is 500
     units.

Monthly costs are:	£	*Variable Cost*:
Direct Labour	2,000	£0.50/Unit
Direct Materials	2,000	100%
Overheads (Fixed)	1,000	—
Costs per month	5,000	
Selling Price:	Mark-up of 25% on Cost	

Required:

(a)   The contribution per unit.

(b)   The estimated profit per month based on 500 units.

(c)   The break-even point per month.
      The break-even revenue per month based on C/S ratio (contribution
      /sales ratio).

(d)   If during the first 6 months revenue reached £42,500, what is the
      estimated profit?

(e)   If sales in a month were £5,950, what is the estimated profit/loss in
      the month?

(f)   Variations due to market changes:
      Propose to reduce the sales price by £1.00 and sales estimated to rise
      by 20% per month or

      increase advertising cost by £250 per month and improve the jeans
      with stronger zip costing £0.30 per unit, with sales estimated to rise
      by 15% per month.

      Which is the better of the two proposals?

(g)   If advertising costs increase by £765 during the first year, how many
      extra units need to be sold to cover this cost?

      Note: Treat as a fixed cost and divide by contribution per unit.

(h)   *Break-Even Chart.* Based on the initial information of 500 units
      output per month, prepare a break-even chart, clearly indicating the
      break-even point.

3. Lillee and Thompson produce sports gear under the trade name 'Down Under'. The present year expects costs to be:

	£
Direct Labour	48,000
Direct Materials	55,000
Production Overheads	22,500
Distribution Costs	15,000
Administration Costs	13,500
Financial and General Costs	4,000
Sales Revenue:	180,000
(expected on 45,000 units)	

Variable Costs:

Direct Labour	75%
Direct Materials	100%
Production Overheads	10%
Distribution Costs	10%

Expected production capacity: 50,000 units.

Required:

(a) A table to show the division of fixed and variable costs based on a capacity of 50,000 units.
(b) Calculate the unit contribution.
(c) If an order for 1,000 units was received, what would the extra cost be, based on marginal costing?
(d) Could the firm accept the above order at £2.80 per unit?
(e) Calculate the break-even point.
    Calculate the break-even revenue based on the C/S ratio.
(f) Calculate the loss on 50 units below break-even.
(g) What is the estimated profit on 50,000 units?
(h) What is the profit/loss on a production of 39,500 units?

4. The following costs relate to a budgeted sales forecast of 30,000 units per year:

Costs	Budgeted	Fixed	Variable
	£	£	£
Production Cost	287,500	25,000	262,500
Administration	35,000	30,000	5,000
Distribution	95,000	62,500	32,500
	417,500	117,500	300,000

Revenue per Unit: £15.00

Required:

(a) The number of units needed to sell to cover costs.
(b) If sales decline to 20,000 units, what is the estimated profit or loss?
(c) If £80,000 is spent on advertising, how many extra units need to be sold to cover cost?
(d) On sales of £345,750 after 10 months, what is the estimated profit/loss at this point?
(e) The following proposals have been made:
  (i) Spend £2.00 per unit improving the product, expecting sales to rise to 40,000 units.
  (ii) Pay £1.00 per unit sales commission, expecting sales to rise to 38,500 units.
  (iii) An additional order of 8,000 units at £12.50 per unit for Export. Export costs £10,000.

  Which of these three proposals do you consider the best?

5. *Situation*: Smith Engineering Ltd has prepared the quarterly budget figures for three months ending 31 March 1986 as follows:

	Budget Forecast Total	Fixed Costs	Variable Costs
	£	£	£
Cost of production	115,000	10,000	105,000
Cost of distribution and Sales	38,000	25,000	13,000
Administration expenses	14,000	12,000	2,000
	167,000	47,000	120,000

Sales forecast:
12,000 units @ £15 each.

As an assistant to the cost accountant you have been asked to calculate the following:

Required:

(a) What is the minimum number of sales units required to cover costs?
(b) If demand was to fall to 8000 units, what is the effect on the forecasted profit?
(c) If an additional £16,000 was spent on advertising the product, how many *more* units need to be sold to cover costs?
(d) Alternative proposals were to be considered:
  (i) Redesign and improve packaging costing £1.50/unit. Test marketing indicates that sales would increase by 25%.

(ii) Reduce the selling price by £1. Research indicates that sales would increase by a third.

Should the company consider one of the above proposals or leave things as they were in the budgeted forecast?   .

6.   As a costing assistant you need to prepare budget estimates for the next financial year. At current production levels, the company produces 6,000 units per year and has the capacity to increase this by another 1,000 units. The firm's pricing policy is to mark-up by 25% on cost.

The estimated costs for the next financial period based on an output of 6,000 units are:

	£
Direct Labour	78,000
Direct Materials	114,000
Factory Overheads:	
Indirect Labour	12,000
Indirect Expenses	33,000
Office Overheads	123,000
	360,000

Your research reveals that Direct Labour and Direct Materials are 100% Variable.

Indirect Labour is 10% Variable as a result of sharing a bonus payment scheme.

Power (Indirect Expenses) is estimated at £1.80 per unit Variable.

All other costs are to be considered Fixed.

Required:

(a)   Prepare a suitable table to show fixed and variable costs based on an output of 6,000 units.

(b)   Calculate:
The contribution per unit.
The Break-even point.

(c)   Prepare a chart based on an output of 6,000 units to illustrate:
The company's break-even point.
The profit/loss based on a production of 6,500 units.
The profit/loss based on a production of 3,500 units.

7. As an assistant to the cost accountant of a manufacturing company, you have been asked to prepare some costing information relating to the launch of the company's new product.

Expected Output:	10,000 Units
Cost per Unit	£
Direct Materials	30
Direct Labour	70
Variable Overheads	40

Total fixed costs attributed to the product is £240,000.
Selling price per Unit: £200.

TASKS

Calculate:

A. The contribution per unit.

B. The break-even point.

*C. The margin of safety, expressed as a percentage.

D. The maximum profit on the expected output of 10,000 units and the estimated profit if production fell to 8500 units.

E. The following proposals have been put forward:

   (i) By reducing the price to £190 per unit, 12,000 units is estimated to be sold.
   (ii) By increasing the price to £210 per unit, 9500 units is estimated to be sold.
   (iii) By retaining the existing price at £200 and an extra £60,000 is spent on advertising, sales being estimated at 11,800 units.

Which of these proposals do you consider is the best? Explain briefly why.

* margin of safety = Output – break-even point
  as a %   = $\dfrac{M/S}{Output} \times 100$

8. The figures below relate to Robertson's PLC.
    Mr Jones, the head of finance, has recently come from a board meeting
    which has discussed two alternative plans for the future growth of the
    company. You have been asked to assist in the submission of a report to
    help evaluate the better of the two proposals.

Profit & Loss Statement, Robertson's PLC
Year ended 30 June 1988

	£	£
Sales (50,000 units) £25 unit		1,250,000
Costs (50,000 units)		
Direct materials £7.5 per unit	375,000	
Direct labour £4.75 per unit	237,500	
Manufacturing OH's:		
Variable £1.25 per unit	62,500	
Fixed	125,000	
Distribution & Sales		
Variable £1.50 per unit	75,000	
Fixed	100,000	
Administration	150,000	1,125,000
Profit		125,000

Plan A

The expansion of sales is expected to be 20% achieved by a vigorous
selling campaign. Representatives to be given specific sales targets and
incentives. Distribution and sales costs to rise by 10p per unit.

Because of overtime and weekend work, direct labour is expected to rise
by 15p per unit.

Fixed costs to increase by 5%.

The selling price per unit to be reduced to £24 per unit.

Plan B

The use of modern plant and equipment outlined for this plan is to boost sales by 50% and take a major share of the market. Both material and labour costs are expected to be reduced because of greater efficiency and economies of scale:

Direct materials: £7.5 unit to £6.5 unit
Direct labour   : £4.75 unit to £4.2 unit

To finance the sales campaign, sales and distribution costs are expected to rise by 30p unit.

Fixed costs will expect to rise by 10%.

The selling price per unit is to be cut by a competitive 15%.

Required:

(a) Calculate the results of the alternative plans put forward by the board.

Include the profit figures to be earned and the break-even points for each plan.

(b) Prepare a forecast profit and loss statement for Plan B for the year ended 30 June 1989.

(c) Briefly comment on the results of your findings and suggest which plan you would recommend to the head of finance to be put into operation.

9. *Situation*

You work on the Costing Section for SuperMacs, an organisation which produces components for the automobile industry and has a capacity to produce 12,500 units per annum.

The cost figures below relate to an estimated production of 10,000 units in the year:

	£	£
Direct Labour	80,000	
Direct Materials	60,000	

Overheads:
  factory   40,000
  distribution   30,000
  office   40,000   250,000

The pricing policy of the organisation is to mark-up by 20%.

The *variable costs* relating to the above figures would be:

  (i) Direct materials 100% variable.
 (ii) Direct labour is to share in a bonus scheme worth £3.5 per unit.
(iii) Factory overheads: power is £1.5 per unit.
(iv) Distribution overheads: Salesman's commission is £1.2 per unit.

The Cost Accountant sets you the following tasks:

TASK A:

  (i) Calculate the prime cost per unit.
 (ii) Calculate the production cost per unit.
(iii) Prepare a table to show fixed, variable and total costs.
(iv) Calculate the contribution per unit.

TASK B

  (i) Prepare a simple break-even chart to illustrate the above information.
 (ii) Indicate the break-even point on your chart.

TASK C

  (i) If estimated sales were £304,650, calculate the estimated profit from these sales.
 (ii) If the selling price was to be reduced by 10% and extra advertising/publicity carried out costing £12,600, market research indicates an increase in sales of 20%. Would you recommend this course of action?

PART 3

Budgeting and Planning

In a well-structured organisation the budget is at the centre of the financial control system. When budgets are being prepared the responsibility for each main section is normally allotted to the functional heads of each department, such as the sales manager, production manager, finance manager, and so forth.

The basic purpose of a budget is to control the organisation's expenditure and to plan ahead for the future. After budgets have been prepared by heads of departments, they should be communicated to all personnel who need to know in order to involve them in the forward planning of the organisation. Budgets assist those in management by motivating them towards the major objectives of the organisation. Expenditure for the year ahead can be planned, profits estimated and targets set. Actual results can then be measured against the budgeted plans and differences (variances) may be analysed, debated and acted upon where appropriate.

Budgets are prepared by management in order to attempt to achieve company policy; their preparation is usually a time-consuming exercise. The main steps may be summarised as follows:

(a) The objectives of the organisation should be clearly stated.
(b) An initial forecast of expenditures and revenues is prepared.
(c) The necessary computations are made in terms of manpower, materials, equipment, overheads, etc.
(d) The initial budget is reviewed and amended where appropriate until it is accepted.

In order to set realistic objectives, management must obtain as much information as it can in terms of both internal and external factors. Externally, the organisation must consider the economic and political climate and obtain as much information as possible about competitors. Internally, it must assess the strengths and weaknesses of its own structure and consider the alternative plans available in order to compete effectively and gain its optimum share of the market.

The main types of budgets are:

Sales budget
Production budget
Personnel budget (or manpower)
Capital expenditure budget
Administration budget
Cash budget

The initial forecast must start with the expected level of sales. Selling is the life-line of an organisation and its cornerstone. Without sales, there is no organisation and therefore it is essential to make an accurate estimation of what sales (for every product) are likely to be. From the sales budget, other budgets should then fall into place.

The production budget must ensure that it can meet the demands set by the sales budget. It must take into account the stocks it already holds and be sure it has the necessary materials, labour, machinery and so forth to meet the appropriate sales demand. It is of little use to budget for a 30% sales increase if production cannot cope with even a 10% increase. If management wants a 30% increase, it must prepare, plan and be ready to finance it.

The personnel budget must ensure that the organisation has the right manpower at the right time, with the appropriate financial support to meet manpower and training needs.

The capital expenditure budget takes into account capital costs and involves the purchase of fixed assets like plant, machinery, equipment, new premises and other items expected to be used in the organisation over the long term. Fixed assets need replacement because they are likely to be worn out eventually or become obsolete. The budget needs to forecast what resources need to be put aside either for replacement or expansion purposes.

The administration budget usually takes into account all the overheads of the organisation from the administrative point of view and involves, largely, the fixed costs like rent, rates, stationery, heating, telephone etc.

The cash budget (or cash flow) is the last but certainly not the least of all the budgets, and is often regarded as the most crucial. It involves all the other budgets in its forecast because it must include all sources of expected revenues in the months ahead (normally 1 year) against all sources of expected expenditure. In other words, it shows the forecast of the flow of cash into and out of the organisation and in so doing, affects the Bank balance. An organisation must have sufficient liquidity (or cash) to meet its day-to-day needs, otherwise it will run into financial difficulties and may have a cash crisis. If it runs out of money because of poor forward planning, how can it pay for wages, materials and a long list of overhead costs? On the other hand, if it can be foreseen that there may be a cash shortage ahead, management can negotiate, ahead of time, the necessary liquidity it needs and, in so doing, it emphasises the financial soundness of the organisation.

The Cash Budget

A new company has gathered the following information for the six months from 1 January, 1988 to 30 June 1988.

(a) Sales (in units) £40 per unit:

JAN.	FEB.	MAR.	APR.	MAY	JUNE	
200	300	200	400	300	400	units

(b) Production is 300 units per month for the whole 6 months.
(c) Fixed overhead costs will be £3,000 per month payable in the month after production.
(d) Variable overhead costs will be £15 per unit payable in the month of production.
(e) Direct wages will be £5 per unit payable in the month of production.
(f) Equipment costing £10,000 will be purchased in February and paid for in March. Once installed, it will allow production to increase to 500 units per month.
(g) Materials will cost £8 per unit and suppliers will be paid in the month following purchases.
(h) All sales of units are on credit. Debtors are expected to pay in the month following their purchase.
(i) Cash at Bank on 1 January = £10,000.
(j) The company expects demand for its products to increase to about 450 units *after* June 1988.

Required:

A schedule of payments and a cash budget.

Schedule of Payments

	JAN. £	FEB. £	MAR. £	APR. £	MAY £	JUNE £
Fixed overheads		3,000	3,000	3,000	3,000	3,000
Variable overheads (300 × £15)	4,500	4,500	4,500	4,500	4,500	4,500
Direct wages (300 × £5)	1,500	1,500	1,500	1,500	1,500	1,500
Equipment			10,000			
Materials (300 × £8)		2,400	2,400	2,400	2,400	2,400
	6,000	11,400	21,400	11,400	11,400	11,400

Cash Budget

	JAN. £	FEB. £	MAR. £	APR. £	MAY £	JUNE £
Bank balance b/f	10,000	4,000	600	(8,800)	(12,200)	(7,600)
+ Receipts*	—	8,000	12,000	8,000	16,000	12,000
	10,000	12,000	12,600	(800)	3,800	4,400
− Payments	6,000	11,400	21,400	11,400	11,400	11,400
Bank balance c/f	4,000	600	(8,800)	(12,200)	(7,600)	(7,000)

*Receipts calculated @ £40 unit sales, allowing for one month credit.

Analysis of the cash budget

The cash budget clearly highlights that the company does not have sufficient capital to finance the above plan. However, if it could lease the new equipment rather than buy it, or obtain more capital by March, the problem would be solved. If the company had not prepared a cash flow budget it would have had a deficit from March to June of a proportion it may not have planned. By preparing a cash flow, the organisation can demonstrate it has some control in its financial affairs and is therefore more likely to accommodate the deficit period by negotiation with its creditors. The cash flow emphasises the common business problem that in order to finance an increasing level of sales, stocks have to be increased, equipment purchased, etc. Extra expenditure is incurred before the revenue from extra sales comes in.

In conclusion, budgets are both a planning and control tool because they help management to evaluate the financial implications of various courses of action ahead of time and to monitor those plans by comparing actual results of budget plans.

Budgets are an example of management by objectives because variations between actual and budgeted results can be highlighted, analysed and debated in order to gain the optimum levels of profits for the organisation.

A Worked Example: Cash Budget Through to Budgeted Final Accounts

This is a testing question and needs to be followed carefully.

You have been asked by a business colleague of yours to 'cost out' his plans to set up a limited company to import and sell mountain bikes, which are apparently the very latest in the U.K.

Information

1) The Company will be called Bikers (Import) U.K. Ltd. and will issue 90,000 × £1 ordinary shares at par on the following terms:

   Jan. 1 on application 20%.
   Jan. 7 on allotment 30%
   Apr. 4 First and Final Call 50%

2) The following is the pattern of Fixed Asset acquisitions:

   January £60,000 by cheque
   and October £20,000 by cheque.

3) Provide depreciation at the rate of 15% – on the total fixed asset value on December 31.

4) Sales are expected to be: Jan. £12,000, Feb. £16,000, Mar – June inc. £20,000 monthly, July – Dec. inc. £25,000 monthly.

5) An initial stock will be purchased on Jan. 1 £20,000 (Selling Value) and subsequent purchases are to be arranged so that the stock at the end of each month will still be at this same figure. The sales margin is to be 30%. Therefore a stock of £14,000 is required in balance each month ending.

6) Estimated wages will be £2,500 each month – payable in that month.

7) Estimated rent and rates will be £1,000 each month – payable in that month.

8) Estimated operating expenses will be £1,500 each month – payable one month in arrears.

9) Trade creditors will be paid in the month after goods are received and Debtors will settle their accounts two months after the sale.

10) Assume that the Directors will propose an Ordinary Dividend of 2 pence per share.

11) Assume that the Directors will provide for Corporation Tax at the rate of 30% of net profit.

TASK A

Prepare a "schedule of payments" for the period January – December inclusive.

TASK B

Prepare a cash budget for the period January – December inclusive.

TASK C

Prepare a Forecast Trading, Profit and Loss and Appropriation Account for the year.

TASK D

Prepare a Forecast Balance Sheet as at 31 December.

Solution
The main problem is to calculate the value of budgeted purchases – notes 4 and 5 give us the detail.

1.   Convert sales figures to cost – i.e. 70% of sales value:-

	Jan.	Feb.	Mar.	April	May	June
Sales £	12,000	16,000	20,000	20,000	20,000	20,000
70% of sales = cost of sales	8,400	11,200	14,000	14,000	14,000	14,000

	July	Aug.	Sept.	Oct.	Nov.	Dec.
Sales £	25,000	25,000	25,000	25,000	25,000	25,000
70% of sales = cost of sales	17,500	17,500	17,500	17,500	17,500	17,500

2. Note 5 tells us that the budgeted stock at the end of each month is to be £14,000 (70% of £20,000). ˙ . The budgeted purchases will be as follows:-

	Jan. £	Feb. £	Mar. £	April £	May £	June £
	8,400					
	14,000					
	22,400	11,200	14,000	14,000	14,000	14,000

	July £	Aug. £	Sept. £	Oct. £	Nov. £	Dec. £
	17,500	17,500	17,500	17,500	17,500	17,500

i.e. in January we purchase our 'base stock' of £14,000 and what we plan to sell in January, then in each month following we plan to purchase what we intend to sell – leaving us with a constant stock at cost of £14,000 at beginning and end of each month.

Note: Many questions actually tell you what the purchases figure is. All you have to do is take note of any credit period given for the cash budget – in this example Bikers expect one month's credit from suppliers e.g. January purchases will be paid for in February.

3. Prepare the *Schedule of Payments* i.e. List what amounts are going to be *paid* in each month:-

	Jan. £	Feb. £	Mar. £	April £	May £	June £
Purchase of F.A.	60,000	–	–	–	–	–
Payments to Suppliers	–	22,400	11,200	14,000	14,000	14,000
Wages	2,500	2,500	2,500	2,500	2,500	2,500
Rent & Rates	1,000	1,000	1,000	1,000	1,000	1,000
Operating Expenses	–	1,500	1,500	1,500	1,500	1,500
	63,500	27,400	16,200	19,000	19,000	19,000

	July £	Aug. £	Sept. £	Oct. £	Nov. £	Dec. £
Purchase of F.A.	–	–	–	20,000	–	–
Payments to						
Suppliers	14,000	17,500	17,500	17,500	17,500	17,500*
Wages	2,500	2,500	2,500	2,500	2,500	2,500
Rent & Rates	1,000	1,000	1,000	1,000	1,000	1,000
Operating						
Expenses	1,500	1,500	1,500	1,500	1,500	1,500*
	19,000	22,500	22,500	42,500	22,500	22,500

*At the end of December £17,500 will be owing in respect of December purchases and £1,500 owing in respect of expenses incurred in December . ˙. These amounts will appear under current liabilities on the budgeted Balance Sheet at December 31.

4. Prepare the *Cash Budget* – in this example there are two sources of revenue:-

   a) The receipts from the initial share issue i.e. £45,000 during January and £45,000 during April.

   b) Receipts from customers – note 9 informs us that Bikers Ltd. intend to give 2 months credit . ˙. January sales will be received in March and so on.

	Jan.	Feb.	Mar.	April	May	June
Balance b/f	Nil	(18,500)	(45,900)	(50,100)	(8,100)	(7,100)
Receipts	45,000	–	12,000	* 61,000	20,000	20,000
	45,000	(18,500)	(33,900)	10,900	11,700	12,700
Payments	63,500	27,400	16,200	19,000	19,000	19,000
Balance c/f	(18,500)	(45,900)	(50,100)	(8,100)	(7,100)	(6,100)

*(i.e. February sales £16,000 + £45,000 balance of share issue)

	July	Aug.	Sept.	Oct.	Nov.	Dec.
Balance b/f	(6,100)	(5,100)	(7,600)	(5,100)	(22,600)	(20,100)
Receipts	20,000	20,000	25,000	25,000	25,000	25,000
	13,700	14,700	17,200	19,700	2,200	4,700
Payments	19,000	22,500	22,500	42,500	22,500	22,500
Balance c/f	(5,100)	(7,600)	(5,100)	(22,600)	(20,100)	(17,600)

5. Prepare the budgeted Trading and Profit and Loss Account for the year.

Bikers (Import) U.K. Ltd. Budgeted Trading and Profit and Loss Account for Year Ending 31 December

	£	£
Sales		258,000
Cost of Sales		
Opening Stock	Nil	
Purchases	194,600	
	194,600	
Closing Stock	14,000	180,600
Gross Profit		77,400
Wages (12 × £2,500)	30,000	
Rent and Rates (12 × £1,000)	12,000	
Operating Expenses (12 × £1,500)	18,000	
Depreciation of Fixed Assets (£80,000 × 15%)	12,000	72,000
Net Profit (b/t)		5,400
Proposed Corporation Tax (30% of £5,400)		1,620
Net Profit (a/t)		3,780
Proposed Ordinary Dividend (90,000 × 2p.)		1,800
P & L c/f		1,980

6. Prepare the budgeted Balance Sheet.

Bikers (Import) U.K. Limited Budgeted Balance Sheet as at 31 December

	£ Cost	£ Depreciation	£ Net
Fixed Assets			
Various	80,000	12,000	68,000
Current Assets			
Stock	14,000		
Debtors	50,000	64,000	
Current Liabilities			
Creditors	17,500		
Accruals	1,500		
Overdraft	17,600		
Taxation owing	1,620		
Dividends owing	1,800	40,020	23,980
			£91,980
Capital and Reserves			
£1 Ordinary Shares			90,000
Profit and Loss Account balance			1,980
			£91,980

Exercises

1. The following is the budget data for J. Robertson and David for the months April to December, 1988:

(in 000's)	Apr. £	May £	June £	July £	Aug. £	Sep. £	Oct. £	Nov. £	Dec. £
Credit sales	20	30	35	34	36	25	26	27	28
Credit Purchases	20	22	22	23	17	18	19	20	30

Rent, Rates paid quarterly in advance, 1st payment due on 1 April, £12,000 per year.
Salaries paid in the month, £2000 per month.
Wages paid in the month, £1,000 per month + 10% increase from 1 September.
General expenses paid in the month, £500 per month.
Opening Bank balance £10,000 overdraft on 1 July, 1987.

Note: Debtors pay at the end of the month following the sale.
Creditors must be paid at the end of the month in which the purchase was made.
A tax payment of £15,000 is to be made in July.

Required:

Prepare a cash budget for July to December inclusive.

2. The following information refers to Jones Ltd and shows the forecast from June 1988 to March 1989.
Sales are £48 per unit: unit sales forecast:

	June	July	Aug.	Sept.	Oct.	Nov.	Dec.	Jan.	Feb.	Mar.
Units	940	980	1,020	1,040	1,080	1,180	1,240	1,280	1,360	1,380

Debtors expected to pay 2 months after invoice.

Production in units:

1,000	1,040	1,040	1,100	1,200	1,240	1,300	1,360	1,400	1,400

Materials cost £20 per unit payable in the month of production.
Labour cost £12 per unit payable in the month of production.
Fixed expenses cost £3,000 per month payable in month *previous* to production.

Variable expenses cost £8 per unit payable in month following production.

Capital expenditure on equipment £15,000 is anticipated in December.

Bank a/c balance estimated in September (1/9/88) is £4,000 Overdraft (agreed bank limit £4,000).

Required:

Prepare a cash budget for the period September 1988 to February 1989 inclusive, showing the cash balance at the end of each month.

3. You work for a firm of Accountants, who have just taken on a client, R. Snall & Co. In addition to the year end accounts, the client requires a 'cash forecast' and has supplied various data.

Information
   (i) Opening Cash (including bank) balance £2,000.
  (ii) Production in units:

(1986)									(1987)	
April	May	June	July	Aug.	Sept.	Oct.	Nov.	Dec.	Jan.	Feb.
480	540	600	640	700	740	760	680	620	520	500

 (iii) Raw Materials used in production cost £10 per unit, which is payable in the month of production.
  (iv) Direct labour costs of £17 per unit are payable in the month of production.
   (v) Variable expenses are £3 per unit, payable $\frac{2}{3}$ in month of production and $\frac{1}{3}$ in the month following production.
  (vi) Sales at £40 per unit:

Mar.	April	May	June	July	Aug.	Sept.	Oct.	Nov.	Dec.
520	400	640	580	800	600	700	800	780	800

Debtors to pay their accounts in the month following the sale.

 (vii) Fixed expenses of £1,200 per month payable each month.
(viii) Machinery costing £21,000 to be paid for in August.
  (ix) Receipt of an Investment Grant of £7,000 is due in November.
   (x) Drawings to be £800 per month.

Required:

(a) Prepare a schedule of payments for the six months to 31.12.86.
(b) Prepare a cash budget for the six months to 31.12.86.
(c) Prepare a draft memorandum to the client, commenting on the results of your cash budget.

4.   Mr Ben is to open a retail shop on 1.7.88. He will put in £70,000 cash as capital. His plans are as follows:

Information

(1) On 1.7.88 to buy and pay for Premises £50,000, Shop Fixtures £7,000 and a motor van £4000.
(2) To employ two sales assistants, each to get a salary of £350 per month, payable at the end of each month (ignore tax and NI).
(3) To buy the following goods:

	July	Aug.	Sept.	Oct.	Nov.	Dec.
(units)	500	540	660	800	900	760

(4) To sell the following goods:

	July	Aug.	Sept.	Oct.	Nov.	Dec.
(units)	345	465	585	705	885	945

(5) Units will be sold for £25 each. One-third of the sales are for cash, the other two-thirds being on credit. Customers are expected to pay their accounts in the month following that in which they buy the goods.
(6) Units will cost £16 for July to September inclusive and £18 thereafter. Suppliers are to be paid in the month of supply.
(7) Mr Ben will withdraw £700 per month as drawings.
(8) His other expenses are estimated at £400 per month payable in the month following.
(9) Stock at 31.12.88 is to be valued £18 per unit.
(10) Provide for depreciation on shop fixtures at 10% p.a. and 25% p.a. on the motor van.

Required:

(a) Prepare a schedule of payments for July to December 1988 inclusive.
(b) Prepare a cash flow budget for the period July to December inclusive, showing the balance at the end of each month.
(c) Prepare a budgeted profit statement for the 6 months ending 31.12.88.
(d) Prepare a budgeted balance sheet as at 31.12.88.
(e) Comment on the expected results of the business, making use of any financial indicators you may wish to illustrate your comments.

5. *Budgeting: Situation*

You work as an assistant to a firm of accountants who deal with a wide variety of financial and management accounts. One of their clients, a partnership called Smith & Jones, have submitted data for your preparation. The information has been placed with you to prepare the draft documents before they are passed on to the client.

Information

Smith & Jones wish to form a new private limited company in the name of S & J Co. Ltd. The new company is to commence its operations with effect from 1st July, 1989. The data estimated for the period from 1 July, 1989 to 31 December, 1989 is as follows:

1. Smith is to put £50,000 into the business bank account on 1 July, 89 and will be issued with 50,000 £1 ordinary shares.

   Jones will put £100,000 into the business bank account on the same date and will be issued with 50,000 £1 ordinary shares and £50,000 of Debenture Stock at 12% interest.

2. The sales will be on a credit basis and are estimated to be:

July	£25,000	Oct.	£50,000
Aug.	£45,000	Nov.	£45,000
Sep.	£65,000	Dec.	£60,000

   All debtors are expected to settle their accounts two months after the month in which the goods are bought.

3. Purchases, all on credit, are estimated to be:

July	£65,000	Oct.	£45,000
Aug.	£35,000	Nov.	£30,000
Sep.	£50,000	Dec.	£45,000

   Creditors' payments are arranged to be paid in the month following the purchase.

4. Wages and salaries are estimated to be £1,750 per month payable on the last week day of each month.

5. Smith & Jones will each draw director's fees of £1,000 per month payable on the same date as in 4. above.

6. Debenture interest is to be paid $\frac{1}{2}$ yearly, the first payment is due in December, 1989.

7. Premises are to be purchased for £85,000 and paid for in August, 1989.

8. Fixed costs are estimated to be £1,500 per month for the first four months of business and then increase by 20% thereafter. These costs are payable one month in arrears.

9. Equipment is to be purchased on 1 July, 89 for £30,000, half of which is to be paid in July and the other in October.
   It is also to be depreciated by 20% per annum on the straight-line basis.

10. Stock is estimated to be valued at £40,000 on 31 December, 1989.

TASK A

Prepare a cash flow budget for the period July to December, 1989 (inclusive).

TASK B

Prepare a budgeted profit & loss account and a balance sheet for the half year to 31 December, 1989.

TASK C

Prepare a draft report to Smith & Jones concerning the importance of budgetary control. Include aspects such as purpose, functions and problems involving the preparation of budgets.

6. *Situation/Information*

You work for a small manufacturing company which is developing a system of budgetary control and the following data is available:

(a) *Balance Sheet as at 31 May 1992*

Fixed Assets	£	£	£
Premises			50,000
Plant (orig. cost £10,000)			6,400
			56,400
Current Assets			
Stock	18,800		
Debtors	11,200		
Bank	600	30,600	
Current Liabilities			
Creditors	18,600		
Proposed Dividend	2,000	20,600	10,000
			£66,400
Capital & Reserves			
£1 Ordinary Shares			50,000
Profit & Loss Account Balance			16,400
			£66,400

(b)

Month (1992)	Credit Sales	Cash Sales	Credit Purchases
May (Actual)	£11,200	£5,600	£18,600
June (Budgeted)	13,400	8,000	19,000
July (Budgeted)	16,400	9,000	20,000
Aug. (Budgeted)	16,000	9,000	10,400

(c) All trade creditors will be paid in the month following receipt of the goods and all trade debtors will take one month's credit.

(d) On 1/6/92 plant costing £5,000 is to be purchased. Depreciation is charged on the straight line basis of 10% p.a. on cost.

(e) The following monthly expenses, to be paid monthly, are estimated as:

Wages £1,800   General Expenses £700

(f) Rent is £3,600 per year, payable in full in June 1992, for the year to 30 June, 1993.

(g) The proposed dividend will be paid in July 1992.

(h) The sales margin is estimated at 20%.

TASKS

  (i) Prepare a schedule of payments for June–August inclusive.
 (ii) Prepare a schedule of receipts for June–August inclusive.
(iii) Prepare a cash flow budget for June–August inclusive clearly showing the balance at the end of each month.
(iv) Prepare a budgeted trading and profit and loss account for the three months, and a balance sheet as at 31st August, 1992.
 (v) Comment upon the resulting profitability and liquidity position.

7. The following information relates to a businessman, D. Balfour, who will be starting his enterprise on 1 July, 1990, with £5,000. He has made a forecast for the next six months concerning his cash flow:

(a) Production will concern the making of an electrical component for the computer industry. His plan is to produce 500 units per month in the first six months.

(b) Sales: each unit has a selling price of £12.50. The sales estimate for 6 months to 31 December is:

July	Aug.	Sept.	Oct.	Nov.	Dec.
400	480	480	560	640	400 (units)

(c) Variable overheads (based on output), will be £1.50 per unit, payable in the month of production.

(d) Fixed costs will be £1,000 per month payable AFTER the month of production.

(e) Production wages (direct) will be £3 per unit payable in the month of production.

(f) Salaries will be £500 per month until October but expected to rise by 10% in the months following.

(g) Equipment, to cost £8,000 will be purchased in September. 25% Deposit will be paid in September with the balance to be paid equally in October and November.

(h) Materials will cost £2 per unit and suppliers will be paid in the month AFTER the purchase.

All unit sales are on credit. Debtors are expected to pay in the month FOLLOWING their purchase. £5,000 was deposited in the business bank account on 1 July.

As Mr Balfour's financial assistant, you have been asked to prepare:

TASK A

A schedule of payments for the 6 months ending 31 December 1990 and a cash budget to cover the same period.

TASK B

An operating budget which will show the Trading & Profit & Loss forecast for the 6 months ending 31 December 1990 and a forecast Balance Sheet as on 31 December 1990. Note: Closing Stock to be valued at £6.50 per unit.

TASK C

A statement which briefly analyses the cash budget.

PART 4

Capital Appraisal

In most organisations, management have certain criteria on which its investment decisions are taken and there are usually more investment proposals than there is finance to back them.

Capital appraisal is a way whereby an organisation can decide which is the best way to invest its money when it comes to capital expenditure. Decisions are made on the basis of:

(a) the sum invested in a capital project,
(b) the estimated returns from the project and
(c) the length of time the project is expected to last.

Three methods of capital appraisal will be discussed. These are:

1. The 'Pay-Back' method.
2. The Return on Investment method (ROI).
3. The Discounted Cash Flow method (DCF).

The Pay-Back Method

This method approaches capital appraisal from the point of view of how long it takes the project to pay back the original sum invested. If an organisation has £10,000 to invest, what could it do with the money? What would be the wisest choice? Note that capital appraisal calculations are only estimations and what may look and seem a good investment on paper may turn out to be a disaster in practice!

An organisation could consider investing its money in new motor vehicles, or in stocks and shares, or in extending its premises or buying another business and so on. Which choice would provide the best return in terms of value for money? How long is it intended the investment last? A bit of a gamble certainly, but with large sums to be invested, investigation into how much the returns will yield is essential in order that management makes the best choice available at the time.

Consider two alternative plans.

Plan A   £10,000 invested in a vehicle appropriate to give driving lessons for a man wanting to be a driving instructor.

Plan B   £8,000 invested in a portfolio of securities estimated to produce about 20% (compound) return on investment.

Which of the two plans will pay back the original investment in the quicker time?

Year		Plan A Driving School Vehicle £	Plan B Portfolio of Securities £	£
	Initial Investment	10,000	8,000	
1	Estimated Return		Estimated	
	(Revenue-Expenses)	3,000	Return 20% 1,600	9,600
2	(Revenue-Expenses)	3,200	" 1,920	11,520
3	(Revenue-Expenses)	3,500	" 2,304	13,824
4	(Revenue-Expenses)		$(9\frac{1}{2}$ months) 2,199	16,023
	(1 month)	300		
			8,023	
		10,000		

Analysis

Plan A is estimated to be the better of the two plans in monetary terms taking 3 years and 1 month to recover the original investment of £10,000.

Plan B is estimated to take about $8\frac{1}{2}$ months longer to recover to recover the initial sum.

Nothing is absolutely certain. These figures can only be estimations. How can it really be possible to calculate with 100% certainty what returns will be in *x* number of years ahead? It may well be that the investor prefers Plan A because it gives him a job as well as income. On the other hand, he may prefer his capital doing the earning on its own.

Return on Investment Method (ROI)

The ROI is the average profit for the project expressed as a percentage of the capital outlay.

For example, a capital project investing £100,000 is estimated to have profits of

		£	£
Year 1		8,000	
2		12,000	
3		24,000	
4		20,000	
5		16,000	80,000

5 years

= 16,000 average

Return on Investment
[ROI]   =   16%

$$\frac{(16{,}000 \times 100)}{100{,}000}$$

Return on Investment is a fairly straightforward method, as is the pay-back method, but both these tend to ignore the fact that any money received in the future will be worth less than it is today. This brings in the third method, discounted cash flow.

Discounted Cash Flow (DCF)

When considering different investments with returns which are not the same, it should be noted that only by discounting the earnings to present values can any valid comparisons be made.

For example, £100 due in one year is only worth £90.91 now if interest rates were 10% per annum:

	£
Current value	90.91
+ 10% interest	9.09
	100.00

£100 due in 2 years time is only worth £82.64 in today's money assuming interest rates of 10%:

	£	
* Current value	82.64	
+ 10% interest	8.26	Year 1
	90.90	
+ 10% interest	9.10	Year 2
	100.00	

* known as 'Net Present Value' (NPV)

The Net Present Value calculated by formulae and by DCF tables

Net Present Value (NPV) using Formulae

$$\text{NPV} \quad = \quad \frac{A}{(1 + r)^n}$$

A   is the amount invested
r   is the interest rate
n   is the number of years

Example 1

If a sum of £8,500 was invested at 10% simple interest over a period of 5 years, what would its net present value be if interest rates are to be assumed at 8%?

	£
Simple Interest £8,500 × 10% × 5 years =	4,250
Add investment	8,500
	12,750

$$\text{NPV} \quad = \quad \frac{£12,750}{(1.08)^5} = \frac{£12,750}{1.469}$$

$$= £8,679$$

DCF tables   = £8,682
(see p. 438)   (12,750 × .681)

The actual increase in the investment using the NPV (that is, how much will a future sum of money be worth in today's money):

	£
Sum Invested =	8,500
Net Present Value =	8,682
	182

Therefore, the actual increase in the investment at NPV was only £182.

Example 2

If an investment in a laundrette amounted to £50,000 and over the next 6 years the expected returns were estimated to be:

Years 1 to 3 at 20%
Years 4 to 6 at 15%

What would the return on the investment be at NPV if interest rates are to be assumed at an average of 10%?

Returns on Years 1 to 3:

$$£$$
$$£50,000 \times 20\% \times 3 = 30,000$$

Returns on Years 4 to 6:

$$£50,000 \times 15\% \times 3 = \underline{22,500}$$

Estimated surplus $= 52,500$

What will the surplus be worth in terms of NPV?

$$NPV = \frac{Amount}{(1 + r)^n}$$

$$\frac{52,500}{(1.1)^6} = \frac{£52,500}{1.77}$$
$$= £29,661$$

DCF tables $= £29,610$
(see p. 438) $(52,500 \times .564)$

The investment in the laundrette over 6 years would bring in a surplus of £29,610 (table figures) at NPV.

Interpreted at today's value, a sum of £29,610, invested at a compound rate of interest at 10% per annum, is estimated to return £52,500 in 6 years time.

Example 3

The following are the net surplus returns for two projects which have an initial capital investment of £300,000:

Project	A £	B £
Earnings Year 1	100,000	80,000
2	120,000	100,000
3	100,000	100,000
4	60,000	100,000
5	40,000	40,000
Total return	420,000	420,000

Pay-Back Method

Project A pays back during the third year whereas Project B pays back during the fourth, and therefore on this basis it appears that Project A is the better of the two.

Return on Investment

Because the total return is the same (average return per year £84,000), both project A and B will give identical returns over the 5 years and therefore there is no basis for comparison here.

$$\text{Return on Investment } \frac{£84{,}000 \times 100}{£300{,}000} = 28\%$$

Discounted Cash Flow (assuming interest rates at 10%)

Year	Project A Earnings £	NPV* £	Discount Factor ·	Project B Earnings £	NPV* £
0		300,000			300,000
1	100,000	90,900	0.909	80,000	72,720
2	120,000	99,120	0.826	100,000	82,600
3	100,000	75,100	0.751	100,000	75,100
4	60,000	40,980	0.683	100,000	68,300
5	40,000	24,840	0.621	40,000	24,840
		330,940			323,560

*NPV (Net Present Value): the earnings are multiplied by the relevant discount factor.

DCF tables are available which relate to variable rates of interest over a period of time in years.

Project A has a superior earnings on a NPV basis than does Project B, a difference of £7,380 in current terms, represented over the 5 year spell (£330,940 − £323,560).

The choice of appraisal method is left to management to decide, but many organisations will use more than one method. Generally, the larger the organisation the more sophisticated the range of methods used. The market standing of the organisation may well influence the choice. For example, a newly formed company may well look for the project with the fastest pay-back while an older company may seek a longer-term view with a steadier return. Note that if the NPV comes out less than the original investment, it is hardly worth considering the project at all.

DCF tables from 1% to 12% over a period of 15 years

% Rate of Discount

Future Years	1	2	3	4	5	6	7	8	9	10	11	12
1	0.990	0.980	0.971	0.962	0.952	0.943	0.935	0.926	0.917	0.909	0.901	0.893
2	0.980	0.961	0.943	0.925	0.907	0.890	0.873	0.857	0.842	0.826	0.812	0.797
3	0.971	0.942	0.915	0.889	0.864	0.840	0.816	0.794	0.772	0.751	0.731	0.712
4	0.961	0.924	0.888	0.855	0.823	0.792	0.763	0.735	0.708	0.683	0.659	0.636
5	0.951	0.906	0.863	0.822	0.784	0.747	0.713	0.681	0.650	0.621	0.593	0.567
6	0.942	0.888	0.837	0.790	0.746	0.705	0.666	0.630	0.596	0.564	0.535	0.507
7	0.933	0.871	0.813	0.760	0.711	0.665	0.623	0.583	0.547	0.513	0.482	0.452
8	0.923	0.853	0.789	0.731	0.677	0.627	0.582	0.540	0.502	0.467	0.434	0.404
9	0.914	0.837	0.766	0.703	0.645	0.592	0.544	0.500	0.460	0.424	0.391	0.361
10	0.905	0.820	0.744	0.676	0.614	0.558	0.508	0.463	0.422	0.386	0.352	0.322
11	0.896	0.804	0.722	0.650	0.585	0.527	0.475	0.429	0.388	0.350	0.317	0.287
12	0.887	0.788	0.701	0.625	0.557	0.497	0.444	0.397	0.356	0.319	0.286	0.257
13	0.879	0.773	0.681	0.601	0.530	0.469	0.415	0.368	0.326	0.290	0.258	0.229
14	0.870	0.758	0.661	0.577	0.505	0.442	0.388	0.340	0.299	0.263	0.232	0.205
15	0.861	0.743	0.642	0.555	0.481	0.417	0.362	0.315	0.275	0.239	0.209	0.183

Exercises

1. The following represents the net returns for two projects which have an initial capital investment of £200,000:

Project Earnings	Year	X £	Y £
	1	40,000	80,000
	2	80,000	120,000
	3	120,000	100,000
	4	80,000	40,000
	5	60,000	20,000

Required:

(a) State which of the two projects pays back the quickest.
(b) Which of the two gives the better ROI?

2. Find out the net Present Values of the following:

Capital Outlay £	Time years	Interest Rates at time %
5,000	4	10
30,000	6	12
100,000	5	8

3. The following are the net surplus figures for three projects which have an initial investment of £400,000:

Project Earning's Year	A £	B £	C £
1	80,000	160,000	100,000
2	160,000	240,000	150,000
3	240,000	200,000	250,000
4	160,000	80,000	120,000
5	100,000	20,000	100,000

Required:

State which project you would recommend and why.
The organisation has a target return on capital of 10%.

4. The following are the net surplus figures for two projects which have an initial capital investment of £500,000:

Project	L	M
	£	£
Earnings Year 1	80,000	60,000
2	120,000	180,000
3	280,000	320,000
4	200,000	200,000

State which project you consider the better and why. (Company target return, 12%.)

5. Calculate the net present value of a pension plan which will earn £20,000 per annum in ten years time at interest rates expected to average 12%. For your calculations, use both the formulae method and the DCF tables.

6. A house is purchased in 1985 for £62,000 and sold in 1990 for £120,000. If interest rates average 11% per annum, in the 5 years, what is the real increase in value of the property taking NPV into consideration?
Use both formulae and DCF tables for your calculations.

7. An investment of £30,000 is expected to earn a sum of £33,460 in Special Bonds over a period of 4 years. This is to be compared with an alternative investment in Unit Trusts, earning £42,580 over a period of 6 years. If interest rates are estimated to be 12% per annum, which of the two investments will give the best return at NPV?

Further Aspects of Accounting

Objectives

To understand the use of Control accounts by organisations having large numbers of debtors and creditors.

To understand that the function of the Trial Balance is limited.

To explain the function of the Journal as a book of prime entry.

To be aware of the use of a suspense account and how errors are corrected.

To be aware that many small business organisations do not keep full records of finance and that final accounts can be prepared from incomplete records.

To understand the importance of Stock Valuation and its affect on profit in the final accounts.

PART 1

The Need to Keep Control Accounts

When an enterprise grows, inevitably the paper work grows with it. The accounting system needs to expand and the work has to be subdivided. Instead of having a single ledger, there may become a need for several ledgers (nominal, sales and bought ledgers).

This is particularly the case where a firm may have numerous debtors and numerous creditors. These will be removed from the main-stream of the general ledger and *personal* ledgers will be used to accommodate debtors and creditors. Some large firms will have several hundred of these personal accounts and therefore a need arises where such individual accounts need to be cross-checked with a 'master' control balance. The control accounts are held in the general ledger and represent the *totals* of debtors and creditors. Whatever happens to an individual personal account, the total effect will be reflected in the Control accounts. The Control accounts not only cross-check the individual accounts, they are also used for management purposes. For example, if the total liability for creditors is required, the Control account should give the answer without the necessity of adding each of the creditor's balances.

Control accounts are only a cross-check with individual balances for debtors and creditors.

If the individual debtors, for example, do not balance with debtors control, detailed checking is required to find the errors. Thus the trial balance should be easier to balance because the Control accounts have 'controlled' individual personal accounts. They are arithmetical proofs of individual ledgers for debtors and creditors.

Examples

1. *Sales Ledger Control* (Debtors Control a/c)

   The following are balances from the ledgers of ABC Company:

	£
Sales Ledger Dr. Balances at 1 June	7,300
Credit Sales (June)	12,500
Cash/Cheques received from Debtors	11,500
Returns from customers	400
Discounts allowed to customers	280
Debtors cheques returned from bank marked 'R/D' (Return to Drawer) — cheques dishonoured	330
Sales Ledger Dr. Balance at 30 June	7,950

   Debtors Control a/c

			Dr.	Cr.	Balance
June	1	Balance			7,300 Dr.
	30	Sales	12,500		19,800
		Bank/Cash		11,500	8,300
		Discounts		280	8,020
		Returns Inward		400	7,620
		Cheques Dishonoured	330		7,950
		Balance (S/L)			7,950

   Note: The 30 June balance from the Sales Ledger is verified with the control balance above. FINE!

2. *Purchases Ledger Control* (Creditors Control a/c)

	£
Purchases Ledger Cr. Balances at 1 June	12,500
Credit purchases for June	19,750
Cheques paid to suppliers	18,200
Discounts received	478
Returns to suppliers	545
Debit Note from suppliers, resulting from undercharge	50
Credit balances from purchases ledger at 30 June	13,427

Creditors Control a/c

		Dr.	Cr.	Balance
June 1	Balance			12,500
30	Purchases		19,750	32,250
	Bank	18,200		14,050
	Discounts received	478		13,572
	Returns outward	545		13,027
	Undercharge		50	13,077
	Balance (B/L)			13,427

Note: There is a discrepancy of £350 between the purchases ledger (£13,427) and the control a/c (£13,077). Somewhere an error has been made and records must be checked until it is found.

Any transaction which affects either a debtor (in the sales ledger), or a creditor (in the bought ledger) must be reflected in the appropriate control account. The control accounts are totals of respective debtors and creditors. They are not part of the double-entry system, they are used as a cross-check of debtors and creditors.

Sometimes it happens that a debtor overpays his account or conversely, a creditor is overpaid, and this temporarily gives rise to

a debtor's account with a credit balance or
a creditor's account with a debit balance

This will be reflected in the control accounts and these may have both debit and credit balances at the beginning and end of the account. For example

	Dr. £	Cr. £
1 March		
Sales Ledger control balances	5,275	130
Bought Ledger control balances	210	2,500
31 March		
Sales Ledger control balances	5,725	85
Bought Ledger control balances	140	1,900
Credit Sales		14,250
Credit Purchases	9,600	
Cheques, cash from customers	13,140	
Returns Inward	175	
Returns Outward		830
Bad debts	380	
Cheques, cash to suppliers		9,240

*Contra entries between debtors and creditors £60.

*Contra entries refer to accounts' 'set off' against each other; for example, where a debtor is also a supplier of goods. One sum may be set off against another by debiting the creditor and crediting the debtor.

Nominal Ledger (accounts shown in traditional style)

Dr.			Sales Ledger Control a/c			Cr.
1 Mar.	Balance b/d	5,275	1 Mar.	Balance b/d	130	
31	Sales	14,250	31	Bad/Cash	13,140	
	Balance c/d	85		Returns In	175	
				Bad Debts	380	
				Transfer (contra)	60	
				Balance c/d	5,725	
		19,610			19,610	
1 Apr.	Balance b/d	5,725	1 Apr.	Balance b/d	85	

Note: The credit balance of £85 b/d has its balance c/d on the debit side. The net figure owing by debtors = £5,640.

If the control account was recorded in the running balance method:

Sales Ledger Control a/c

		Dr. £	Cr. £	Balance £	
1 Mar.	Balances	5,275	130	5,145	Dr.
31	Sales	14,250		19,395	
	Bank/cash		13,140	6,255	
	Returns Inward		175	6,080	
	Bad debts		380	5,700	
	Contra		60	5,640*	
1 Apr.	Balances (S/L)	5,725	85	5,640	Dr.

*Net result of Dr. and Cr. balances.

Back to the traditional two-sided ledger for the purchases control a/c (bought ledger control).

Dr.			Bought Ledger Control a/c			Cr.
1 Mar.	Balance b/d	210	1 Mar.	Balance b/d	2,500	
31	Bank/cash	9,240	31	Purchases	9,600	
	Return Outward	830		Balance c/d	140	
	Contra	60				
	Balance c/d	1,900				
		12,340			12,340	
1 Apr.	Balance b/d	140	1 Apr.	Balance b/d	1,900	

Note: The debit balance of £140 has its corresponding c/d balance on the debit side. The net figure owing to creditors = £1,760.

If the control account was recorded in the running balance method:

Bought Ledger Control a/c

		Dr. £	Cr. £	Balance £
1 Mar.	Balances	210	2,500	2,290 Cr.
31	Purchases		9,600	11,890
	Bank/cash	9,240		2,650
	Returns Outward	830		1,820
	Contra	60		1,760*
1 Apr.	Balances (B/L)	140	1,900	1,760 Cr.

*Net result of Dr. and Cr. balances.

Exercises

1. From the following details for the month of January, prepare Freddy Smith's sales ledger control account and purchases ledger control account.

    The opening balances in the purchases ledger and sales ledger were £4,420 credit and £2,420 debit respectively.

	£
Credit purchases from suppliers	36,480
Credit sales to customers	30,500
Cash paid to creditors	36,840
Receipts from trade debtors	26,175
Discounts received	825
Discounts allowed	720
Purchases returns	815
Debit note to debtor	119
Bad debt written off	730
Credit balances in purchases ledger transferred to sales ledger	180
Returns inward	414

    On 31 January, the purchases ledger had a balance of £2,240 and the sales ledger £5,080. Check these figures with your control accounts.

2. The following information has been taken from the books of Harry Jones relating to the year ended 31 December 1988:

	£
Sales Ledger balance 1 January 1988	2,246
Bought Ledger balance 1 January 1988	1,608
Credit Sales	38,127
Cash Sales	9,750
Purchases on credit	27,121
Receipts from customers	27,560
Payments to suppliers	19,422
Discount allowed	810
Dishonoured cheques from customers	925
Returns Outward	316
Returns Inward	1,427

Required:

Prepare the sales and bought ledger control accounts for the year ended 31 December 1988.

3. The following figures for the month of May relate to the Sales Ledger of George Harrison:

Balances brought forward from	£
30 April	13,740
31 May	16,996
Sales	12,450
Returns Inward	150
Cash from customers	9,208
Discounts allowed	245
Bad Debts	222
Cheques returned from Bank marked insufficient funds	442
Cash Sales	4,173
Debit notes to customers	154
Interest charged to customers (on overdue accounts)	58
Debit balances in Sales Ledger transferred to Purchases ledger	42

Required:

(a) Prepare the Debtor's Control account for the month of May.
(b) From the figures you have prepared, what conclusions do you arrive at?

4. *Situation/Information*

You work as an accounts clerk for a manufacturing company, Rock Ltd., and have to write up the Control Accounts for the month of February 1990. Details of transactions are as follows:-

		£
Feb 1 Purchase Ledger (Credit Balance)		26,100
Purchase Ledger (Debit Balance)		460
Sales Ledger (Debit Balance)		51,400
Sales Ledger (Credit Balance)		630

Total Transactions in the month:

	£
Bad Debts written off	420
Credit Purchases	37,590
Cash Purchases	5,200
Returns Outwards	510
Returns Inwards	1,480
Cheques paid to Creditors	24,270
Cheques received from Debtors	47,360
Contras	800
Dishonoured cheques (ie. from Debtors)	140
Credit Sales	74,900
Cash Sales	9,250
Discount Allowed	1,840
Discount Received	960
Cheque received from a Supplier	460

TASK A

Prepare the Sales Ledger Control Account for February.
[The Sales Ledger schedule total was £73,910]

TASK B

Prepare the Purchase Ledger Control Account for February.
[The Purchase Ledger schedule total was £37,200]

TASK C

Describe one other system of internal check which can be used to ensure accuracy of posting.
Which of the two control accounts agreed?
How much was the discrepancy in the control account which failed to balance?

5. *Situation/Information*

You work as an accounts clerk for a wholesale company Zarak Ltd. and have to write up the Control Accounts for the month of August 1990. Details of transactions are as follows:

		£
Aug 1	Sales Ledger (Debit Balance)	48,000
	Sales Ledger (Credit Balance)	520
	Purchase Ledger (Credit Balance)	24,200
	Purchase Ledger (Debit Balance)	350

Total Transactions in the month:-

Credit Sales	61,740
Cash Sales	5,210
Credit Purchases	34,720
Cash Purchases	3,905
Discount Allowed	760
Discount Received	980
Returns Inwards	1,750
Returns Outwards	430
Cheques received from Debtors	51,720
Cheques Paid to Creditors	23,890
Dishonoured Cheques (i.e. from Debtors)	880
Contras	750

TASK A

Prepare the Sales Ledger Control Account for August.
[Sales Ledger schedule total was £54,300]

TASK B

Prepare the Purchase Ledger Control Account for August.
[Purchase Ledger schedule total was £32,520].

TASK C

Briefly explain why Control accounts are used.
Which of the two Control accounts did not balance with the schedule?

TASK D

Briefly explain the purpose of an aged Debtor List.

6. *Situation*: You are an assistant in the accounts office responsible for nominal ledger entries in a firm of Wholesalers, Smith & Jones. The following information is available to you from which it is proposed to prepare control accounts for both sales and bought ledgers for the month ended 31 March 1990.

Balances at 1 March:		£
Bought ledger balances	(CREDIT)	149,940
Bought ledger balances	(DEBIT)	320
Sales ledger balances	(DEBIT)	311,100
Sales ledger balances	(CREDIT)	425
Sales		130,155
Purchases		65,250
Bad Debts written off		225
Dishonoured cheques		485
Discount to customers		310
Discount from suppliers		395
Cash repayments to customers		120
Contra entries between debtors and creditors		765
Returns Inward		2,155
Returns Outward		580
Cheques, cash from customers		127,255
Bills payable		150
Cash Sales		1,575
Cheques, cash to creditors		62,350
Cheques received from suppliers		125
An increase in the provision for bad debts		277

At 31 March, the following balances were taken from the personal ledgers:

Sales ledger balances	(DEBIT)	309,545
	(CREDIT)	140
Bought ledger balances	(CREDIT)	152,655
	(DEBIT)	150

Required:

(a) Prepare the sales ledger control account and the purchases ledger control account for the month of March.

(b) Comment on any discrepancy that may appear in your figures.

7. As a member of the accounting team of ABC Co. Ltd you are asked to prepare the Control Accounts of both the sales ledger and bought ledger for the month ended 31 March 1990.

The following were balances taken from the books of ABC Co. Ltd for the month March 1990:

1 March		£
Bought Ledger	Cr. balance	12,860
Bought Ledger	Dr. balance	225
Sales Ledger	Dr. balance	34,755
Sales Ledger	Cr. balance	372

31 March	
Purchases Journal	23,805
Sales Journal	37,215
Discount Received	621
Discount Allowed	558
Cheques received from customers	29,950
Cash/Cheques to Suppliers	22,140
Contra entries between debtors and creditors	420
Cash purchases	1,285
Bad Debts written off	470
Returns Outward Journal	950
Dishonoured cheques from customers	155
Interest charged to customers on overdue accounts	85
Returns Inward Journal	1,472
Received from creditor in respect of overpayment	25
Bills receivable	1,150
Cash refund to customer	50
Provision for bad debts	750

The balances extracted from the personal ledgers of ABC Co. Ltd on 31 March were:

		£
Bought Ledger	Cr. balance	12,484
Bought Ledger	Dr. balance	150
Sales Ledger	Dr. balance	38,124
Sales Ledger	Cr. balance	456

Required:

(a) Prepare the Bought Ledger Control Account and the Sales Ledger Control Account for the month ended 31 March 1990.

(b) From the figures you have prepared for (a), what conclusions can you draw?

(c) Briefly explain, by means of memorandum to the junior accounts clerk, why in some business enterprises there is a need to keep control accounts.

The Trial Balance and its Limitations. The Journal and the Use of the Suspense Account

The trial balance is used to check the arithmetical accuracy of the double-entry system. At frequent intervals, ledger account balances are listed to see if total debits equal total credits. If the trial balance fails to balance, the ledger accounts need to be checked to locate the errors and to correct them.

The trial balance is not a fool-proof system because some types of error will not be disclosed.

Errors which the trial balance fails to disclose:

    (a) Errors of compensation.
    (b) Errors of principle.
    (c) Errors of omission.
    (d) Errors of commission.

The following are examples of errors made in the ledgers where the use of a trial balance has failed to disclose them.

(a) *An error of compensation*
    This refers to an error where the *same* mistake has been made to both sides of a transaction.

    A cheque of £451 was received from a debtor, T. Smith, but was entered incorrectly as £415 in the records:

Entry: Dr. Cash Book   £415
       Cr.   Smith a/c (Sales Ledger)   £415

Both debit and credit entries have recorded the same error and the trial balance would fail to disclose it and therefore would still balance.

Correction of error:

      Dr.   Cash Book   £36
       Cr.   Smith a/c   £36
      (making up the under-stated £415 to the correct £451)

(b) *An error of principle*

This refers to an error where a transaction has been posted to the wrong group of accounts. An asset account incorrectly posted as an expense is a good example.

Office equipment bought on credit from ABC Suppliers Ltd, at £2,500, was incorrectly posted to the purchases account instead of office equipment:

Entry: Dr. Purchases a/c   £2,500
       Cr.   ABC Suppliers Ltd   £2,500

Correction of error:

      Dr.   Office Equipment a/c   £2,500
       Cr.   Purchases a/c   £2,500
      (this will clear the over-stated purchases of £2,500 and correctly increase the asset by £2,500)

(c) *An error of omission*

This refers to an error where a transaction has been omitted altogether — a sales or purchase invoice mislaid, a gas or electricity bill neglected or missing. No transaction would be entered in the books and the trial balance would fail to disclose the omission and still balance, of course. A sales invoice to J. Jackson had been misplaced and no entries were made in the books:

Entry: Dr. J. Jackson a/c (Sales Ledger)   £200
       Cr.   Sales a/c   £200

Correction of error:

When the invoice has been found, the above entry is required in the Sales and Nominal Ledgers.

(d) *An error of commission*

This refers to an error where a transaction has been posted to the wrong account, but to the same group of accounts — a nominal account like a gas bill incorrectly posted to another nominal account like office expenses. The trial balance would still balance because both are debit entries to the expense account.

A gas bill of £185 had been incorrectly entered in office expenses instead of light and heat account:

> Entry: Dr.   Office Expenses a/c   £185
>   Cr.   Cash Book   £185

Correction of error:

> Dr.   Light & Heat a/c   £185
> Cr.   Office Expenses a/c   £185.
> (this clears the over-stated office expenses by £185 and correctly increases the light & heat account by £185)

All these types of error will not be disclosed by the trial balance and therefore as a checking device it has its limitations. The trial balance is still an essential part of the accounting system because some check on the ledger system must be made frequently to ensure that the double-entry principle is used in the recording of transactions. What has to be borne in mind, however, is that not all trial balances which balance are automatically correct!

In the following section which looks at the Journal, the above type of errors can be corrected by using Journal entries.

The Journal

The Journal is used for those transactions which are normally outside the scope of the other subsidiary books.

When the book-keeping system was in its early stages of development, the Journal acted as the only subsidiary book in use. All transactions were entered in the Journal prior to ledger posting. Later on, as the book-keeping system developed, it was found that the use of the Journal as the only book of original entry was inadequate. There were so many repetitious entries to be made that separate subsidiary books were soon in use. The day books gave the answer for sales, purchases and returns, and the cash book for those transactions of a cash/cheque nature.

The Journal has now a far lesser role than when it was first in use. It is left with the function of *providing some original entry for those miscellaneous type of transactions* that do not quite 'fit in' to the other subsidiary books.

For example, purchasing plant and machinery on credit. This cannot be entered in the Purchases Day Book because the asset, plant and machinery is not for resale, neither can it be entered in the Cash Book because the transaction is not in cash.

The answer: use the Journal.

Some of the more common uses of the Journal include the following:

(a) Correcting errors.
(b) Transfer of revenue and expenditure accounts.
(c) Opening entries in a new accounting period (that is, a list of assets, liabilities and capital).
(d) Making accounting adjustments.

Note that the Journal has a debit and credit column to facilitate the double-entry. The debit entry is always entered first. The credit entry is entered underneath and slightly indented. There is also a very brief comment which offers some explanation of the entry.

The following page show the journal entries of G. Harrison where the trial balance errors are recorded.

The Journal: Correction of Errors

THE JOURNAL: G. Harrison

No. 2

		Dr. £		Cr. £	
June					
8	Cash Book (Bank)	36			
	T. smith (Sales Ledger)			36	
	Error of compensation.				
	£451 cheque entered as £415.				
10	Office Equipment	2,500			
	Purchases			2,500	
	Error of principle:				
	An asset incorrectly entered				
	as an expense.				
14	J. Jackson (Sales Ledger)	200			
	Sales			200	
	Error of omission:				
	Sales Invoice No. 2176 omitted				
	no entries in the books.				
26	Light & Heat	185			
	Office Expenses			185	
	Error of commission:				
	Gas bill incorrectly entered				
	as office expense.				

Ledger entries recording corrected errors:

	Folio	Dr. £	Cr. £	Balance £	
Sales Ledger:					
T. Smith a/c					
June 1 Balance				451	Dr.
2 Bank	CB 5		415	36	
8 Bank	J 2		36	—	
J. Jaokson a/c					
June 1 Balance				50	Dr.
14 Sales	J 2	200		250	
Nominal Ledger:					
Office Equipment a/c					
June 1 Balance				1,000	Dr.
10 Purchases	J 2	2,500		3,500	
Light & Heat a/c					
June 1 Balance				350	Dr.
26 Office exps.	J 2	185		535	
Office Expenses a/c					
June 1 Balance				595	Dr.
26 Light & Heat	J 2		185	410	

On the following page, Journal entries are recorded for:

(a) The commencement of a new accounting period, 1 January.
(b) The transfer of revenue and expense accounts and stock account, to trading and profit and loss account, 31 December.
(c) The purchase of a Motor Van on credit on 31 December.

JOURNAL G. Harrison

No. 3

			Dr.		Cr.	
			£		£	
(a)	Jan. 1	Premises	12,000			
		Fixtures & Fittings	1,500			
		Equipment	2,480			
		Motor Van	1,000			
		Stock	1,500			
		Debtors	765			
		Bank	400			
		Prepaid Expenses	120			
		Creditors			950	
		Accrued Expenses			88	
		Mortgage on Premises			8,000	
		Bank Loan			1,000	
		Capital: G. Harrison			9,727	
			19,765		19,765	
		Assets, Liabilities & Capital				
		of G. Harrison on 1 January . . .				
(b)	Dec. 31	Sales	11,000			
		Trading a/c			11,000	
		Trading a/c	5,000			
		Purchases			5,000	
		Transfer of sales and purchases				
		to trading				
		Trading a/c	1,000			
		Stock (1/1)			1,000	
		Stock (31/12)	1,500			
		Trading a/c			1,500	
		Transfer of stock (beg.) and				
		stock (end) to trading				
		Profit & Loss a/c	884			
		Salaries			884	
		Transfer of expense to				
		profit & loss				
(c)	Dec 31	Motor Van	7,500			
		Jake's Garage				
		Purchased on credit			7,500	
		over 3 years				

The Suspense Account and the Correction of Errors

The purpose of using a suspense account is to balance the trial balance temporarily. When errors are made which produce an incorrect trial balance because the totals disagree, a suspense account may be entered in the trial balance by inserting the difference between the trial balance totals. A suspense account is opened in the Nominal Ledger and is written off when the error or errors are located. The Journal is used to make the appropriate corrections.

Extract of Trial Balance taken from the books of G. Harrison 30 June . . .

Account	Dr. £	Cr. £
Sales		18,600
Purchases	12,500	
Furniture & Fittings	4,200	
General Expenses	150	
Discount		35
	36,660	36,500
Suspense		160
	36,600	36,600

Errors must eventually be found and corrected. When they are found, Journal entries are necessary to correct them and the appropriate accounts adjusted to their correct value. The following errors were located in the books of G. Harrison:

(a) Sales were under-valued by £100 in cash sales when posted to sales account.
(b) General Expenses of £40 had been omitted from Cash Book posting to the nominal account, General Expenses.
(c) The purchase of furniture of £300 was wrongly debited to the Purchases account.
(d) Discount received of £100 had not been posted to the discount account in the nominal ledger.

Required:

(a) Open a Suspense a/c in the Nominal Ledger on June 30 with an opening balance of £160 Cr.
(b) Make the appropriate Journal entries to correct the errors.
(c) Adjust the accounts in Harrison's Nominal Ledger.
(d) If Harrison had a Net Profit on 30 June of £8,500, how would the above errors affect the profit?

(e) One of Harrison's debtors, J. Smith, had been written off as bad. He owed £250. Show how this would be entered in the Journal.

JOURNAL *G. Harrison*

No. 4

			Dr. £		Cr. £	
June						
30	Suspense a/c		100			
	Sales				100	
	Sales a/c under-valued					
30	General Expenses		40			
	Suspense a/c				40	
	Failed to complete double-entry					
	from Cash Book					
30	Furniture & Fittings		300			
	Purchases				300	
	Error of Principle. Furniture					
	incorrectly posted to purchases.					
30	Suspense a/c		100			
	Discount Received				100	
	Failed to complete double-entry					
	from Cash Book					
30	Bad Debts		250			
	J. Smith				250	
	Debtor written off as bad					

Nominal Ledger

		Folio	Dr. £	Cr. £	Balance £
Suspense a/c					
June 30	Trial Balance			160	160 Cr.
	Sales	J 4	100		60 Cr.
	General Expenses	J 4		40	100 Cr.
	Discount	J 4	100		—
Sales a/c					
June 30	Balance				18,600 Cr.
	Suspense	J 4		100	18,700
General Expenses a/c					
June 30	Balance				150 Dr.
	Suspense	J 4	40		190
Furniture & Fittings a/c					
June 30	Balance				4,200 Dr.
	Purchases	J 4	300		4,500
Purchases a/c					
June 30	Balance				12,500 Dr.
	Furniture & F	J 4		300	12,200
Discount Received a/c					
June 30	Balance				35 Cr.
	Suspense	J 4		100	135 Cr.

How Profit is Affected

If the Trading & Profit & Loss a/c had already been prepared before the errors were located, the correction of the above would have changed the value of net profit:

Net Profit (before errors)			£8,500	
Add	Sales (undercast)	£100		
	Discount Received	£100		
	Purchases	£300	500	£9,000
Less	General Expenses	£ 40		40
Net Profit (after errors)				£8,960

Exercises

1. Make the appropriate JOURNAL entries to correct the following errors:

    (a) An amount of £300 had been included in the Salaries a/c for a job which involved repairing the proprietor's garage (J. Jones).
    (b) A cheque of £350 from P. Smith had been credited to R. Smith in error.
    (c) The purchase of calculators for the office staff, costing £125, had been posted to the purchases a/c.
    (d) An invoice for rates owing to Wimborne D.C. for £178 had been mislaid.

2. On 1 January, Tom Jones had the following assets and liabilities:

	£
Premises	20,000
Vehicle	500
Equipment	2,100
Stock	1,860
Debtors	675
Mortgage on Premises	15,000
Bank (Overdrawn)	450
Creditors	1,155

    Prepare an Opening JOURNAL entry of 1 January showing Tom Jones assets, liabilities and capital as at this date.

3. Make the necessary JOURNAL entries for the following:

    (a) A debtor, Harry Smith, failed to pay his account of £256 and it was decided to write the debt off.
    (b) A machine valued £500 was purchased on credit terms from Equipment Supplies Co. Ltd.
    (c) The motor vehicle (cost £2,800) was to be depreciated by 25% of cost.
    (d) Sales £14,500 and Purchases £9,850 are to be transferred to the trading account for gross profit calculation.
    (e) A gas bill of £85 had been wrongly posted to the rates account.

4. An extract of Harry's Trial Balance:

	DR. £	CR. £
Suspense a/c		247
	20,534	20,534

Subsequently the following errors were found:

(a) Goods £285 to R. Smith had been posted to J. Smith in error.

(b) Accounting equipment sold for £600 credited to Sales account.

(c) Cash discount of £8 allowed to J. Jones and credited to him, but no entry was made to the discount a/c.

(d) The addition of the Sales Day Book was undercast by £200.

(e) Salaries accrued £55 at the end of the previous year had not been brought forward to the new accounting period.

(f) A Sales Invoice of £275 had been misplaced. No entries had been made.

Required:

(a) Journal entries necessary to correct the books.

(b) The Suspense account entries.

5. The accounts of a business were extracted on 30 June as follows:

	£	£
Bank Account	1,245	
Capital Account		34,900
Stock	3,400	
Premises	20,000	
Furniture and Fittings	900	
Wages and Salaries	15,400	
Office Expenses	1,060	
Purchases	13,900	
Sales		21,900
Drawings	3,800	
Debtors	2,600	
Creditors		3,230
	62,305	60,030

It was subsequently discovered that the following errors had been made in the listing of the balances:

(i) The Bank Account was overdrawn £1,245.

(ii) A sum of £200 drawn out by the Owner for his personal use had been included under 'Office Expenses'.

(iii) Purchases totalling £1,000 had not passed through the books.

(iv) The balance of the Discount allowed account, £160, had been omitted.

(v) £2,400 included under Wages and Salaries and £600 included under Purchases represented extensions to Premises.

(vi) Office Cash of £55 had been omitted from the list of balances.

Required:

(a) A suspense account in the ledger.

(b) A corrected trial balance for the month ending 30 June.

6. *Situation/Information*

You work as a senior accounts clerk for R. Underwood, and have been assisting in the preparation of the final accounts. The trial balance as at 30th April 1986 did not agree, and a suspense account was opened for the difference. The following errors have now been traced:

(i) The total of the Returns Outward Book, £248, had not been posted to the ledger.

(ii) An invoice received from a supplier, A. Biggs, for £200 had been mislaid, so entries for this transaction had not been made.

(iii) A payment for repairs to vehicles, £72, had been entered in the vehicle repairs account as £70.

(iv) When balancing the account of G. Bradford in the ledger, the debit balance had been brought down in error as £28, instead of £82.

(v) £100 received from the sale of Office Equipment had been entered in the Sales Account.

(vi) A private purchase of £230 by R. Underwood had been included in the business purchases.

(vii) The Purchase Day Book was undercast by £92.

TASK A

Show the requisite journal entries to correct the errors.

TASK B

Write up the suspense account showing the correction of the errors.

TASK C

If the originally calculated profit was £10,500, show your calculation of the correct figure.

TASK D

State four types of errors which do not affect the agreement of the trial balance – giving an example of each.

7. *Situation/Information*

Hawkers & Pedlar have produced a Trial Balance for the year ended 31 March, 1990, which does not balance. A Suspense Account was opened for the difference. An examination of the firm's books disclosed the following errors:

1) An invoice from R. Pitman amounting to £300, for goods purchased, has been omitted from the Purchase Day Book and posted direct to the Purchases Account in the Nominal Ledger but not entered in the Purchase Ledger.

2) The Sales Day Book has been undercast by £450.

3) Discount allowed for the month of March, amounting to £242, has not been posted to the nominal ledger.

4) A cheque, amounting to £540, for the purchase of furniture and fittings had been correctly entered in the Cash Book but entered in the Nominal Ledger Account as £450.

5) A Sales Invoice, amounting to £730, sent to J. Knight, has been omitted from the books completely.

6) A payment, amounting to £233, for heating and lighting had been correctly entered in the cash book but posted, in error, to the motor expenses account at £322.

7) An invoice regarding the purchase of a new printer included £180 in respect of computer stationery. The total invoice value had been posted to the Equipment Account in the nominal ledger.

TASK A

Write up the Journal entries, where necessary, to correct the errors. (Narratives not required).

TASK B

Draw up the Suspense Account.

TASK C

If the net profit for the year excluding the seven errors was £22,031 produce a statement showing the corrected profit figure.

PART 3

Accounting for Incomplete Records

Many small business organisations do not keep a full set of adequate accounting records because they have neither the time nor the necessary accounting experience to do so.

Sole-traders in particular, only keep partial or 'incomplete records' and rely on the services of an accountant to write up their accounts at the end of the financial year. This is required for the purpose of calculating the taxation due to the Inland Revenue and also to have some idea of how the business has performed.

Some financial data are available, of course, because all businesses need to have essential information such as:

how much they owe suppliers
how much customers owe them
how much cash is available
how much VAT is payable to Customs and Excise

and so forth. Because of these reasons the accountant is able to use the financial information which may be available, like invoices, credit notes, till rolls, bank statements, cheque stubs, receipts for cash, etc., to prepare a set of accounts (that is, the trading and profit and loss account and balance sheet).

From incomplete financial data, therefore, it is still possible to reconstruct accounts by relating and piecing them together in order to prepare the final accounts.

Procedure

The procedure for reconstructing accounts is varied. Many accountants like to use a work sheet which shows a logical sequence of workings extending to a trial balance. Any adjustments such as accruals and pre-payments may also be included and the final accounts can then be prepared. The following method is a basically simple procedure which pieces the accounts together without necessarily resorting to a work sheet.

1. Establish the owner's capital (net worth) at the beginning of the financial year by listing his assets against his liabilities.
2. Prepare a bank/cash summary in the form of a simplified cash book which will identify receipts and payments of money into and out of the business. The accountant would do this from records such as bank statements, till rolls, cheque stubs etc.
3. Establish the sales and purchases for the year from the reconstruction of debtors' and creditors' accounts. Financial data available to the accountant could come from invoices, credit notes, cheque stubs, statements, cash receipts, etc.
4. Prepare the trading and profit and loss accounts including items for adjustments, and the balance sheet for the year under review.

The role of the accountant in this capacity is to prepare the final accounts of the business as accurately as possible from the given financial data available. He does not audit the accounts. The accounts may be checked by other accountants expressing, in their view, the trueness and fairness of them.

A Worked Example

1. *Establishing the owner's capital*
    E. T. Gibbs is a sole-trader in business as an electrician. He uses his garage as a small workshop but most of his business is on contract with clients which takes him to various parts of the locality where he works.
    On 1 January 1988 his statement of affairs at the beginning of the financial year was

	£	£
Tools and Equipment	250	
Motor Vehicle	950	
Debtors	2,150	
Bank balance	1,970	
Stock	3,180	8,500
Creditors		2,800
Capital January 1, 1988		5,700

Note: This information could have been taken from his balance sheet as at year ended 31 December 1987.

2. *Preparing a bank/cash summary*

From bank statements, till rolls, cheque book records and other sources, it is possible to draw up a bank summary to establish where money has come from and where it has gone, as well as calculating the bank/cash balance at the end of the financial year. From the records of E. T. Gibbs, the following bank summary was available on 31 December 1988:

A Bank Summary E. T. Gibbs

Receipts	£	Payments	f
Bank balance (1 Jan. 1988)	1,970	Payments to suppliers	30,125
Receipts from customers	39,750	Personal drawings	3,880
Cash Sales	2,185	Wages (assistant's)	4,375
		General expenses	560
		Motoring expenses	835
		Insurance	160
		Telephone and rates	395
		Light and heat	170
		Advertising	350
		Bank balance (31 Dec. 1988)	3,055
	43,905		43,905

The figures from the bank summary are used to help reconstruct the final reports. At the end of the financial year, E. T. Gibbs had £3,055 in the bank, an increase of £1,085 from the beginning of the year.

3. *Establishing sales and purchases for the year*

Because receipts from debtors and payments to suppliers do not necessarily correspond with the sales and purchases totals, it is therefore required to reconstruct the debtors' and creditors' accounts in order to arrive at the sales and purchases totals. The accountant may get this information from invoices sent to customers and invoices received from suppliers plus credit notes, bank statements, cheque stubs, and so forth. Many sole-traders actually write on invoices and statements the dates when settlement of accounts occurred, including any cash discounts paid or received.

The following reconstructions relate to E. T. Gibbs:

Debtors

Dr.			£	Cr.		£
1988				1988		
Jan. 1	Balance		2,150	Bank/cash		39,750
				Discount Allowed		650
Dec. 31	SALES*		41,125	Returns Inward		200
				Dec. 31		
				Balance		2,675
			43,275			43,275

Note: *To reconstruct debtors in order to find the sales, the opening Dr. balance of debtors (£2,150) is subtracted from the total of the Cr. column (£43,275) = £41,125.

Bank/cash was taken from the Bank Summary Dr. side, discount allowed and returns inward from debtors' statements.

Any unpaid invoices at the end of the year would represent the debtors closing balance on 31 Dec., £2,675.

Creditors

Dr.	£	Cr.		£
1988		1988		
Bank/cash	30,125	Jan. 1	Balance	2,800
Discount received	875			
Returns Outward	1,350	Dec. 31	PURCHASES*	32,720
Dec. 31				
Balance	3,170			
	35,520			35,520

Note: *To reconstruct creditors in order to find the purchases, the opening Cr. balance of creditors (£2,800) is subtracted from the total of the Dr. column (£35,520) = £32,720.

Bank/cash was taken from the Bank Summary Cr. side, discount received and returns outward from creditors' statements.

Any unpaid invoices to suppliers at the end of the financial year would represent the creditors closing balance on 31 Dec., £3,170.

Once the figures have been reconstructed from debtors and creditors, they can be transferred to the trading account.

4. *Preparing the final accounts: trading, profit and loss account and balance sheet*

The only further information required before preparing the final accounts is to check on any adjustments such as accruals, pre-payments and depreciation. The stock position at the end of the financial year must also be calculated by the owner.

On 31 December 1988 the following information was available relating to E. T. Gibbs:

	£
Stock	3,246
Electricity owing	35
Depreciation on tools and equipment and	20
Motor vehicle	100
Debtors' balances	2,675
Creditors' balances	3,170

Trading and Profit and Loss a/c
E. T. Gibbs for year ended 31 December 1988

	£	£
Sales (credit)	41,125	
Other	2,185	
	43,310	
− Returns Inward	200	43,110
− Cost of Sales		
Stock (Jan. 1)	3,180	
+ Purchases	32,720	
	35,900	
− Returns Outward	1,350	
	34,550	
− Stock (Dec. 31)	3,246	31,304
Gross profit		11,806
− Other Expenses		
Wages (assistant)	4,375	
General expenses	560	
Motor expenses	835	
Telephone and rates	395	
Light and Heat (+ £35 accrued)	205	
Advertising	350	
Discount allowed	650	
Depreciation (tools, motor)	120	
Insurance	160	7,650
		4,156
+ Discount received		875
Net Profit		5,031

Balance Sheet
E. T. Gibbs as at 31 December 1988

	£	£	£
Fixed Assets			
Tools & Equipment	250		
– Depreciation	20		230
Motor Vehicle	950		
– Depreciation	100		850
			1,080
Current Assets			
Stock	3,246		
Debtors	2,675		
Bank	3,055	8,976	
less			
Current Liabilities			
Creditors	3,170		
Accrued expenses	35	3,205	
Working Capital			5,771
			6,851
Financed by			
Capital			
E. T. Gibbs (Jan. 1)	5,700		
+ Net Profit	5,031		
	10,731		
– Drawings	3,880		6,851

Note: Mr Gibbs made £5,031 profit calculated from the figures he forwarded to
his accountant. For personal use, he withdrew £3,880 during the financial
year thereby increasing his net worth in the business to £6,851, an increase
of £1,151.

The profit of £5,031 will be the basis of his tax liability to the Inland
Revenue, less the appropriate taxable allowances as per his tax coding.
His tax liability is therefore

	£		
Profit	5,031		
– Allowances	4,200		
Taxable Income	831	@	30% tax
Tax payable		=	£249.30

Illustrated Example to Final Accounts

Preparation of a Trading & Profit & Loss Account Balance Sheet from Incomplete Records

Situation

You have just completed a Business Studies Course and have been asked by an old school friend, J. Starky, to have a look at his books. J. Starky has been running a retailing business for the past year and needs to know what his 'state of affairs' is for taxation purposes.

Information

J. Starky's summary cash book for the year ended 31 March 1990 is as follows:

	£		£
1/4/89 Balance b/f	10,000	Payments to	
Cash Sales	50,000	Suppliers	157,340
Cash Received from	219,500	Cash Purchases	7,880
debtors		Rent	22,500
		Rates	900
		Salaries	13,080
		Wages	30,500
		General Expenses	22,000
		Drawings	15,000
		31/3 Balance c/f	10,300
	£279,500		£279,500

His assets and liabilities were:-

	1 April, 1989	31 March, 1990
Creditors for Goods	28,400	30,010
Rent Owing	1,000	500
Stock	54,000	53,000
Debtors	46,600	55,700
Prepaid Rates	170	295
Fixtures and Fittings	10,000	10,000
Vehicle	7,500	7,500

In preparing the accounts you decide:

(i) To depreciate the vehicle by $33\frac{1}{3}\%$
(ii) To depreciate the fixtures and fittings by 10%
(iii) To make a provision for bad debts of 5%
(iv) To assume (based on J. Starky's estimate) that J. Starky has taken *£1,000 worth of goods* from the business for his own use.

Solution

Calculation of sales and purchases:

As per the requirements of the matching (accruals) concept we should include the cost of purchases made in the year and the value of sales generated in the final accounts – which is not the same as payments made and cash and bank receipts.

Control account to find value of sales:

Total Debtors

1/4 Balance b/f	46,600	Cash from debtors	219,500
∴ credit sales =	228,600*	31/3 balance c/f	55,700
	275,200		275,200

Total sales = £228,600 + £50,000 (cash sales) = £278,600

* i.e. the balancing figure.

Control account to find value of purchases

Total Creditors

Payments to suppliers	157,340	1/4 Balance b/f	28,400
31/3 Balance c/f	30,010	∴ Credit purchases	158,950*
	187,350		187,350

Total purchases = £158,950 + £7,880 (cash purchases) = £166,830.

J Starky Trading and Profit & Loss A/C for year ending 31 March, 1990

	£	£	£
Sales			278,600
Less cost of sales:-			
Opening Stock		54,000	
Purchases	166,830		
Less goods for own use	(1,000)	165,830	
		219,830	
Closing Stock		53,000	166,830
Gross Profit			111,770
Rent (22,500−1000+500)*		22,000	
Rates (900+170−295)*		775	
Salaries		13,080	
Wages		30,500	
General Expenses		22,000	
Depreciation − Vehicle		2,500	
Depreciation − Fixtures & Fittings		1,000	
Provision for bad debts (5%)		2,785	94,640
Net Profit			£17,130

*Both rent and rates figures have to be adjusted in respect of opening and closing accruals and prepayments.

J. Starky Balance Sheet as at 31 March, 1990

Fixed Assets	£ Cost	£ Depn.	£ Net
Fixtures and Fittings	10,000	1,000	9,000
Vehicle	7,500	2,500	5,000
	17,500	3,500	14,000
Current Assets			
Stock	53,000		
Debtors (55,700 − 2,785)	52,915		
Prepayments	295		
Bank	10,300	116,510	
Current Liabilities			
Creditors	30,010		
Accrued Rent	500	30,510	
			86,000
Working Capital			£100,000

Financed by

Capital at (1/4/89)*	98,870
Add Profit $\left(\dfrac{\text{cash} \quad \text{goods}}{15{,}000 + 1{,}000}\right)$	17,130
Less Drawings	16,000
	£100,000

*Calculation of opening capital:-

Assets on 1/4 £54,000 + £46,600 + £170 + £10,000 + £7,500 + £10,000

$\hspace{8cm}$ = 128,270

Liabilities on 1/4 £28,400 + 1000 $\hspace{3cm}$ 29,400

$\hspace{10cm}$ £98,870

Exercises

1. The Balance Sheet of Harry Jones, a trader was as follows on 1 January, 1988:

	£		£
Capital	7,000	Equipment	2,900
Creditors	560	Stock	3,100
		Debtors	950
		Balance at Bank	610
	7,560		7,560

The information given below relates to Harry's business transactions for the year to December 31 1988.

	£
Payments to suppliers	39,950
Payments received from customers	49,645
Bank drawings for private use	2,310
Salaries and wages	4,165
Expenses	2,242
Discounts allowed	150
Discounts received	585

At 31 December the stock in trade was valued at £4,850. Expenses paid in advance amounted to £200, trade debtors to £4,845 and trade creditors to £3,550. Depreciation of equipment is at 15% per annum.

Required:

(i) The total account for debtors and the total account for creditors for the year — and thus ascertain the sales and purchases for the year.

(ii) A summarised bank account for the year.

(iii) The Trading and Profit and Loss account for the year ended 31 December 1988.

(iv) The Balance Sheet at 31 December 1988.

2. The following information relates to Freddy Smith at the commencement of the accounting period 1 January 1988:

	£	
Stock	3,200	debit balance
Debtors	3,850	debit balance
Creditors	2,460	credit balance
Rates in Advance	70	debit balance
Capital	6,500	credit balance

Smith did not keep proper books of account but from his cheque butts it was possible to draw up a summary of his bank details for the year:

		£		£
(1/1)	Balance (beg.)	1,840	Rent, Rates	1,050
	Cash received	68,375	Suppliers for	
	from customers		materials etc.	43,955
	Interest from		Light & Heating	545
	bank	150	Wages, Salaries	8,825
			Insurances	490
			Misc. Expenses	2,240
			Motoring Expenses	1,985
			Advertising	650
			(31/12)	
			balance	10,625
		70,365		70,365

At the end of the year the following balances were extracted

31 December, 1988	£
Stock	4,750
Debtors	8,242
Creditors	5,465
Rates in Advance	55

Freddy also took £5,000 from the bank for his own Christmas present at the end of the year!

Required:

Prepare a Trading and Profit and Loss account for the year ending 31 December and a balance sheet as at that date.

3. The following information was extracted from the books of Jack Rogue at 31 December 1988:

	£		£
(1/1) Opening balance	1,120	Cash paid to suppliers	40,800
Cash received from		Rent and rates	2,155
credit customers	58,750	Lighting and Heating	325
		Salaries	6,450
		Insurances	120
		General expenses	1,145
		Drawings	6,525
		Motor Vehicle expenses	875
		Closing balance (31/12)	1,475
	59,870		59,870

Balances:	1 January	31 December
	£	£
Stock	3,955	4,555
Debtors	3,525	4,625
Creditors	3,410	4,150
Motor Vehicle	2,750	2,500
Insurance paid in advance	60	75

Required:

Jack's Trading and Profit and Loss Account for the year and Balance Sheet as at 31 December 1988.

4. The following balances represent the accounts of F. Smith, a sole-trader who does not keep a full set of accounts:

	1 January 1988	31 December 1988
	£	£
Premises	25,000	25,000
Tools & Equipment	2,150	
Motor Vehicle	2,500	1,950
Debtors	1,750	2,780
Stock	2,565	3,425
Bank	—	
Mortgage on Premises	15,250	13,295
Creditors	3,150	4,825
Overdraft	1,765	—

Smith's Receipts and Payments for the year were as follows:

Receipts	£	Payments	£
From credit customers	42,720	Light and Heat	350
Cash Sales	5,400	Wages to assistant	3,240
		Rates	390
		Insurance	270
		Telephone	120
		Drawings	5,160
		Payments to suppliers	33,470
		New Equipment	2,000
		Motor Expenses	450
		Miscellaneous Expenses	375

Further information

(a) Discount to customers £545, discount received from suppliers £425.
(b) Tools and Equipment to be depreciated 10% including new purchases.
(c) Debtors are to be provided against going bad by 5% (from 31 December balance).
(d) Wages to assistant owing £55.
(e) The owner took stock for personal use valued £750.
(f) The Mortgage repayment (£1,955) has not been included under payments for the year.

Required:

(a) A summarised bank account for the year ended 31 December 1988. Assume all cash is paid direct into the bank and all payments are by cheque.
(b) A trading and profit and loss account for the year ended 31 December 1988 and a balance sheet as at that date.

5. The following information relates to the books of J. Archer who has been running a retailing business for the past year and needs to know what his state of affairs is for taxation purposes.

The summary of his receipts and payments for the year ended 31 March 1988 was:

	£		£
(1/4/87)			
Bank balance	10,000	Payments to suppliers	157,340
Cash Sales	50,000	Cash purchases	7,880
Receipts from debtors	219,500	Rent and Rates	22,900
		Salaries	13,580
		Wages	30,500
		General Expenses	20,500
		Light and Heat	1,500
		Telephone	850
		Motor Expenses	2,150
		Drawings	12,000
		Bank balance	
		(31/3/88)	10,300
	279,500		279,500

J. Archer's assets and liabilities were:

	1 April 1987 £	31 March 1988 £
Creditors	28,400	30,010
Rent Owing		500
Stock	54,000	53,000
Debtors	46,600	55,700
Pre-paid Rates		295
Fixtures & Fittings	10,000	9,000
Motor Vehicle	7,500	6,450

In preparing the accounts it is decided to:

(a) Depreciate the fixtures by a further 10% *of the 31/3/88 value.*
(b) Make a provision against bad debts of 5%.

Required:

(a) Prepare a trading and profit and loss account for the year ended 31 March 1988 and a balance sheet as at that date.
(b) Make a brief assessment of Archer's trading performance using any accounting ratios you think are necessary.

6. *Situation/Information*

Jack Jones is a retailer who does not keep a proper set of accounts. He keeps a record of receipts and payments through the bank, and documents such as invoices and bills, relating to the business.

On 1 January, his statement of affairs showed the following balances (other than his bank account):

	£
Premises	15,000
Fixtures & fittings	2,500
Motor Van	1,350
Debtors	2,750
Stock	3,000
Creditors	2,600
Bank Loan (5 years)	4,000

His summarised bank account for the financial year:

Receipts	£	Payments	£
Bank balance (Jan. 1)	2,000	Wages (casual)	1,550
Shop takings + receipts		Light and Heat	295
from debtors	47,250	Advertising	300
Commission	500	Rates and Water	250
		Personal drawings	2,875
		Payments to Suppliers	38,550
		Motor Van expenses	750
		Shop Equipment	1,300
		Telephone	290
		Bank + Interest charges	215
		General expenses	500
		Repairs to property	700 .
		Bank balance (Dec. 31)	2,175
	49,750		49,750

Note: Discount Allowed to customers £225.
Discount Received from suppliers £550.

Further Information

(a) Balances at the end of the financial year, 31 December 1987, other than bank account:

	£
Debtors	1,800
Creditors	2,465
Stock	3,815

(b) The owner took £800 goods for his own use during the year.
(c) Depreciation: The motor van is revalued to £1,000.
    Fixtures are to be reduced by 20%.
    Premises remain at cost.

(d) Rates in advance £40. Advertising pre-paid £50. Casual wages due to be paid £75.

(e) A provision for bad debts to equal 5% of current debtors is to be made.

Tasks

A Prepare a statement of affairs on 1 January, to show Jack Jones's financial position.

B Reconstruct debtors and creditors accounts in order to calculate sales and purchases for the financial year.

C Prepare the trading and profit and loss account for the year ended 31 December 1987. Also a Balance sheet as at this date.

D Write a short report to Jack outlining the financial results for the year. Use any accounting ratios you feel appropriate.

7. *Situation/Information*

You work as a self-employed Accountant and are about to draw up the final accounts for a client, D. White. D.White does not keep a full set of accounts but has kept a receipts and payments book for the year.

Data extracted on 31/12/92:

Summary of Receipts and Payments Book

		£		£
1/1/92	Balance b/f	1,488	Cheques to	
	Cheques from		Suppliers	148,992
	Debtors	208,500	Salaries & Wages	27,800
			Rent & Rates	6,700
			Lighting & Heating	1,420
			Misc. Expenses	5,255
			Drawings	14,900
			Purchase of	4,000
			Equipment	
			Balance c/f	921
		209,998		209,988

	1/1/92	31/12/92
	£	£
Stock	11,900	12,850
Debtors	15,210	16,930
Creditors (for purchases)	11,840	13,120
Accruals for salaries & wages	490	560
Prepayment of rates	810	900
Fixed assets	56,000	?

N.B. Fixed assets held on 31 December 1992 are to be depreciated by 15%.

TASK A

Prepare the Trading and Profit and Loss Account of D. White for year ending 31/12/92.

TASK B

Prepare the Balance Sheet of D. White as on 31/12/92.

8. *Situation/Information*

Justin Harris carries on a retail business and does not keep his books on a double entry basis. The following particulars have been extracted from his books.

	1 July 1991 £	30 June 1992 £
Fixtures and fittings	48,000	?
Stock in trade	32,000	36,000
Trade debtors	4,000	6,400
Trade creditors	14,000	12,000
Cash in hand	720	1,440
Balance at bank	9,800	8,800

At 1 July 1991, the only outstanding expense items were lighting accrued £160 and rates in advance £400.

At 30 June 1992, there was £1,000 owing for rent, rates had been paid in advance by £480, wages accrued amounted to £360, and there was a stock of heating fuel valued at £600.

The following cash and bank transactions took place during the year ending 30 June, 1992:

Carriage inward	3,360
Wages	18,360
Sundry expenses	1,000
Printing, stationery and advertising	2,240
Rent and rates	5,000
Heating and lighting	2,760
Cash received from customers	205,000
Cash paid for purchases	160,400
Cash withdrawn from business for own use	12,160

During the year Harris had taken goods from his business for his own consumption amounting to £30 per week, and had not paid any money into the business for them.

Depreciation of fixtures and fittings to be charged at 10 per cent. There have been no sales or purchases of fixtures and fittings during the year.

TASKS

Prepare a Trading and Profit and Loss Account for the year ended 30 June 1992, and Balance Sheet at that date.

9. You work for a firm of accountants which prepares the accounts for Murry Limited. During the night of 2nd June 1987, MurryLimited suffered a fire which destroyed all the company's stock records and a quantity of stock. The stock was covered by insurance against loss by fire. You have been asked by your firm to assist with preparing the insurance claim for Murry Limited.

You have ascertained the following information:

	On 1.1.87	On 2.6.87
	£000	£000
Stock at cost	264	?
Trade Debtors	78	94
Trade Creditors	90	106

The following transactions took place between 1.1.87 and 2.6.87

	£000
Cash purchases	34
Payments to Creditors	548
Cash received from Debtors	628
Cash sales	160
Discount received	20
Discount allowed	16

The physical stock-take, carried out first thing in the morning on 3.6.87, showed the remaining stock (undamaged) to have a cost value of £182,000. Murry Limited operate a standard margin of 30% i.e. a gross profit of 30% on selling price.

Required:

(a) Calculate the total value of purchases for the period.
(b) Calculate the total value of sales for the period.
(c) Use the information in tasks (a) and (b) to calculate the cost of the damaged stock.

PART 4

The Importance of Stock Valuation

The buying of stock is of great importance to the business. Whether the stock is described as raw materials or components or partly finished or finished goods, it must be the right stock, bought at the right price, in the right quantities, at the right time.

The optimum level of stock must be carried, otherwise an organisation can either run out of stock and lose orders, or it may carry too much stock and absorb working capital which could be used for alternative purposes. Stock can quickly become obsolete in some areas of business (like fashions) and may have to be marked down in price, in some cases lower than its cost.

A good buyer of stock should know his buying market well. He should keep a list of his suppliers and should ensure that his purchases are competitive and reliable.

When goods arrive from suppliers they should be checked carefully with the original order and the delivery note to make sure there is confirmation relating to quantity and description. When the invoice for the goods is received it should be checked with great care to ensure that all details comply with the terms of the order.

Stock is an important asset. In the final accounts it affects the value of profit in the period under review. If stock is over-valued or carried to the next period at more than its cost price, it will overstate the value of profit in the current period; or if it is under-valued, the effect will be to understate the current year's profit.

The matching concept in accounting should ensure that the value of revenue matches the value of expenses in the financial year they occur. If stock is over-valued or under-valued, it tends to distort the measurement of profit.

Stock is normally valued at its cost price and many small organisations tend simply to itemise the stock at the end of the financial year and value it at its cost price. SSAP No. 9 (Statement of Standard Accounting Practice), which recommends methods of practice, states that stock should be valued at its cost or, if lower than cost, at its net realisable value (its expected selling price). In other words, if some stock items are valued lower than their cost because of age or damage, etc. the expected selling price should be stated rather than cost, to give a more realistic assessment of stock value in the financial period under review.

If an organisation uses a computer, there are programs available to maintain stock records which have various functions like keeping up to date stock records, minimum and maximum stock levels, re-order levels and current balances of each stock type. Effective stock control should ensure that computer records are checked with actual physical records to avoid cases of fraud or pilfering of stock.

Here is an example of stock valuation showing 'at cost or lower of net realisable value':

Lower of Cost and Net Realisable Value

Stock valuation at December 31 1988

Stock Code	No. in Stock	Cost price £	Value at Cost £	Net Realisable Value (NRV) £	Lower of Cost or NRV £
EO 145	10	5.00	50.00	40.00	40.00
EO 146	20	10.00	200.00	250.00	200.00
EO 147	5	12.00	60.00	60.00	60.00
EO 148	25	5.00	125.00	100.00	100.00
EO 149	10	2.50	25.00	10.00	10.00
EO 150	2	25.50	51.00	20.00	20.00
			511.00	480.00	430.00

In the final accounts for the year ended December 31 1988, the figure in the final column, £430, would be taken along with other stock valuations as the stock end value. This indicates that the items of stock valued at less than their cost should be assessed against the profit for the current period.

Costing Direct Materials

In manufacturing concerns the valuation of direct materials (materials used in producing a product) is usually straightforward in that the quantity used is valued at the supplier's price. For example

```
500 units   @ 50p each   =   £250
100 units   @ 40p each   =   £ 40
```

Stocks of materials are normally held in stores and issued to production as and when required. Stock cards or computer records (on VDUs — visual display units) are used to show what has come in and gone out of stock and the balance on hand.

When costly parts (such as car engines or gear boxes) are valued, the cost price of each part is clearly known and used for stock valuation purposes. However, for items of stock having a *low-value* and bought frequently in large quantities (such as nuts, bolts, brackets, screws, washers, etc.), it may not be possible or desirable to itemise the value of each item, particularly when costs may vary from time to time.

To cost these low-value items in production there are three distinct methods of valuation which basically consider the stock being issued in a particular order. The three methods are:

FIFO   First-in, First-out
LIFO   Last-in, First-out
AVCO   Average cost of stock

In actual physical terms, the order of movement of stock does not matter. It does matter how the stock is valued.

FIFO   assumes that stock in first is the first stock out
LIFO   assumes that stock in last is the first stock out and
AVCO   takes the weighted average of units in stock

and each method is valued accordingly.

Example

Stock received: 300 @ £1   = £300   January
                     200 @ £1.20 = £240   March
Stock issued: 400 between January to March

Using the three methods of stock valuation, what is the value of the stock still in hand for each method?

(a) FIFO   100 × £1.20 = £120
(b) LIFO   100 × £1.00 = £100
(c) AVCO   100 × £1.08 = £108   (£540/500 = £1.08)

So, for valuation purposes the FIFO method in this case values stock the highest (when prices rise) and LIFO and lowest. AVCO is in between the two.

Most organisations tend to use either the FIFO or AVCO methods. LIFO is rarely used because in times of rising prices it values stock the lowest and therefore has the effect of understating profit.

Remember an important concept in accounting from a previous section? The concept referred to is 'consistency'. Once a method has been chosen it should be consistently used and in this way stock valuation in one period can be accurately and fairly compared with another.

The following pages illustrate the stock record sheets or cards of the same item of stock (25 mm bolts) using the three distinct methods of valuation. Note that the stock end is 28 February and that

FIFO	values the balance in stock at £7,680
LIFO	values the balance in stock at £7,120
AVCO	values the balance in stock at £7,303

Clearly, the prices of the stock item rose because the FIFO valuation is the highest and LIFO the lowest, as one would expect.

S T O C K   R E C O R D   C A R D

UNIT: BOLTS (25mm)   QUANTITY LEVEL: Minimum: 100
CODE: 17484 TW   Maximum: 750
SUPPLIERS: Spaldings (Lincs)   Re-order
                                                                    level: 200

| | Received | | | Issued | | | BALANCE | | | |
DATE	Qty	Unit Price £	Cost £	Qty	Unit Price £	Cost £	No in Stock	Unit Price £	Value £	
Jan 5	150	12–	1800				150	12	1800	
7	125	10–	1250				125	10	1250	
							275		3050	
10				150	12	1800				
				25	10	250	100	10	1000	
21	200	14–	2800				200	14	2800	
							300		3800	
28				100	10	1000				
				20	14	280	180	14	2520	
Feb 1	500	16–	8000				500	16	8000	
							680		10520	
27				180	14	2520				
				20	16	320	480	16	7680	Stock (end) 28/2

STOCK RECORD CARD

UNIT: BOLTS (25mm)
CODE: 17484 TW
SUPPLIERS: Spaldings (Lincs)

QUANTITY LEVEL: Minimum: 100
Maximum: 750
Re-order
level: 200

DATE	Received			Issued			BALANCE			
	Qty	Unit Price £	Cost £	Qty	Unit Price £	Cost £	No in Stock	Unit Price £	Value £	
JAN 5	150	12–	1800				150	12	1800	
7	125	10–	1250				125	10	1250	
							275		3050	
10				125	10	1250				
				50	12	600	100	12	1200	
21	200	14–	2800				200	14	2800	
							300		4000	
28				120	14	1680	100	12	1200	
							80	14	1120	
							180		2320	
FEB 1	500	16–	8000				500	16	8000	
							680		10320	
27				200	16	3200	100	12	1200	
							80	14	1120	
							300	16	4800	
							480		7120	Stock end 28/2

STOCK RECORD CARD

UNIT: Bolts (25mm)
CODE: 17484 TW
SUPPLIERS: Spaldings (Lincs)

QUANTITY LEVEL: Minimum: 100
Maximum: 750
Re-order level: 200

| DATE | Received | | | Issued | | | BALANCE | | | AVCO Notes |
	Qty	Unit Price £	Cost £	Qty	Unit Price £	Cost £	No in Stock	Unit Price £	Value £	
JAN 5	150	12-	1800				150	12	1800	
7	125	10-	1250				125	10	1250	3050/275
							====		====	unit price = value div. by stock.
							275	11.09	3050	
10				175	11.09	1941	100		1109	
21	200	14-	2800				300	13.03	3909	3909/300
28				120	13.03	1564	180		2345	
FEB 1	500	16-	8000				680.	15.21	10345	10345/680
27				200	15.21	3042	480	15.21	7303	Stock end 28/2

Trading Account Showing the Importance of Stock Valuation

Using stock (end) 28 February
valuation from stock record cards:

Method	A FIFO	B LIFO	C AVCO
	£	£	£
Turnover	80,000	80,000	80,000
Less Cost of Goods Sold			
Stock (beg.)	7,500	7,500	7,500
Purchases	42,000	42,000	42,000
	49,500	49,500	49,500
− Stock (end)	7,680	7,120	7,303
	41,820	42,380	42,197
Gross Profit	38,180	37,620	37,803
	80,000	80,000	80,000

Note: Method A has a greater stock value at the end of the month than either Methods B, which means that by using Method A the gross profit is greater.

However, the opening stock balances for March will be the closing balances from February. Because of this, there will be no further differences in profit, the different methods cancelling each other out. What is important, is that businesses apply the *same* method of valuation of stock over and over again to ensure consistency in the recording of accounts. Not only is accounting conservative in nature because it tends to take a pessimistic view of accounting by anticipating losses, but it also has views that businesses should apply adopted policies with rigorous consistency.

UNIT: *Quantity Level*:   Minimum: _____

CODE: Maximum: _____

SUPPLIERS: Re-order Level: _____

DATE	Received			Issued			BALANCE			NOTES
	Q	Unit Price £	Cost £	Q	Unit Price £	Cost £	No. in Stock	Unit Price £	Cost £	

Exercises

1. The goods listed below were in stock at Jack's Store on 31 December.
    Record the items on a stock card/sheet and calculate the value of stock
    at the end of the year, 31 December.

Code No.	Items	Quantity	Cost per Unit	NRV per Unit	*Lower* of Cost or NRV
			£	£	£
427	Jeans	50	10.5	12.5	525.
428	Jeans	10	15.20	14.	
859/1	Sweaters	120	8.75	7.5	
859/2	Sweaters	60	12.50	15.95	
859/3	Sweaters	15	9.95	12.50	
870	Men's socks	50	1.15	1.50	
870/1	Men's socks	5	3.90	1.00	

2. The stock issues of a manufacturer for the months June to August
    inclusive were as follows:

Stock Issues — June, July, August

		Quantity (units)	Cost per Unit £	Value of stock £
1/6	Balance	200	2.00	400.
15/6	Purchases	100	1.95	
30/6	Purchases	200	2.10	
		500		
30/6	Issues	150		
1/7	Balance	350		
21/7	Purchases	200	2.15	
		550		
30/7	Issues	200		
1/8	Balance	350		
10/8	Purchases	150	2.20	
21/8	Purchases	100	2.20	
		600		
31/8	Issues	250		
1/9	Balance	350		

Required:

Write up a stock record card for the months June to August and calculate
the value of stock on 1 September in terms of both FIFO and LIFO order
issues.

3. Complete the stock record card by entering the 'balance in hand' figure on the right of the card. Calculate the value of stock end if purchases were £2.50 per ream up to 12/9 and £3.00 after 12/9 (use FIFO method).

STOCK RECORD CARD

MONTH: Sept

Item: Typewriting Paper – Size A4
Suppliers:1 ABC Co Ltd 2
         3 XYZ Ltd 4

Quantities
MIN:100 Ream
MAX:200 Ream
Re-order level:

DATE	ORDERED			RECEIVED			ISSUED		BALANCE
	Supp.	O/No.	Qty	Supp.	O/No.	Qty	Dept.	Qty	130 Reams
Sept 1	1	347	150						
3	2	348	125						
6							P.	36	
6							A	20	
9				1	347	150			
10							T	25	
12				2	348	100			
14							B	55	
14							M	60	
16	2	349	100						
18							A	25	
19				2	349	90			
20							P	79	

4. Use FIFO and AVCO methods to value the following stock:

Jan.	1	Balance	50 units @ £3 unit
	10	Purchased 100 units @ £3	
	16	Purchased 100 units @ £3.20	
	24	Issued 80 units	
Feb.	7	Purchased 200 units @ £3.50	
	14	Issued 240 units	
	20	Issued 80 units	
	28	Purchased 50 units @ £3.40	

Required:

(a) Prepare two stock cards to illustrate FIFO and AVCO methods of stock recording
(b) What effect would these methods have in the trading a/c?

5. *Situation/Information*

The purchase of stock is of great importance to a business. It must be bought in the right quantities, at the right time, at the right price and at the right quality. Stock record cards may be kept to keep an accurate record of both quantity and value in stock.

At the end of the financial year, physical stock-taking should take place to value the unsold stock, which is then transferred to the trading account. The value of the stock influences the gross profit: the higher the value of closing stock, the greater the value of gross profit.

Task A

Complete the stock card below by showing the value in the end column. When the stock is sold, it is on the basis of first-in first-out (FIFO). This means that for value purposes, the stock first in is assumed to be the first sold out.

Type of			Stock Level		150–200
Goods	Unit 5		Re-Order Level		100
Code No.	11/13				
Supplier	Arena, Metro				

Date	Quantity Received	Unit Value £	Sales	Stock Balance	Unit Value £	Value £
June 1	Balance			200	4.00	800
5			80	120	4.00	480
12	Arena 200	4.25		200	4.25	850
				320		1330
15			140			
18			50			
20	Metro 120	4.00				
28			145			

Note: As a check, you should have 105 units in stock value on 28 June.

Task B

The end of the firm's financial year is 30 June. The value of the unsold stock, Code No. 11/13, is entered on a stock sheet along with other stocks in order to calculate the value of unsold stock at the end of the accounting period.

The firm values its unsold stock at the 'lower of cost or net realisable value'. This basically means that if the expected selling price is less than the cost price, then the lower figure will be used to asses the stock value.

Complete the Stock Sheet Sheet as on 30 June:

Code No. & Comments	Stock Balance Quantity	Unit Value £	Value £	Net Realisable Value £	£	Value £	Lower of Cost or Net Realisable Value
11/13	105			105	5.00	525	
11/27 (old stock)	215	10.00	2150	215	7.00	1505	1505.00
11/33	150	6.50		150	7.50		
11/42 (damaged)	10	8.50		10	2.00		
11/50	85	12.75		85	15.50		
					total	_____	

Task C

Completion of Trading and Profit and Loss account.

Sales for the financial year were   £38,850
Purchases for the financial year were £27,500
Stock (1/7) commencing   £ 2,650

Distribution Costs   £ 3,750
Administration Expenses   £ 1,225

Prepare the firm's trading and profit and loss account for the period ending 30 June. Use the stock valuation from the stock sheet above.

An Assignment Programme

Preparation of Balance Sheets and Calculation of Current Ratios

Situation

You have been given a summary of the Balance Sheet of your organisation for the last four years from your supervisor, the Finance Manager. He wants you to produce separate balance sheets for the purpose of calculating working capital and current ratios.

Information

Use the data from the table below relating to the last four years balance sheets.

BALANCE SHEET FIGURES OVER THE LAST 4 YEARS

	£ 000's			
	Year 1 £	Year 2 £	Year 3 £	Year 4 £
Premises	100	100	100	110
Plant, Machinery & Equipment	60	80	85	90
FIXED ASSETS	160	180	185	200
Stocks	70	80	100	115
Debtors	30	42	75	75
Bank/Cash	65	38	—	10
CURRENT ASSETS	165	160	175	200
Creditors	85	95	100	120
Bank Overdraft			35	
CURRENT LIABILITIES	85	95	135	120
Loans more than 12 months:	50	65	50	85
NET ASSETS	190	180	175	195

TASK A

Prepare separate Balance Sheets for each of the 4 years and clearly indicate the working capital in your presentation.

TASK B

Calculate the working capital ratio (current ratio) for each of the four years and prepare brief notes to your superior to indicate your findings.

TASK C

If the above organisation is a public limited company, outline how the company could be financed.

Construction of Final Accounts in Private and Public Sectors of Business — A Contrast

Situation

You are to assume that you are employed by a group of accountants in private practice and you have been given draft figures to prepare accounts for two distinctive types of business organisations, one from the private sector, the other from the public sector.

Information

Enterprise No. 1. The following information refers to a large organisation, for the year ending 31 March 1988:

Profit & Loss a/c	£ 000's
Net Trading Profit	2,560
Taxation provision	200
Profit & Loss balance (1 April 1987)	100
Dividends provided	515
Transfer to Reserves	1,500

Balance Sheet as at 31 March, 1988

	£ 000's
Fixed Assets	3,275
Current Assets:	
Stock	10,336
Debtors/Pre-payments	1,530
Bank/Cash	172

Current Liabilities:
Creditors/Accruals 2,800
Bank Overdraft (secured) 244
Loan (short-term) 2,125
Taxation provision 200
Dividends provision 515

Bank Loan (over 10 Years)
(secured) 2,850

Ordinary Shares Issued & Paid 2,980
Share Premium a/c 512
Reserves 2,642
Profit & Loss 445

Task A

Prepare the Profit & Loss Appropriation a/c of Enterprise 1 for the period ended 31 March 1988.

Prepare a Balance Sheet as at that date, showing clearly the working capital (net current assets) and capital employed.

Information

Enterprise No. 2. The following information refers to the second organisation, for the year ended 31 March 1988.

Revenue & Expenditure Programme 1987–1988

	£	£ (millions)
Current Expenditure		19,692
+ other Expenditure		2,615
Total Expenditure		22,307

Resources:

	£	£ (millions)
Specific Grants		2,366
Block Grant	8,730	
Domestic Rate Relief	686	
RSG		9,416
Aggregate Exchequer Grant:		11,782
Funding from Local Precepts		10,525
Total Resources		22,307

Task B

Calculate the percentage of the Exchequer Grant as a proportion of the total expenditure for the year.

What does RSG mean? How many p/£ is it at the present time?

Balance Sheet as at 31 March 1988

	£ 000's
Fixed Assets (net)	26,350
Current Assets	
Stock	66
Debtors' Mortgagors	2,512
Investments (short)	2
Bank/cash	5
Revenues Accrued	2,135
Current Liabilities	
Creditors	745
Bank Overdraft	625
Temporary Loans	3,740
Provisions	880
Long-Term	
Loan — Public Loan Works Board	8,510
Capital Structure:	
Capital funds	10,518
Capital receipts	4,325
Revenue Account Surplus	1,727

Task C

Prepare the Balance Sheet of Enterprise No. 2 as at 31 March 1988, showing clearly working capital and capital employed.

Task D

List the items which indicate the difference between a public sector organisation from one in the private sector.

An Investigation into Different Forms of Business Organisations in Your Area

Situation

You are to assume you are currently employed by a Market Research Agency. The agency has been approached by one of the major US banks in this country, who wish to expand their financial services to a wide range of UK business enterprises. The bank has just established its new head offices in your area and requires the agency to undertake a number of surveys about business in this area as a pilot project. The assignment is based on the collection of data on four organisations found in the area, namely

(a) A *Public* Limited or a *Private* Limited Company.
(b) A *Partnership* and a *Sole-Trader*.
(c) A *Public Sector* organisation.

TASK 1
Collect information individually or in groups about the organisations you have selected by using a variety of sources including:

> Public Reference Library
> College Library
> Careers Office
> PRESTEL
> Employees of organisations known to you

When you have completed the initial research you should arrange for speakers from selected organisations to address the class and answer questions.

Under the guidance of your lecturers you should, as a class:

(a) Decide upon the different types of business you will use for this task and which speakers or companies will be approached.
(b) Draft a letter of invitation.
(c) Complete any other necessary correspondence.
(d) Make arrangements for rooms, times, etc.
(e) One member of class should welcome and introduce the speaker and another propose the vote of thanks.
(f) You should *all* prepare written questions to be asked after the talk, which will be submitted to the lecturer for assessment.

TASK 2
Using the information collected in Task 1 each student should write a report to the Marketing Manager to describe, compare and contrast the different types of organisations in terms of

(a) How the organisation was legally established.
(b) Where it obtained (and in what form) finance for its establishment.
(c) The ownership of the organisation.
(d) Its management and operation.
(e) Control exercised over the organisation.
(f) Its organisational structure.

TASK 3
Individually, you should give a brief oral presentation on any one of the organisations studied and be prepared to answer questions from the class.

TASK 4
To ensure the prospective clients are viable, long-term customers worthy of support and help, the bank requires detailed financial information about the organisations. Your Market Research Agency is required to:

(a) Prepare Balance Sheets for each of the organisations chosen or in the case of the Public Sector Organisation, a similar document indicating sources of finance and a programme of expenditure for the current financial year. Present the figures in vertical form.
(b) From the figures you have prepared in (a) calculate accounting ratios to evaluate the liquidity, where relevant, of each of the organisations and briefly comment on the organisation's ability to cover its debts, as an appendix to the Balance Sheet.

(c) The bank often has customers who forward complaints about unaudited accounts. Write a brief memorandum to the Marketing Manager stating which of your organisations have their accounts audited and explain why it is important to audit accounts.

TASK 5

To assist the bank in its marketing strategy, it needs to know the aims and objectives of each of the organisations selected. Write a memorandum to the Marketing Manager setting out clearly the aims and objectives of each of your organisations.

Construction of Manufacturing Account to Balance Sheet

Situation

Robert David Company Ltd is a business which manufactures electrical components for the car industry. Production output is 50,000 units per annum but they have the capacity to increase this by about 15–20%. The following information has been taken from their books on 31 December, from which you are to compile a draft of their final accounts:

Information

The trial balance of the company as on 31 December 1988 was as follows:

	£	£
Ordinary Share Capital:		
70,000 @ £1 shares issued and paid		70,000
Share Premium Account		7,000
Profit & Loss (1 January 1988)		5,820
Premises (cost)	86,000	
Plant, Equipment, Machinery (cost)	12,000	
Provision for Depreciation:		
Plant, Equipment, Machinery		6,000
Debtors	10,498	
Creditors		58,409
Stock: Raw Materials (1 January, 1988)	5,892	
Finished Goods (1 January, 1988)		
2,500 units	8,500	
Provision for bad and doubtful debts		210
Bad Debts written off	528	
Bank/Cash	2,910	
Direct Wages	56,804	
Purchases of Raw Materials	156,820	
Sales: 48,000 units in year		204,000
General Overheads ($\frac{1}{2}$ factory)	2,944	
Rates and Insurance ($\frac{1}{2}$ factory)	610	
Office salaries	5,220	
Carriage Outwards	2,713	
	351,439	351,439

Further information on 31 December, 1988

(a) The value of unsold stock of raw materials was £20,893.
(b) In the year, 50,000 units were produced. The unsold stock in the warehouse is to be valued at production cost.
(c) Depreciation of Plant, Equipment and Machinery is to be at 10% of Net Value.
(d) The provision for Doubtful Debts is to be increased to £750.
(e) The Directors have recommended a 5% ordinary dividend and a General Reserve is to be created by the transfer of £4,000.

Task A

You are to prepare the Company's Manufacturing Account, Trading and Profit & Loss Account and Appropriation Account for the year ended 31 December 1988.

Task B

Prepare the Company's Balance Sheet as at 31 December 1988, showing clearly the net current assets of the company as well as the capital employed.

Task C

Based on the number of units produced in the year, make calculations to show:

(a) The Direct Labour cost per unit
(b) The Direct Material cost per unit.
(c) The *total* Overheads per unit (factory & office).
(d) Using the trial balance figures for the selling price per unit, calculate the mark-up on cost per unit.

Costing Forecast

The budget figures for the following year 1989 are estimated as follows:

		£
Production Output:	60,000 units	
Direct Labour:		63,500
Direct Materials:		147,000
Factory Overheads:		15,000
Service (office) Overheads:		14,500

Variables:

Direct Materials:	100% variable.
Direct Labour:	30p per unit as a productivity bonus.
Factory Overheads:	2p per unit for Power.
All other costs:	Fixed.

Task D

Prepare a suitable table to show fixed, variable and total costs based on the figures above. Calculate the Contribution per Unit.

Task E

Calculate the Break-Even point. Prepare a Break-Even Chart to illustrate the break-even point. On your chart show:

Profit/Loss	on	42,000 units produced.
	on	30,000 units produced.

Baldwin & Son Ltd Jean Factory — A New Product

Situation

Baldwin & Son Ltd have been given the opportunity by their existing customers to produce an 'up-market' type jeans rather than the existing standard model that they now produce. Profit is very marginal on the standard type and the market is extremely competitive. It is the company's belief that the new product will improve profitability, given that it can increase its share of the market.

The development of the new product will require new machines, some retraining of staff and also a reorganisation of the works itself. If the plan does go ahead, an additional two new members of staff will be required in production.

The staff have been pressing for a pay increase. Mr Baldwin has responded by stating that any increase in pay be met by appropriate increases in output. Workers want at least £1.00 per unit bonus, double the current £0.50 they earn at present.

Mr Baldwin wants to be sure that productivity is increased by 25% on present output before any increase in bonus is offered. Current output per month is 800 units. He would like to see this increased to around 1,000 units per month.

The cost of retraining staff is estimated to be £100 per worker and at least five members will need training. The purchase of new machines will also increase the monthly cost of overheads.

The Trial Balance figures for March were:

	£	£
Premises	35,000	
Equipment and Machines	4,000	
Motor Vehicle	4,750	
Stocks	3,680	
Bank		2,422
Petty Cash	200	
Debtors, Creditors	4,050	4,785
Mortgage on Premises		22,450
Bank Loan (5 years)		4,725
Sales (776 units)		9,700
Purchases	5,617	
VAT		248
Gross Wages	4,425	
Light, Heat	55	
Telephone, Insurance	105	
Petty Cash Expenses	148	
Fixed Overheads	800	
Drawings	1,500	
Capital		20,000
	64,330	64,330

Note: Stocks are valued £5,297 as on 31 March. Wages — a bonus of £83 is outstanding on the same date.

TASK I

As the book-keeper/accounts person of the company, Mr Baldwin requires a number of tasks of you:

Task A

Prepare the Trading & Profit & Loss Account of the firm for the month ended 31 March.

Prepare a Balance Sheet as on that date. Show working capital as part of the presentation and calculate the current ratio.

The Costing figures relating to March are as follows:

Output:	800 Units
Direct Materials:	£5.00 per Unit (variable cost)
Direct Labour:	£0.50 per Unit (variable cost) bonus scheme, additional to fixed £4,500 wages.
Overheads:	£1,200.
Selling Price:	Calculate price from the sales figures.

Task B

Draw up a table of costs for the month of March, indicating the total, fixed and variable costs.

Estimate the profit/loss for the month based on the above figures. Calculate the point where all costs are covered. What is the current Mark-Up % on costs?

Producing the New Product — Estimated Costs for April

The cost of retraining staff is estimated to cost £100 per employee and five staff will be retrained. The workforce will be increased by two new members who will earn £80 per week each. Fixed overheads are expected to increase by 10% per month. Calculations are based on 4 weeks.

Output:	An increase of 25% on March figures.
Direct Materials:	£8.00 per Unit.
Direct Labour:	£1.00 per Unit bonus scheme. Wages £4,500 + 2 new staff members.
Overheads:	£1,200 + 10% increase + costs of retraining.

Task C

Draw up a similar table of costs for April (as in Task B).

The selling price of the new product is estimated to be £16.50 per unit. Calculate the estimated profit/loss for April. Calculate the break-even point.

Should Mr. Baldwin go ahead? Briefly comment on the results of your calculations.

TASK II

In order to produce and market the new type of jeans profitably, the company will require a significant amount of information. Draw up a report to be submitted to Mr Baldwin which explains what type of information will be needed and how this information should be obtained.

TASK III

Assuming the information collected reveals an increasing expectation of new consumers wanting to purchase the new product, use demand and supply diagrams to show how this would influence the market situation.

TASK IV

The information also reveals the likely expectation of a large inflow of cheap, high-quality 'up market' jeans from South East Asian countries. With the aid of demand and supply diagrams show how this would influence the market situation.

TASK V

As part of a preliminary investigation you are asked to survey a number of people in your age group about their requirements when buying jeans. Working in groups, draw up suitable questions about such things as cost, quality, styles and the extent that people are influenced by advertising. After conducting the survey present the results individually, in diagramatic form and comment on the findings.

TASK VI

For some time now the workforce of Baldwin and Son has considered becoming unionised. You have been asked to investigate this and produce explanatory notes which:

(a) Describe some of the potential problems which may arise if the new product is manufactured and how these may lead to the workforce becoming more dissatisfied (for example, changes in organisation structure, job descriptions, working conditions).
(b) Describe the potential benefits of union membership
(c) Summarise your own position — that is, whether you would consider joining a union in the present circumstances.

The Baldwin & Son Ltd Jean Factory — Relocation

Since the last assignment, Baldwins have improved their stock control system, and this has helped to reduce costs and improve the small profit margin the business makes. Other problems do exist however. Industrial relations could be better. Although the company has a small work force, the staff has considered joining a union to be a little more assertive in its demands.

Cheap foreign imports continue to affect the company adversely and make it difficult for Baldwins to compete effectively, except possibly in the more 'up-market' jeans.

The company has not found a major bulk supplier of materials in the north and it is having to purchase its materials from a variety of suppliers and so fails to obtain bulk discounts which would reduce costs. There is a materials supplier in the south of England which could solve the problem of bulk purchase.

Another serious and more recent problem has come from just over the Pennines in Leeds, where the Government has established an Enterprise Zone and a new factory has been set up, one of its main products being jeans. It is now proving to be a strong competitor to Baldwins and recent sales have shown a downward trend.

The continuing fall in incomes in the north of England because of the high levels of unemployment has meant, in any case, that demand is 'sluggish' for the present. Moreover, sales of an up-market product which Baldwins has always been keen to pursue, are not very promising in the north.

As a result of these problems, Mr Baldwin has put to his fellow share-holders a proposal which he asks them to consider:

> "That Baldwins should close down and sell its premises in Manchester and move to the more affluent south of England."

The local authority is keen to encourage new industry into its area and employment, incomes and demand are substantially higher than in the north.

The tasks which follow are based on the consideration of such a move to the south. You are to consider yourself in the position of an employee being offered an opportunity to move house, home and job to the south of England.

From the management's point of view, you will also be asked to consider the 'pros and cons' as to whether a move to the south is desirable economically as well as socially.

TASK I

Personal Finance

As an employee of Baldwin & Son Ltd you have been approached by management with a proposal to move to the south of England with the company and to receive £500 towards your relocation costs, given that the move goes ahead.

Your average gross income is £100 per week and your partner earns a gross income of £150 per week employed as a bus driver. It is assumed that a similar job as a driver will be available in the south on the same wages. You have no children.

Your existing property in Manchester is valued at £25,000 with an outstanding mortgage repayment of £7,000. You would like to buy a similar semi-detached or terraced house in the south within the price range of £35,000 to £45,000. The building society has agreed that you may borrow up to $2\frac{1}{2}$ times your joint income.

Moving Expenses:

For your calculations consider the following costs:
  (i) Solicitor's fees.　　　　Buying: £440 + VAT and 1% Stamp Duty.
  　　　　　　　　　　　　　　Selling: £340 + VAT.
 (ii) Selling Agents:　　　　A commission of $1\frac{1}{2}$% + VAT.
(iii) Society's Survey:　　　A fee of £75.
 (iv) Removal Expenses:　　Manchester–south of England. £500 + VAT.
  (v) Any further costs you feel appropriate.

Task A

Find information from Estate Agents relating to suitable accommodation within the price range stated above. (Attach literature indicating the choice of dwelling to your assignment.)

Calculate the total cost of the move from Manchester to the south of England, presenting the information in a clear, statement form.

Task B
Prepare a Personal Cash Budget for the first six months (March to August 31) assuming you have moved into your new home. Take the months of May and July as having 5 weeks, the other months as 4 weeks.

Expenditure Items

(i) The mortgage repayments per month.

(ii) General Rates (paid monthly). £1.95/ in the £.
Water & Sewerage (paid monthly). £0.40/ in the £.

(iii) Light and Heat: average weekly cost £6.

(iv) Food: average weekly cost £30.

(v) Entertainment: cigarettes/pubs/clubs . . .. You decide!

(vi) Clothes: . . .. You decide.

(vii) Miscellaneous . . .. You decide.

Revenue:

Your combined net wages each week are the only source of income. Take into consideration tax and national insurance and tax allowances. Mortgage interest relief is currently 30%. Overtime and bonus payments should net an extra £25 per week on average.

Start your bank balance on March 1 with the figure you have calculated after the costs of relocation.

Assume you had £850 in the bank *before* you moved.

TASK II

Relocation factors

Task A
You are required to prepare a report to the Managing Director, Mr Baldwin, evaluating the case for and against the suggested relocation from Manchester to the south of England both from the employers' and employees' point of view.

Task B
If the suggested move goes ahead, the company will require adequate finance to fund the relocation.

Prepare a well presented written statement for your superior with your reasons, the four most suitable methods by which this could be achieved.

TASK III

Preparing a presentation

Each class should now divide into two groups, one group to assume the role of management representatives who are *in favour* of the relocation; the other to assume the role of staff representatives who are *against* the relocation.

Working together, prepare a spoken presentation of your reasoned arguments to be given to your opposite numbers. The presentation should include appropriate audio visual aids. Be prepared to answer any questions which may arise.

Note

Assessment of this task will include:

(a) assessment of the effectiveness of the presentation.
(b) assessment of each individual's contribution to the working of the group.

This task should be negotiated with your lecturers.

TASK IV

You are now approached by your immediate superior, Mr Lewis, who asks you to investigate one *alternative locality* for relocation by using Prestel. Carry out the investigation and write an informative memorandum for Mr Lewis. The memorandum should preferably be produced by using a word processor and include a comment on how helpful the information on Prestel proved to be.

Allied Components Plc – Diversification

Situation

Allied Components makes electrical components used in the production of electrical appliances. Because of intense competition, especially from the Far East, the Board has taken a decision to diversify Allied's business interests.

Two plans are put forward:

1. To produce other products using existing plant and equipment. This plan is favoured by the Production Director because his research and development team has devised new plans for other products.

2. To purchase another manufacturing organisation in order to give Allied a wider product range and diversify its markets. This plan is favoured by the Finance and Sales Directors who would like to use the company's funds to acquire subsidiaries. Particular interest has been shown in purchasing one of two private companies which specialise in producing circuit boards used in a wide variety of products. Both companies appear to be sound financial investments.
The companies are:

Arrowsmith Ltd   An older, well established company having a stable record of production and profits over a number of years; good labour relations record.

Hardcastle Ltd   A relatively new company which has rapidly become established. Only a few years trading figures available but early trend shows rising profits. Young and more aggressive management but more strained labour relations.

The Financial Director has been able to secure the most recent figures of both these organisations and you have been asked as one of his assistants to prepare a draft of the final accounts of the two companies and to give a reasoned assessment of them. You have also acquired accounting ratios from 'Inter-Firm Comparison Ltd' provided by the British Institute of Management.

On page 516 information is made available to you relating to Arrowsmith Ltd and Hardcastle Ltd . . .

Accounting data to Year ended December 1989

	Arrowsmith Ltd £	Hardcastle Ltd £
Turnover	356,000	327,000
Stock (1/1/89)	62,000	58,750
Cost of Production	256,500	201,500
Stock (31/12/89)	84,000	68,750
Sales & Distribution Costs	28,100	44,800
Administration Expenses	44,400	38,700
Interest Payable	4,000	5,500
Taxation Provision	15,500	14,500
Transfer to Reserves	20,000	25,000
Dividends Proposed	9,000	2,500
Fixed Assets (Net Values)	156,500	135,100
Debtors	84,200	76,750
Bank/Cash	4,800	(10,800) O/D
Prepayments	–	500
Accruals	500	4,900
Creditors	86,500	89,400
Loans (Long-term)	40,000	52,000
Issued & Paid Up Capital		
Ordinary @ £1 Shares	100,000	50,000
Reserves [1/1/89]	57,500	27,500

Accounting ratios provided by the British Institute of Management on electronic industries. The figures have been supplied for guidance as to financial performance.

Accounting Ratios:	%
Gross Margin	40.
Net Profit (b/t)/Sales	14.5
Net Profit (a/t)/Capital Employed	20.75
Net Profit (a/t)/Net Worth	29.55
Production Cost/Sales	60.5
Sales & Dist. Cost/Sales	9.5
Administration Exp./Sales	11.0
Current Ratio	Deci. 1.85 :1
Acid Test	Deci. 0.95 :1
Capital Gearing	80 %
Current Assets/Sales £1,000	£450
Fixed Assets/Sales £1,000	£421

Investment Ratios

Earnings per share	£0.55
Cover	8 times
Dividend per share	£0.05
Yield	Not available
P/E ratio	Not available

The current market value per share for Arrowsmith is 174p and for Hardcastle 256p.

TASK A

Prepare a draft copy of the trading and profit and loss accounts of the two companies for the year ended 31 December 1989. Prepare the balance sheets as at that date.

TASK B

Using the Inter-Firm Comparison ratios as a guide, prepare accounting ratios of both companies on which to form your assessment. Include investment ratios for both companies, as listed.

TASK C

Evaluate the case for and against the company which appears to be the better of the two investments. Draw attention to the limitations accounting ratios tend to impose on the assessment of financial performance.

Glossary of Terms

ACCOUNT — A formal record of one or more business transactions expressed in money and kept in a ledger/journal.

ACCRUAL — The accounting treatment of expense incurred in one financial year but paid in the next financial year.

ADVICE NOTE — Note accompanying the delivery of goods.

ASSET — Any resource owned by a business, tangible or intangible.

AUDIT — An examination of the accounts and supporting records by an independent accountant.

AUDITOR — The person who carries out the audit.

BAD DEBT — An amount receivable but deemed to be uncollectable.

BALANCE — The difference between the debit and the credit entries in an account.

BALANCE SHEET — A statement of assets held in a business at a particular time — the Position Statement.

BANK RECONCILIATION — A statement explaining the difference between the cash book and the statement issued from the bank.

BOOK VALUE — The original cost of an asset less the cumulative depreciation.

BOOK-KEEPING — The process of recording financial transactions in the ledger/journal.

BOOKS OF PRIME ENTRY — Books into which transactions are first recorded before transfer to the ledger.

BUDGET — The expression of a business plan in money terms.

CAPITAL — Usually refers to the owner's net worth: that is, the total capital employed minus long-term liabilities.

CASH BOOK — A book in which is recorded all the cash/bank receipts and payments.

519

CASH DISCOUNT	An amount allowed for prompt settlement of an invoice.
CONTRA	The setting off of matching debit with credit against each other.
CREDIT NOTE	The document which shows the amount and other particulars regarding the reduction or cancellation of the amount originally invoiced.
CREDITOR	One to whom money is owed.
CURRENT ASSET	An asset held for less than one year which can be converted to cash, such as Stock, w.i.p., or Debtors.
CURRENT LIABILITY	A short-term debt which must be repaid before the anniversary of the next balance sheet.
DEBTOR	One who owes money to the business.
DEPRECIATION	The estimated loss in value of a fixed asset as a result of wear and tear or obsolescence.
FINAL ACCOUNTS	The profit and loss account and balance sheet drawn up at the end of the financial year.
FIXED ASSET	An asset held for more than one year, such as land, buildings, plant and machinery, office equipment.
FUNDS FLOW	*See* STATEMENT OF SOURCES AND APPLICATIONS OF FUNDS.
GOODWILL	The excess paid for a business over the book value of assets minus liabilities being acquired on purchase.
INTANGIBLE ASSET	An asset which has no physical substance but possesses a value, such as goodwill or development costs.
IMPREST SYSTEM	Most usually associated with petty cash, whereby a fixed amount of money is advanced to the Petty Cashier who is reimbursed on a regular basis for the amounts paid out on petty cash vouchers.
INVOICE	The document which shows the quantity, price, terms and other particulars regarding goods or services provided.
LEDGER	The main book of account in which entries are recorded and divided into the purchases, sales and nominal ledgers.
LIABILITY	Amount owing to third party.
MARGIN	Profit expressed as a percentage of selling value.
MARK-UP	Profit expressed as a percentage of cost value.
PAR	The nominal or face value of a security.
PETTY CASH BOOK	A book kept by the Petty Cashier in which small cash disbursements are recorded. It's a subsidiary of the Cash Book.

PETTY CASH VOUCHER	Document supporting an entry in the Petty Cash Book.
POSTING	The act of transferring entries from the books of prime entry to their separate accounts in the ledger or cash book.
PRE-PAYMENT	The accounting treatment of expenses incurred in the current financial year which relates to the next financial year.
PROFIT AND LOSS ACCOUNT	A summary account which nets off all revenue expenditure against income showing as its balance the net profit for the accounting period.
PROVISION	Amount written off or retained out of profits to provide for depreciation or known liability.
RECEIPT	A written acknowledgement of payment for goods or services received.
STATEMENT OF ACCOUNT	A statement prepared to show the amount due. Usually a statement will show only the amounts and dates of transactions between the two parties since the preparation of the previous statement.
STATEMENT OF AFFAIRS	A report, usually prepared from incomplete records, that show the assets, liabilities and net worth of a business.
STATEMENT OF SOURCES AND APPLICATIONS OF FUNDS	A statement which summarises the inflow of funds and the outflow of funds during a specific time period — usually the financial year.
STOCK IN TRADE	Goods held for subsequent sale in the ordinary course of business.
TANGIBLE ASSET	*See* FIXED ASSET.
TAXABLE INCOME	Earnings that are subject to tax.
TRADE DISCOUNT	A reduction that is allowed to certain customers on a list price. Usually the greater the quantity of items purchased the higher the discount.
TRIAL BALANCE	A list of all the balances in the ledgers of a business to prove the arithmetical accuracy of the debit and credit balances before preparing final accounts.
TURNOVER	Net sales — that is, Sales less returns inwards.
VALUE ADDED TAX	Tax levied by H.M. Customs and Excise on the supply of some goods and services.
WRITTEN DOWN VALUE	*See* BOOK VALUE.

Abbreviated Answers to Text Questions

Section I

Parts 1 and 2   An Introduction to Finance

Q1 Book-keeping's main function is the recording of financial information on a day-to-day basis and to classify and group this information into sets of accounts.

Accounting needs book-keeping records for the purpose of preparing financial statements, such as Profit and Loss A/C, Balance Sheet, to provide the interested parties with essential information about the financial aspects of the organisation.

Q2 The size of capital relates to the size of an organisation because the potential to raise capital depends on either one or more persons subscribing the initial finance. A sole-trader has only his own resources while a PLC can raise vast sums because it can invite the public, through its prospectus, to buy shares.

Other factors: the size of market available, the nature of the goods or services provided, the personal wealth of the entrepreneur.

Q3 (a) Personal wealth, resources available, such as bank loan.

(b) Share capital, debentures, retained profits and loans.

Q4 The private sector refers to economic activity in the hands of private individuals, providing goods and services in order to gain individual benefit.

The public sector refers to economic activity in the hands of the state, providing goods and services for the benefit of the nation.

Q5 The Community Charge (poll tax) and borrowing from various sources, but mainly from the Government's Works Loan Fund.

Q6 PSBR – Public Sector Borrowing Requirement.
PSDR – Public Sector Debt Repayment.
Yes, in times of a budget surplus.
No, in times of a budget deficit, where borrowing is needed to balance total expenditure.

Q7 Government revenue: Direct and Indirect taxation.
Government expenditure: Social Security, Health, Education.
Defence and other government departments, such as Environment.

Q8 To regulate the economy, mainly by using taxation as a means of influencing DEMAND for goods and services. To keep inflation under control. To invigorate the economy by providing subsidies and incentives for growth and investment. To stimulate employment through training programmes or financial initiatives. To direct the economy which will respond to the needs of the market.
Direct tax — taxes on income, such as income tax, corporation tax.
Indirect tax — taxes on goods and services, such as VAT, Customs and Excise tax.

Q9 By earning revenue through the sale of its goods or services, by retaining profits for growth, from Government subsidies, grants and loans.
The more finance central government give, the more influence it will exert.

Q10 Management of the office. Control of day-to-day recording of financial information. Control of wages and cash. Preparing of financial statements. Advisor to the organisation on financial matters.

Part 3 Balance Sheets

Q1 J. Smith
Assets: fixed £10,400, current £1,550, total £11,950.
Liabilities: deferred £7,500, current £115, total £7,615.
Capital £4,335. (a) C = A – L   (b) Mortgage £7,000.
$£4,335 = £11,950 - £7,615$
(c) Bank £5 Creditors NIL. (d) On credit: stock £125, creditors £125.
(e) C = A – L
$£4,335 = £11,960 - £7,625$

Q2 John Jones
Bank £1,760.   (c) Assets: fixed £3,340, current £3,260, total £6,600.
Liabilities: deferred £1,000, current £1,800, total £2.800.
Capital £3,800. (d) Working capital £1,460. WC ratio 1.8 — adequate.

Q3 M. Crooks
   (a) Assets: fixed £53,200, current £16,375, total £69,575.
        Liabilities: deferred £33,500, current £16,075, total £49,575.
        Capital £20,000.
   (c)   C = A − L   (d) Just, working capital £300.
        £20,000 = £69,575 − £49,575 (e) Sell stock.

Q4 R. David
   (a) Fixed assets £16,000. Working capital £7,485. Total £23,485.
        Deferred liabilities £11,500. Net assets £11,985.
        Capital £13,985 *less* Drawings £2,000 = £11,985.
   (c) Need sufficient 'liquid' funds to pay current debts.

Q5 H. Smith
   Balance Sheet: Assets: fixed £34,050, current £7,370 (working capital
                    £950)
                    Liabilities: current £6,420. Deferred £24,000
                    Net assets £11,000. Capital £12,000 *less* drawings
                    £1,000 = £11,000.
   (a) Liabilities of £30,420 against £11,000 of capital. A strain to repay
        debts within 5 years.
   (b) No. Only £100 cash available.
   (c) Most of resources tied up in fixed assets.
   (d)   C = A − L

        £11,000 = £41,420 − £30,420

Q6 R. James
   (a) Fixed assets £44,000, working capital £5,750 = £49,750.
        Less deferred liabilities £26,000 = £23,750.
        Capital £20,000 − Drawings £4,500 + Profit £8,250 = £23,750.
   (b) Good working capital: WC ratio 1.9.
   (c) Yes — a very good return of 41.25%.
   (d) Independence, challenge, self-motivation, etc.

Q7 Capital (1/1) £24,500. Fixed assets £18,100, Working Capital £20,393 =
   £38,493 − Deferred Liabilities £20,753 = £17,740. Capital £17,740. A
   poor trading year. Capital reduced due to Net Loss and Drawings.

Q8	Year 1	Year 2	Year 3
Working capital	£700	£920	£1720
Working capital ratio	1.5	1.8	1.9

Year 2 probably best [Year 3 carries too much stock and has bank o/d].

Section II

Part 1 Ledgers + Trial Balance

Q1 Balances: credit, creditors, mortgage, overdraft and capital. All others debit.

Q2 Green A/C Nil balance, Bank A/C £135 Dr. Goods A/C £1,600 Dr.

Q3 R. David: Bank £3,950, Stock £1,800, Equipment £300, Briggs £350 all Dr. Capital £2,600, XYZ £1,300, Loan £2,500 all Cr. MV A/C Nil.

Q4 J. Bird: Bank £35,000, Premises £26,000, Fixtures £1,250, MV £5,000 all Dr. Capital £60,000, Jackson £5,000, Loan £4,000 all Cr.

Q1 Trial balance totals = £19,965.

Q2 Trial balance totals = £13,800.

Q3 Trial balance totals = £7,318: Bank £64, J. Jones £148, H. Belafonte £1,175, Purchases £632, Stock £2,150, MV £2,750, Equipment £399 all Dr. Diamond £100, Jake's £2,475, Manilow £584, Capital £4,159 all Cr.

Q4 Trial balance totals = £1,260: Smith £415, Lillee £201, Thomson £156, Purchases £345, Bank £143 all Dr. Capital £18, May £195, Cowdrey £152, Sales £895 all Cr.

Q5 Trial Balance totals £25,950. Premises £15,000, Stock £2,150. Purchases £2,325, Equipment £2,275, MV £2,400, Bank £200, Gordon £500, Jones £287, White £813 all Dr. Loan £10,000, ABC £1,000, Jake's £1500, Jackson £953, Brown £1,297, capital £11,200 all Cr.

Part 2

Error in example: J. Randle A/C £350 not £450.

Trial Balance totals £6,597.

Q1 (a) D. Robert. Trial Balance totals: £40,840.
   (b) The personal A/Cs Dr. — sales ledger: Smith & Hunt.
       The personal A/Cs Cr. — bought ledger: Jones & Fox.
       All other A/Cs in the nominal ledger.
   (c) Purchases, sales, wages and general expenses.

Q2 R. Lee: Trial Balance totals: £3,852.
   Purchases £2,585, Jackson £250, Fanshawe £300, Bank £717 all Dr.
   Capital £221, Sales £3,198, Newman £433 all Cr.

Q3 F. Smith: Trial Balance totals: £29,051, Premises £20,000, MV £1,875, Stock £1,900, Bank £1,277, Rollin £500, Vines £450, Purchases £2,850, General expenses £115, Insurance £84, all Dr. Capital £6,263, Mortgage £16,750, Boston £2,950, Turner £600, Sales £2,488 all Cr.

Q4 J. Briggs: Trial Balance totals: £26,380, Bank £265, Premises £17,000, Fixtures £1,000, Cash £595, Collins £2,850, Smith £720, Purchases £1,870, Salaries £600, Repairs £260, Stock £1,200, Drawings £20 all Dr. Capital £20,000, Jones £1,055, Sales £5,325 all Cr.

Q5 G. Harrison: Trial Balance totals: £3,605. Cash/Bank £1,226, Lloyd £250, Jones £268, Purchases £1,195, General Expenses £57, Salaries £165, Insurance £54, MV £350, Drawings £40, all Dr. Capital £1,860, Bloggs £250, Sales £915, T. Jones £580 all Cr.

Q6 L. Dawson: Trial Balance totals £44,980.
Debits: Bank £14,258, Cash £2,658, Purchases £9,500, F+F £6,200, Advertising £56, Rent £6,000. Wages £170, Insurance £400, P+S £38, Drawings £500, Redhill £3,100, Shaw £2,100.
Credits: Capital £30,000, Sales £11,480, Green £3,500.

Part 3 Sales Day Book

Q1 (a) A. Smith SDB totals: sales £1,690, VAT £253.5, total £1,943.5.
(b) Sales ledger Dr. (c) Nominal ledger, sales and VAT Cr.
Debtors total Dr. (d) To cross-check accuracy of sales ledger.
Double-entry already completed.

Q2 (a) Sales £890. (b) Arthur £450, Brian £160, Colin £280 all Dr.
Sales A/C £2,130 Cr.

Q3 (a) Sales £890, VAT £133.5, total £1,023.5.
(b) Arthur £517.5, Brian £184, Colin £322, all Dr.
(c) Sales A/C £2,130 Cr. VAT £8.5 Cr, Sales ledger control £1,023.5 Dr.

Q4 (a) Sales £2,460, VAT £369, total £2,829.
(b) Debtors: Bremner £1,667.5, Gray £422, Lorimer £1,175, Jones £629.5, Giles £115 all Dr. in Sales Ledger.
(c) Sales ledger control £4,009 Dr.

Q5 Totals: Total £1,109.55, bats £755, balls £111.75, pads £242.8.
Debtors: Brearly £420.46, Botham £99.75, Boycott £415.85, Bailey £188.38, Benaud £335.5 all Dr.
Debtors control: £1,459.94 Dr.

Part 4 Purchases Day Book

Q1 (a) Purchases Day Book. R. Jones.
(b) Net purchases £157.87. VAT £23.09. Total £180.96.
(c) Purchases and VAT Dr. Harrison A/C Cr. £180.96.

Q2 Purchases Day Book — G. Harrison.
(a) Purchases £1,007.10, VAT £149.79, total £1,156.89.

(b) Bought Ledger (or purchases ledger). Credit. Because they represent liabilities to Harrison.

(c) Nominal Ledger: Purchases and VAT Dr. total creditors Cr.

(d) Cross-check the Bought-ledger.

(e) Rocco.

Q3 Purchases Day Book: Purchases £880.
Bought ledger Dick £500, Eric £380, Fred £160 all Cr.
Purchases A/C £1,980 Dr.

Q4 Purchases Day Book: Purchases £880, VAT £132, total £1,012.
Bought ledger Dick £560, Eric £437, Fred £175 all Cr.
Nominal ledger: VAT £257 Dr. Purchases £880, Bought Ledger control £1,172 Cr.

Q5 (a) Purchases Day Book £4,497.5, Sales Day Book £2,420.
(b) Bought ledger: ABC £3,937.5 XYZ £560 Cr.
Sales ledger: Green £1,575, Jones £495, Smith £350 Dr.
Sales A/C £2,420 Cr, Purchases A/C £4,497.5 Dr.

Q6 Purchases Day Book. Purchases £1,605, VAT £240.75, total £1,845.75.
Bought ledger: Mellows £632.5, Hudson £638.25, Paterson £460, Moorcroft £115 all Cr. Bought ledger control A/C £1,845.75 Cr.

Part 5 Returns Day Books

Q1 Returns Inward Day Book. Returns inward £130, VAT £19.5, total £149.5.
Sales Ledger: Arthur £77, Brian £51, Colin £92.5 all Dr.
Nominal Ledger: Returns Inward A/C £387 Dr. VAT A/C £144.5 Dr.
Sales Ledger control A/C £220.5 Dr.

Q2 Returns Outward Day Book. Returns Outward £188, VAT £28.2, total £216.20.
Bought Ledger: Dick £188, Eric £44.8, Fred £51 all Cr.
Nominal Ledger: Returns outward A/C £540 Cr. VAT £96.8 Dr.
Bought ledger control A/C £283.80 Cr.

Q3 Purchases Day Book: Total £7,736.50 (No Vat).
Returns Outward Day Book: Total £892.5 (No Vat).
Dunlop's A/c £2,628 Cr.
Sondico's A/c £921 Cr.

Q4 Purchases Day Book: Purchases £2,580, Vat £337.5, total £2,917.5
Returns Outward Day Book: Returns Out £96.30, Vat £14.44, total £110.74.
Purchase Ledger: Truman £1,757, Statham £580, Tyson £1,285.5, Snow £938, Illingworth £654.26, Old £667. All credit balances. P/L control a/c £5,881.76

Q5 Sales Day Book: Sales £510, Vat £76.5, total £586.5.
Purchases Day Book: Purchases £730, Vat £109.5, total £839.5.
Returns Outward Day Book: Returns Out £200, Vat £30, total £230.
Sales Ledger: Hunt £149.5, Speedie £247, Milton £230. All debits.
Purchase Ledger: Ball £287.5, Carlson £184, Smith £138. All credits.
S/L Control a/c £626.5.
P/L Control a/c £609.5.

Part 6 Cash Book

Q1 Cash A/C £50, Bank £730 Dr. Dis. All. £17 Dis. Rec. £1.
Q2 Cash A/C £661, Bank £1,597 Dr. Dis. All. £6, Dis. Rec. £40.
Q3 Cash A/C £369.31, Bank £932 Dr. Dis. All. £50.65, Dis. Rec. £28.
Q4 Cash A/C £388, Bank £336.80 Dr. Dis. All. £15.20, Dis. Rec. £7.
Personal A/Cs all Nil balances.
Q5 Cash A/C £62, Bank £101 Dr. Dis. All. £13, Dis. Rec. £9.
Q6 Bank A/C £62.85 Dr. Dis. All. £22.5 Debtors £502.5, Record Sales
£225.36. Other Sales £901.44. Dis. Rec. £15, Creditors £1,435, Wages
£280, Other £427, Drawings £275.
Q7 R. Lees : Wine £830, Beer £1030, Spirits £290, Other £134.
Total Sales £2,284. Vat £342.6. Total Cash £2,626.6.
Both Sales and Vat totals are posted on the credit side of their ledger
accounts.
To be aware of which lines are selling. Better control of buying and
marketing.

Part 7 Bank Reconciliation Statements

Q1 Bank A/C £253 Dr. BRS: £420 + £90 − £257 = £253.
Q2 Bank A/C £699 Dr. BRS: £864 + £205 − £370 = £699.
Q3 Bank A/C £2,791 Dr. BRS £3,084 + £404 − £697 = £2,791.
Q4 Bank A/C £377.5 Cr. BRS £379.4 − £24 + £22.10 = £377.5 O/D.
Q5 Bank A/C £206.35 Dr. BRS £625.15 + £156.20 − £575 = £206.35.
Q6 Bank £630 Cr. (Overdrawn) BRS £893 (Overdrawn) − Deposits Cr.
£1,215. = £322 Cr. − Unpresented cheques £952 = £630 (overdrawn).
Cashbook errors: Debit £426, £500.
Credit £840, £19, £23, £215, £99, £1,700.
Q7 Cash Book: Debits: £600, £420, £122. Credits: £79, £1,353, £90, £200,
£70. Balance £2,200.
BRS £1,935 + £1,800 − £1,535 = £2,200.

Part 8 The Petty Cash Book

Q1 Petty Cash balance £0.61, VAT £17.70, Postages £29.84, Stationery £36.66, Travel £81.18, Cleaning £20, Sundries £14.01, Reimbursement £199.39, Cash float £200.

Q2 Petty Cash balance £23.15, Cleaning £27.59, Stationery £31.31, Postages £8.35, Sundries £9.60, No VAT, Reimbursement £76.85, Cash float £100.

Q3 Petty Cash balance £13.93, VAT £4.80, Cleaning £24.32, Stationery £37.65. Postages £17.80, Sundries £19.50, Packing Materials £32, Reimbursement £136.07, Cash Float £150.

Q4 Petty Cash Balance £39.26, VAT £4.30, Travel £8.35, Cleaning £16.30, Postages £13.28, Stationery £12.40, Refreshments £3.76, Sundries £2.35, Reimbursement £60.74, Cash Float £100.

Q5 Petty Cash balance £9.80, VAT £4.19, Travel £13.27, Stationery £10.53, Cleaning £4.36, Refreshment £4.85, Postage £3, Reimbursement £40.20, Cash Float £50.

Part 9 Computer-based Accounts

Q1 Printouts of accounts, including statements. Analysis of accounts e.g. aged debtors and creditors. Automatic double-entry. Instant up-dating and review on screen. Integration with other aspects such as invoicing and stock control.

Q2 Example: Sales Ledger menu: Ledger Processing. Gives access to any customer a/c. Functions include up-dating files and the input of day to day information such as invoices and receipts.

Q3 Ledger Processing. Function No. 2 Ledger Posting – for entering day to day details relating to any account.

Q4 Invoices and Credit Notes. The Sales and Purchases Day Books provide the same information.
Customer and supplier accounts give more details such as address, turnover to date, invoice and cheque numbers, aging of debts etc.

Q5 Have you tried hands on a computer yet?
If not, why not?

Section III

Part 1 Trading & Profit & Loss (without adjustments)

Q1 Wright, J. Gross profit £8,350, Net Profit £5,975. Fixed Assets £25,325, Working Capital £3,900. Capital employed £29,225.
Capital £25,000 − Drawings £1,750 + Net Profit £5,975 = £29,225.

Q2 Armstrong. Gross Profit £31,950, Net Profit £9,100. Fixed Assets £34,300, Working Capital £1,800. Capital employed £36,100 − Deferred liabilities £20,000 = £16,100. Capital £7,000 + Net Profit £9,100 = £16,100.

Q3 Smith, F. Gross Profit £3,280, Net Profit £2,000. Fixed Assets £2,700 + Working Capital £1,300. Capital employed £4,000. Capital £2,000 + Net Profit £2,000 = £4,000.

Q4 White. Gross Profit £6,057, Net Profit £3,128. Fixed Assets £14,410, Working Capital £248. Capital employed £14,658.
Capital £12,730 − Drawings £1,200 + Net Profit £3,128 = £14,658.

Q5 Robert. Gross Profit £15,820, Net Profit £6,780. Fixed Assets £18,100, Working Capital £3,880. Capital employed £21,980. Capital £18,000 − Drawings £2,800 + Net Profit £6,780 = £21,980.

Q6 Chappell, G. Gross Profit £904.88, Net Loss £240.29.
Fixed Assets £1,225, Working Capital £2,387.48, − £402.77 = £3,209.71. Capital £4,050 − Net Loss £240.29 − Drawings £600 = £3,209.71.

Part 2 Trading + Profit & Loss (with adjustments)

Q1 Wright, H. Gross Profit £7,770, Net Profit £1,373. Fixed Assets £15,010. Working Capital (−£1837) insolvent. Capital employed £13,173. Capital £16,000 − Drawings £4,200 + Net Profit £1,373 = £13,173.

Q2 Hunt. Gross Profit £4,950. Net Profit £403. Fixed Assets £1,900. Working Capital £4,003. Capital employed £5,903. Capital £8,000. − Drawings £2,500 + Net Profit £403 = £5,903.

Q3 Chappell. Gross Profit £3,285. Net Loss £545. Fixed Assets £8,375. Working Capital £490. Capital employed £8,865. Capital £9,950 − Drawings £540 − Net Loss £545 = £8,865.

Q4 Lloyd, J. Capital £170,350. Totals of trial balance £344,310. Gross Profit £9,787, Net Loss £28,883, Fixed Assets £125,320. Working Capital £1,907. Capital employed £127,227. Capital £170,350 − Drawings £14,240 − Net Loss £28,883 = £127,227.

Q5 Dooley, T. Trial balance totals £28,393. Gross Profit £7,437. Net Profit £2,039. Fixed Assets £3,456, Working Capital £7,631. Capital employed £11,087. Capital £9,048 + Net Profit £2,039 = £11,087.

Q6 Jones, A. Gross Profit £37,500, Net Profit £11,125. Fixed Assets £75,600. Working Capital £5,725. Capital employed £81,325. Capital £71,000 − Drawings £800 + Net Profit £11,125 = £81,325. Note: Carriage Inwards in Trading A/C.

Q7 ABC Co. Gross Profit £9,700, Net Profit £4,022. Fixed Assets £31,350. Working Capital £4,072. Capital employed £35,422 Deferred Liabilities £15,500 = £19,922. Capital £18,000 − Drawings £2,100 + Net Profit £4,022 − £19,922.

Q8 Jones, J. Gross Profit £3,440, Net Profit £2,005. Fixed Assets £15,580. Working Capital £5,249. Capital employed £20,829 − Deferred Liabilities £12,100 = £8,729. Capital £7,574 − £850 + Net Profit £2,005 = £8,729.

Q9 Lewis, D. Provision for BD a/c: Debit £550, Credit £600, £660. Balance £710 cr.
1990: P & L a/c £600 (expense). BS Debtors £11,400 (net).
1991: P & L a/c £660 (expense). BS Debtors £13,490 (net).

Q10 Premises a/c £1,500,000 Debit. Plant & Machinery a/c £900,000 Debit. Provision for Depreciation a/c £423,500 Credit.
Asset Disposal a/c Debit £10,000 to P+L a/c (as surplus on sale).
Balance Sheet: Fixed Assets: Cost £2,400,000, Depreciation £423,500, Net Book Value £1,976,500.
Revaluation Reserve a/c not used for distribution (of dividends).
Details of the revaluation: name of valuers, basis, date, etc.

Q11 Mitchell, F. Gross Profit £110,615, Net Profit £16,667, Fixed Assets £104,400, Working Capital £28,320, Capital Employed £132,720. Capital £131,653 + Net Profit £16,667 − Drawings £15,600 = £132,720. A sound WC ratio of 2:1.

Q12 Walker, M. Capital £27,908. Gross Profit £65,409, Net Profit £31,632. Fixed Assets £43,025, Working Capital £6,095 = £49,120.
Capital £27,908 + Net Profit £31,632 − Drawings £10,420 = £49,120.

Part 3 Partnership Accounts

Q1 A & B. Appropriation A/C: Net Profit £14,680 − Salaries £6,000 − Interest on Capital £1,200 + Interest on Drawings £460 = £7,940. Profit Share £3,970 each partner.
Balance Sheet: Capital A/Cs £24,000. Current A/Cs A £3,470, B £2,245, both Cr.
Balance Sheet: Capital A/C A £15,000, B £15,000, C £10,000,
Total £40,000.
Profit Sharing Ratio 3:3:2.

Q2 Smith & Jones: Gross Profit £10,012, Net Profit £5,691. Appropriation A/C: Net Profit £5,691 – Salary £1,000 + Interest on Drawings £369 = £5,060. Profit Share 3:2. Smith £3,036, Jones £2,024. Current A/C balances: Smith £101. Dr. Jones £824. Cr.
Balance Sheet. Fixed Assets £27,500. Working Capital £3,223 Capital employed £30,723, Capital Accounts £30,000. Current Accounts £723 = £30,723.

Q3 Lee and Crooks: Gross Profit £14,565, Net Profit £5,097. Appropriation A/C: Net Profit £5,097 – Salaries £2,500 + Interest on Drawings 549 = £3,146. Profit Share £1,573 each partner. Current Accounts Lee £626 Dr. Crooks £955 Dr. Balance Sheet: Fixed Assets £20,680, Working Capital £5,738. Capital employed £26,418. Capital A/Cs £28,000. Current A/Cs £1,582 Dr. = £26,418.

Q4 May and Cowdrey. Gross Profit £6,299. Net Profit £3,495. Appropriation A/C: Net Profit £3,495 – Salary £1,046 – Interest on Capital £700 = £1,749. Share of Profit: May £1,311.75, Cowdrey £437.25. Current A/Cs: May £561.75 Cr. Cowdrey £733.25 Cr. Balance Sheet: Fixed Assets £9,164, Working Capital £6,131. Capital employed £15,295. Capital Accounts £14,000, Current A/Cs £1,295 = £15,295.

Q5 Jones, Smith & Brown. Gross Profit £60,970. S & D costs £6,767. Admin. costs £17,202. Net Profit £37,001. Appropriation A/C: Net Profit £37,001 – Salary £2,750 – Interest on capital £3,000 + Interest on Drawings £550 = £31,801. Share of Profit 5:4:1. James £15,900.5, Smith £12,720.4, Brown £3,180.1 Total £31,801.
Current A/Cs Jones £12,342.5, Smith £14,085.4, Brown £2,393.1 all Cr. Balance Sheet: Fixed Assets £72,800, Working Capital £33,021. Capital employed £105,821 – Deferred liabilities £27,000 = £78,821 (net assets). Capital A/Cs £50,000. Current A/Cs £28,821 = £78,821.

Q6 Smith, Jones & Rogers.
Appropriation A/c: Net Profit £7,300 – Salary £900, – interest on capital £510, £480, £450, + interest on drawings £165 = £5,125. Profit share: Smith £2,050, Jones £2,050, Rogers £1,025.
Current a/c's: Smith £1,095 Cr. Jones £1,075 Cr. Rogers (£370) Dr.
Fixed Assets £30,700, Working capital £50, Capital employed £30,750, – Loan £4,950 = £25,800. Capital £24,000 + Current a/c's £1,800 = £25,800.

Q7 French & Saunders.
Appropriation A/c: Net Profit £19,800 – interest on capital £3,600 + interest on drawings £800 = £17,000. Profit share £8,500 each partner.
Current a/c's: French £2,100 Cr. Saunders (£7,160) Dr.
Fixed Assets £61,000, Working Capital (£1,060), Capital employed £59,940, – Loan £20,000 = £39,940. Capital £45,000 + Current a/c's (£5,060) = £39,940. WC ratio 0.87 (insolvent). Reduce Saunders Drawings of £15,000?

Q8 Wooldridge & James.
Appropriation A/c: Net Profit £38,650 – salary £21,000 – interest on capital £8,300 + interest on drawings £1,550 (W £650, J £900), = £10,900. Profit share: Wooldridge £6,540, James £4,360.
Current a/c's: Wooldridge £7,990, James £2,660, both Cr.
Fixed Assets £114,000, Working Capital £5,650, Capital employed £119,650, – Deferred Liab. £29,000 = £90,650.
Capital £80,000 + Current a/c's £10,650 = £90,650.

Part 4 Accounting for Companies

Q1 XYZ Co. Ltd. Net Profit (before Tax) £15,500 – Provision for tax £3,760 = £11,740, Net Profit (after Tax). + P & L balance £5,000 = £16,740 – provision for dividends £11,750 and Reserve £2,000 = P & L balance (31/12) £2,990.
Balance Sheet. Fixed Assets £144,000. Current Assets £13,000, – current liabilities £22,010. Working capital (insolvent) £9,010 Capital employed £134,990. Capital £130,000. Reserve £2,000, P & L A/C £2,990 = £134,990.

Q2 ABC Ltd. Net Profit (before tax) £18,750 – Provision for tax £1,500 = £17,250, Net Profit (after tax) + P & L balance £5,460 = £22,710 – Provision for dividends £9,000 and reserves £10,000 = P & L balance (31/12) £3,710.
Balance Sheet. Fixed Assets £94,250, current assets £27,670 – current liabilities £18,210 = working capital £9,460. Capital employed £103,710. capital £60,000, Reserve £40,000, P & L A/C £3,710 + £103,710.

Q3 Bournemouth T Co. Ltd. Gross Profit £31,310, Net Profit (before tax) £9,505 – Provision for tax £500 = £9,005 net profit (after tax), + P & L balance £1,300 = £10,305 – Provision for dividend £9,000 – Reserve £600 = £705 P & L balance (31/12). Balance Sheet: Fixed Assets £53,900, current assets £33,931 – current liabilities £15,526 = working capital £18,405, capital employed £72,305 – Deferred liabilities £5,000 = £67,305. Capital £60,000, Premium A/C £6,000, Reserve £600, P & L A/C £705 = £67,305.

Q4 Robertson & David Co. Ltd. Gross Profit £151,800, Net Profit (before tax) £43,033, Provision for tax £19,200. Net Profit (after tax) £23,833 + P & L balance £7,780 = £31,613 – Dividends £22,400 – Reserve £4,000. P & L balance (31/12) £5,213. Balance Sheet. Fixed Assets £322,330. Current assets £102,169 – current liabilities £110,286. Working capital (insolvent) −£8,117. Capital employed £314,213 – deferred liabilities £40,000 = £274,213 (net assets). Capital £240,000. Reserve £29,000, P & L A/C £5,213 = £274,213.

Q5 G. Chappell & Sons Ltd. Gross Profit £19,324. Net Profit (before tax) £6,305. Provision for tax £1,250. Net Profit (after tax) £5,055 + P & L balance £1,170 = £6,225, − dividends £4,125 − Reserve £2,000 = P & L balance £100. Balance Sheet: Fixed assets £113,000, current assets £28,567 − current liabilities £9,967. Working Capital £18,600. Capital employed £131,600. Capital £125,000, Premium A/C £2,500, Reserve £4,000, P & L A/C £100 = £131,600.

Q6 Harrison Ltd. Gross Profit £94,225, Distribution cost £40,414, Admin. expenses £40,595. Interest payable £5,000, total expenses £86,009. Net Profit (before tax) £8,216. Provision for tax £3,750. Net Profit (after tax) £4,466 − Provision for dividends £3,750 + P & L balance (31/12) £716. Balance Sheet: Fixed assets £101,300, current assets £52,160, Current liabilities £60,744. Working capital (insolvent) − £8,584. Capital employed £92,716. − Deferred liabilities £40,000 = £52,716 (net assets). Capital £50,000, Reserve £2,000, P & L A/C £716 = £52,716.

Q7 Jason Ltd.
Appropriation A/c: Net Profit £40,600 − tax £8,400 + P+L bal. £19,200 − Dividends £2,400, £9,000 = Reserves £40,000.
Fixed Assets £160,000, Current assets £45,000, Current liabilities £30,000
Working Capital £15,000, Capital employed £175,000.
Share capital £130,000 + Reserves £45,000 = £175,000.

Q8 Compton Ltd.
Appropriation A/c: Net Profit £108,000 − tax £30,000 + P+L bal. £22,000, − Dividends £16,000, £48,000 − Reserves £20,000 = P+L bal. 31/3, £16,000. Fixed Assets £554,000, Working Capital £16,000, Capital employed £570,000. Share Capital £500,000, Reserves £54,000, P+L a/c £16,000 = £570,000.

Q9 J P Davies, PLC
Appropriation A/c, Net Profit (after interest) £67,500 − tax £20,000, + P+L bal. £40,000 − Dividends £15,000, £40,000 − Reserves £25,000 = P+L bal. 30/6, £7,500.
Fixed Assets £355,000, current assets £419,000, current liabilities £296,500, Working Capital £122,500, Capital employed £477,500 − Deferred Liab. £100,000 = £377,500. Share Capital £300,000 + Reserves £70,000, P+L a/c £7,500 = £377,500.

Part 5 *Sources and Application of Funds*

Q1 Jones Ltd. Sources: £5,700, Application £4,510 = £1,190.
Working capital + £770. Liquid funds + £420 = £1,190.

Q2 ABC Co. Ltd. Sources £77,150, Application £83,500 = (£6,360) deficit.
Working capital − £5,125, Liquid funds − £1,225 = (£6,360) deficit.

Q3 Jackson Ltd. Sources £27,750, Application £21,100 = £6,650.
Working capital £7,070. Liquid funds – £420 = £6,650.

Q4 Jones, Rogers PLC (a) WC Ratio: 1987 2:1, 1988 2.5:1 liquidity good.
Increase due to issue of shares and debentures. (b) Sources: profit &
depreciation £50,000, other sources £92,000 = £142,000. Application
£108,000 = £34,000. Working capital £26,000, liquid funds £8,000 =
£34,000.

Q5 Balance Sheets: Yr 1 Fixed assets £28,904, Working Capital £2,000,
Capital employed £30,904, Deferred liabilities £5,000 = £25,904. Capital
+ Reserves £25,904. Yr 2 Fixed Assets £38,244. Working capital
(insolvent) – £1,500, capital employed £36,744. Deferred liabilities
£2,500 = £34,244. Capital + Reserves £34,244. Sources of funds
£31,090. Application £27,940 = £3,150. Working capital £5,276. Liquid
funds – £2,126 = £3,150.

Q6 XYZ Ltd.
Sources £14,800 (Net Profit £10,000 – Gain £2,500).
Application £15,000 = (£200) deficit.
Working Capital £800, Liquid funds (£1,000) = (£200) deficit.

Q7 Aspen Ltd.
Sources £88,460, Application £97,520 = (£9,060) deficit.
Working Capital £4,140, Liquid funds (£13,200) = (£9,060) deficit.
Current ratio (both years) 2.7:1. ROCE 17.6%.

Q8 Rads Ltd.
Sources £340,000 (Profit £155,000 + Depreciation £25,000 – Gain
£20,000). Application £375,000 (Fixed Assets £180,000, £120,000,
Dividends £75,000). = (£35,000) deficit. Working Capital (£3,100),
Liquid funds (£31,900) = (£35,000) deficit.

Part 6 Public Sector Accounts

Q1 Central Government. Provides the nation with essential needs and
services, Health, Social Security, Education, Defence and also about
30% of expenditure goes to help finance local government expenditure.
Local Government. Provides the local community with services including education, police and housing, financially supported by Central
Government around 50% of expenditure (RSG).

Q2 Rates, Rate Support Grant (RSG) and Borrowing. Current expenditure
— day-to-day running expenses — most going to pay wages and salaries
of public employees. Capital expenditure — capital projects — roads,
buildings, shopping precincts, community centres.

Q3 Balance Sheets are very similar in terms of assets and liabilities. Under
the 'financing' section there is *NO* share capital only items such as capital
funds, grants, receipts and surplus accounts — that is, the 'net worth' of
the authority.

Q4 Local rates £131,800,000. Expenditure £226,280,000 = Revenue from rates £131,800,000, Grants of £94,380,000 + other sources £100,000 = £226,280,000.

Part 7 Social Organisations

Q1 Profit from Bar £2,475. Revenue £9,330, Expenditure £8,675, Surplus £655. Fixed assets £26,950, current assets £4,855, Current liabilities £550, Working capital £4,305. Capital employed £31,255. Accumulated funds £30,600 + Surplus £665 = £31,255.

Q2 Revenue £15,175, Expenditure £7,878, Surplus £7,297. Fixed assets £13,500, Working capital £5,397. Capital employed £18,897. Accumulated funds £11,600 + Surplus £7,297 = £18,897.

Q3 Bank Account (31/3) £4,115. Revenue £7,827, Expenditure £3,842 = Surplus £3,985. Fixed assets £8,550. Working capital £3,735. Capital employed £12,285. Deferred liabilities £5,000 = £7,285. Accumulated funds £3,300 + Surplus £3,985 = £7,285.

Q4 Refreshment surplus £1,640.
Revenue £4,715, Expenditure £3,496 = surplus £1,219. Fixed Assets £19,299. Working Capital (£1,625), Capital employed £17,674, – Loan £5,955 = £11,719.
Accumulated funds £10,500 + surplus £1,219 = £11,719.

Q5 Bank A/c £2,825. Refreshment surplus £515. Revenue £3,980, Expenditure £1,953 = surplus £2,027. Fixed Assets £17,750, Working Capital £2,827, Capital employed £20,577 – Loan £2,000 = £18,577.
Accumulated funds £16,550 + surplus £2,027 = £18,577.

Section IV

Part 1 Accounting Ratios

Q1 Gross Profits £10,000, £12,000, £13,050. Net Profits £3,850, £5,050, £4,675.
Gross Profit %'s £33.33%, 33.33%, 29%. Net Profit %'s 12.8% 14% 10.4%. Expense %'s Distribution 10%, 8.9%, 9.1%.
Administration 10.5%, 10.4%, 9.5%.
Stock turnover = 10, 9.6 and 8 times per annum.
Credit days taken 73 — Yr 1 and Yr 2, 89 days Yr 3.
Return on capital 14.5%, 16.8%, 14.7%.

Q2

	Co. A	Co. B		Co.A	Co. B
Gross Profits	£4,000	£13,500	Fixed Assets	£7,000	£10,000
Net Profits	£2,450	£6,000	Working Capital	£2,275	£3,250
				£9,275	£13,250
Gross Profit %	44.4%	56.25%			
Net Profit %	27.2%	25%			
Return on capital	26.4%	45.3%			
Working capital ratio	2.14	1.9			

Q4

	Yr 1	Yr 2	Yr 3
Gross Profit %	40%	33.33%	40%
Net Profit %	22%	13.33%	17.5%
Return on Capital Inv.	35.5%	19.0%	29.5%
Return on Capital Empld	22.9%	15.6%	27.3%
Current ratio	2.1	1.3	1.25
Net worth/total assets	72.5%	68%	65.3%

Year 2 inferior in all respects.
Big improvement in Year 3.

Q5

	Ball Bearings Ltd	Rocco Bank Ltd
Net Profit (after tax)	£1,500,000	£1,600,000
Earnings/Share	15p	80p
Dividend/Share	7p	20p
Cover	2.1	4
Current ratio	0.98	0.95
Acid test	0.5	0.95
Capital gearing	0.3 (high)	4 (low)
Net worth/total assets	11%	7.5%

Q6

	Sales	Cost of Sales	Gross Profit		Expenses	Net Profit	NP%
Yr 1	£36,000	£27,000	£9,000	25%	£8,400	£600	1.67%
Yr 2	£54,000	£40,500	£13,500	25%	£9,500	£4,000	7.4%
Yr 3	£78,000	£58,500	£19,500	25%	£11,500	£8,000	10.3%
Yr 4	£120,000	£96,000	£24,000	20%	£19,000	£5,000	4.2%

Q7

	1986	1987	1988
Gross Profits	£36,000	£50,000	£70,000
Net Profits	£1,600	£7,000	£16,000
Profit Returns			
Gross Profit %	30%	$33\frac{1}{3}$%	35%
Net Profit %	1.33%	4.67%	8%
ROCE	2.67%	6.67%	10%
Stock Turnover	10.5	11.8	13

Steady improvement over the 3 year period. Sales and turnover of stock has increased each year to give a ROCE of 10% [still moderate]. Reduction of fixed costs and cost of sales for further improvement in 1989.

Q8

	A	B	C
Net Profit (after interest)	£695,000	£695,000	£645,000
Net Profit (after tax)	£451,750	£451,750	£419,250
Retained Profit (after dividends)	£41,750	£31,750	£59,250
E.p.s.	13.4p	12.9p	13.9p
Capital gearing	16.6%	0%	16.6%

Scheme C may be worth pursuit, having greater retained profits and marginally the highest eps.

Part 2 Capital and Revenue Expenditure

Q1 (a) (b) (f) (g) (l) = capital expenditure.
(c) (d) (e) (h) (i) (j) (k) = revenue expenditure.

Q2 Capital expenditure: vehicle (basic) £800 + fittings £300 + lighting £50 + new seat £100 + new tyre £55. The other items revenue expenditure. If new tyres are changed *within* 12 months, then revenue expenditure. Motor vehicle value (with tyre) £1,305.

Part 3 Accounting Concepts

Q1 Chairman's Report:
Accruals (1st line), consistency (depreciation)
prudence (stock, lower of cost), going concern (whole report).
Other: cost & materiality.

Q2 Peter Drucker suggests: market standing, product leadership, staff development and public responsibility.
Profit motivation still the most significant aspect.

Q3 See pages relating to 4 concepts.

Q4 a) cost concept, realisation (turnover), consistency (depreciation) prudence (stock), going concern (whole accounting policy).

b) check manufacturing accounts and the importance of stock value.

Section V

Part 1 Personal Finance and Taxation

Q1 Smith: Gross Pay £162. Deductions £54,34. Net pay £107.66.

Q2 Gross Pay: Jack £134.40. Fred £123.90. Harry £151.90.

Q3 Piece-rates on 1650 units £28.75. Basic pay £50. Total pay £78.75.

Q4 Robbin's: Time allowed 54 hours. Time taken 39 hours. Time saved 15 hours. Bonus hours 50% of 15 hours = 7.5 hours. Gross pay 46.5 × £3 = £139.50.

Q5 Clock Card $44\frac{1}{2}$ hours. Overtime = $6\frac{1}{2}$ hours. Basic pay £91.20. Overtime pay £23.40. Total Gross pay £114.60.

Q6 Tax liability: Bigs £7,405 × 25% = £1,851.25.

Q7 Tax liability: Jarman £11,195 × 25% = £2,798.75.

Q8 Tax liability: Hale £9,495 × 25% = £2,373.75.

Q9 Basic Pay £180 + O/time (7 hrs. × £1.25) £43.75 = £223.75 Gross Pay. Deductions: NIC £16.92, Tax £41.49. Net Pay = £165.34.

Q10 Married Couple: 1) Gross pay £285 per week.
Deductions: NIC £22.43, Pension £11.40, Tax £45.68.
Net Pay £205.49.
2) Gross Pay £120 per week. NIC £7.58, Tax £15.55. Net Pay £96.87.

Part 3 Personal Cash Budgeting

Q1 June £240, July £340, August £430 — monthly balances. Savings suggested: June £200, £100 July, £80 August.

Q2 January £340, February £440, March £330 — monthly balances. Savings: January £140, February £240, March £130.

Q3 April £625, May £350, June £85 — monthly balances. Open-ended suggestions for part (b).

Q4 a) Gross salary £153.85
Net salary £103.86 (£104 for budget).
b) Bank c/f Jan £176, Feb. £322, March £572.
c) Saving £572 over 3 months, he could spend an average £190 per month.
d) £90 month, £65 month.
e) Finance from bank, h–p co. or even credit card. Bank, a specific loan over 3 years probably the best.

Section VI

Part 1 Manufacturing Accounts

Q1 F. Smith. Prime Cost £58,925, Factory OHs £10,102, Factory Cost £69,117. Gross profit £25,578, Net profit £15,384.25.

Q2 J. Jones. prime Cost £108,025, Factory OHs £17,044, Factory Cost £125,089. Gross Profit £31,891, Net profit £28,051.

Q3 Harry. Prime Cost £57,549, Factory OHs £11,759, Factory Cost £69,308, Factory Profit £8,692, Gross Trading Profit £25,505, Net Loss £389. DL/Unit £7.75, DM/Unit £21.02, FOHs/Unit £5.88, Prod. Cost/Unit £34.65. Yes — manufacturing was cost-effective, by £4.35/Unit. *Note*: Total Gross Profit £34,197.

Q4 ABC Co. Ltd. Prime Cost £73,185, Factory OHs £11,760, Factory Cost £84,415. Gross Profit £39,299, Net Profit £15,519. Prime Cost/Unit £6.97, FOHs/Unit £1.12, prod. Cost/Unit £8.04, Total cost/unit £10.30, Mark-up % 18.1, Margin % 15.3.

Q5 Fred's Co. Ltd. Prime Cost £49,005, Factory OHs £10,470, Factory Cost £59,475. Factory Cost/Unit £5.95. Gross Profit £24,212.5, Net Profit £17,515.

Q6 P. Jackson.
Prime Cost £100,958, Factory OH's £14,745, Factory Cost £115,703.
Gross Profit £64,793, Net Profit £38,717.
Fixed Assets £43,025, Working Capital £10,272, Capital employed £53,297.
Capital £25,000 + Net Profit £38,717 – Drawings £10,420 = £53,297.

Q7 XYZ Co. Ltd. Prime Cost £198,623, Factory Cost £201,000, Cost/Unit £4.02. Finished goods stock 31/12 £18,090. Gross Profit £12,590, Net Profit £1,802. P & L C/F £1,382, Fixed Assets £91,400, Working capital − £11,018 (insolvent). Capital employed £80,382. Shareholders funds: £80,382.

Cost Classification

Q1 ABC Co. Ltd. Cost Sheet DL £21,000, DM £47,600, Fact. OHs £54,885, Dist. OHs. £35,370, Admin. OHs £27,045. Factory Cost/Unit £81.72. Prime Cost £67,700, Factory OHs £54,885, Factory Cost £122,585. Gross Profit £89,723. Net Profit £27,308.

Q2 J. Jones. Cost sheet: DL £20,300, DM £15,575, DE £675, Factory OHs £19,455, Dist. OHs £17,220, Admin. Ohs £12,870. Factory Cost/Unit £11.194.
Prime Cost £36,440, Factory OHs £19,455. Factory Cost £55,970. Gross Profit £34,076. Net Profit £3,986.

Part 2 Marginal Costs

Q1 (a) Table: Fixed costs £56,000, Variable costs £44,000. (b) Contrib./ Unit £38 (£60 − £22). (c) Profit on 2000 units, £20,000. (d) 2100 units, £23,800, on 1950 £18,100. (e) Break-even 1474 units. Profit (1 above) £38. Loss (1 below) £38. (f) Variation: £14,400 profit.

Q2 Baldwin (a) C/Unit £8. (b) Profit £1,250. (c) B/E 344 units, £4,300 revenue. (d) Profit £10,700. (e) £1,058. (f) £1450 profit first, £1,427.5 profit second, first best. (g) 96 extra units.

Q3 Lillee, Thompson (a) Table; Fixed costs £63,250, Variable cost £94,750. (b) C/Unit £2.105. (c) £1,895 extra cost. (d) Yes. (e) B/E 30,048 Units. £120,192 revenue. (f) Loss £104.2. (g) £42,000. (h) £19,897.5 profit.

Q4 (a) B/E 23,500 units. (b) £17,500 loss. (c) 16,000 units extra. (d) £2,250 loss. (e) (i)£2,500 profit, (ii) £36,500 profit, (iii) £10,000 extra profit — total profit £42,500. (iii) is best proposal.

Q5 1. 9400 units. 2. £7,000 loss. 3. 3200 units. 4. (i) Profit £5,500. (ii) Profit £17,000. (ii) is best proposal, current profit only £13,000.

Q6 (a) Fixed costs £156,000. Variable costs £204,000. (b) C/Unit £41. B/E 3805 units. (c) 6,500 units = £110,500 profit. 3500 units £12,500 loss.

Q7 Contribution £60. Break-even 4000 units.
Margin of safety 6000 units, 60%.
Estimated profits £360,000 and £270,000.
Proposals: 1. £360,000 profit, 2. £425,000 profit, 3. £408,000 profit.
. · . No. 2 has best profit potential.

Part 3 Budgeting & Planning

Q1

Cash Budget:	July	Aug.	Sept.	Oct.	Nov.	Dec.
Bal. b/f	(10,000)	(19,500)	(6,000)	8,400	7,800	10,200
Receipts	35,000	34,000	36,000	25,000	26,000	27,000
Payments	44,500	20,500	21,600	25,600	23,600	33,600
Bal. c/f	(19,500)	(6,000)	8,400	7,800	10,200	3,600

Q2

Cash Budget:	Sept.	Oct.	Nov.	Dec.	Jan.	Feb.
Bal. b/f	(4,000)	(3.480)	(4,720)	(7,080)	(24,760)	(25,040)
Receipts	47,040	48,960	49,920	51,840	56,640	59,520
Payments	46,520	50,200	52,280	69,520	56,920	58,680
Bal. c/f	(3,480)	(4,720)	(7,080)	(24,760)	(25,040)	(24,200)

Q3

Cash Budget:	July	Aug.	Sept.	Oct.	Nov.	Dec.
Bal. b/f	2,000	4,040	(7,900)	(8,060)	(4,840)	11,680
Receipts	23,200	32,000	24,000	28,000	39,000	31,200
Payments	21,160	43,940	24,160	24,780	22,480	20,660
Bal. c/f	4,040	(7,900)	(8,060)	(4,840)	11,680	22,220

Q4

Cash Budget:	July	Aug.	Sept.	Oct.	Nov.	Dec.
Bal. b/f	70,000	2,475	1,660	1,925	1,350	2,475
Receipts	2,875	9,625	12,625	15,625	19,125	22,625
Payments	70,400	10,440	12,360	16,200	18,000	15,480
Bal. c/f	2,475	1,660	1,925	1,350	2,475	9,620

Gross Profit £30,910. Net Profit £23,460. Proprietor's capital 31/12 £89,260.

Q5

Cash Budget:	July	Aug.	Sep.	Oct.	Nov.	Dec.
Balances c/f	£131,250	(24,000)	(39,250)	(64,500)	(49,750)	(38,300)

Gross Profit £60,000, Net Profit £21,900.
Fixed Assets £112,000, Working Capital £59,900,
Capital employed £171,900 – Debentures £50,000 = £121,900.
Capital £100,000 + Profit £21,900 = £121,900.

Q6

Cash Budget.	June	July	August
Balance c/f	(9,900)	(11,000)	(8,100)

Sales £71,800 – COS £57,440 = Gross Profit £14,360.
Stock value £10,760. Net Profit £5,585.
(*Note:* Depreciation £375, Rent £900).
Fixed Assets £61,025, Working Capital £10,960, Capital employed £71,985.
Capital £50,000 + P+L a/c £21,985 = £71,985.

Part 4 *Capital Appraisal*

Q1 (a) Y. (b) X = 38%. Y = 36%.

Q2 NPV: (a) £5,000 = £3,415. (b) £30,000 = £15,210. (c) £100,000 = £68.100.

Q3 Payback method: B is fastest.
Return on investment: A 37% B 35% C 36%   A best.
NPV: Earnings: A £556,500. B £560,940. C £546,610   B best.
Project B.

Q4 Payback method M is fastest.
Return on investment: L 34% M 38%.
NPV: Earnings L (£493,640) M £552,080.
Clearly project M is best.

Q5 NPV formulae £20,000/$(1.12)^{10}$ = £20,000 × 3.1058 = £6,440.
tables £20,000 × 0.322 = £6,440.

Q6 NPV formulae £58,000/$(1.11)^5$ = £58,000 × 1.6851 = £34,419
tables £58,000 × 0.593 = £34,394

Q7 NPV formulae £33,460 $(1.12)^4$ = £33,460 × 1.5735 = £21,265
(Bonds) tables £33,460 × 0.636 = £21,280
NPV formulae £42,580 $(1.12)^6$ = £42,580 × 1.9738 = £21,572
(Trusts) tables £42,580 ×0.507 = £21,588

Unit trusts marginally more profitable, £308 (tables).

Section VII

Part 1 Control Accounts

Q1 F. Smith: Sales ledger control £4,820 Dr. A discrepancy of £260 with sales ledger.
Bought ledger control £2,240 Cr. Agrees with bought ledger balance.

Q2 H. Jones: Sales ledger control £11,501 Dr. Bought ledger control £8,991 Cr.

Q3 G. Harrison: Sales Ledger Control £16,977 Dr. A discrepancy of £19 with sales ledger.

Q4 Rock Ltd.
Sales Ledger Control. Balance £73,910. (Debits £126,440, Credits £52,530). Purchase Ledger Control. Balance £37,150 (Debits £27,000, Credits £64,150). S/L control agrees. P/L control, £50 discrepancy.
The trial balance and bank reconciliation are two other methods of cross-check and control.

Q5 Zarak Ltd.
Sales Ledger Control. Balance £54,320. (Debits £109,820, Credits (55,500). Purchase Ledger Control. Balance £32,520. (Debits £26,400, Credits £58,920). P/L control agrees. S/L Control £20 discrepancy.

Q6 Smith & Jones
Sales Ledger Control. £310,865. £1,320 discrepancy with Sales Ledger. Purchase Ledger Control. £150,905. £1,750 discrepancy with Purchase Ledger.

Q7 ABC Co. Sales ledger control £38,324 Dr. £456 Cr. A discrepancy of £200 with sales ledger. Bought ledger control £12,484 Cr. (same as Bought Ledger) £150 Dr.

Part 2 Trial Balance Limitations, Journal & Suspense A/C.

Q1 Journal entries: (a) Drawings Dr. Salaries Cr. (b) R. Smith Dr. P. Smith Cr. (c) Office Equipment Dr. Purchases Cr. (d) Rates Dr. Accrued expenses Cr.

Q2 Journal entries: Premises £20,000, Vehicle £500, equipment £2,100, Stock £1,860, debtors £675, all debit entries. Mortgage £15,000, Bank O/D £450, Creditors £1,155 and capital — T. Jones £8,530 all credit entries.

Q3 Journal entries (a) Bad debts £256 Dr. H. Smith £256 Cr. (b) Equipment £500 Dr. Equipment Supplies Co. £500 Cr. (c) P & L £700 Dr. Provision for depreciation of MV £700 Cr. (d) Sales £14,500 Dr. Trading A/C £14,500 Cr. Trading A/C £9,850 Dr. Purchases £9,850 Cr. (e) Light and Heat £85 Dr. Rates £85 Cr.

Q4 Journal entries (a) R. Smith Dr. J. Smith Cr. (b) Sales £600 Dr. equipment £600 Cr. (c) Discount allowed £8 Dr. Suspence A/C £8 Cr. (d) Suspense A/C £200 Dr. Sales £200 Cr. (e) Suspense A/C £55 Dr. Salaries £55 Cr. (f) Debtors A/C £275 Dr. Sales £275 Cr.

Suspense A/C	Dr. Sales	£200	T. Balance	£247 Cr.
	Salaries	£55	Dis. All.	£8
		£255		£255

Q5 Suspense A/C Dr. Bank £2,490, Cr. T. Balance £2,275 Discount £160, Cash £55.

(b) Corrected Trial Balance: Bank £1,245, Capital £34,900, Sales £21,900 and Creditors £4,230 all Credit balances. Stock £3,400, Premises £23,000, Furniture £900, Wages and Salaries £13,000, Office Expenses £860, Purchases £14,300, Drawings £4,000, Debtors £2,600, Discount All. £160, Office cash £55 all Debit balances. Totals: T.B. £62,275.

Q6 R. Underwood. a) Suspense a/c £248 Dr. Returns Out. £248 Cr., Purchases £200 Dr. Biggs £200 Cr., Vehicle Repairs £2 Dr. Suspense £2 Cr., Bradford £54 Dr. Suspense £54 Cr., Sales £100 Dr. Office equip. £100 Cr., Drawings £230 Dr. Purchases £230 Cr., Purchases £92 Dr. Suspense £92 Cr.
b) Suspense a/c £248 Dr. Credits: £100, £2, £54 and £92.
c) £10,584.

Q7 Hawkins a) Suspense a/c £300 Dr. Pitman £300 Cr., Suspense £450 Dr. Sales £450 Cr., Discount Allowed £242 Dr. Suspense £242 Cr., F+F £90 Dr. Suspense £90 Cr., Knight £730 Dr. Sales £730 Cr., Heat & Light £233 Dr. Suspense £89 Dr. Motor Expenses £322 Cr., Stationery £180 Dr. Equipment £180 Cr.
b) Suspense a/c Dr. £300, £450, £89. Credits: £507, £242, £90.
c) £22,878.

Part 3 Incomplete Records

Q1 H. Jones. Debtors — to reconstruct sales £53,690. Creditors to reconstruct purchases £43,525. Bank A/C £1,588. Gross Profit £11,915. Net profit £5,708.
Balance Sheet: Fixed assets £2,465, Working capital £7,933. Capital employed £10,398. Capital £7,000 — Drawings £2,310 + Net Profit £5,708 = £10,398.

Q2 F. Smith. Bank A/C £10,625 — Cash Drawings £5,000 = £5,625. Sales A/C £72,767. Purchases A/C £46,960. Gross Profit £27,357. Net Profit £11,707. Balance Sheet: Fixed assets Nil. Current assets £18,672, current liabilities £5,465, working capital £13,207. Capital £6,500 — Drawings £5,000 + Net Profit £11,707 = £13,207. *Note*: Rates £1,065 in P & L A/C.

Q3 Jack. Capital = £8,000 (Assets £11,410 — Liabilities £3,410). Sales A/C £59,850, Purchases A/C £41,540. Gross Profit £18,910. Net Profit £7,605. Balance Sheet: Fixed assets £2,500. Working capital £6,580. Capital employed £9,080. Capital £8,000 — Drawings £6,525 + net Profit £7,605 = £9,080. *Note:* insurance £105 in P & L A/C.

Q4 F. Smith. Bank A/c commence payments with O/D £1,765 and include £1,955 mortgage repayment. Balance on 31/12 = £1,425 overdrawn. Sales A/C £49,695, Purchases £35,570. Gross Profit £15,735, Net Profit £9,261.
Balance Sheet: Fixed assets £30,685, Current assets £6,066, current liabilities £6,305, working capital (insolvent) − £239, capital employed £30,446. Deferred liabilities £13,295. Net assets £17,151. Capital £13,800 — drawings £5,910 + Net Profit £9,261 = £17,151.

Q5 J. Archer. Capital £99,700. Sales A/C £228,600. Purchases £158,950. Gross Profit £110,770, Net Profit £12,850. Fixed assets £14,550. Working Capital £86,000. Capital employed £100,550. Capital £99,700 — Drawings £12,000 + Net Profit £12,850 = £100,550. *Note*: Depreciation of fixtures £1,900.

Q6 J. Jones. Capital £20,000. Sales £46,525, Purchases £38,965. Gross Profit £9,175, Net Profit £4,225.
Fixed Assets £19,300, Working Capital £5,250, Capital employed £24,550 – Loan £4,000 – £20,550. Capital £20,000 + Net Profit £4,225 – Drawings £3,675 = £20,550.

Q7 D. White. Gross Profit £60,898, Net Profit £10,742. Fixed Assets £51,000, Current assets £31,600, Current Liabilities £13,680, Working Capital £17,920, Capital employed £68,920.
Capital £73,078 + Net Profit £10,742 – Drawings £14,900 = £68,920.

Q8 Justin Harris. Gross Profit £51,200, Net Profit £16,520.
Fixed Assets £43,200, Current assets £53,720, Current Liabilities £13,360, Working Capital £40,360, Capital employed £83,560.
Capital £80,760 + Net Profit £16,520 – Drawings £12,160, £1,560, = £83,560.

Q9 Murray Ltd. Credit purchases £584,000. Credit Sales £660,000. Sales £820,000 – COS £574,000 = Gross Profit £246,000. Closing stock £308,000 (£882,000 – £574,000).
Stock Loss £126,000. (£308,000 – £182,000).

Part 4 The Importance of Stock Valuation

Q1 Jack's store: Lower of cost or NRV £525, £140, £900, £750, £149.25, £57.50 and £5. Total stock value = £2,526.75.

Q2 Using FIFO: value of stock 1/7 £715 1/8 £745 1/9 £765 = 100 units × £2.15 = £215. 250 units × £2.20 = £550. Total value = £765.
Using LIFO: value of stock 1/7 £700 1/8 £700 1/9 £700 = 200 units × £2 = £400. 100 units × £1.95 = £195, 50 units × £2.10 = £105. Total value £700.

Q3 Stock Card: 12/9 299 reams × £2.5 = £747.5 20/9 Balance 170 reams: FIFO 80 × £2.5 = £200, 90 × £3 = £270. Total value £470.

Q4 FIFO: 24/1 Balance 100 units × £3.2, 70 units × £3, total 170 units value £530. 28/2 Balance 50 units × £3.40, 50 units £3.50, total 100 units value £345.
LIFO: 24/1 Balance 150 units × £3, 20 units × £3.20, total 170 units value £514. 28/2 Balance 50 units × £3, 50 units × £3.40, total 100 units value £320.
LIFO's stock value is £25 *less* than FIFO. Therefore gross profit would be £25 less if LIFO stock value used.

Q5 a) Stock Card: 28/6 105 units @ £4 unit = £420 stock value.
b) Stock Sheet: Total £4,003.75 (rounded up to £4,004).
c) Gross Profit £12,704.
   Net Profit £ 7,729.

Index